Exit and Voice

Exit and Voice

The Paradox of Cross-Border Politics in Mexico

Lauren Duquette-Rury

UNIVERSITY OF CALIFORNIA PRESS

University of California Press
Oakland, California

Suggested citation: Duquette-Rury, L. *Exit and Voice: The Paradox of Cross-Border Politics in Mexico*. Oakland: University of California Press, 2020.
DOI: https://doi.org/10.1525/luminos.84

Cataloging-in-Publication Data is on file at the Library of Congress.

Library of Congress Cataloging-in-Publication Data

Names: Duquette-Rury, Lauren, author.
Title: Exit and voice : the paradox of cross-border politics in Mexico /
    Lauren Duquette-Rury.
Description: Oakland, California : University of California Press, [2020] |
    Includes bibliographical references and index.
Identifiers: LCCN 2019024344 (print) | LCCN 2019024345 (ebook) | ISBN
    9780520321960 (paperback) | ISBN 9780520974203 (epub)
Subjects: LCSH: Transnationalism—Political aspects—Mexico. | Mexican
    Americans—Political activity. | Immigrants—Political activity.
Classification: LCC JV7402 .D86 2020 (print) | LCC JV7402 (ebook) | DDC
    304.80972—dc23
LC record available at https://lccn.loc.gov/2019024344
LC ebook record available at https://lccn.loc.gov/2019024345

29 28 27 26 25 24 23 22 21 20
10 9 8 7 6 5 4 3 2 1

For Aaron, Maxwell, and baby Finn with love

CONTENTS

FIGURES

MAP

ACKNOWLEDGMENTS

A theme that runs through this book is changing conceptualizations of community, collective action, and the transcendence of physical space where social relationships take root, grow, and blossom into something else entirely. I owe a debt of gratitude to my mentors, advisors, friends, family, and migrant confidants in the United States and Mexico who showed me a new meaning of community and working together while I researched and wrote this book.

I appreciate the unwavering support of Steven Wilkinson (Yale University) and John Padgett (University of Chicago) for empowering me to follow my intuition. Although neither of them studied international migration, they cared about me and my ideas and encouraged me to find my own path. Forging my own path ultimately led me to sociology, but the unparalleled training I received in political science at Chicago continues to ground my research and pushes me to require my advisees to immerse themselves in literatures across the artificial disciplinary walls that separate the social sciences. Before leaving for Princeton and Yale, Carles Boix and Sue Stokes inspired me a great deal. I thank Carles for showing me how to question everything and ingraining in me the benefits of a comparative approach. I thank Sue for modeling how to be critical and generous simultaneously when offering feedback and for being a visionary leader in comparative politics. And while I have never met Peter Evans or Judith Tendler and will never meet Elinor Ostrom or Albert O. Hirschman, they are my academic heroes and muses. Insights from their canonical works have made a deep impression on this research.

Most people say it in jest, but it is true: the University of Chicago is an odd bird, or a unicorn, or something else unique and hard to describe. It is an institution whose inhabitants celebrate intensity, rigor, unflagging curiosity, and critical dialogue, but it is also a place where big ideas are given the light, food, and space they need to be cultivated from root to fruit. I am certain that luck went into my matriculation there, but I am a better scholar for having attended it and a better person because of the people I befriended while there. My graduate cohort became very close thanks to Cathy Cohen's data analysis course and many sherry hours. Loren Goldman, Zac Callen, Marissa Guerrero, Jon Caverley, Negeen Pegahi, John Dobard, Sevag Kechichian, and the rest of our crew treaded water together and (eventually) started to swim. Deva Woodly-Davis, Anthony Davis, Sina Kramer, Andrew Dilts, Joe Fischel, Igor De Souza, Jenna Jordan, Emily Nacol, Bethany Albertson, Jon Rogowski, Mara Marin, Mona Mehta, Sondra Furcajg, and my academic "siblings" Jon Obert and Sarah Parkinson helped turn the need for work and parties into many memorable work-parties and provided laughter and guidance along the way. Patchen Markell, Dan Slater, and Iris Marion Young also provided support at critical moments. While in Chicago, I also found my bar, the Map Room, and there I met my husband. The owners, Mark and Laura, created a space for great conversation and fun. When I think of Chicago I think of many happy times at the Map Room and the friendships I built with Amanda Keleman Stump and Billy Stump, Jessica Kenney, Sara Elder, may she rest in peace, and Dave Neville.

Receiving a University of California President's Postdoctoral Fellowship changed the course of my academic life. With this postdoc, I was able to transition into the UCLA Sociology Department and was afforded the luxury of time to publish articles and remap my overly ambitious and clunky dissertation into this book. It also cemented the friendships I hold dear with Annie Ro and Renee Luthra, two women who I immensely admire and with whom I shared the experience of learning how to be an academic mama for the first time.

The postdoc came about because in spite of my anxiety, I closed my eyes and hit Send on an email to Roger Waldinger, asking him for coffee when he came to give a talk at Chicago. He responded and said yes despite my conviction that this request would be ignored. Over the last eight years, our relationship has bloomed. Roger became a generous mentor, valued colleague, creative collaborator, but most importantly a treasured friend. Over many meals and coffees, backyard picnics, office and faculty meetings, sharing and critiquing of each other's work, phone calls, and emails, Roger has showed me what it means to give of one's time and attention in the pursuit of someone else's goals. His mind is sharp, his words honest and direct, his heart and actions humane and sincere. I am so thankful he saw my potential to make a mark and buoyed me along the way. For any graduate students reading this, I implore you to push through your worries of being a burden and ask your senior colleagues and those you admire in academia to meet up and talk about your ideas. "Make the ask!" as the influential Kerry Ann Roquemore would say.

The UCLA Sociology Department was my home while writing this book and for that I am forever grateful. My colleagues there are the finest in the discipline and I learned so much from each of them. I thank Roger Waldinger, Rubén Hernández-León, Gail Kligman, Stefan Timmermans, Judy Seltzer, Steve Clayman, Rob Mare, Marcus Hunter, Abigail Saguy, Ka-Yuet Liu, Cesar Ayala, Hannah Landecker, Rebecca Emigh, Bill Roy, David Lopez, Patrick Heuveline, Darnell Hunt, C.K. Lee, Tanya Stivers, Lynne Zucker, Gabriel Rossman, Ed Walker, Jennie Brand, Stephen Bargheer, Megan Sweeney, Jacob Foster, Karida Brown, Vilma Ortiz, Jeffrey Prager, Rogers Brubaker, Min Zhou, Aliza Luft, and Jeff Guhin for their warmth and collegiality. Gail, Abigail, Roger, Rubén, and Karida deserve special thanks for reading all or parts of the manuscript and providing constructive, thoughtful comments. Roger, Rubén, Gail, Vilma, Darnell, Steve, Megan, Marcus, and Stefan were sources of inspiration and wise counsel while at UCLA and I am so grateful to have had their support during our institutional transition.

Several others at UCLA deserve special thanks for giving me feedback on this project, providing encouragement, and helping me become a better instructor. I thank graduate students Peter Catron, Molly Fee, Zhenxiang Chen (Zeke), Joel Herrera, Ana Oaxaca, Mirian Martinez-Aranda, Carla Salazar Gonzalez, Jesse Acevedo, Deisy Del Real, Leydy Diossa-Jimenez, and Diana Morales for their support. Zeke provided outstanding research assistance when I decided to expand parts of the quantitative analysis. He was willing to learn new methodological approaches alongside me and taught me new STATA coding too. His good nature and conviviality made the additional data hurdles all the more rewarding in the end. Ana Oaxaca, sharp and talented graduate student in political science, is also an incredible artist. Together we conceived the cover art for this book and Ana expertly made our vision come to life. Every time I look at it, I will think of the immense value that DACAmented and undocumented students bring to our universities, communities, and personal lives. The staff in the UCLA Sociology Department is the absolute best and helped lighten my load in so many ways. I thank Michael ONeill, Julie Huning, Simbi Mahlanza, Herumi Baylon, Irina Tauber, Wendy Fujinami, Hahan Rahardjo, Allan Hill, and Michelle Fielder for their magnanimity and kind dispositions.

While at UCLA, the Provost, Division of Social Sciences, and Sociology Department graciously organized a book manuscript workshop for me. Esteemed scholars Peggy Levitt, Emilio Parrado, and Devesh Kapur read and provided constructive feedback on the entire manuscript along with UCLA colleagues Roger Waldinger, Matt Barreto, Rubén Hernández-León; from Colef, Rafael Alarcón; and from UCSD, Abigail Andrews. The event was incredibly rewarding and the comments and suggestions I received helped improve the quality of the manuscript. Thank you all for your time and generosity. I also appreciate insightful comments from David FitzGerald and Filiz Garip, migration scholars whose books are required reading across the discipline and beyond. At UC Press I thank Naomi Schneider for believing in this book from the first day we met and Benjy Malings for helping it all come together.

I am fortunate to have a robust network of scholars and friends who have been willing to engage my work and cheer me on. I thank Clarisa Pérez-Armendáriz, Sophia Wallace, Dana Moss, and Abigail Andrews for being in my corner and Cecilia Menjívar, Leisy Abrego, Hiroshi Motomura, Rocío Rosales, Annie Ro, Patricia Morton, Renee Luthra, Shirin Montazer, Krista Brumley, Covadonga Meseguer, Katrina Burgess, Filiz Garip, Natasha Iskander, Irene Vega, Xochitl Bada, Sylvia Zamora, Adrìan Felix, and David Meyer for their support.

A lot of life happened in the years I was writing and finishing up this book that gave new direction to my career and reinforced the importance of nurturing friendships and family. Three of our parents received cancer diagnoses and we lost two dear friends. Additionally, my mother and mother-in-law had organ transplants. I had surgery to remove a tumor a week before I sent the complete manuscript to readers. We found out later it was benign. And Aaron and I made the difficult decision to move our family across the country from LA to Detroit to solve the tricky challenge of dual academic careers. While it is not customary in many professions to share these kinds of intimate life details, I hope that some who are reading these words feel a little less alone if they experience challenging circumstances while trying to produce great work. I have been fortunate that I genuinely love my job and found that research and writing sustained me and provided a respite of sorts when the going got tough. I thank my friends, family, and the NCFDD for reminding me that making time for pleasure and enjoying rewards to punctuate achievements is necessary to restore our energy wells and feel human.

Marissa Guerrero, my best girlfriend and titi to my boys, has been a loyal, trusted friend, intellectual companion, dance partner, thrift store mate, dispenser of advice, and reservoir of joy and humanity for the entirety of this project from seed idea to dissertation to book. I am a better person because she is my friend. I hope everyone has a friend like her in their lives to make the days sunnier and storms more navigable. Iljie Fitzgerald was a true gem to me in my last two years in LA. We played hooky together and went to the spa, ate delicious Korean food, plotted, laughed endlessly, and worked together to make the Fernald daycare a better place for all of UCLA's faculty and staff children. I would also like to thank Betty and Miguel at the UCLA faculty club for making me smile every morning while I wrote. Our daily conversations and sharing memories of Mexico were truly delightful.

My academic mamas group is a daily source of inspiration, reciprocity, and accountability. I am so grateful to the National Council of Faculty Development and Diversity for bringing us together though the Faculty Success Program (aka Faculty Bootcamp). Abigail Andrews, Mary Doyno, Maria Alejandra Perez, and Rachel Haywood-Ferreira have been my rocks over the last three years and I treasure the camaraderie and safety net we have created for each other. Together we are becoming better parents, partners, and colleagues and we push each other to take leaps. Abigail has become a cherished friend and book buddy. She is a careful researcher, devoted mama, and fabulous person all around. I am so lucky to have her in my professional and personal life. Sweet Mary is my cross-country bestie. She has shown me that personal tragedy can help willing people grow into the best versions of themselves. She has offered me grace, love, and light at every turn and for that I feel blessed.

Wayne State University wisely recruited Aaron and I am grateful they were willing to create a position for me too. I thank Jeff Kentor, Wayne Raskind, and Ratna Naik for bringing us on board and our lovely colleagues in Sociology and Chemistry for welcoming us with open arms.

This research would not have been possible without the generous financial support from the Ford Foundation and the National Academies, the Tinker Foundation, the National Science Foundation Dissertation Improvement Grant (SES-0819245), and a UC President's Postdoctoral Fellowship that gave me funds to travel to Mexico and conduct fieldwork, design and disseminate the original survey, and grant me leave from teaching to revise my dissertation into a book manuscript. I was also fortunate to receive a research grant from the Department of Political Science, the Center for Latin American Studies, and a Harper/Visiting Committee Fellowship while at the University of Chicago. At UCLA, a Hellman Fellowship, Early Career Faculty Grant from the Center at the Study of International Migration, and an Academic Senate Faculty Grant provided funding for a research assistant to complete additional empirical analysis and also released me from teaching obligations to finish the book.

I have tremendous gratitude for my parents who have always believed in me and encouraged me to follow my bliss even if it meant moving far away from them. They made huge sacrifices for my education. I am the first in my mother's family to attend college and I am so thankful for this privilege. I hope I have made them proud. My love for my sister is borderless and effortless. She brings so much joy and laughter into my life. Thank you, Kelly, for always being you and being my beacon. You are what is right and good in the world.

My husband, Aaron, is my partner in life, my best friend, my champion, my co-parent. Together we have built something truly magical that sustains me and gives me room to grow and evolve. He assumed more of the household and parenting responsibilities when I needed time to write and helped me believe I could succeed even when my confidence waned from time to time. I am so thankful for his love and support of my career. Our son, Maxwell, arrived my first year at UCLA and made writing this book more meaningful. He is such a curious, joyful, and goofy child. Being his mommy and playing with him is a beautiful release. And my baby Finn, who coos on my chest while I write these words, you, our sweet boy, are the next chapter. Thank you for coming into our lives at exactly the right time and completing our family.

Finally, to the migrants and families who opened up their homes to me in Mexico and the U.S., thank you for sharing your stories and showing me what true sacrifice looks like. You gave me a place to stay, fed me, danced with me, and told me stories about your experiences, culture, and communities. Learning from all of you has been one of the greatest gifts of my life. Thank you.

Introduction

On a clear day in the winter of 2009, I boarded a bus leaving Guadalajara, the second-largest city in Mexico, and headed toward the municipality of Comarga nestled high in the northern mountains of Jalisco. The bus hugged the shoulder of the two-lane highway and zigzagged its way through switchbacks along Route 23. Agave fields, old Catholic churches, and rural villages punctuated the rural countryside. Every so often the bus stopped to collect and drop off travelers. I welcomed these little pauses in the journey, precious moments to recover from vertigo, take in the local scenery, and buy fruits and veggies soaked in lime and chilies from sellers who hopped on the idling bus. Each town we passed had its own history and feel— San Cristóbal de la Barranca, Teul, Tlatenango, and Momax. Rows of tomatoes, beans, greens, and livestock farms lined the road leading into the municipal town center where local residents congregated in plazas with round pavilions and market stalls.[1] Chickens, goats, and lambs milled about the courtyards of adobe and concrete flat-roofed houses that lined the roads. I saw cars and trucks with license plates from California, Texas, and Illinois. And peppered throughout the towns, alongside more modest dwellings, sat renovated houses with grand new additions, gable roofs, circle driveways, and buffed wooden garage doors. Many of these improvements were funded with remittances earned in the United States and sent home to migrant families in Mexico. In each town we passed, signs of northern migration to the U.S. commingled with familiar features of the rural countryside.

Along the bus route I also saw big placards that noted sites of new public infrastructure. In connection with the Mexican government, migrants also financed public goods and services with remittances. They pooled resources in the U.S. and built schools, bridges, and health clinics in their hometowns. They paved roads

FIGURE 1. Road pavement project completed through 3x1 Program in Guanajuato. Photo by author.

and sidewalks; supplied school buses and ambulances; constructed parks; and extended public electricity, water, and drainage for residents left behind. Between 2002 and 2016, migrants implemented more than 26,000 public works projects in half of all Mexican municipalities, many in localities classified as "poor" and "very poor" by the Mexican government. Some migrants in the United States from a common place of origin have formed voluntary associations where they express shared ties to the people and places they leave behind and invest collective resources back home. These hometown associations (HTAs) (*clubes de oriundo*) exist around the globe—from Ghana to Germany, Japan to Cuba—and go by different names—*sons and daughters of the soil, landmanshaftn, kenjinkai, cabildos de naciones*.[2] But Mexican HTAs are different in one important way. In response to their collective, grassroots mobilization, these migrant groups and the Mexican government developed a federal social spending program that matches migrants' collective resources to coproduce local public goods and services. The program is called the 3x1 Program for Migrants (*Programa 3x1 para Migrantes*) (hereafter "the 3x1 Program").

While scores of studies have documented migrant hometown groups and their role in development,[3] little is known about how partnerships with the sending state affect local democratic governance. What are the political consequences that result from migrant transnational partnerships with the sending state? Who is involved in these transnational partnerships and how do they differ from place to place and over time? What can migrant participation in public goods provision tell us about who makes decisions in local governance and how those decisions are made? This is why I came to study in Mexico.

The answers to these questions lie in the underlying social and political conditions in which transnational partnerships are situated because they contribute to partnerships being organized differently. Some migrants remain socially embedded in the hometown by maintaining diverse social ties and constructing new social relationships with important stakeholders. Migrants who are more socially embedded also practice meaningful cultural repertoires that confer their community membership even while living abroad. In the political sphere, the bureaucratic capacity and electoral considerations of local governments also affect the organization of transnational partnerships. Together, these social and political factors determine how involved local residents and political officials are in the provision of transnational public goods and yield different political consequences. For example, when broadly inclusive of the local citizenry and when local government is also engaged, partnerships induce a form of transnational participatory governance in which both territorial and extraterritorial citizens articulate interests, exercise rights, meet obligations, and mediate conflicts[4] through deliberation and cooperative decision-making. This kind of synergetic partnership entwines migrants, local citizens, and government representatives in a network of democratic decision-making, which leads to more socially accountable and responsive government authorities. Participatory governance also expands the array of nonstate actors who are involved in democratic decision-making and empowers many local citizens to participate in local civic and political processes for the first time.

By contrast, different combinations of community inclusion and government engagement reflect more corporatist, substitutive, and fragmented types of transnational partnership and are associated with different political outcomes such as outright corruption and partnership failure. For example, in many cases of corporatist and fragmented coproduction, political clientelism results.[5] Broadly conceived, clientelism refers to the exchange of goods for political support and involves an asymmetric power relation between patrons and clients in which clients receive targeted, nonprogrammatic spending (e.g., bags of rice, gift cards, cash) in exchange for their political support come election time. In more substitutive cases of coproduction, local political officials offload responsibility for public goods provision entirely onto migrant groups. And in cases of corruption, resources that migrants commit to cofinancing public goods "disappear" from state coffers, which often leads to project and partnership failure.

Over the last eight years, I examined when, why, and how people who left their countries of origin collaborated with state actors to provide public goods back home through transnational partnerships. During my fieldwork, I visited municipalities across Mexico and studied the interactions between government officials, migrant groups, and residents as they unfolded over time. I listened to residents, current and former migrants, priests, business owners, mayors, political party officials, civic leaders, state and federal political officials, and learned that migrants' involvement in public goods provision had unintentional, yet profound political effects. I found that migrant actors, when more socially embedded, facilitated new modes of inclusive, democratic engagement that made local government more responsive to the citizenry. A focus on how migrants organize transnational partnerships reveals not only the conditions under which public service delivery increases and democratic participation and government performance improves in high-migration locales, but also how the process of coproducing public goods across national borders changes relations between state and society.

MOTIVATING EMPIRICAL PUZZLES

Although official Mexican statistics classified the municipality of Comarga as middle-income, like many of the 196,000 localities in Mexico with less than 2,500 inhabitants, the village of Atitlan was much poorer and greatly in need of public goods, especially when compared to the more densely populated county seat.[6] Atitlan is one of Comarga's five main localities and home to 340 residents. Despite democratization and decentralization reforms over the last 30 years, residents could not recall a single public works project in Atitlan since the late 1970s. As soon as I got off the bus this was evident—little improvement could be seen. Unlike the county seat where streets and sidewalks were paved, most streets in Atitlan were compacted dirt that flooded during the rainy season and swelled with garbage and sewage. Since the public drainage system reached just half of the households, those without access either purchased piping with their own money or disposed of sanitation in the old stone latrine that snaked its way through the back part of town. There were also few light posts in the village. Residents gave me a flashlight to navigate the streets at night. I had never experienced such darkness before my first night in Atitlan. But for the stars in the sky, it was pitch black. It was hard to tell where one's body ended and blackness began.

In 2004, the mayor (*presidente municipal*) of Comarga traveled to U.S. cities to meet paisanos, fellow countrymen and women, who had emigrated abroad.[7] During dinners and meet and greets, the mayor asked migrants to form clubs, raise money, and help the municipal government provide public works through the 3x1 Program. Four clubs formed after the mayor's trek across U.S. cities. Emilio and Esme, migrants from Atitlan, agreed to form a club and worked with the mayor on his proposed project: a concrete vehicle bridge. The mayor proposed the bridge project because the town was separated by a river. The only way for residents on the west side to access the main route into town was to cross a rickety, wooden footbridge or wade through the river on horseback or donkey and in small boats, which often capsized. After they recruited other paisanos, Club Atitlan planned the bridge project with the mayor's administration.

When the bridge was finished, club members in the United States were proud and felt like they contributed something important in their absence that locals appreciated. I was a bit taken aback, then, when residents told me they resented migrants' involvement. Many locals were initially confused—who were these migrants? Why had the paisanos not discussed their plans with leaders of the town's most important civic association, the *Patronato*, the patron saint festival group? Why did locals not have the same privileges, the ability to access political officials and get them to deliver goods and services they needed in their town? Residents felt slighted. After all, they lived there, they had voted for this mayor, and they had their own ideas about what the village needed. Relations further deteriorated when residents who were left out of discussions about 3x1 projects became increasingly suspicious of migrants' intentions. At the height of tensions, residents of Atitlan prohibited the club from participation in local public affairs and mobilized to vote against the incumbent mayor's political party to punish the administration for their alliance with the migrant club.

The turmoil unleashed by Club Atitlan's cross-border participation in public goods provision had several unanticipated impacts on political participation and relations between local government and Atitlan society. Residents mobilized a collective effort and punished the incumbent's party for privileging migrants' voices over that of local citizens. Their social exclusion from project governance motivated short-term political activism. Atitlan voters banded together and cast ballots for the opposition in the 2010 election, which likely played some role in the defeat of the incumbent in a close race. But the initial wave of political activity petered out and turned into political disenchantment. Frustrated with members of the migrant club who residents perceived as allies of the local government, residents turned away from politics and refocused their energy on the social and religious activities of the community.

The case of Atitlan and its paisanos in the U.S. raises important questions about how international migration reconfigures local democratic engagement in origin countries. Migrants who use material resources collected abroad mobilize new mechanisms of voice and make political decisions in their places of origin that affect migrant and nonmigrant households alike. The cross-border participation of migrants and migrant groups upends traditional modes of local governance because although migrants have exited, some never really leave. Migrant loyalty and social connectivity to the hometown catalyzes the collection of newfound resources acquired abroad, which they use to participate in public affairs back home.

A 30-minute drive along a potholed road took you from Atitlan to El Mirador, another locality in Comarga. Because a bus could not safely navigate the high mountain road, El Mirador was only accessible by all-terrain vehicles such as trucks or jeeps, or on horseback. It was also a poor village with a substantial portion of its population living abroad, mostly in Chicago and southern Indiana. I hitched a ride to El Mirador with a local crew going up to finish the most recent transnational project between Club El Mirador and the municipal government; the last bits of corrugated metal roofing were being installed on a new recreation court (*cancha*). More geographically remote and higher up in the Sierras, I thought El Mirador would be worse off than Atitlan because the town's geographic isolation meant the provision of public goods was more difficult to implement up in the mountains. But after entering through the tall gates of the long paved road into town, I saw this was not the case at all. Every street in El Mirador was newly paved with a hydraulic drainage system underneath. Almost every house was connected to the electricity grid. A new kindergarten school room was recently constructed. And while only half the town had use of the public water system every other day, a well had recently been installed to meet local needs. In addition to the new recreation area, a new rodeo ring (*lienzo charro*) was built for neighbors to enjoy horseback competitions and festivals. All of the new infrastructure was provided through the collaboration between migrants from El Mirador and the local government with matching funds from state and federal 3x1 Program partners.

Yet, none of the tension or political turmoil between residents, migrants, and political officials in Atitlan was present in El Mirador. Residents spoke highly of HTA members—as friends, paisanos, and community members—and said their relationship with the club was copacetic. Local residents of El Mirador were actively engaged in the selection and implementation of projects and visited the municipal government building (*ayuntamiento*) in Comarga. There they discussed project budgets, timelines, materials, and labor contracts with political officials. Local residents even fundraised and donated resources to a few projects. The first year into the transnational partnership, residents formed their own public works committee in El Mirador, the first of its kind in recent memory. The contrast in number of public services between Atitlan and El Mirador was stark. The nature of the interactions between key social and political actors was also qualitatively different. The Atitlan partnership was mired in conflict and cleavages that divided residents, migrants, and municipal officials. After a short burst of political interest and activity, citizens recoiled from politics and from involvement with "outsiders" (dubbed *fuereños*). In contrast, citizens of El Mirador formed a civic association, solved local problems through deliberation, and became more politically aware and active through the process of providing public goods.

Why were transnational partnerships between organized migrants and local government in the two communities within the *same* municipality so different? The same mayor organized and worked with the clubs. Both villages were similar in terms of population size and level of economic development. Both villages had high rates of out-migration. And both villages were "strongholds" of the incumbent party in which a plurality of voters regularly turned out to support the National Action Party (*Partido Acción Nacional,* PAN). Furthermore, El Mirador did not benefit from any favoritism from the mayor, who, in fact, had been born and raised in Atitlan. Unlike in Atitlan, Club El Mirador recruited local residents to participate in public goods projects and residents regularly engaged in deliberations with municipal officials. Since El Mirador was more geographically isolated, there was more trust and cooperation among neighbors,[8] and migrant club members regularly engaged in festivals, home ownership, the local Catholic church, and maintained the dress, traditional customs, and mannerisms of their rural community. Migrants, in other words, continued to practice cultural repertoires of community membership while living abroad in ways that were meaningful to friends, family, and strangers who remained behind. Despite their physical distance, they remained socially embedded in the local community from beyond national borders.

In comparison, migrant club members from Atitlan did not remain well integrated into the social life of the hometown after exit. Time away from Atitlan taxed the breadth and depth of social ties, and migrants' quest for social status and an alliance with political authorities created animus with residents. Migrants still felt connected to Atitlan even though they had emigrated. They also had a common bond with each other in the U.S. as they shared a migration experience. But their physical absence and social location outside the hometown network prevented them from exercising legitimate voice in the community in which they were no longer inhabitants. In turn, the process of public goods provision created contests for recognition between migrants, migrant families, and residents in relation to the municipal government in Atitlan, while the process broadened civic engagement in collective decision-making practices in El Mirador.

The transnational partnership case of El Cerrito, a larger locality in the municipality of Selvillo, Guanajuato, was organized differently and produced different political dynamics over time. Unlike in Atitlan and El Mirador, where political officials were enthusiastic about coproducing public goods with migrant groups, the PAN administration in Selvillo was initially inactive. Club El Cerrito produced its first few projects without the involvement of local government because the mayor who had promised support never delivered on it. The migrants relied on cofinancing from state and federal tiers of the Mexican government and implemented projects on their own. Club El Cerrito selected the projects, hired the contractors, sourced the materials, and coordinated all facets of project implementation. In the early years of migrants' investment in El Cerrito the club substituted for local government provision with limited involvement of El Cerrito residents.

Living far away from their homelands, migrants from El Cerrito were able to improve public goods without support from local officials and community residents, but doing so presented two challenges. The first obstacle was logistical. Accountable to the migrant members who invested their own scarce resources to better conditions back home, club leaders feared that poor management and inadequate implementation of projects discouraged future investments. Since the club leaders and members had moved far away from their hometowns, they lacked the capacity to monitor projects during and after implementation. Moreover, monitoring was crucial, as the projects were targets of predators of various sorts, whether laborers or contractors who shirked on quality and failed to supply materials on time or outside parties who tried to seize the materials bought for the projects that the association funded. Club El Cerrito, like many hometown clubs, faced the constant risk that unscrupulous local actors, such as local political bosses referred to as *caciques* and organized gangs connected to criminal drug-trafficking networks, would take advantage of the migrants' absence.

The second obstacle concerned legitimacy.[9] While the migrants' distance from their hometowns made them vulnerable to local opportunists, it also potentially undermined their legitimacy, as they claimed to belong to a community in which they no longer resided. Just as in Atitlan, residents in El Cerrito were suspicious of the club's motives and publicly challenged the migrants' involvement in the delivery of public goods. The migrants still had family and friends in El Cerrito, but they had limited social ties beyond their immediate social circles and only a few residents knew those migrant leaders who served as the visible ambassadors of the club. Since migrants were no longer embedded in hometown social life, residents did not initially recognize them as social actors with a legitimate voice to make decisions in public affairs. Moreover, low levels of trust that were pervasive in the town spilled over into migrants' efforts. However meritorious Club El Cerrito's project proposals were to the migrants and their close circle of familiars, since a broader swath of local residents did not have a direct stake in the outcome and they did not believe that migrants represented their interests, the proposal was insufficient and illegitimate.

But just three years later the local government and residents were active contributors in the transnational partnership. By 2013, close to 30 public works projects had been completed throughout El Cerrito such as road pavement, sidewalks, electricity, street lamps, a computer lab, and a recreation area for the elementary school to name a few. Migrants' horizontal ties in the community and vertical ties to local government facilitated new modes of interaction and deliberation between local citizens and elected representatives through the process of coordinating public goods with migrants. Migrants constructed meaningful social ties with different citizen groups in El Cerrito through social events such as rodeos, dances, and fundraising dinners and actively recruited residents into project governance. Three new civic associations were created to work with Club El Cerrito, but they also completed their own projects and solved local problems on their own. In turn, when they witnessed increased involvement of residents (voters) and experienced fiercer competition from opposition political parties, local government scaled up its engagement in the process and continued to be supportive even as the administration switched political party from PAN to the Institutional Revolutionary Party (*Partido Revolucionario Institucional*, PRI) and then back to PAN. The completion of highly visible public projects in which incumbents claimed credit became a politically expedient method that shored up public support in hotly contested municipal elections. The case of El Cerrito shows that the organization of transnational partnerships is not set in stone. Community inclusion and government engagement change in response to social outreach and political conditions in the hometown.

These cases generate important questions for researchers of international migration, political sociology, and participatory development. Who has the legitimate authority to speak for whom in a political community? Can migrants who exit use their voice in hometown public affairs as if they were still residents? What are the political consequences of doing so? Does it matter if cross-border political participation is materially conditioned by remittances? How does "doing" development enable and foreclose opportunities for political inclusion, activism, and equality in places with high migration? These questions motivate this book.

HOME-COUNTRY LOYALTIES AND MIGRANT TRANSNATIONAL PRACTICES

Many of the 244 million migrants located around the world who leave their homelands for economic opportunity and safe haven abroad realize their dreams in a promised land.[10] Individuals and families leave their countries of origin when staying is no longer a sensible option and when an economic and political system in which they feel they have no ability to change strips them of security and opportunity.[11] Many people do not want to go but do so when it seems like they have no choice. When the price of crops plummets, when cities overflow, when factories cut wages and stop hiring, when children need food to eat, and when families are threatened by violence, migrants make the difficult decision to leave loved ones behind. They do what Albert O. Hirschman and others call "voting with their feet."[12] Given the choice between staying and using their voice to induce political change and availing themselves of the freedom to exit, many individuals see the latter as the chance for a better life, albeit a life abroad.

Once migrants cross a border into a destination country, they do not cease to feel attached, to meet social, ethnic and religious obligations, and to express solidarity with the people and places they leave behind. As Rainer Baubock explains, migration is an international phenomenon between states insofar as it involves a movement of persons across the territory of sovereign states; however, it becomes transnational when it creates overlapping memberships, rights, and practices that reflect migrants' belonging to two different political communities.[13] Not all migrants are "transmigrants" who regularly communicate, exchange resources, ideas, and behaviors, and visit the origin country.[14] Loyalty to the hometown and the people in it takes various forms and is felt to different degrees. Some migrants remain fervently engaged transnationally, others more sparingly. Some keep up with the major news of the day back home and speak their mother tongue. Others send their children back in the summer so that their kids know what life is like in their parents' and grandparents' hometowns. Other migrants return to attend annual community festivals and ethnic and religious holidays. For many, though, the strangeness of a new land, the foreignness that shadows them, and the discrimination they face create trepidation, a longing for home, and generate new kinds of political interests that can be channeled to the hometown.[15] Many migrants simply hope to return one day to the place of their birth and where their parents are buried. Feelings of separation and nostalgia grow with time and compound when immigrants face exclusion in their adopted countries. Motivated by different rationales, many migrants remain loyal and engage in multiple "ways of being" and "ways of belonging" in transnational social and political spaces.[16]

Migrant cross-border engagement is not a new phenomenon. Before Western Union, social media platforms, cheaper air travel, and long-distance telecommunications, Italian, German, Chinese, and Polish immigrants wrote letters to family, kept up with news from the homeland, formed mutual aid societies, and sent money via post or in person on steamships.[17] While people today are more likely to exchange messages on social media platforms and through text and video messaging, migrants' dual loyalties spanning borders are a modern facsimile of earlier historic periods. But the advance of the internet and ability to see the faces of loved ones, old neighbors, and government partners on device screens in the palm of one's hand means that cross-border practices occur with greater ease and in real time. In the case of Latinx migrants in the United States, the majority sustain some degree of cross-border engagement, with only a minority detaching from the homeland altogether.[18]

THE FORMATION OF MIGRANT HOMETOWN ASSOCIATIONS

Migrant hometown associations are a common transnational practice enabled by international migration that allows migrants to act out their loyalty to the homeland. HTAs arise in destination countries around the world and date back to the industrial era of migration and even earlier.[19] Hometown clubs arise because, in addition to economic motivations, social network ties lead migrants to concentrate in destination places where other members of their social network reside.[20] The social-networked nature of international migration results in the formation of "daughter" or "filial" communities.[21] In these filial communities, migrants fortify a social connection based on a shared sense of belonging and attachment to a common origin. Paisanos come together in voluntary spaces to chat, dance, play, reminisce, celebrate holidays, and provide support to each other. Massey and colleagues refer to this kind of social organization as *paisanaje*:

> Origin from the same place is not a meaningful basis of social organization for people while they are at home. In general, within the community itself, the concept of *paisanaje* does not imply any *additional* rights and responsibilities to other paisanos that are not already included in the relationships of friend, family member or neighbor. It is not a meaningful concept until two paisanos encounter each other outside their home community. Then the strength of the *paisanaje* tie depends on the strangeness of the environment and the nature of their prior relationship in the community.[22]

The concentration of migrants from a common place of origin and shared *paisanaje* form the seedbeds for the emergence of migrant hometown associations.

Not all HTAs are involved in financing public works in their hometowns. Some are more akin to mutual aid societies of the past, which are societies, organizations, or voluntary associations that provide mutual aid, support, and benefits to their members. Other HTAs focus more on promoting culture and folk traditions, recreation, and social gathering. And those migrant HTAs that do become involved in cross-border development projects often begin with a more social or cultural mission and adopt public goods provision as a secondary goal.[23]

Migrants who are members of development-focused HTAs do so for many reasons. Some do so for purely altruistic reasons and a love of the homeland. Others finance public goods to fulfill ethno-religious obligations. And there are those who contribute resources for instrumental reasons such as securing better living conditions for when they eventually return home and having their social status elevated and valorized by acting as patrons for resident clients who remain behind.[24] But the motivations of migrants are not static. The reasons for participating in HTAs and the goals of the associations change over time as people's circumstances change—increased social mobility, assimilation into the destination society, new obstacles encountered in their adopted countries, natural disasters striking back home. The motivation to create HTAs and invest in public goods is also encouraged by actors in the sending state eager to channel remittance resources toward public ends.

TRANSNATIONAL PRACTICE OF FINANCIAL AND SOCIAL REMITTANCE SENDING AND EFFECTS

In addition to hometown clubs, migrants engage in other ways across borders and their practices have numerous effects. Financial remittance sending is perhaps the most visible and quantifiable transnational practice. Since migration enables a modicum of social mobility, migrants can save a portion of their savings and send it home. In 2016, migrants sent more than $601 billion across borders to support families, of which $441 billion went directly to developing countries.[25] If informal remittances flows could be captured, totals are estimated to be much higher. India,

China, Mexico, and the Philippines are the top recipient countries with remittances ranging from \$73 billion (India) to \$27 billion (Mexico). But as a share of gross domestic product (GDP), smaller countries including Tajikistan and Kyrgyz Republic (30 percent), Nepal (28 percent), Tonga (28 percent), and Moldova (26) are the largest recipients.[26] A stable form of international finance, remittances are more than three times the size of official development aid (ODA) and mitigate the adverse effects of economic shocks and natural disasters as demonstrated by the massive influx of remittances to the Philippines in the wake of two typhoons in 2009 and Super Typhoon Haiyan in 2013.[27]

Migrant remittances finance household consumption such as educational expenses, medicine, food, clothing, housing construction, appliances, and electronics. They also go toward productive investments and savings[28] and have myriad effects on the political economy of origin countries including economic growth and poverty alleviation; inequality; monetary policy; skill formation; and institutional quality.[29] Given the sheer volume of remittance flows globally, it is no wonder this source of foreign income has been hailed by the development banking community and policymakers alike as a new panacea for development in sending countries.[30]

Beyond economic transfers, migrants also exchange ideas, behaviors, norms, and social capital between origin and destination referred to as *social remittances*.[31] Migrants remit cultural, social, political, and economic worldviews and practices they acquire abroad back to their places of origin through their roles in families, communities, and organizations.[32] Social remittances affect how people rear their children, divide labor in the household, and determine right from wrong. Social remittances also alter political attitudes and behaviors, religious rituals, and burial practices.[33] While distinct, social and financial remittances are also intimately linked.

Financial transfers are "communicative acts"[34] that relay information about migrants' social positioning in places of origin and sustain social ties between migrants and nonmigrants.[35] Like other forms of monetary transactions, financial remittances are motivated by social relations, and social relations, in turn, affect financial remittance sending practices.[36] When transfers assume a collective form and are sent by transnational migrant associations for public goods provision, the ideational and material effects go beyond interpersonal relationships; they also affect social relations and local politics. Remittances have these community-wide social and political effects because they enable migrants to use voice in decision-making about public goods in the hometown. Collective remittances convey information about migrants' experiences in the destination country and are situated in preexisting social relationships that affect how collective resources are used and who else is involved in determining their use.[37] These decisions are distinctly political acts in that public goods provision is a core function of government, especially subnational governments in decentralized political systems such as Mexico.

As such, a small but growing area of research is focusing more on the political consequences of different facets of international migration, most notably individual out-migration, remittances, and their effects on domestic politics in the homeland. Research on "political remittances" suggests migration can have democratizing effects and stabilize authoritarian regimes at the national level.[38] Micro-level research shows that as more migrants leave their places of origin, formal political participation, such as voting in elections, decreases while other studies show no effect on nonmigrant political behaviors.[39] Other research argues that migrants can be agents of democratic diffusion who transfer ideas back to their hometown communities through their social ties, which improves nonmigrants' social tolerance and civic engagement.[40] While rich and instructive, how *individual* pathways of migration affect national and subnational politics is still up for debate.

Research on how migrant *collective* participation affects politics at home is also incipient and similarly mixed. Studies marshal evidence that cross-border participation can be both "good" and "bad" for democracy.[41] Migrant-led development projects have been shown to have democratizing effects when migrant groups demand higher political standards from authorities,[42] introduce fiercer political competition,[43] and ensure political accountability.[44] By contrast, migrant clubs have been found to work at cross-purposes with the state and local citizens,[45] and local government often pursues partnerships with an eye toward electoral payoff in lieu of development goals.[46] Research on the effects of migrant associations on democracy has come a long way, but we know little about the *conditions* under which migrant associations produce more positive (or negative) political effects for local democracy.

SENDING-STATE MIGRANT OUTREACH

The migrant population's desire to stay connected to the people and places they leave behind and their ability to send money home is not lost on sending country governments. While migrants maintain social ties "here" and "there," sovereign states also fundamentally shape the relationships between migrants and their countries of origin.[47] The exit of individuals from state control poses a constraint on sending states. Since migrants are no longer territorial residents, sending states have limited capacity to use coercion, extract resources, and make migrants comply with state demands.

As a result of these constraints on control, sending country governments reach out to their nationals abroad and attempt to attract remittances and homeland engagement through both symbolic tools and public policy initiatives. States acknowledge emigrants as "absent sons and daughter" and "heroes" in national discourse. Political officials visit expatriates abroad, expand consular presence and services in destination countries, lobby banks to lower transaction fees for sending money home, adopt dual citizenship policies, and host specials events with migrants to cultivate ties. Sending states' proactive efforts to encourage their expatriates to remain connected and channel resources home have been instantiated in diverse ways from cabinet positions to federal ministries. In the case of economic development in Mexico, the 3x1 Program was developed with migrants to direct their resources toward public ends. For every project that receives approval, each tier of the government—local, state, and federal—matches migrant resources, three-for-one, for the provision of local public goods and services. The matching grants schema creates an interesting tension for migrant HTAs and public agencies in the sending state.

Migrants, through the process of emigrating to new political jurisdictions, partially invert the power relationship between "state" and "society" because migrants' evolving resource base generates new sources of political leverage back home. The sending state has no administrative authority to instruct private parties, even if citizens, on how to spend income earned abroad that is sent back directly to households. Household financial remittances are private resources for private use and all the sending state can do is encourage migrants to maintain social connections and continue sending those remittances back to families. But collective remittances amassed by migrant HTAs are different. Since collective economic remittances are intended for *public goods* provision, it not only creates the opportunity for migrants to use voice in local public affairs, it also creates new political opportunities for sending states to determine, in part, how collective resources are used. When sending-state actors become coproduction partners in the provision of public goods and match migrants' remittances with public funds, the sending state regains some control over how those resources are used in the homeland for community and, potentially, personal political gain. Political officials often claim credit for public goods that are conjointly funded by extraterritorial migrant citizens living abroad.

But sending states that want to harness collective remittance resources toward public ends must relinquish some control and negotiate with migrants when investing in development projects for public use. Local government cannot completely dictate how funds are used, what projects are chosen, and how labor and supplies are coordinated without some input from migrant actors because each party contributes resources. For organized migrants, emigration grants them access to U.S. wages that generate resources to use voice in local public affairs. Emigration also liberates migrants to express a voice that might otherwise be constrained or coerced at home.

The devil, however, is in the details. In decentralized systems like Mexico, how migrant and state actors navigate the transnational relationship is not the same across partnerships because local-state capacity and electoral incentives vary and motivate local political actors differently. Moreover, these incentives may not align with the goals of federal and state authorities providing matching contributions to public works projects in programs like the 3x1 Program.[48] Furthermore, while a growing number of countries have adopted matching grants programs similar to

Mexico's 3x1 social spending program, many others have no administrative oversight with regard to migrant investment in local projects or an institutionalized method of organizing public-private partnerships between migrant groups and the sending state. In Mexico's 3x1 Program and in other countries where HTAs are active, local, state, and federal authorities respond to migrant remittance-led investments according to their own political incentives, which drives the extent of their participation and cooperation with migrant groups differently across geography and time. Research has yet to fully account for the ways in which government actors' participation varies across transnational coproduction partnerships.

Understanding why and how migrant involvement in public goods provision varies is important because it tells us a great deal about the quality of governance in origin countries with substantial emigration. The origin and evolution of matching grants programs that draw on external migrant resources for development projects serves as an important window into social and political institutional dynamics in local democracy. It also reveals how migrant nonstate actors, with and without the support and involvement of local citizens and the state, propel new modes of civic and political interest and engagement in public service delivery.

POLITICS OF PUBLIC GOODS PROVISION AND LOCAL GOVERNANCE

Public goods and services such as potable water, electricity, health services, safety, education, sidewalks, and roads are intrinsic components of people's well-being. Inadequate provision of clean drinking water, sanitation, and hygiene, for example, often leads to disease outbreaks. Access to quality healthcare services reduces complications during maternal childbirth and infant mortality rates. Paved, easily navigable roads connect important market centers where agricultural producers locally sell commodities and export them abroad to earn a living. In short, public service delivery is an essential component of economic development and poverty alleviation everywhere.

Traditionally, the state provides public goods to people in exchange for their quiescence to authority and taxation.[49] Assuming a group of interested citizens has the requisite time, energy, skills, and resources, they could cooperate to build water wells, put up street lamps, pave roads, and erect bridges themselves. However, because public goods benefit everyone, private provision suffers from classic free-rider problems of collective action.[50] When everyone can benefit from clean drinking water whether or not they contribute to get the system up and running, few are willing to sacrifice private time and resources to supply a public good that others will enjoy for free. Certainly, a limited number of goods can be provided this way and citizens have found creative solutions to collective action problems including informal institutions that govern common pool resources.[51] But generally, private provision of public goods leads to underprovision. This is why government is tasked with supplying public service delivery—to ensure that citizens gain access to the basic goods and services they need to live healthy, productive lives.

In consolidated and recently transitioned democracies, citizens vote in elections and hold officials to account for public goods delivery. Participating in free, fair, and contested elections informs representatives of constituents' preferences and serves as the central mechanism to demand political change.[52] But many democracies suffer from political and institutional distortions that undermine formal instruments of political accountability.[53] First, casting a ballot is a less informative instrument for public officials to learn what kinds of public goods citizens want and need. Second, decentralization reforms that devolve authority over public goods to lower tiers of government frequently fail to improve efficiency and bring citizens closer to the political process. Inefficiencies result because resources transferred from state and federal governments are politically manipulated.[54] Throughout the world, decentralization is unevenly implemented and fiscal authority to collect income taxes and finance social spending lags behind reforms that decenter administrative and political responsibility to subnational governments.[55] Getting government to provide public goods is indeterminate in recently transitioned democracies and nondemocracies because local electoral institutions are absent or are often weak instruments of what political scientists call "vertical political accountability." By vertical accountability I am referring here to the means through which citizens, mass media, and civil society enforce standards of good performance on political authorities through popular control.[56]

A lack of political accountability fuels skepticism among the citizenry that electoral institutions can *do* anything to improve their lives and leads some to fret over a crisis of faith in political parties and the return of more authoritarian forces.[57] In periods in which participation and contestation are in flux, nonelectoral forms of political participation and coproduction arrangements become critical in the provision of public services.[58] Migrants, with their newfound collective resources earned and pooled abroad, leverage their remittances and become political actors who decide what kind, how much, and where public goods are provided in conjunction with and in place of local government authorities.

PARTICIPATORY DEMOCRACY AND THE
COPRODUCTION OF PUBLIC GOODS

Citizens counteract the weakness of electoral institutions through informal, that is, nonelectoral forms of participation in which they communicate information, demand political action, and engage directly with political officials and help make decisions about how the local government operates. These informal forms of civic and political engagement introduce a measure of social or horizontal accountability—an approach toward building good governance that relies on ordinary citizens and civil society organizations participating directly or indirectly in exacting accountability through bottom-up, demand-based efforts.[59] However, not all citizens participate equally. Some citizens have more resources, are more motivated, and are part of recruitment networks that create and foreclose opportunities for engagement.[60] Some civic cultures are more propitious for civic engagement while others emphasize private entitlements.[61] The large social capital literature shows how norms of trust and reciprocity are imbued in social relationships that promote cooperation and membership in civic associations, and this civic associationalism, in turn, correlates with good government in liberal democracies.[62] But who or what nurtures social trust and reciprocity and brings about citizens' engagement in politics is rather elusive. And the mechanisms through which social networks of trust, reciprocity, and cooperation cause government officials to behave better while in office also remain an open question.[63]

In many cases, citizen participation in public life is determined by costs, benefits, and expectations of democratic engagement[64] and shaped by states. States have enormous power to scale up citizen engagement by opening up new spaces in which citizens propose, deliberate, and help make public decisions alongside elected officials.[65] These participatory spheres not only improve service delivery, but also nurture the emergence of new actors and subjectivities involved in local governance. And as citizens' interest and exposure to political life increases, so too may their sense of personal political efficacy, that is, the belief that they can understand and influence political affairs and bring about a more responsive government through purposeful action.[66]

Since this kind of participatory sphere brings ordinary people into government decision-making, it also has the transformative potential to improve social inclusion and more equitable allocation of public resources. Drawing on citizens' local knowledge and resources harnesses their agency to make them what Gaventa calls "makers and shapers" rather than simply "users and choosers."[67] And being open to the role of "co-governance" or "coproducer" in providing public goods and services creates opportunities for citizens to "cut their political teeth"[68] and be more inclined to engage in other arenas that bring about social and political change. Public goods are a kind of problem that sometimes cannot be solved by government actors alone, but also may not be solvable without them.

In turn, citizens and the state can create new institutional arrangements for public goods delivery when either entity is incapable or unwilling to do so alone. These public-private partnerships between state and society arise to coproduce public goods and services.[69] Each public (state actors in public agencies) and private (social actors in civil society) entity supplies complementary resources to conjointly organize the provision of public goods. Coproduction partnerships between public and private actors can also have democratizing effects when the quality of deliberation and who is engaged in public decision-making expands to include more marginalized, previously excluded voices.

While ostensibly beneficial for local democracy, our collective understanding of how public-private partnerships emerge, are structured, and affect political and civic engagement from beyond national borders remains undertheorized and empirically systematically underexamined. To date, research on coproduction partnerships has not fully examined the transnational dimensions of public goods provision and the conditions under which this kind of transnational institution injects political change in places with extensive emigration. This book does just that.

WHY TRANSNATIONAL PARTNERSHIPS MATTER FOR LOCAL DEMOCRATIC GOVERNANCE

The great variety and significant effects of transnational public goods projects are most fruitfully understood when they are situated in the preexisting social and political contexts of both the destination and place of origin. While prior research has emphasized how transnational practices are embodied in larger social structures and political institutions, few studies have systematically linked how these spheres of influence interact to structure the ways in which transnational practices are forged and organized and lead to success and failure.

My observations do not depart from the voluminous migrant transnationalism research that emphasizes the role of social ties and relations in facilitating cross-border practices, specifically transnational development and public goods provision. It is the case that migrants' "multipolarity" in two social worlds, the society of origin and destination, widens their field of existence such that they embody new identities and assert rights and duties of belonging and citizenship both "here and there."[70] Asserting continued belonging and attachments to places of origin is the very foundation of many migrant social groups' involvement in public goods provision. Migrants, through the translational act of sending collective remittances through hometown organizations, relay messages about increased social position, status, and prestige to nonmigrants at home while simultaneously claiming what Carling and Lacroix refer to as the "repayment of communality" and "lifeworlds" and the reassertion of "villageness" that helps migrants meet their social and ethnic obligations to community and allegiance to the hometown through the provision of development projects.[71]

However, my project is not an excursus of migrants' multidimensional motives to engage in this particular form of cross-border engagement with the homeland. Rather, this is my point of departure. All of the migrant actors I observed were involved in hometown associations and remain, to varying degrees, "loyal" to the homeland to borrow Hirschman's canonical language.[72] How I build on previous research is to start from the premise that all transnationally engaged migrants and their hometown clubs are not similarly situated in the hometown social network after departure. This is the half of the equation that needs to be explained. I heed

Levitt and Glick Schiller's call to focus on spatially embedded relations or networks, which puts the emphasis on the fluidity and openness of social relations. In doing so, it is incumbent on me to explain why migrants' social embeddedness in the hometown varies from place to place and over time and how this variation produces different kinds of cross-border partnership. By theorizing and testing how the structure of migrant social ties varies, I am able to show when local citizens are included in transnational development activities in ways that improve democratic participation and governance. Drawing on the migrant transnationalism literature provides a starting point for analyzing what kinds of migrant social relations structure how public goods projects are carried out, who is involved in selecting and managing projects, and how interactions are negotiated over time to expand the range of actors participating in and influencing decisions about goods and services that directly affect their lives.

But unpacking the variation in migrant social embeddedness to discern who is involved in making decisions about public goods provision in origin locales is just half of the analytic puzzle that requires explanation. The transnational practice I study necessarily involves state actors and government agencies in the sending state who become more or less engaged in the coproduction of public goods with migrants according to key political incentives and institutional climates. Across space and time, the political institutional context stymies and encourages local, state, and national government actors to forge public-private ties to emigrants and their organized groups abroad. It is thus also incumbent on me to theorize and empirically examine the political factors that structure coproduction partnerships. By disentangling the political *and* social conditions that interact to structure the transnational partnerships in which migrants, nonmigrants, and government actors provide public goods across national borders, I account for how different transnational partnerships shape and transform local democratic governance.

While there is a large and growing literature on the relationships between migration and development and the political consequences of international migration for both sending and receiving countries, we lack a good answer for why some partnerships are better or worse for local democracy. I argue the lacuna stems from three sources. First, the focus on single cases for exploratory theory and confirmatory analysis cannot test how conditions varying across different migrant-sending communities affect the transnational partnerships that migrant associations seek to promote.[73] Comparative analysis is better suited to isolate and contrast factors that influence the nature of transnational partnerships and catalyze political dynamics in diverse hometown settings.

Second, when research does capture variation in migrant development efforts, it examines either the role of political institutions or social factors without considering how both arenas interact to affect outcomes or change the nature of transnational partnerships over time.[74] In other words, how might social and political relations between relevant state and migrant actors change as a function of coproduction activities? There is very little research that theorizes and empirically examines why and how social and political conditions at origin shape and are shaped by transnational partnerships and how these partnerships are responsive to changes in relations at home and abroad.[75]

There are reasons to be concerned with how political and social institutions interact to successfully coordinate public goods with migrant groups. Public goods decisions made between state and migrant actors may not be compatible with the needs of *local citizens* who are not passive recipients of public projects, but actors with a stake both in their voices being heard (the democratic process) and in policies that directly affect their quality of life (development outcomes). Moreover, government engagement in partnerships cannot be taken as a given since political officials face fiscal constraints, shirk responsibilities onto migrant groups, and use matching resources for personal gain. And changing conditions in both origin and destination locales including rising violence and economic recession may tax migrants' capacity to engage in coproduction regardless of any favorable initial conditions that create more synergetic partnerships. Explaining how partnership types change over time and break down in response to changing social and political conditions at origin and destination requires systematic and in-depth, micro-level exploration.

Finally, compared to their household counterparts, *collective* remittances sent by migrant groups are a drop in the bucket and virtually impossible to systematically track. Few researchers have examined the conditions under which HTAs and their development partnerships with the sending state alter democratic participation because there is skepticism that the small sums invested in public goods, when compared to household remittances, have observable political effects. Additionally, the lack of large-n data limits the ability of researchers to challenge this skepticism.[76] But the empirical gap in research does not mean that the political effects are negligible. As I show in the chapters ahead, migrant groups and their transnational partnerships with the sending state are a fruitful window for assessing how external nonstate actors, and the intermediary arrangements they help create, change the way people take part in government and its operation by "doing" development. It is not the amount of money sent across the border that matters as much as how that money affects and is affected by social and political structures and agency in origin and sending communities.[77]

SCALING UP DEMOCRATIC ENGAGEMENT FROM ABROAD BY DOING DEVELOPMENT

People are on the move engaging in politics across national borders. So who is involved in development and how development happens are no longer confined within the domestic walls of the nation-state. Using newly acquired resources abroad made possible through the act of emigrating, transnational migrants and their social groups upends traditional modes of political engagement because while people exit, some still use voice.[78] Spaces for civic and political participation are created with one purpose in mind such as public goods provision, but during the process social actors renegotiate boundaries of recognition, belonging, and community membership. And once migrants (re)negotiate their membership in the hometown community by creating and replenishing social ties and overcoming perceived status differences with hometowners, local and transnational citizens work together to directly and indirectly oblige political officials to answer for their actions while in office and sanction them for poor performance. The increase in civic and political participation of citizens supplements their role as voters and watchdogs of government to create more social actors involved in local governance.

Spearheaded by transnational migration, the widening of deliberation and inclusion constructs a politics of engagement in which previously excluded and dormant citizens and citizen groups have the opportunity to use voice in the local democratic process. In doing so, citizens make their concerns legible to the state through political participation in formal electoral institutions as well as informal modes of engagement including participation in protest activities, petitions, political campaigns, rallies, marches and protests, town halls, and civic associations.[79]

But since some migrants do not remain embedded in the social base of the hometown after exit and some local officials are unwilling and unable to engage migrant partnerships, competition for resources and recognition can lead to friction between migrants, residents, and political officials. While sometimes bursts of political activity occur in response to contests for power, contests for status and recognition between social actors, more often than not, lead to political disengagement. Apart from the substantive merits of a project proposal, be it a schoolhouse or health clinic, when residents and migrants do not share mutually intelligible meanings of community membership required of decision-making authority in public affairs, migrant-state partnerships may be deemed illegitimate and suffer contention and breakdown.

Furthermore, not all civic associations have democratic ideals. Migrant groups fall prey to opportunism, much like political officials, and transnational partnerships devolve into patronage for the local government or succumb to outright corruption. Migrant groups use resources acquired abroad and invest in public goods across national borders, improving citizens' access to essential services,[80] but the organizational structure and social learning inherent to ongoing relations in transnational partnerships reveals when it is effective at deepening political engagement and inducing more responsive governance.

The political dynamics unleashed by migrant groups' investment in local public goods are not the goal of transnational partnerships with the state. Rather, I argue they are unintended consequences. As I show in the chapters ahead, migrant actors are overwhelmingly apolitical and the principal objective for most clubs is implementing the project—building the school, paving the road, and constructing the bridge. But through the complicated process of coordinating projects in transnational space, migrants, local citizens, and political officials realize different motivations for participating (or not) and they become constrained and enabled by social relationships and local-state capacity. In other words, public goods provision through transnational partnerships is a window into seeing how actually existing local democracies work. The process shows who is involved in making decisions about goods and services essential for well-being, whose interests are being represented by whom, and who is excluded. It also shows how institutional arrangements emerging from outside the boundaries of the nation-state can scale up political participation but also exclude marginalized groups. And finally, the transnational process shows when and how political authorities are willing to shirk their primary responsibilities and offload service provision to migrant groups abroad that wield resources acquired through the act of emigrating abroad.

THE STRATEGIC CASE OF MEXICO

In few places are issues related to public goods provision, migration, and democratization more salient than in Mexico. Over the last century, Mexican migrants have crossed the 2,000-mile border into the richest country in the world to find jobs and reunite with love ones abroad. As of 2016, the Mexico–U.S. migration corridor is considered the most heavily traveled in the world.[81] Between 1970 and 2013, more than 10 million Mexican immigrants came to the U.S., an increase of about 1,000 percent, and are the largest share of the foreign-born population. While out-migration from Mexico was traditionally concentrated in states in the rural, central-western part of the country, as of 2010, few municipalities in Mexico remain untouched by U.S.-bound migration.[82]

Over the same period, Mexico has also experienced subnational changes in political development. Subnational democratization occurred throughout the 1990s and culminated in national democratization in which the PAN defeated the PRI after 71 years of uninterrupted rule. During this time in which more opposition parties effectively competed for state and local office, the federal government adopted decentralization reforms. These decentralization reforms introduced important variation in subnational political authorities' interest and ability to provide public goods. First, there are subnational differences in levels of economic development, which a vast literature has shown is highly influential in shaping public goods provision and democratic governance.[83] Second, while civil society organizations have strengthened over time after being lulled by decades of authoritarian rule, recent evidence suggests a stall: only 16 percent of all municipalities report the presence of a citizen assembly; 27 percent, a citizen council or board; 12 percent, representation of municipal delegations (*delegados*) in localities; 20 percent, a comptroller for social welfare and public works projects; and just over a third of municipalities report the presence of citizen committees of any kind.[84] Since previous levels of political engagement and social capital inherent to civic associations shape and are shaped by transnational partnerships, observing variation across these dimensions is key.

Given the complete lack of systematic data on collective remittances, annual data kept by the Ministry of Social Development (Sedesol) that administers the 3x1 Program provides a rare opportunity to assess the political effects of transnational coordination in a variety of local settings. Between 2002 and 2013, HTAs helped alleviate municipal poverty and increased citizens' access to drainage, sanitation, and water compared to places without active HTAs.[85] Moreover, since three tiers of the Mexican government (local, state, and federal) match migrants' resources, funds for public works are significantly amplified; in a quarter of 3x1 participating municipalities, remittances and matching contributions from the government accounted for more than half of local public works budgets.[86] Many municipalities have come to rely on the 3x1 Program to fund public works. And although collective remittances dwarf household remittances in sheer volume of flows, since these resources are used for public goods they benefit not just migrant households but also those citizens who cannot or choose not to go. Mexico provides an unparalleled opportunity and critical case for analyzing the emergence, variation, and effects of transnational processes in different social and political settings while holding macrostructural features constant.

EMPIRICAL STRATEGY: AN INTEGRATIVE MULTI-METHOD APPROACH

Findings for this book are based on original qualitative and quantitative data used in a multi-method research design. This strategy can be thought of as *integrative* in that one method provides an initial summary of knowledge about a problem of causal inference, while the additional methods test assumptions behind the initial summary but also discover new material.[87] I used each method for what it is especially good at, which helped overcome the inherent weakness in the other methodological approaches. Data was collected from a representative original survey of Mexican hometown associations, comparative fieldwork in Mexico, publicly available data for panel analysis of Mexican municipalities, and longitudinal survey data sourced from the Mexican Family Life Survey (MxFLS).

TRANSNATIONAL SURVEY INSTRUMENT, CASE SELECTION, AND COMPARATIVE FIELDWORK IN MEXICO

The process of data collection and analysis followed a specific sequence. First, I developed and disseminated a survey to all Mexican hometown associations registered with the Institute for Mexicans Abroad (IME). The survey instrument was informed by 30 face-to-face and telephone interviews with hometown association leaders in North Carolina, California, Illinois, and Texas and pilot tested with two clubs. The survey respondents were migrant club leaders located in 25 U.S. states from 23 states in Mexico (and the federal district) and 230 different municipalities.

I then collected additional data that situated clubs in transnational space; that is, I gathered a sociodemographic, political, and fiscal statistical profile of each U.S. destination and Mexican sending municipality that corresponded to migrant club respondents. This transnational data effort represents, to my knowledge, the first survey to link migrant associations with places of origin and destination.[88] This additional step of data collection was important to decipher how destination and origin characteristics made transnational partnerships both more common and more successful while informing the organizational features of migrant clubs. For example, migrant clubs in U.S. rural locales were more isolated and unable to join state-level federations of migrant clubs that aided the dissemination of best practices regarding fundraising, membership recruitment, and leadership know-how for improving club capacity to deliver public works.

Additionally, in Mexican places of origin, long histories of local authoritarianism and escalating violence related to the drug trade and the spread of criminal organizations exacerbated distrust in political officials. In turn, local citizens were more reticent to work with migrant partners in transnational partnerships with the state. U.S. and Mexican place-based characteristics informed how migrant clubs emerged and were structured, but also the extent to which partnerships were likely to be more inclusive of local residents and local government more fully engaged.

Initial analysis of survey responses showed that community inclusiveness and government engagement varied across clubs and were highly correlated with political outcomes. To understand why these factors differed across clubs, I selected five municipalities from three traditional migration states to conduct fieldwork. The geographic locations of the field sites are mapped in Map 1. Guanajuato, Jalisco, and Zacatecas have in common a storied history of migration to the U.S., active HTAs, and participation in the 3x1 Program. In these three states alone, 10,405 coproduction projects were completed between 2002 and 2013, representing over half of all 3x1 projects across Mexico and 44 percent of 3x1 Program expenditures.[89] Over the full time period, approximately $288 million (USD) was spent on 3x1 projects in just these three states.

The transnational partnerships I selected in each municipality maximize differences in community inclusiveness and government engagement and are exemplary of different organizational types. Some key factors including club capacity such as resources, time, energy, and interest of the club membership base were held constant, but the cases were initially stratified by economic development and local political conditions at origin. Four of the municipalities selected for fieldwork

MAP 1. Geographic location of field research sites in Zacatecas, Guanajuato, and Jalisco, Mexico. Source: ArcGIS Mexican Administrative Level Boundaries, Municipalities, ISO-19139 Metadata.

were of active migrant clubs and one municipality was the site of a failed transnational partnership. More detailed information about the case selection process, including a distribution of the cases by organizational type, and the transnational survey appears in Data Appendixes A and B.

After the cases were selected, I conducted fieldwork during 2009 and 2010. In every municipality I visited, I spoke to past and present government officials, the director of the office of migrant outreach (if there was one), local residents, leaders of civic associations, business and shop owners, migrant households, political party candidates and operatives, church pastors, locality delegates to the municipal government,[90] and members of local public works committees. I also regularly attended local public works meetings, town halls, assemblies, social and religious events, and ceremonies for public works installations. In most cases, I stayed with host families and participated in social events and weekly Catholic mass to build familiarity and trust with locals. The fieldwork generated 60 semi-structured interviews with key informants and hundreds of informal chats. I followed up with individuals with whom I had been unable to meet during fieldwork over email and telephone and participated in several HTA fundraising events and meetings in Illinois and California. This was necessary because in one case, Santa Catarina, drug violence made it unsafe for me to stay as long as I had planned.

I also interviewed state and federal political officials in Jalisco, Guanajuato, and Zacatecas, and the director of the 3x1 Program in Mexico City. In the U.S., I interviewed 3x1 Program officials at the Chicago and Los Angeles Mexican consulates and several migrant HTA leaders, club members, and HTA federation leadership. Many states have organized state-level federations composed of several hometown clubs from the state across U.S. cities. The states of Michoacán, Jalisco, and Zacatecas have the oldest and most well-organized federations in Texas, California, and Illinois, but most states in Mexico have at least one state-level federation of migrant clubs in the U.S.

The multi-sited fieldwork and interview data offered support for my initial intuitions about the factors that shape transnational partnerships. But the qualitative data revealed to me more concretely that migrant social embeddedness and continuous interactions between migrants, political officials, and residents that led to social and political learning were the key underlying mechanisms that explained why and how community inclusion and government engagement changed over time and accounted for different political outcomes. The comparative fieldwork also showed me that in places where social ties between migrants and local residents had decayed or were limited to begin with, social ties could be constructed when migrants recruited locals into the coproduction process and when they reengaged in repertoires of community membership. The kinds of membership activities included, for example, meetings with civic association leaders and pastors, participation in social and religious events including festivals, rodeos, dances, church meetings, dinners, and town halls, and social interactions in person and over social media, video chats, texting, and phone calls with residents in the hometown. Thus the survey and fieldwork were complementary. The survey helped to identify cases for in-depth analysis of micro-processes while the fieldwork provided evidence in support of the initial hypothesis and unearthed new information about causal mechanisms, which I could then test using additional data sources and methods.

SURVEY, PANEL DATA, AND STATISTICAL ANALYSIS

With fresh insights garnered from fieldwork, I then revisited the survey data and more closely examined organizational variation in transnational partnerships using cluster analysis and determined whether organizational types were linked with civic and political engagement before and after the start of transnational partnerships. Since the survey data is cross-sectional, I also evaluated aggregate effects of transnational partnerships across all Mexican municipalities from 1990 to 2013 to assess the effects longitudinally. In the final phase of the analysis, I compiled data on the sociodemographic, political, fiscal, and migration characteristics for Mexican municipalities and assessed, with statistical techniques tailored to the quasi-experimental nature of the data, how places with and without transnational partnerships differed in political participation and government responsiveness. Additionally, I looked to the Mexican Family Life Survey (MxFLS), a longitudinal survey, and analyzed how transnational partnerships affected more informal forms of civic engagement and nonelectoral modes of political participation across a representative sample of Mexican municipalities.

The integrative multi-method research strategy provides compelling evidence that migrant transnational partnerships improve political and civic engagement under certain conditions. The comparative case study method, initially selected to confirm hypotheses, became more exploratory when it revealed new information about why the structure of transnational partnerships varied, which then required closer scrutiny. The close examination of the micro-process of public goods provision showed that migrant social networks and political institutions shaped how involved local actors and political officials were in the transnational partnership with migrant groups. Moreover, observations of variation within cases over time showed me how different organizational forms of partnership were linked to different political consequences for local governance. Examination of cases like El Cerrito brought to light how migrant actors who lacked social embeddedness in the hometown constructed social ties to community stakeholders through outreach across multiple projects, which culminated in a process of social learning.

While the small-n method can neither be used to generalize effects in the aggregate nor control for the great variation that exists in the real world, without it, I would not have known to examine processes of social learning or even have known to look for it in the large-n data had I used that method alone. Without the large-n data, I would not be able to say with confidence that the political consequences I observed on the ground were not confounded by other factors I could not account for in the field. The integrative multi-method design allowed each method to complement the other methods and each was crucial to the demonstration of how transnational partnerships shape and transform local democratic participation through the process of public goods provision in migrant places of origin.

THE CHAPTERS AHEAD

In chapter 1, I describe why coproduction has different organizational forms and how this variation affects political and civic participation and government responsiveness. This part of the book provides a foundation upon which to then analyze the process and effects of transnational partnerships across and within Mexican communities. In chapter 2, I use a historical institutional approach, original qualitative interviews, and secondary data to present the evolution of the Mexican 3x1 Program and sending-state outreach policies with the Mexican migrant population in the U.S. The goal of this chapter is to present a macrostructural analysis of why and how transnational partnerships emerge.

The next four chapters comprise the empirical heart of the book. Chapters 3, 4, and 5 provide a bird's-eye view of the social and political contexts that organize partnerships and draw on six comparative case studies in five municipalities in Zacatecas, Jalisco, and Guanajuato. In each of the cases, I trace how community inclusion and government engagement interact to produce four organizational partnership types—synergetic, corporatist, fragmented, and substitutive—and the associated political consequences. In chapter 6, I scale up from micro-analysis to the meso-level of the migrant association. Here, I draw on original survey data to describe how partnerships vary across survey respondents using cluster analysis. Using the transnational survey data, I also test how club-specific factors affect the organization of partnerships. I next turn back to the hometown community and examine how transnational types observed in the survey data are associated with political changes on the ground in Mexico. The chapter then moves beyond cases in which transnational coproduction is known to occur to assess the systematic effects of partnerships in places with and without them over a 30-plus-year period (1990–2013) using statistical analysis.

The conclusion summarizes the central findings based on the case of Mexico. I situate transnational partnerships in Mexico with contemporary issues related to organized crime and violence spreading into more regions of the country and assess how voluntary return and deportations from the U.S. interior back to Mexico may affect local governance. I also contemplate what remittance-led development means in the globalized world. Finally, I discuss how well the framework I offer may travel beyond Mexico to decentralized democracies and authoritarian countries with substantial emigration.

Local Democratic Governance and Transnational Migrant Participation

While mobilized from abroad, migrant partnerships with the sending state are coordinated in preexisting social and political conditions in places of origin. Local social relations and political factors shape who becomes involved in partnerships, whose interests are represented, and the quality of the deliberations during project negotiations. How involved local citizens and government authorities are in the transnational process with migrant partners organizes partnerships differently. In this chapter, I argue that the combination of community inclusion and government engagement shapes transnational arrangements, creating four main types of partnership: synergetic, corporatist, substitutive, and fragmented.

The central argument is that transnational partnerships that are broadly inclusive of residents' input and reflect the full engagement of local political officials facilitate new modes of interaction between local citizens and elected representatives. This interactive process entwines state and society in local governance. Migrants' horizontal ties in the community and vertical ties to local government create conditions ripe for a more politically engaged local citizenry and more responsive governance. Other factors such as the length of time migrants have been abroad, the intensity of emigration in the hometown, and the size of the origin community are important, but these factors neither straightforwardly determine successful coproduction of public works nor determine changes in local political and civic engagement. Rather, the ability of migrant leaders to overcome the array of challenges inherent to collective action from abroad hinges on social and political institutions and resources in the hometown and are captured through the concepts of community inclusion and government engagement.

COORDINATION OF TRANSNATIONAL PARTNERSHIPS
IN THE SOCIAL BASE OF THE HOMETOWN

The coordination of public goods provision between migrant actors (and their groups) and political officials is a fluid process that occurs in the social base of the hometown.[1] By "social base" I am referring to the structure of the relational setting composed of a set of social ties and interactions among a set of actors that enables them to act collectively.[2] Migrants' collective remittance resources create vertical ties to government actors that contribute complementary resources for local public goods provision, which forms the organizational basis for transnational coproduction to occur. But migrants are also socially embedded in their places of origin to varying degrees. I argue the extents to which migrants maintain and construct horizontal ties and practice cultural repertoires that confer community membership are the most important determinants of the breadth and depth of community inclusion in the coproduction process. When migrants participate in public goods provision, how well they remain integrated into the social base of the hometown and their ability to overcome perceived differences in status brought about by migrating abroad play significant roles in how effective their partnerships with sending state actors will be and the political outcomes that result.

EFFECTS OF INTERNATIONAL MIGRATION ON
SOCIAL TIES AND COMMUNITY MEMBERSHIP

Distance from the place of origin and exposure to new influences, attitudes, behaviors, and customs create separation from people remaining behind. Some migrants are fundamentally changed by the migratory experience, which introduces modes of disconnection between sojourners and stay-at-homes. The length of time abroad attenuates migrants' web of contacts in the home place, constricting individual ties to more narrow circles of familiars. Demands on time, cost of travel, and legal status barriers to regular home-country visits reduce HTA members' exposure to and knowledge of conditions in the home place. Migrants' social and physical distance from the hometown leads to ideational gaps between "here" and "there" that likely constricts migrants' social ties to a diverse set of social actors and stakeholders in the hometown community.

The social distance created by emigration is not so different from other kinds of departure. Take, for example, changes in social status that occur when people go away for college. While going to college is a privilege in its own right, some high school graduates have the additional luxury of being able to go to a school in a different part of the home state or in a different state altogether. Time away in some different place exposes sojourners to new experiences, ideas, and behaviors. College-goers meet new friends across campus from different parts of the country, they become more mature, and they learn new things about themselves and about the world they live in. As people get older, work, and play together, they develop meaningful relationships that continue to inform who they are and where they want to go. Like college-goers, migrants often see their hometowns and the people remaining behind through a new lens after experiencing life in a new place.

Sometimes the distance produces nostalgia and a strong desire to return to familiar ways of life. But for others the psychological and emotional journey to somewhere else and the experiences afforded to them in new places create social divisions and noticeable differences between those who go and those who stay. When migrants, like college grads, have achieved some upward mobility because of their emigration, their material resources and ideas about the world that result from living abroad may affect social status at home. Migrants' experiences living abroad and acquisition of income lead some to adopt new attitudes and enables them access to land, new language, manners, customs, and dress.[3] These differences between here and there arising from migration may exacerbate social divisions already present and generate new cleavages between those who stay and those who go, which complicates migrants' claims to continued membership in the hometown community after they go abroad.

Places of origin are not frozen in time during migrants' absence either. While migrants work and live in the destination, people go on living, working, and engaging in the social, economic, cultural, and political life of the sending community. Children go to school. Political incumbents win and lose. Families invest in housing improvements, start businesses, and care for the sick and elderly. Couples marry and break up. Scandals, gossip, festivals, celebrations, traditions, and all manner of social and cultural life continue even as migrants come and go, video chat with family and friends, and build more permanent lives in the destination.

In some places, as emigration increases, communities become more transnationally oriented.[4] Residents with migrant ties or in places with high rates of emigration become more aware of and interested in the culture and society of the destination country. Substantial emigration changes many immigrants and it changes people remaining behind as well. These changes that accompany substantial emigration mean that some migrants are more likely to be embedded in the social base of the hometown after exit while others are less so.

Moreover, it is not enough to have social connections. Migrants must also be able to overcome perceived status differences between them and the stay-at-homes. When migrants continue to partake in cultural norms and values that are meaningful for group solidarity in the homeland, they signal to those at home that even though they have left and have become more prosperous they still belong. Migrants who are more socially embedded have both breadth and depth of social network ties in the hometown community and they are more likely to include local residents as active partners in the transnational process of coproducing public goods. Community inclusion has important consequences for civic and political engagement in local governance.

MIGRANT SOCIAL EMBEDDEDNESS AND MEMBERSHIP IN THE HOMETOWN COMMUNITY

Migrant embeddedness depends on the maintenance and construction of social ties and continued engagement with cultural repertoires that signal community membership. In this context, the relevant migrant actors are those individuals who are the active leaders or ambassadors of the migrant club in the hometown. Migrants' social embeddedness is key to understanding which residents are active participants in the coproduction process because it informs whose interests are being represented in negotiations with local government actors. This inclusiveness has important implications for the scaling up of local civic and political engagement in project governance and the likelihood that local participation spills over into other forms of democratic engagement.

Embeddedness is also crucial because it mitigates legitimacy issues that arise when migrants make decisions in town affairs from abroad. I expect that migrants who are more socially embedded will be able to substantively participate in the public affairs of the hometown as if they were territorial citizens because residents and community leaders still perceive them as members of the social and political community. In other words, making legitimate political decisions in public affairs from beyond borders is predicated on the belief of those remaining behind that migrants still belong to the community in a meaningful way. Migrants who maintain or construct more extensive social ties in the hometown, fulfill social, religious, and ethnic obligations, and practice quotidian cultural repertoires of social solidarity are more likely to be perceived as group members regardless of their territoriality and to include residents in the coproduction process. And while migrant individual characteristics and cultural practices matter for their belongingness so too does the structure of social ties in the hometown community.

By "community," I am referring to territorial (local resident) and extraterritorial (migrants who live abroad) citizens who share common attachment to the territory of the municipality or locality where public goods projects are provided in the coproduction process.[5] In this context, the concept of community extends beyond the confines of the political territory of the nation-state to those who are citizens abroad and who have a juridical claim to citizenship based on *jus solis* (birthright citizenship, or "right of the soil") and *jus sanguinis* (one or both parents being citizens, or "right of blood") laws. The important distinction here is that while migrants may retain juridical citizenship claims to participate in their places of origin, their absence calls into question whether or not they still belong.

Since public goods decisions are not binding on migrants because they live abroad, when migrants take an active, collective role in making decisions regarding public projects by mobilizing their remittance resources, residents may not perceive those decisions as legitimate if they have not had a meaningful part in their formation.[6] To increase the likelihood that public goods project decisions have legitimacy when they are transnationally coordinated, either local citizens are included in the decision-making process, or migrants who represent community interests are perceived as social and political members of the hometown such that when they make decisions about public goods projects, their decisions are articulations of local residents' interests.[7] There is an inherent tension in extraterritorial migrant citizens acting on their juridical citizenship claims to substantively participate in local political decisions in places where they no longer physically reside. As such, the recruitment of local citizens into the coproduction process is an important factor in determining the successes and failures of projects and possibilities for more democratic participation in local governance. We need to know who is involved in helping migrants and political officials make public goods decisions to know how egalitarian the process is. Understanding the structure of migrant social ties in the hometown shows us the way.

MIGRANT BONDING AND BRIDGING SOCIAL TIES IN THE HOMETOWN

The structure of migrant social ties in the hometown determines the degree of community inclusion. Migrant ties are best characterized by a combination of two types of social ties: bonding and bridging ties. The migrant bonding network includes people who are similar in terms of their demographic characteristics such as kin (consanguine and affinal) and fictive kin relationships.[8] Most often, migrants are bonded to family and close friends remaining behind as well as other migrant households in the origin community as these relationships entail trust and reciprocity. Bonding social ties are also the most likely to endure after emigration. When migrants needed help with transnational public projects, they most often initially recruited from this network.

By contrast, bridging ties are social ties to people who do not share many characteristics and tend to be beyond migrants' immediate social circles.[9] Bridging ties are more outward looking and encompass people with diverse socioeconomic characteristics, whereas bonding ties are more inward looking and reinforce exclusive identities and more homogenous, similar characteristics. Bonding ties undergird reciprocity and mobilize solidarity, but bridging ties serve as links to external assets and improve information diffusion by generating broader identities and nurturing relationships of reciprocity.[10]

The bonding and bridging ties[11] that make up migrants' social base are not either-or categories that neatly divide social networks. Rather, the membership of migrant HTAs has both bonding and bridging ties; however, bridging ties tend to be in shorter supply. Assessing the inclusiveness of coproduction in terms of the extent of bonding and bridging social ties in the hometown is key to understanding how reflective the coproduction process is of different interests and needs in the hometown setting, especially those of more marginalized citizens and citizen groups.[12]

Robert Putnam argues that without bridging ties, such as those that cross various social divides based on religion, class, ethnicity, gender, and socioeconomic status, bonding ties can become the basis for the pursuit of narrow sectarian interests.[13] Community inclusion that is reflective of both bonding and bridging ties is indicative of greater representation of societal interests. Smaller communities and those with strong ethno-religious institutions like *usos y costumbres,* a traditional self-governance system based on indigenous customary law, may be more likely to have preexisting bridging ties with migrants abroad. Moreover, destination country place-based characteristics, including the size of the hometown clubs' membership base, may influence the extent of the bonding and bridging ties in the social base that migrants can draw on to coordinate public goods projects.

In sum, the extent to which migrants are socially embedded in the hometown is defined by the social ties they retain after their departure. Those ties are most often bonding social ties to family, close friends, and neighbors. While some migrants maintain social connections to a wider network of people in the hometown, these ties are often in shorter supply and most likely in places with ethno-religious institutions. The combination of bonding and bridging social ties connects migrants to their hometown community and determines the initial recruitment of local citizens in the transnational process of planning and implementing public goods. The overall structure of these ties matter for understanding the effect of transnational partnerships on changes in political and civic participation in the hometown because who is involved in the process determines whose interests are represented and which groups gain access to political officials.

If bridging ties are limited or nonexistent in the migrant social base they can still be created. Some migrant club members may forge new bridging ties through community outreach and recruitment initiatives through existing institutions, elites, and infrastructures.[14] In other instances, local residents may request access to project planning or insert themselves into the coproduction process if they feel excluded. Locals who are stakeholders or leaders in public affairs in the hometown may challenge the legitimacy of migrant club involvement in public goods provision if club members do not seek their consultation or respect their social status. Recruitment of bridging ties with key stakeholders in the community is critical if migrants want their hometown investment and participation to have broad support and they want to thwart contests for power and authority.

Social interactions with residents outside migrants' bonding network in the hometown may lead to the expansion of bridging ties and the incorporation of a broader swath of societal interests into the coproduction process. Through recruitment initiatives, introductions, and repeated social interactions with local residents beyond migrants' immediate social circle, bridging ties are often constructed. And these new social actors representing diverse interests in the community are incorporated into the public goods process.

To summarize, the construction of new bridging ties in the migrant social network that accompanies repeated, cumulative interactions over the course of coproducing public goods projects enables migrants and stay-at-home citizens to learn ways to confront conflict and problem-solve through deliberation and negotiation. Since the construction and maintenance of both bonding and bridging ties that embed migrants in the social fabric of the hometown community can be quite challenging, community inclusion is more likely to reflect migrants' narrower bonding network to the exclusion of others. While I argue that, on average, community inclusion is more likely to be narrower, I also emphasize that social learning through repeated coproduction projects does allow for the expansion of social network ties that leads to increases in community inclusion in the coproduction process. The construction of more heterogeneous social ties in the hometown is possible, even if migrant social embeddedness is rather limited at the outset.

CULTURAL REPERTOIRES, COMMUNITY MEMBERSHIP, AND MUTUAL RECOGNITION

Social relations between migrants and territorial residents are important, but the basis of social membership is also instantiated, in part, on the practice of cultural repertoires that are meaningful to community members. By "cultural repertoires" I am referring to cultural ideas, rituals, customs, traditions, activities, pastimes, and practices that convey social solidarity and community. Social ties and interactions between migrants and residents in the social base of the hometown are easier to have when migrants continue to practice cultural repertoires that are meaningful to the residential members of the hometown.

In this formulation, cultural repertoires emphasize what Amy Binder and colleagues refer to as the constitutive elements of culture, including "the diverse meanings and beliefs that individuals and groups adopt to interpret their life experiences and, equally important, how such life experiences are in turn consequential in their social lives."[15] Migrants' who continue to participate in different materialist and recreational activities, ways and manner of communication, and social institutions including the Catholic Church and neighborhood associations while abroad reproduce and, therefore, reaffirm their membership in the social life of the hometown. Engaging in cultural repertoires of community also deemphasizes perceived or actual status differences that often accompany migrants' upward social mobility brought about by living and working abroad. Since the migration experience changes the material status of migrants, individuals who participate in club activities in the hometown have to strike a delicate balance in how they display their wealth and social status difference and maintain social solidarity and mutually recognized ideas of community with residents.

For example, when migrants go abroad they often learn a new language (e.g., English), adopt a new style of dress typical of the destination country, adopt new cultural practices perceived as "modern" (e.g., tattoos, piercings), and engage in conspicuous forms of consumption that together signal ascendance to a new social location, which may create social distance and sometimes jealousy. The social status differences affirmed by the migration experience are partially counteracted by practicing cultural repertoires and sharing their wealth and success with hometowners. When migrants maintain residences, visit frequently or for extended periods, continue to operate businesses from abroad, send remittances, bring home gifts for family, close friends, and acquaintances during visits, speak their native tongue, meet ethnic obligations (e.g., *tequios* or *faenas*) and wear traditional dress, they communicate solidarity, even if the activities are enabled by social mobility abroad. Migrants also partake in and host parties, rodeos, and church celebrations, financially support cultural traditions and community festivals (e.g., the annual patron saint festival) from abroad, and buy drinks and dinners for friends and acquaintances. These activities help preserve solidaristic ties with residents and influence recognition of social membership in the hometown community when membership is no longer tied to territorial residence. Engaging in cultural repertoires helps preserve imagined meanings of community that trespass national political borders in places that experience and are influenced by international migration.[16]

The reproduction of cultural repertoires enables migrants who achieve new levels of social mobility abroad to preserve their social position as a member of the community even while residing abroad. I expect that those migrants who practice cultural repertoires are also those who are more likely to have or are willing and interested in constructing bridging ties.[17] Those migrants who have wider social network ties or are able to construct ties anew, and who participate in cultural practices, norms, and values that communicate solidarity, are those most likely to have the highest degree of community inclusion in transnational partnerships despite achieving new levels of wealth and experience relative to those remaining behind.

COMMUNITY INCLUSION IN TRANSNATIONAL PARTNERSHIPS

Community inclusion refers to the extent to which locals are involved in the transnational coproduction of public goods—selecting, volunteering, monitoring, negotiating, planning, and donating labor and resources to projects. Community inclusion is important to transnational partnerships for two reasons. First, the social base provides migrant club leaders absent from the hometown with local resources that help achieve project goals. Migrants' social ties support the coproduction endeavor in migrants' absence in several important ways. Local citizens monitor coproduction projects, ensure timely completion and quality standards, volunteer labor and contribute personal and community resources, put pressure on local officials to meet matching contributions, and regularly interface with local officials regarding project selection, materials and machinery, implementation, and technical planning. Without local support from the social base, migrant clubs must attempt to manage coproduction partnerships entirely from abroad or have the means to visit (e.g., legal status, time, energy, resources to cross the border) to meet with officials and plan and execute public goods projects. Without the "eyes and ears" of local citizens, transnational projects are vulnerable to corruption by local government and other nonstate actors.[18] Reliable local community partners provide an important check on public agents and improve the likelihood that transnational collective action achieves the desired project goals.

Second, community inclusion, especially the inclusion of bridging social ties, increases the legitimacy and representativeness of the coproduction process since it includes more social actors and interests of different social segments of the community. Limited bridging ties can be problematic for a couple of reasons. Limited bridging ties may mean migrant club members are more likely to be perceived as social outsiders who lack information about norms of reciprocity and obligation, and the needs of the local citizenry. These "social gaps" of trust beyond migrants' social base of support undermine collective action efforts because citizens may rally to challenge the HTA as the representative voice of the community and work at cross-purposes.[19] When social ties are lacking, the selection of coproduction projects with the local government reflects migrant desires and those of their close social ties to the exclusion of other societal interests. This exclusion may renew or create social divisions between migrant and nonmigrant households in the hometown and ignite questions about who belongs and who is really a member of the community with the authority to make decisions in public affairs when territorial residence is not the only factor that determines membership.

From the perspective of territorial citizens, exclusion from the coproduction process may undermine their social and political location. Exclusion from coproduction sends the message that political participation is hierarchical, and that one's access to and influence in political deliberations is materially conditioned. And because coproduction involves the state, when elected representatives privilege the voice of migrants over their constituents, they diminish the inherent value of (territorial) participation in politics. In places with substantial emigration, an active, organized group of migrants with resources to wield power and influence can diminish political membership and participation of territorial residents when residents are excluded from the coproduction process. When the voices of emigrants are louder than the voices of territorial citizens, or when they represent a narrow group of interests based on migrants' close social ties, migrant groups' transnational collective action becomes an instrument of what Weber called social closure—the process by which social collectives seek to maximize rewards by restricting access to resources and opportunities or in which resources and opportunities are restricted to a limited circle of social actors who are eligible.[20] Transnational coproduction creates social closure when migrants act as if they are still territorial residents of the hometown without renegotiating their social membership in the community through the maintenance and construction of a wide array of social ties and practice of cultural repertoires and speak on behalf of the community of territorial residents without the legitimate authority to do so.

When emigrants exercise political voice after exit and that political voice is not predicated on mutual recognition of community membership, coproduction distances residents from making the decisions that affect their quality of life. Migrant transnational collective action that is exclusionary may displace residents from participation in the democratic political process, which is supposed to serve as a vehicle for interest representation and mechanism of social and political accountability in local governance. To overcome the inherent paradox in exercising voice and exit simultaneously, migrants must renegotiate their membership in the hometown community, which is facilitated by their degree of social embeddedness in the hometown community and includes local residents in coproduction; the broader the social network, the more successful the partnership.

LOCAL GOVERNMENT ENGAGEMENT IN TRANSNATIONAL PARTNERSHIPS

The structure of the social base in origin communities explains the degree to which transnational partnerships are inclusive of a broad, representative group of local citizens. However, since coproduction is a public-private partnership between organized migrant groups and local government, I also consider the factors that incentivize (and disincentivize) local government authorities' engagement in the process. Since coproduction requires complementary public financing from local government it is also necessary to assess what factors affect the quality of government engagement.

The degree to which local government provides complementary inputs to coproduction in the form of monetary and in-kind resources, project selection and planning, technical support, labor, and quality control is likely to vary across hometown settings. I argue two distinct but related factors affect local government engagement. First, government capacity determines political officials' ability to provide complementary inputs and their capacity depends, in part, on the organizational competence of local officials such as the public resources in the budget, their level of expertise, training, and professionalism. Second, when political officials are facing the possibility of their political party gaining or losing office and voters are actively engaged in making requests (or demands) for public goods, local political officials are likely to be more engaged in coproduction projects. In democratic systems with multiparty elections, government officials' incentives to cooperate with HTAs are likely shaped by local electoral incentives.[21] In the Mexican system, local officeholders cannot run for reelection for municipal president. As a result, competition between political parties is an important factor in determining when local government takes an active approach toward the transnational partnership. Taken together, both demand-side and supply-side factors explain the degree to which local government officials engage in the coproduction project process.

On the supply side, government contributions to partnerships are most often shaped by local budget constraints and the size of the origin community, but also the training and professionalism of local government officials and staff.[22] Government engagement suffers if local officials do not have the training and skills to provide technical plans and organize project budgets, or the ability to maintain authority and provide security over their political territory. In short, government engagement in coproduction is more likely in political contexts in which local government has what Michael Mann calls "infrastructural power." Infrastructural power refers to the capacity of the state to actually penetrate civil society and implement logistical political decisions through those realms.[23] Furthermore, as Wendy Pearlman argues, state capacity is an important factor to be evaluated rather than a property to be assumed when analyzing sending-state experiences with mass migration.[24] Explaining variation in local government engagement necessitates a description of the real and effective authority of the government, which is captured by the size of the origin community, fiscal budgetary constraints, and the degree of professionalization of political officials and their staff.

On the demand side, attention to the ways in which electoral systems channel societal interests for social spending and public goods delivery determines when local government officials are more likely to be engaged. Since electoral competition has become fiercer with subnational democratization, incumbent political parties interested in electoral victory may use public spending and remittance matching for public goods as a strategy to curry political favor in local political districts. Incumbent political officials may respond to increasingly competitive elections by using spending strategies that either win over swing voters or reward loyal party supporters.

Whether incumbents use broad, programmatic, or targeted spending to garner political support happens according to two separate logics according to the distributive politics literature. According to the first logic, incumbents use programmatic spending on public works to win over swing voters in highly competitive districts.[25] Programmatic spending increases public goods provision, which benefits everyone including both loyal constituents and swing voters. We should expect, then, that in highly competitive municipalities, incumbent political officials will by more engaged in transnational partnerships that provide public goods to win over a larger share of the electorate in order to win elections. According to a second logic, in political party strongholds incumbent parties may choose to reward core supporters with targeted spending because they only need to win by a small margin called the *selectorate*.[26] Targeting goods directly to core constituents allows incumbents to reward those who consistently turn out to the polls to support them. If political officials follow this strategy, we should expect less government engagement in party strongholds where incumbent officials need not rely on programmatic spending on public goods as a winning strategy. To understand the variability in municipal engagement in coproduction projects, I also assess how municipal officials respond to changing municipal electoral pressures and the competitiveness of multiparty elections.[27]

In short, understanding the variation in local government engagement requires a careful evaluation of the political conditions that incentivize officials' degree of participation and the real and effective authority that they have while holding office. Local government must use public resources and know-how to meet their obligations in coproduction projects, but how much they complement the coproduction process with time, energy, and resources is a function of their capacity and the perceived political payoff of doing so. But why can't HTAs simply provide public goods and services on their own? Why do they need government partners and the support of public agencies in the sending state?

There are a few reasons why HTAs need some engagement from the local or subnational government in decentralized political systems. First, migrant HTAs are made up of immigrants in the destination country who volunteer their free time, energy, and resources to improve social welfare in their hometown communities. While some associations have become formal organizations with 501c(3) status and maintain high levels of capacity (e.g., stable and growing membership and resource base, skills in organizing and fundraising, membership in state-level federations of clubs with information and resources to draw from), very few HTAs are likely to have the requisite training, support, energy, resources, and economies of scale to independently coordinate public goods without input and support from government authorities. Most HTAs are social groups that range in size but have a core group of leaders with a less involved membership base. This means that club leaders are most often the ones who do the bulk of the activities required to produce public projects back in the hometown. Migrant leaders organize, fundraise, and oversee development projects often in their spare time, on weekends, over telephone and email, and in meeting places at one another's houses. These club leaders are rarely professionally trained engineers and public administrators and typically do not have a full-time staff to support transnational efforts. HTAs need the financial and technical support of local government in order to meet the demands of implementing public works projects from beyond national borders.

Second, local government in many decentralized federal systems bears the administrative and political responsibility to provide public goods and services to the citizenry. Local government is the entity charged with caring and administering public lands. For many public goods projects, HTAs, at a minimum, need the approval and legal permission from local government to access public territory to build cemeteries, bridges, roads, sidewalks, water pipes, light poles, and the like, in the hometown.

Third, as competition for local public office becomes more competitive, local incumbents must build a base of support to secure electoral victory. If migrant HTAs are providing public goods without the cooperation of local government, elected officials may perceive migrant groups as a challenge to their legitimate authority and work to demobilize HTA development efforts or seek to offload responsibility completely onto migrant groups. In this vein, the size of the origin community where coproduction projects are proposed and carried out is a likely factor in the degree of local government engagement. In larger, wealthier communities in which political officials face fewer fiscal constraints to spend on public goods, local government actors may be less inclined to commit resources to the coproduction effort because officials do not need migrants to fulfill their administrative and political obligations. It may be more likely the case that smaller communities and those with more restricted social spending budgets are more inclined to support transnational coproduction projects with migrant groups abroad in order to subsidize local social spending initiatives with complementary resources from abroad.

Finally, if migrants' social bases are diffuse networks of engaged citizens and their civic associations, lack of government engagement signals to a segment of the voting public that local administration is wanting, which may harm incumbents come election time or create more discord and distrust in politicians. The local political context, including the preexisting character of political competition and institutional capacity, helps explain the extent to which local government engages in coproduction projects with migrant transnational partners.

HOW COMMUNITY INCLUSION AND GOVERNMENT ENGAGEMENT ORGANIZE PARTNERSHIP TYPES

How do partnerships organizationally vary? I conceive of the coproduction process as a relational space in which migrant and political actors interact in different social and political settings.[28] Figure 2 represents a conceptual space in which community inclusion (horizontal axis) and government engagement (vertical axis) intersect at different points and times along the two dimensions. The two dimensions of coproduction are dynamic, as are the interactions between different sets of agents (migrant groups, political officials, local citizens, and citizen groups). I emphasize that it is this dynamism, this variation, that determines political outcomes.

Different combinations of community inclusion and government engagement yield coproduction "types" identified in the four quadrants of the diagram. When

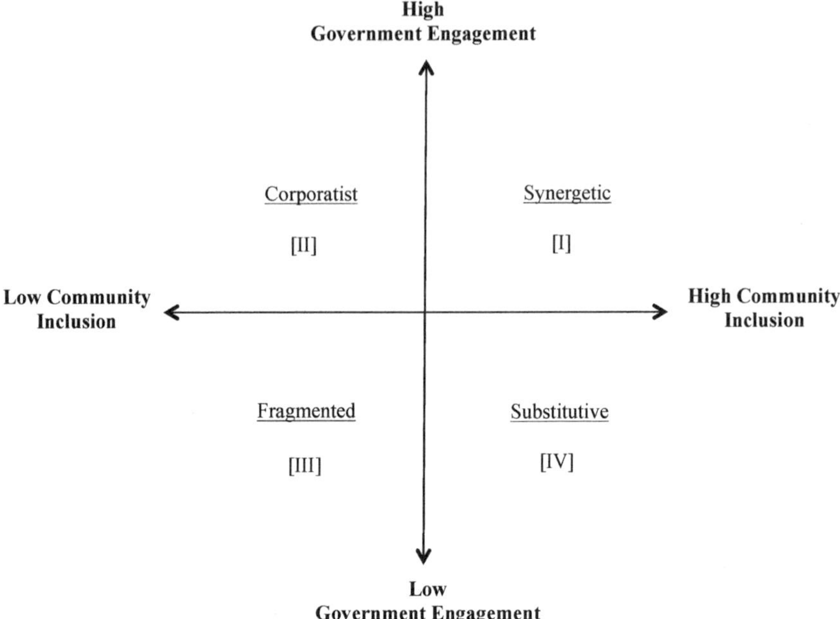

FIGURE 2. Conceptual diagram illustrating how community inclusion and government engagement interact to produce four organizational types of transnational coproduction.

inclusion and engagement are high (quadrant I), I call this a *synergetic partnership*. Synergetic coproduction is characterized by cooperative engagement among migrant HTAs, local government, and local citizens. All groups collaborate to coordinate projects, including deliberation over project selection, implementation, and oversight. I argue that as coproduction partnerships become more cooperative and inclusive, the likelihood that positive spillovers from coproduction affect civic and political participation in the hometown beyond project governance increases. In turn, as more local citizens participate in civic and political institutions—for example, voting and community associations—more citizens' interests will be represented in the political sphere of decision-making and government responsiveness will improve.

Synergetic coproduction is more likely to lead to greater civic and political engagement because citizens and government actors become embedded in more routinized forms of interaction and participation. Since citizens are more involved in making and shaping social welfare decisions that directly affect their lives, they are more likely to engage in politics as they learn what the democratic process can do to improve their lives and solve local problems that affect the citizenry. In other words, more participation in coproduction is likely to increase the political efficacy and mobilization needed for political participation in other spheres, including local elections. More civic and political engagement of the citizenry, in turn, will yield a more responsive government apparatus since citizens are willing to put pressure on government actors through social mechanisms. Information that citizens have about public budgets and the kind of decisions government actors make occur in closer proximity to their constituents. When citizens, migrants, and elected representatives are more enmeshed in decision-making over public goods and services, more local democratic engagement and responsive governance ensues.

By contrast, when both indicators are low (quadrant III), a *fragmented partnership* emerges. This form is inherently vulnerable to co-optation by the state and, in some instances, the HTA. The exclusion (intentional or unintentional) of local residents and low government engagement coupled with migrants' interrupted presence or physical absence from the hometown during project activities often leads to project mismanagement, appropriation of funds, and ultimate failure. Fragmented coproduction is most often associated with a worsening of state-society relations and a decline in citizen trust and engagement in local political life.[29] Fragmented partnerships signal less information sharing between migrants and residents about local government. When citizens are less involved in the coproduction process there are fewer social actors to monitor local government and provide oversight in project planning, implementation, and quality control. The lack of monitoring by residents and migrants who live abroad makes corruption and rent-seeking behaviors more likely, which often leads to the failure of the transnational partnership.

I discuss two additional intermediary cases in which either inclusion or engagement is low (or high) along the continuum of the axes. These intermediary forms I refer to as *corporatist partnerships* (quadrant II) and *substitutive partnerships* (quadrant IV). Corporatist coproduction is an organizational form in which high government engagement but low citizen inclusion links migrants' organized interests directly with the decisional structure of the local government. Cooperative relations between HTAs and local government grant HTAs privileged access to political officials to set the local public policy agenda. When migrants' public goods preferences predominate, the unequal distribution of resources toward migrant- and state-preferred public projects crowds out the voices of residents with a stake in public goods decisions that directly affect their lives. I hypothesize that corporatist coproduction affects local democratic engagement in two ways: political disengagement or short-run political activism.

Corporatist coproduction, characterized by low levels of community inclusion but high government engagement, suggests a narrow representation of interests reflected in project selection and implementation. If the migrant club lacks the ability or desire to retain some autonomy from the state, then migrant and state interests become the same and migrant groups may be vulnerable to clientelistic capture. On the one hand, citizen exclusion may trigger short-run political activism. When citizens perceive migrant groups' participation being privileged by the local government or perceive migrants as agents of the state, this crowding out may induce greater political awareness, interest, and mobilization to participate in formal politics. Citizen exclusion may introduce more short-term political participation at the local level as opposition political parties seize the opportunity to garner disaffected citizen voters. Citizens may be more encouraged to use the ballot box to punish incumbents for poor performance while in office (and reward incumbents who perform well) because they witnessed government mismanagement firsthand. On the other hand, citizen exclusion from the coproduction process may lead locals to distrust political (and migrant actors) and politics more generally. This decline in political interest may create disenchantment with local politics and a decline in political engagement.

Finally, substitutive coproduction refers to low government engagement and high community inclusion. In substitutive coproduction, local government provides some, albeit minimal, complementary inputs to public projects. Since cofinancing from other levels of government (state and federal) often accompanies coproduction, higher tiers of government and migrant HTAs subsidize local government provision. HTAs, in coordination with local citizens and citizen groups, organize project selection, planning, and implementation, leaving local government largely off the hook for service provision. In substitutive coproduction, government responsiveness is likely to wane as HTAs, citizens, and state and federal cofinancing partners subsidize local public works provision through coproduction.[30] In extreme cases, migrant groups may begin to challenge local officials for political power and authority and become the apex provider of local public goods and services. Substitutive coproduction is most likely to affect government responsiveness in public goods provision. If migrant groups subsidize social welfare spending and complete the lion's share of effort in coordinating public works, local governments are likely to allocate less resources for public social welfare, thus allowing them to shift spending patterns to alternative budget categories.

It is important to stress that coproduction cases are likely to be situated at other points along the conceptual continuum. The four cases I analyze reflect extreme combinations of inclusion and engagement and provide a set of testable hypotheses for the empirical chapters that follow. Additional cases of coproduction include transnational partnerships that come together for the purpose of one and only one project. I do not discuss such cases of *one-off coproduction*, but they frequently emerge. Other cases of coproduction are also likely affected by local factors that are not directly related to political institutions and social embeddedness including, for example, economic crisis and drug-related violence, which affected the United States and Mexico in the period of study. These hybrid cases are likely closer to reality than the stark characterizations I present here. I explore the role of economic crisis and public insecurity and violence more in the qualitative empirical chapters ahead.[31]

HOW U.S. AND MEXICAN CHARACTERISTICS SHAPE TRANSNATIONAL PARTNERSHIPS

Certainly, other factors are important to coproduction processes, including migrants' length of stay in the destination country, ecological features of the destination locale such as membership size, network dynamics, proximity of HTAs to other clubs and home country consulate, membership in state-level federations (especially in the Mexican case), as well as the internal structure of club decision-making. All of these factors vary across transnational partnerships. The point is not that other factors are irrelevant. Rather, I argue they are most likely to affect the configurations of partnerships through their effect on community inclusion and government engagement. In other words, the role of HTA capacity and U.S. and Mexican place-based characteristics, for example, may be endogenous to the community inclusion and government engagement that structure transnational partnerships.

One could imagine that the capacity of HTAs to carry out coproduction activities, most notably their fundraising ability and club internal organizational structure, is conditioned, in part, on the very factors that I argue affect migrant social embeddedness and thus community inclusion, including the size of the U.S. destination membership base. HTAs with more club members have access to more social ties from which to draw support. Since they are embedded in larger social bases they may expand community inclusion beyond their immediate bonding network. And because they have larger social networks to draw on for fundraising and coproduction support, they may also have a larger resource base to invest in public works from abroad.

Additionally, clubs that are members of state-level federations may develop more direct vertical links to political officials in the home country, enabling more opportunities to interface with elected representatives in the origin and destination country. More opportunities to interact with political authorities through state-level federations may, in turn, encourage more government engagement by way of leveraging bargaining power over municipal authorities with the collective power and voice of many migrant clubs from the same state of origin. In the theoretical framework I offer here, I hold HTA club capacity constant in an effort to maintain parsimony. I analyze greater variation in HTA capacity and the size of the membership network of the HTA abroad, among other factors, in the upcoming empirical chapters and report their effects on the organization of partnerships in chapters 4 and 6.

SUMMARY

In this chapter, I lay the foundations for the subsequent empirical analysis of migrant collective engagement in local public goods provision. I propose that transnational partnerships produce systematic effects on local political engagement and responsive governance. The typological theorizing I present describes the reasons why partnerships vary and how more synergetic, corporatist, substitutive, and fragmented partnerships change local democratic governance including state-society relations and political engagement. The argument advanced here is not meant to be a model that replaces the role of other factors that affect civic and political engagement and government responsiveness. Rather, I seek to bring greater attention to the role of transnational migrant actors and the variation in organizational forms of a transnational institution (coproduction partnerships) to better understand how civic and political engagement waxes and wanes in local democracies experiencing international migration. This theory is not meant to replace theories of electoral institutions, economic development, and social capital whole cloth but is instead intended to complement existing theories and explain more variation in political participation and the sources of change in government performance.

In the next chapter, I describe the macrostructural factors that gave rise to the Mexican sending state's outreach policies with the migrant diaspora in the United States, which culminated in the 3x1 matching grants program. The 3x1 Program administers coproduction projects between migrant clubs and the local, state, and federal governments in Mexico.

Decentralization, Democratization, and the Feedback Effects of Sending State Outreach

In 2002, the Mexican federal government unveiled the 3x1 Program. The 3x1 Program is a national social spending program whereby each level of government—local, state, and federal—matches the collective remittances that migrant clubs send home, peso for peso, for public goods provision. Between 2002 and 2017, more than 28,000 public goods projects have been financed through transnational partnerships between migrant clubs and the Mexican sending state and range from urbanization and public infrastructure to parks and schools. These public goods projects are overwhelmingly implemented in poorer, rural localities in middle-income municipalities where many Mexican migrants originated and public goods are lacking. Mexico is a pioneer in the creation of public policy in which the sending state matches migrant resources for local development purposes. Since its inception, the 3x1 Program has served as a social spending public policy model to emulate in other countries with substantial emigration interested in tapping the diaspora for hometown investment.

When are transnational partnerships between organized migrants abroad and political officials representing the sending state more likely to occur? Specifically, why did the Mexican sending state, which historically had a laissez-faire policy toward the migrant diaspora, cultivate ties with migrant clubs to spur development in Mexico in the late 1980s and 1990s? In this chapter, I show that transnational partnerships with migrant clubs are not automatic outgrowths of international migration despite the prevalence of HTAs around the world. Rather, the processes that encourage the formation of HTAs in destination countries are affected by the particular history of migratory waves out of the origin country. I use the strategic case of Mexico to trace the historical institutional conditions that explain the emergence of transnational coproduction partnerships in the 1980s and 1990s and the formalization of these partnerships into the federal 3x1 Program in 2002 that continues through 2018.

First, migrant grassroots organization predated Mexican sending-state outreach. The networked nature of Mexican immigration to the United States reached a tipping point in the 1980s and 1990s and led to concentrations of Mexicans with shared ties to places of origin, which helped create HTAs and paved the way for political mobilizations in hometown communities. Moreover, during this period, factors internal to the country led to democratization and decentralization and changed conditions in ways that facilitated migrant HTA intervention in local public goods provision. In doing so, organized migrants' mobilization impelled political officials at the subnational level of government to craft new ways of engaging migrants abroad in informal coproduction schemas and later in state-level matching grants programs. Subnational cross-border partnerships between organized migrant clubs and state-level federations of migrant clubs preceded a series of federal outreach initiatives beginning in President Salinas de Gortari's administration. The convergence of interests between migrant groups who were eager to effect change in their hometowns and that of the Mexican state led to an iterative process of negotiation that shaped the nature of the federal 3x1 Program that was eventually implemented. Eager to mobilize migrant resources toward public ends and appease migrants' discontent with the sending state, political officials at all levels of government in Mexico seized upon migrant hometown associations' bottom-up organizing and responded with top-down outreach at a critical juncture in Mexico's specific institutional history.

Data for this chapter is based on secondary data, in-person interviews, and transnational survey data. From 2009 to 2011, I interviewed local mayors in Mexico, directors of state-level 3x1 Programs, and political officials in local and state migrant affairs offices in Guanajuato, Jalisco, and Zacatecas. Additionally, I interviewed the director of the federal 3x1 Program in Mexico City and 3x1 Program coordinators and migrant outreach officers at the Los Angeles and Chicago Mexican consulates. Finally, I conducted participant observation at 3x1 project validation committee meetings (called COVAM) in Guanajuato's namesake capital and the Zacatecas State Federation building in Chicago, Illinois.

THE MEXICAN–U.S. MIGRATION CORRIDOR

Over the last century, Mexican migrants crossed the 2,000-mile border into the richest country in the world to find higher-paying jobs and reunite with family who had previously made the sojourn abroad. Recruited by American industry during World War II, *braceros* (manual laborers from Mexico) worked in factories and agricultural fields throughout the Southwest, Chicago, and California on guest worker contracts. Many laborers came on guest worker visas for temporary, seasonal stretches and other workers permanently stayed. Many of these individuals, almost exclusively men, were directly recruited by U.S. employers. The Bracero Program brought close to 4.6 million immigrants to the U.S. and another 3 million entered in the same period without guest worker status.[1]

After the Bracero Program (1942–64) ended, many migrants made the brutal, dangerous journey across the Sonoran Desert and Rio Grande without papers to try and improve their lot in life. During this period, emigration from the traditional states of the rural center of Mexico was predominantly undertaken by male "pioneers" who left the countryside for jobs in the north where they made more money working the same kind of job and diversified their family income.[2] Up until 1965, U.S. immigration policy restricted Mexican immigration through formal channels. But with the passage of the Hart-Cellar Act that eliminated national origins quotas for U.S. entry and the Immigration Control and Reform Act (IRCA) in 1986, more Mexicans applied for travel visas to the U.S. through family reunification provisions. Many more migrants crossed into the U.S. without documentation.

Concomitant with U.S. immigration policy changes, a series of economic shocks occurred in Mexico including the oil crisis in the late 1970s, debt crisis in the 1980s, peso currency devaluation, and passage of the North American Free Trade Agreement (NAFTA) in the 1990s. These economic shocks and the trade agreement not only imperiled the Mexican economy, but also had substantial consequences for international migration. Between 1965 and 2012, about 5–7 million Mexicans immigrated to the U.S. in search of economic opportunity and family reunification.

The IRCA was passed by Congress during the Reagan administration and was the first large-scale legalization program in U.S. history. The policy legalized the status of 2.7 million immigrants who met requirements and created a path to citizenship. Once naturalized, immigrants were granted the right to petition for family members to join them in the U.S., which had large unanticipated consequences for the number of Mexican persons immigrating through formal channels.[3] Additionally, the policy increased border security, established penalties for hiring undocumented laborers, and made it a criminal offense to cross into the U.S. with fraudulent documentation or without papers. Despite enhanced border security and immigration enforcement, the structural demand for low-wage immigrant labor in the U.S., family reunification concerns, and economic crises in Mexico encouraged significantly more emigration to the U.S. after 1986.

Changes to U.S. immigration policy coincided with the financial crisis in Mexico referred to as "The Lost Decade" (*La Década Perdida*). Until then, the Mexican economy largely relied on windfalls from crude oil and a strategy of import substitution industrialization in which high trade barriers protected domestic companies against foreign competition. The country suffered severe setbacks when the price of petroleum plummeted in the late 1970s and Mexico's entry into the General Agreement on Tariffs and Trade in 1985 exposed the economy to increased financial risk. Rampant inflation led to currency devaluation (peso crisis) and subsequent restructuring of the economy to an export-led growth strategy and loans from international banks that required conditions including scaling back federal social spending, a policy shift known as state retrenchment. The further penetration of the Mexican economy into international trade occurred in 1994 when NAFTA—the trilateral trade agreement among Mexico, the United States, and Canada—went into effect.

The elimination of trade barriers between the North American countries had important consequences for international migration. While the treaty benefitted several aspects of the Mexican economy, it was controversial legislation for the Mexican agricultural industry. Farmers were displaced from the land when staples of Mexican agriculture such as corn, beans, strawberries, and livestock could not compete with cheaper, heavily subsidized U.S. crops. Agricultural production and livestock that were once mainstays of states in the central-western region of the country ceased to be tenable employment. In response to sagging agricultural wages, droves of Mexicans left for the U.S. during this period. By 2012, about 11.4 million Mexican foreign-born persons resided in the U.S.[4]

The negative effects of economic instability were felt throughout Mexico and expanded the number of states sending Mexican nationals abroad in search of economic opportunity. Between 1920 and 2010, the Mexican states of Michoacán, Zacatecas, Jalisco, Guanajuato, San Luis Potosí, Durango, Guerrero, Aguascalientes, Nayarit, and Colima accounted for about half of all Mexican immigrants to the U.S.[5] However, as the economic crisis spread and affected more regional economies in Mexico, emigration rates increased in the southern states such as Veracruz, Yucatán, Chiapas, and Oaxaca in the latter half of the 1990s and early 2000s. Just as the spatial distribution of Mexican migrant sending states changed, so too did immigrant destinations in the U.S. Previously, Mexican immigrants to the U.S. were concentrated in the Southwest border states and the Chicago metropolitan region. These popular immigrant destinations are referred to as traditional immigrant gateways.[6] Before 1990, 85 percent of all Mexican immigrants lived in three states—Texas, Illinois, and California[7]—but after 1990, migrant settlement expanded beyond traditional gateways into the Southeast, Northwest, and Northeast regions. New immigrants went directly into new destinations including Georgia, North Carolina, Utah, Washington, Iowa, Nebraska, Tennessee, and Oregon. And those immigrants already in the U.S. moved internally to new destination states and especially to the suburbs with the acquisition of more social mobility. Mexican migration became less regionalized and more of a mass phenomenon on both sides of the U.S.-Mexican border.[8]

Understanding the causes of international migration in the contemporary period are important for understanding the formation of hometown associations in the United States. Mexican-based immigrant organizations were first documented in the 1920s and 1930s in the U.S., but these early organizations focused mostly on support and aid to Mexican immigrants in the U.S. and Mexican cultural appreciation such as folk art, dance, sports, other recreational activities, and religion.[9] These early associations were not organized around hometown ties as Mexican migration to the U.S. had not yet amassed concentrations of people who shared *paisanaje*— meaningful social connections based on a shared sense of belonging and attachment to a common origin that emerges when immigrants encounter each other outside of the homeland. *Paisanaje* is a necessary and sufficient condition for the formation of migrant hometown clubs. While a few early transnational immigrant clubs were documented in U.S. gateway cities in the late 1960s and early 1970s, it was not until the passage of U.S. immigration policy legalizing immigrant status in the U.S. that migrant transnational social networks diversified and concentrations of immigrants from the same places of origin built up over time and matured, leading to the formation and multiplication of hometown associations across U.S. cities.

MEXICAN MIGRANT HOMETOWN ASSOCIATIONS IN THE UNITED STATES

Generally, the formation of voluntary civic associations based on *paisanaje* is a particular feature of social networked–based migration. In the Mexican context, the social network character of international migration was a dominant feature of U.S.-bound migration but reached an apex in the 1980s and 1990s. Once migrant transnational social networks expanded and matured and concentrations of migrants from the same hometown communities proliferated, more HTAs emerged in diverse destinations across the U.S. The social network nature of U.S.-Mexican migration created the conditions for filial communities in the U.S., and when it reached a tipping point, there was a widespread formation of Mexican hometown associations.

By 2003, over 600 Mexican migrant HTAs had formed in 17 U.S. states from 26 states of origin and the Mexican federal district.[10] Ten years later, over 1,200 different Mexican clubs had partnered with the Mexican government for a public goods project at least once through the federal 3x1 Program, although more than 3,000 HTAs are registered with the Institute for Mexicans Abroad.[11] Contemporary migrant clubs did not begin with the singular focus of investing in the development of their hometowns. Rather, collective resources were sent back initially to support the annual patron saint festivals and church renovations in migrants' hometowns. The Catholic Church and ethno-religious institutions were an important catalyst for the formation of migrant clubs. Itinerant priests sought out paisanos from predominantly rural hometowns in the U.S. and asked them to become partners in church improvement projects.[12] Other HTAs, predominantly from Chiapas and Oaxaca, formed clubs around ethno-religious obligations to the community of origin as part of the system of *usos y costumbres*.

The system of *usos y costumbres* in indigenous Mexican communities is a system of village-based traditional governance that requires community members abroad to meet social obligations called *faenas* and *tequios* despite their physical absence.[13] Making cross-border investments through hometown clubs allowed absent migrants to meet their ethno-religious obligations from the U.S., which was often a requirement for maintaining membership in the social community.[14] Many migrant groups also came together on their own, first, as social, cultural, and prayers groups, soccer clubs, and rotating credit associations (referred to as *tandas* or *cundinas*). Clubs later changed their primary focus and adopted cross-border development projects, especially after emergencies and natural disasters in their hometowns. Survey data I collected of a representative sample of Mexican HTAs shows that the majority of HTAs formed on their own (67 percent) after 1990, while other clubs said they formed at the request of the Mexican local government (17 percent). Prior to 1990, before select states adopted state-level matching grants schemes, migrant clubs that supported projects in their hometowns did so on a more informal and spontaneous basis and projects were small in scale.[15]

WHY DO MEXICAN MIGRANTS PARTICIPATE IN HOMETOWN ASSOCIATIONS?

The reasons for migrant participation in HTAs are multifaceted and often change over time with social mobility and experiences in the destination and origin society. While such participation is often motivated by altruism and loyalty to the hometown, it also reflects the adoption of new views brought about by the migratory process.[16]

Movement to a richer country provides migrants with better access to public services in addition to higher wages. As they acclimate more into U.S. society they come to expect, for example, that in an emergency a phone call to 911 summons an ambulance that will take them to a hospital. In many rural Mexican towns, there are no ambulances. In El Cerrito, Guanajuato, residents told me they had to "wait and ask a friend for a ride" or "ride horseback" to get to the closest hospital when there was an emergency. Migrants also observe and adopt new norms of behavior while living in U.S. society, bringing into starker contrast the lack of public goods provision in their places of origin. Living in the U.S. alters migrants' expectations about what kinds of public goods and services citizens in Mexico should have access to, and many start or join HTAs to modernize their hometowns in accordance with these new views.

But while speaking the language of community, migrant HTA activities also articulate that they are no longer the same as those remaining behind.[17] For some migrant groups, sending money home is more akin to patronage and residents are viewed as the beneficiaries of migrant generosity. This view of HTA participation as a strategy for personal or group advancement is not typically the primary objective when forming or joining a club, but many migrants come to derive social status and enjoy their newfound prestige over time. Migrant clubs' development efforts sometimes come to reflect a calculated strategy aimed at cementing social differences in the origin community.[18]

The context of reception in U.S. society plays another role in shaping the formation of HTAs. Since many immigrants live in precarious and exploitative working conditions in the U.S. in which their identities are criminalized and marginalized, HTA engagement helps combat the vagaries of how they are perceived in the destination place. This "reactive transnationalism," as it is sometimes called, is an opportunity for migrants to feel socially connected and valued in a social community while managing the rigors of daily life abroad.[19]

Finally, HTA engagement may be based on the prospect of future return to the hometown. Some migrants invest in public projects for future enjoyment or to ensure that their good deeds obligate community members to care for them in old age. Migrants form HTAs to celebrate culture and play soccer and eventually adopt development projects as the central mission. Once development goals are adopted, collective remittance sending also does "relational work" for migrants.[20] It signifies migrants' expressive, affective ties and serves as a tool for social status valorization in towns in which they want to eventually return.

The degree to which Mexican immigrants are involved in HTA activities also varies. For some people, occasional donations to fundraising efforts or attendance at club meetings and social events constitutes the whole of their participation in the club. Others assume a leadership role, which requires significant time, energy, skills, and resources to coordinate projects across borders. The core leadership of migrant clubs is most likely male, married, between the ages of 30 and 44 years old, with a high school degree or equivalent, and living in the U.S. between two and ten years (55 percent), although a sizable percent of the survey sample had lived in the U.S. just two years (18 percent) and longer than 11 years (25 percent). Legal status and the size of the paisano social network are all factors that help determine the scale of HTA participation. While some clubs negotiate public goods provision from afar without visiting, those individuals with legal status and who can visit the homeland more easily are more likely to be involved in the day-to-day activities of their HTA. The degree of formality of club organization and overall membership activity also varies across clubs. On average, clubs had around 100 members, but some clubs were made up of just a few families and some had up to 5,000 active members. The largest clubs were most likely to be located in California, Texas, and Illinois with a long history of Mexican immigration from the traditional sending states of Jalisco, Guanajuato, Michoacán, and Zacatecas. More information about Mexican HTAs is presented in chapter 6 and Data Appendix B.

FROM A "POLICY OF NO POLICY" TO SENDING-STATE OUTREACH INITIATIVES

During the period of mass Mexican immigration to the U.S., Mexican emigration policy changed from a "policy of no policy" to *acercamiento*—the adoption of several state outreach initiatives intended to bring Mexican immigrants back into the national imaginary. Mexican state outreach policies eventually culminated in the federal 3x1 Program in 2002 for reasons only tangentially related to migration. Economic crisis spelled the beginning of the end of the PRI's 71 years of uninterrupted control of the presidency when opposition political parties began to effectively compete for state and local government. In an effort to retain national control, the PRI adopted a series of decentralization reforms devolving authority to subnational government over three terms (*sexenios*).[21]

Subnational democratization and decentralization represented two critical periods in Mexico's historic-institutional context that help explain the formation of Mexican sending-state outreach initiatives. Because of these internal political developments, Mexican leaders looked to migrants abroad and extended the reach of the corporatist state beyond the border in an attempt to appease migrants' political discontent.[22] The Mexican sending state's *acercamiento* project, in turn, increased the capacity of migrants to bring additional pressure on Mexican political officials to have migration programs reflect their needs and interests. The negotiation between organized migrants and state and federal Mexican officials led to the adoption of remittance matching grants programs and subsequent changes in how the programs operated.

Prior to World War II, the Mexican government's emigration policy restricted emigration through exit controls. Mexican migrants were often castigated by Mexican officials and called *pochos*, a derogatory term designated for "deserters" who left the homeland and lost their Mexican culture.[23] In the postwar period, restrictive emigration gave way to more careful attention to those who left to participate in the Bracero Program in the U.S. labor market. However, the end of the Bracero period and failure of emigration policy to control departure ushered in a more laissez-faire attitude toward emigration that was accompanied by what many have dubbed an emigration "policy of no policy."[24] The lack of policy was itself a policy that performed both as an economic, political, and demographic escape valve following severe macro-economic crises and a political crisis for the long-standing PRI, and as an interest in releasing the pressures of rapid population growth.[25]

Rather than attempting to regulate departure through exit controls, emigration policy in the 1980s and 1990s focused instead on embracing emigrants already beyond the border. The discursive shift from denigrating emigrants as *pochos* to extolling them as *hijos ausentes* (absent sons) and *heroes* was accompanied by changes to emigration policy that encouraged and nurtured social, political, and economic ties to the Mexican homeland. It is in this period of *acercamiento* that Mexican emigration policy concentrated more on promoting development through remittances, extending dual nationality and absentee voting, and cementing a Mexican ethnic lobby in Washington, DC.[26]

Thus the ramped-up efforts of Mexican outreach to the emigrant population in the U.S. was precipitated by decentralization reforms and democratization, two critical junctures internal to Mexico that paved the way for formal development partnerships with migrants and the 3x1 Program. First, changes to the system of intergovernmental relations brought about by a series of decentralization reforms devolved political and administrative authority over public goods provision to local government. While these reforms de-centered decision-making over public service delivery to local (municipal) political officials, authorities still had to rely heavily on federal and state revenue-sharing arrangements to finance public expenditures. Looking abroad to their paisanos, municipal, state, and eventually federal tiers of government capitalized on the changing resource base of migrants abroad to help fund public works investment through transnational partnerships. Second, the opening of the political system to opposition parties at the subnational levels of government in the late 1980s and 1990s created political opportunities for government actors to further encourage migrant investment in hometown development. As political competition became fiercer and incumbent parties faced legitimate threat from the opposition, delivery of public goods took on greater importance for local electoral victory. For many municipal leaders, providing public goods with matching funds from state and federal partners closed the gap in funding constraints and allowed municipal leaders to adopt more programmatic spending agendas with migrant partners.

DECENTRALIZATION AND THE PROVISION OF PUBLIC GOODS IN MEXICAN MUNICIPALITIES

The De la Madrid Sexenio (1982–88)

Prior to the defeat of the PRI in the 2000 national presidential election by the popular PAN candidate Vicente Fox, the Mexican political system was dominated by one-party rule. Mexico was a strong central state with a weak federal system. Subnational political units lacked autonomy and resources and political power was concentrated in the presidency with the PRI. Until 1988, the PRI controlled all Senate seats and before 1989 no opposition party had ever won a gubernatorial election. Between 1982 and 2000, however, the PRI's lock on political control changed. Mexico experienced dramatic changes to its political institutions, spearheaded by President de la Madrid's 1984 Municipal Reform in the wake of the 1982 debt crisis.

De la Madrid's presidency initiated a profound shift from the import-substitution industrialization policies of his predecessors, which could no longer be supported by loans financed by international capital investors. During this period in which the economic system shifted to a neoliberal export-led growth strategy,

Mexico had zero economic growth, unemployment reached 35 percent in 1985, income inequality worsened, and workers' salaries and real wages dropped to 1966 levels. While the economic crisis that began in 1982 had somewhat abated by 1990, the economic woes that crippled Mexico during the "Lost Decade" were exacerbated again with the 1994 currency devaluation of the peso. The PRI's mismanagement of the economy galvanized calls for democratization and affected the ruling party's iron grip on political power. The national election in 1988 brought these demands to a head. Incoming president Salinas de Gortari, who succeeded De la Madrid, confronted the difficult task of restoring the PRI's power while continuing to implement free-market economic reforms and scale back the welfare state as a condition of financial loans from Washington and the international development banking community. The strategy deployed by the PRI administration was to decentralize authority to subnational levels of government in order to maintain central power and authority in the presidency.[27]

The economic crisis that rattled Mexico in the 1980s had iterative effects on pluralist representation at state and local levels. It also catalyzed De la Madrid's decentralization reforms. Rodriguez recalls, "by the 1980s, the façade of Mexican democracy had deteriorated so badly that the entire political system was in dire need of a facelift."[28] The 1984 Municipal Reform was the regime's first response to regional economic and political imbalances that were a threat to political stability and the strength of the PRI. The processes of political opening, recognizing opposition party victories, and fiscal decentralization policies of the De la Madrid administration were pursued on the general premise that by strengthening governments at the subnational level the power and stability of the PRI presidency could be preserved. To accomplish this, the PRI recognized a smattering of opposition victories in the 1980s and responded to demands to decentralize administrative responsibility over the delivery of public services and social welfare. The devolution of power to subnational units of government was best characterized as "unintended decentralization" and a reactive strategy: to maintain political power, the PRI had to give some away.[29]

The De la Madrid decentralization reforms of 1984 granted greater autonomy to municipalities and fundamentally changed the character of intergovernmental relations in Mexico. However, it was far less risky politically because it could be selectively implemented. The municipal reforms were ostensibly to pacify municipal desires for financial and political autonomy, but while the reforms granted some political power to municipal governments, lower levels of government never received full financial autonomy; subnational government did not receive an increased percentage of revenue-sharing allocations but were responsible for social spending on public goods and services.

Officially, the initiative to reform Article 115 of the Constitution, which deals with municipalities, granted administrative responsibility in the domain of public service provision for the following services: potable water and drainage, street lighting, street cleaning, markets and supply centers, graveyards, slaughterhouses, street paving and maintenance, parks and gardens, public security and traffic. The reform also granted municipal governments all revenues collected from property taxes (*predial*), fees and licenses but these revenues were marginal. Additionally, the reforms gave municipalities administrative power to design and implement development initiatives and the freedom to make formal assistance and cooperative agreements with the state and federal governments for the efficient provision of public services, if necessary. According to De la Madrid, the decentralization reforms emphasized: "Centralization in an earlier périod [that] allowed the country to accelerate its economic growth and social development has outlived its usefulness and become a serious limitation on the country's national project . . . Centralization has seized from the municipality the ability and the resources needed for development and the moment has come to stop this centralizing tendency" (Cámara de Diputados 1983: 8).

In practice, decentralization reforms transferred administrative authority to subnational governments but ultimately allowed the PRI to maintain control. The national presidential election held in the midst of economic crisis in 1988 and calls for more political aperture culminated in the greatest threat to the PRI's power since the creation of the party. During this period of economic and political crisis, the incoming administration looked to the Mexican migrant community abroad as one of the foreign policy strategies to improve domestic relations.

The Salinas de Gortari Administration (1988–94)

The electoral victory of Carlos Salinas de Gortari in 1988 was one of the most controversial presidential elections in Mexican history. Many people cried foul, both inside Mexico and across the border in the U.S. When Cuauhtémoc Cárdenas, former governor of Michoacán and longtime member of the PRI, failed to be nominated as the PRI's presidential candidate, he splintered from the party and coordinated a coalition to run an opposition party ticket under the National Democratic Front. The party later become the Party of the Democratic Revolution (*Partido de la Revolución Democrática*, PRD), a major political party contending for power at all levels of government. Veteran Chicano groups, Mexican labor unions in the U.S., exiled students and activists from the 1968 antigovernment revolt, grassroots organizations, human rights advocates, and others rallied behind Cárdenas's campaign. Cárdenas was an outspoken supporter of absentee voting rights for Mexicans in the U.S., workers' rights, economic stability, and democratization in Mexico. Cárdenas also traveled several times across the border to large emigrant and Mexican American communities in the U.S., where he campaigned in the run-up to the election.

In California and the southwestern states of Arizona and New Mexico, Cárdenas energized and mobilized an international democratic movement in his favor, enough to establish formal branches of his opposition party in the U.S. called *comités de base* (base committees). These PRD base committees fundraised extensively in select U.S. cities and encouraged PRD immigrant supporters to persuade family and friends in Mexico to cast their vote for Cárdenas. Absentee suffrage was not extended to the Mexican emigrant community during the 1988 election, despite Cardenas's efforts. However, Cárdenas's project to mobilize an active and vocal oppositional voice to the PRI on both sides of the border was effective. His engagement with migrants and Mexican Americans made it difficult for the PRI to ignore the mobilized population after 1988.

The defeat of opposition candidate Cuauhtémoc Cárdenas created widespread political division. Especially vocal were immigrants and Chicanos in the United States who supported the Cárdenas presidential campaign. While *cardenismo* started as a social movement, the support garnered from "discontented and disaffected" Mexicans living throughout the U.S. culminated in the emergence of the PRD as a major political party and greater support for national democratization in Mexico mounted.[30] Mexican immigrants in the U.S. driven from Mexico because of economic and political problems became a natural constituency of the PRD and Cárdenas. This mobilization around the PRD forced Mexican PRI officials to recognize resentments in the Mexican community in the U.S. that felt forgotten and disenfranchised by their government.[31] Cárdenas's presidential campaign in 1988 created competition between the parties for the loyalty of their compatriots as both parties searched for constituencies and allies in the U.S.

In an effort to reinforce the exceedingly fragile legitimacy of his electoral victory, Salinas revived and broadened the Mexican federal government's historically on-again, off-again *acercamiento* with the Mexican emigrant population. Salinas resuscitated the Mexican federal government's emigrant incorporative strategy, although he used a different mode of incorporation than in the post-revolutionary period.[32] Whereas the 1917–32 period was characterized by a policy of encouraging return, the Salinas administration directly courted migrants and their resources abroad. Salinas's contentious electoral victory mobilized opposition voices on both sides of the border that unleashed new pressure on the PRI administration to appease discontent.

The strategy adopted by the PRI was to extend services to the immigrant population in the U.S. through a series of policy initiatives including the International Solidarity Program and the Program for Migrant Communities Abroad (*Programa para las Comunidades Mexicanas en el Extranjero,* PCME). Salinas conceived of the International Solidarity Program as a way to create coproduction partnerships between civil society (nonstate private actors) and state officials and agency (public actors and agencies) in the Mexican government. This strategy sought to enhance state legitimacy in a way that previous coproduction programs had undermined.[33] The PCME was created in 1991 as part of the division of the Ministry of Foreign Relations (SRE). The PCME was directed by ministry staff in conjunction with consulates and Mexican cultural institutes abroad and officials regularly reached out to Mexican immigrants throughout the U.S. The program delivered education, community outreach, culture, recreation, and business services to migrants in the U.S. The community program, in particular, focused on helping migrants form HTAs and state-level federations of clubs and promoted state offices for migrant affairs. One of the chief activities of Mexican state offices for migrant affairs was to collect information on immigrants' whereabouts in the U.S. and publicize state-level matching funds programs to them in the states of Zacatecas, Guerrero, Jalisco, Guanajuato, and Durango.[34] It is no coincidence that the number of migrant clubs surged during this period of Mexican state outreach through the PCME and International Solidarity Programs.[35]

The social spending cornerstone of the Salinas administration was the National Solidarity Program (Pronasol, Spanish acronym). Pronasol was originally conceived as a poverty alleviation and regional development program. The objectives of the Solidarity Program were to improve living conditions in marginalized groups, promote balanced regional development, and strengthen the participation of social organizations and local authorities through further decentralization.[36] The Solidarity Program ("Solidarity") established community participation in the selection and implementation of projects through local Solidarity committees that provided a mechanism for greater citizen involvement. It also led to the creation of municipal Solidarity councils. These councils promoted greater municipal and state control over fiscal resources, autonomy over public service delivery, and social welfare programs.[37] Solidarity decentralized fiscal resources and decision-making authority by allocating federal funds directly to project committees and their municipal councils instead of going through state government. While Solidarity did provide some fiscal resources directly to the municipalities for social investment, the federal revenues from income taxes were allocated to states and then to municipal government. Even as municipal governments obtained more autonomy over the administration of local budgets, they were almost entirely dependent on state and federal revenue sharing to run their jurisdictions.

The system of state-to-municipality revenue sharing called *participaciones* was problematic for some municipal authorities, namely rural municipalities, because of considerable variation in the actual proportional allocation of resources they received from state governments. Urban municipalities, for example, tended to receive the largest allocations of fiscal transfers, and municipalities governed by political parties other than the dominant PRI did not fare as well. Some political officials decried that the program was a mechanism for the PRI to exercise political manipulation. By rewarding PRI strongholds with public resources, municipalities financed public goods in areas with potential swing voters to capture a plurality of votes to win local elections, allegations that have been supported by extensive research on the Pronasol program.[38] Solidarity funneled resources directly to municipalities for the production of public works; however, they still relied extensively on state and federal governments for financing, and the funds were politically manipulated in places with different state and municipal political party affiliation.

The International Solidarity Program was one of the central, although less publicized, components of Pronasol and directly engaged the Mexican migrant diaspora in the U.S. International Solidarity was administered as a separate branch of PCME that offloaded a significant portion of infrastructure development costs to organized migrants interested in being partners in hometown development. Salinas's Solidarity programs replaced a large component of the social safety net, which was abandoned during the neoliberal shift. The programs also led to the creation of citizen committees, which contributed 50 percent to financing and implementing projects in a public-private partnership schema best described as an early form of coproduction. Migrant hometown associations were not viewed differently than citizens living in Mexico; migrant HTAs regularly served on citizen committees (albeit in the U.S.) and entered into collaborative public-private partnerships with the federal government. Between 1993 and 1997, International Solidarity coproduced 211 projects transnationally with migrant HTAs predominantly from the traditional sending state of Zacatecas.

While several migrant hometown associations predate the creation of PCME, the outreach program was another important reason why the number of HTAs and public-private partnerships increased throughout the 1990s. Immigrants who visited consulates for regular business were given information about the International Solidarity Program and PCME and how they could help develop their places of origin with collective remittances in partnership with the Mexican government. In addition, the PCME hired staff to document existing HTAs and created a directory of sports, social, religious and cultural clubs that could be converted to clubs that supported infrastructure development.[39] PCME, in conjunction with the Mexican consulates, also arranged visits between governors of migrant sending states, municipal presidents, and their paisanos in the U.S.

According to my survey, almost a quarter of club respondents reported forming HTAs at the request of local and state Mexican officials and officials at Mexican consulates in the U.S. Moreover, PCME was responsible for the administration of applications for the consular identification cards to Mexican migrants called *matricula consular* cards. Federal officials collected the names and contact information of migrants who had applied for the ID cards in the U.S. That contact information was then shared with state-level agencies in Mexico, and states then combined this information with their own registries of paisanos abroad in order to have a comprehensive list of the whereabouts of migrants from home states of origin across the U.S. Additionally, at lower tiers of government, municipal administrations interviewed relatives and neighbors of emigrants to learn where they had settled in the U.S.[40] Together, state officials and municipal presidents coordinated efforts, contacted their paisanos abroad, and encouraged collaborative partnerships for public goods provision using collective remittance resources.

The PCME acted as the organizational vehicle through which municipal, state, and federal officials tapped into the financial resources of migrants for development purposes in the 1990s. The Mexican federal government's outreach efforts, administered through the PCME, were a central catalyst of migrant-state coproduction of public works through transnational partnerships with Mexican migrant HTAs. This state outreach coalesced during a period of political and economic turmoil in Mexico. During the 1980s and 1990s, municipal governments had greater political and administrative responsibility, but lacked fiscal autonomy. Creating collaborative partnerships with migrant hometown associations and using collective remittances to finance local public works was an effective strategy for many municipalities searching for innovative ways to liberate additional resources for use at local levels of governance.[41]

Municipalities had extraordinary opportunities to introduce changes into their political jurisdictions because of the weak institutional context in which they worked.[42] During the 1990s newly elected municipal officials had little of what Merilee Grindle referred to as "institutional memory": lack of useful records of expenditures, few instructions of how offices were to be run, lack of organizational manuals and information about pay structures for public officials or the debts of previous administrations, and no documentation of civil registry.[43] These limitations inspired many municipal presidents to seek creative alternatives to the system of revenue transfers to finance public works as electoral competition increased at the local level. Even as municipal and state governments were responsible for more than half of national expenditures, they only collected around 5 percent of revenue and needed to depend on federal transfers for most of their fiscal budgets. Incomplete fiscal decentralization to subnational levels of Mexican government created the impetus for municipal and state political authorities to find creative solutions to finance their public goods mandate.

Zedillo and Nuevo Federalismo (1994–2000)

By the mid-1990s Salinas's successor, PRI president Ernesto Zedillo, continued the decentralization reforms of his predecessors with the introduction of the Program of New Federalism (*Nuevo Federalismo*). Mexican municipalities were, by and large, responsible for the design, selection, and implementation of public service provision for their territorial jurisdiction, but still relied heavily on the fiscal resources from the state government to realize local development goals and public service delivery. The decentralization reforms that began after the economic crisis in 1982, again in 1994, and through the New Federalism under the Zedillo administration, granted municipalities more political and administrative autonomy than ever before. While political conditions changed rapidly during the 1990s as a result of top-down changes, the federal system of revenue sharing did not change in step; political institutional changes were not part of an overarching fiscal scheme to link local, state, and federal levels of government in a strong federal system.[44]

Zedillo's decentralization strategy extended not only to lower tiers of government, but also to other branches including the judiciary and legislative branches. His administration also implemented other reforms including several procedural rules that changed the composition of Congress to reflect more proportional representation and public financing increases for opposition parties. Additionally, the access of opposition parties to mass media increased; the National Electoral Institute, the autonomous electoral management authority, became fully independent; and the powers of the federal electoral court were enhanced. The Zedillo administration continued to pursue decentralization as a means of holding onto power—in order to maintain power in the presidency they further devolved power to local and state levels of government.[45]

Decentralization was a politically expedient method of PRI survival. But by the midterm elections in 1997 the PRI faced a serious threat. For the first time in PRI's history they had lost control of the lower house to opposition parties. They also lost six gubernatorial elections including the important states of Jalisco, Nuevo Leon, and Guanajuato, six state legislatures, and nearly all of the largest Mexican cities to the PAN; and they also lost Mexico City to Cárdenas and the PRD. The Chamber of Deputies and other important elections to opposition parties ushered in new mandates for further dispersion of power and fiscal resources to subnational units of government. As opposition party politicians took office, they demanded more autonomy and resources from the federal government. By this point, the PRI had to concede to opposition party demands.

The economic crisis that rattled Mexico in the Lost Decade of the 1980s and early 1990s caused a series of political, fiscal, and administrative decentralization reforms that gave subnational governments more power and autonomy than ever before. The market-oriented reforms implemented during the Zedillo administration changed political incentives for the ruling elites and made it more necessary to pay increased attention to the needs of the poor. The electoral competition at the subnational level required political candidates to honor the wishes of the electorate in order to preserve party success in future elections. By 1999, the major opposition parties governed 45.5 percent of Mexico's population at the municipal level, more than 10 state governors, and the Federal District. And, state and municipal government carried out more than half of all national expenditures through the system of federal revenue sharing and transfers.[46]

By the end of the Zedillo administration, the PRI's protracted rule in Mexico had started to severely wane. In order to keep the presidency, De la Madrid, Salinas, and Zedillo decentralized power to subnational levels of government. But by the late 1990s, opposition parties governed municipalities across Mexico and were directly responsible for the provision of public goods and services to the electorate, although autonomous sources of income were hard to come by. Collective remittances from migrant HTAs became a new source of revenue that municipal and state governments tapped into through the development of public policies directed at organized migrants in the U.S. Decentralization and democratization across local and state governments were critical antecedents in the cultivation of transnational partnerships in the provision of public works between Mexican public agencies and migrant hometown clubs abroad.

STATE REMITTANCE MATCHING FUNDS PROGRAMS

Migrant hometown associations' sponsorship of small-scale infrastructure and other community social welfare projects predate Mexican federal, state, or municipal outreach. Migrant transnational collective action was principally a grassroots phenomenon that was fairly informal and project support was sporadic across Mexico in the 1980s. But as a result of federal emigrant incorporative strategies described above, the number of HTAs and the scope of their projects increased throughout the 1990s. One of the most important reasons why hometown associations multiplied was sending state outreach and the development of state matching funds programs.

The first matching funds program originated in the state of Zacatecas. In 1986, when Genero Borrego took office as PRI governor of Zacatecas, the long-term state engagement with Zacatecano migrants in the U.S. began. Borrego actively courted migrant support for his election and during his campaign made several trips to Los Angeles and Chicago to meet with migrants and discuss the problems they confronted in the destination. One of the central tenets of his platform was to protect and advance the issues that faced Zacatecano migrants. After Borrego became governor he kept his word to migrants, declaring, "I am the governor of Zacatecas over here [in the United States] just as much as I am the governor of the Zacatecanos over there [in Zacatecas]."[47] He declared November 11 the Day of the Migrant (*dia del migrante*) and promised to return every year to celebrate with Zacatecanos in the U.S.[48]

Working with a coalition of Zacatecano migrant clubs in Los Angeles, which would later become the powerful Federation of Zacatecan Clubs in southern California, Borrego and migrant leadership developed a series of matching funds programs. The state matching funds program first started with a 1x1 program in which the state cofinanced public works projects with Zacatecan migrant clubs. The state programs planted the seed for the federal 3x1 matching funds program still active today. During the Borrego administration, the informal 1x1 program would coproduce about 100 projects in 35 municipalities with 20 migrant clubs. The entire state budget for the program was only about $200,000.[49]

Borrego's successor, Governor Romo, was determined to continue the state relationship with organized migrant clubs. Romo met with Zacatecan HTAs early in his governorship and expanded the nascent matching funds program to an additional matching contribution from the federal government, which turned the informal 1x1 program into the official 2x1 state program. Both Borrego and Romo lobbied President De la Madrid and President Salinas to develop programs for Mexicans abroad. To combat the abuse and discrimination migrants were facing in the U.S., Romo advocated the expansion of the matching funds program to include a municipal contribution. Close to the end of his tenure, Romo's suggestions were heard. In 1997, the 3x1 matching funds program was formally launched in the state of Zacatecas and soon after other states including Guanajuato, Guerrero, and Jalisco followed suit.

The state 3x1 program in Zacatecas formalized an existing relationship between migrant clubs and the state of Zacatecas and was the beginning of a contractual commitment from the state to support migrants in the U.S. and their communities of origin. Zacatecas officially adopted a model of local economic development that not only explicitly recognized migrants, but also built on migrants' economic and social connection to their communities of origin in order to provide basic services and reduce the isolation of villages throughout the state.[50] Other states including Guerrero, Jalisco, and Guanajuato implemented versions of the Zacatecas matching program during the late 1990s. Migrants were no longer passive recipients of Mexican government services. Through the matching grants programs organized migrants became active negotiators in the development of social spending policies. Migrant leaders worked directly with municipal and state authorities to include provisions in the program that would give them a voice in the selection and implementation of projects.

FEDERAL 3X1 PROGRAM FOR MIGRANTS

Before he became the opposition candidate to defeat the PRI in the presidency, Vicente Fox was the PAN governor of Guanajuato. Fox built relationships with paisanos from Guanajuato, although the mode of emigrant incorporative relations was different than that employed by the PRI and PRD governors of Zacatecas. Augmenting the outreach initiatives of his predecessor, Fox was more focused on tracking, tabulating, and measuring migration and remittances. His strategy sought to channel the resources of migrants to meet state-centered priorities for economic growth and political development. For example, Fox championed the *Casas Guanajuato* initiative launched in 1992. *Casas* were a series of centers placed in large emigrant communities in the U.S. that provided services to Guanajuatense migrants similar to services provided by consulates.[51] Fox's administration also established the *Direccion General de Atención a Comunidades Guanajuatense en el Extranjero* (DAGCE). The DAGCE was a separate state government agency that helped migrants "connect, communicate, support, and serve" their communities of origin.[52] In reality, it tracked emigration and assessed the impact on high migration communities in Guanajuato. During his governorship, Fox created 18 Casas Guanajuato.[53]

Governor Fox also launched the *Mi Comunidad* program in addition to the state 2x1 matching funds program. *Mi Comunidad* directed remittances toward investment for small *maquiladoras* (*maquilas*) to be established in migrants' communities of origin. Maquilas are production plants that employ Mexican workers and import U.S. materials and equipment duty-free and tariff-free in order to assemble and finish products for export back to the U.S. The state raised initial capital investment for the *maquilas* and migrant clubs invested an initial $60,000. Of the 13 *maquilas* that opened, 10 failed almost immediately and three continued for a couple of years after Fox left office, but only through additional subsidies from migrant clubs. Guanajuato's 2x1 remittance matching grants program created a similar arrangement in which transnational partnerships between migrant groups and the state government worked together to coproduce public works, although the state program did not include a federal matching contribution. By this point, Fox was in the throes of a heated contest for president against the PRI and the interim governor did not wish to ask for federal resources for state-migrant investment.

While the Guanajuato state 2x1 program was not as successful as other matching funds programs in Zacatecas, Guerrero, and Jalisco, for example, it was an important part of Fox's presidential campaign platform. Fox promised to take the 2x1 program nationwide and proposed to raise the matching funds to three pesos for every peso contributed by migrant HTAs. In an informal public opinion survey taken after Fox won, the promise to expand the matching funds program and existing programs for migrants in the U.S. was one of the main reasons respondents cited for backing the PAN.[54] Fox was known to have invoked the 3x1 Program during presidential campaign stops in Chicago and California.[55] Fox seized upon his predecessor's outreach with organized migrants abroad who wanted to engage in cross-border public goods provision in their hometown and scaled up programmatic initiatives to affect all migrants across the U.S. and their engagement with local, state, and federal levels of government.

Fox kept his promise to nationalize the 3x1 Program. Once he was elected to the presidency, he set up a cabinet position to address the demands and needs of migrants directly. Several hometown association leaders were also invited to inaugural activities and 15 leaders attended the inauguration itself. When the federal 3x1 program was launched in 2002, initially titled the *Programa 3x1 Iniciativa Ciudana* (Citizens Initiative), it was met with opposition from migrant HTA leadership. The migrants claimed the program was another watered-down version of Salinas and other presidents' poverty alleviation programs such as Pronasol.

The initial version of the federal program, formally administered by the Ministry of Social Development, allowed local citizen groups to also propose public goods projects and receive matching funds from municipal, state, and federal governments in addition to migrant HTAs. But this upset organized migrants' groups who had negotiated the program to be exclusively for migrants at the state level. In response, many migrants traveled to state capitals in Mexico to remind state government authorities how the program originated and pressured authorities to change the rules of operation. Guadalupe Gomez, president of the Federation of Zacatecan Clubs in southern California, told the state governor: "Keep the projects for the migrants. This is our program. We started it and we negotiated it … you need to help us out."[56] Raquel Sandoval, HTA president and a founding member of the Zacatecan federation, recalls: "We told them that clubs were disbanding because they no longer felt motivated to participate in a program that didn't take our voices seriously. We were frustrated with all the red tape."[57] Migrants' concern was that the federal government would become further co-opted by other social and political actors and resources would be redirected from migrant-initiated projects to other groups.

Early collaborative partnerships between state authorities and migrant groups were instructive as to how a federal version of the program would be implemented. Migrants I interviewed that participated in the early years of the Zacatecan matching grants program were frustrated that state officials made decisions on project selection and implementation without much input from migrant actors. Organized migrant groups felt like they were there to subsidize the political officials' preferred projects without any decision-making authority. Early promoters of the matching grants programs wanted assurances that their autonomy would be preserved. In order to put pressure on political officials, migrant hometown association leaders threatened a remittance boycott as Fox and the 3x1 program lost credibility with the influential and increasingly organized migrant emigrant community in the U.S. Juan Hernandez, president of the Office for Mexicans Abroad, was heard telling the minister of foreign relations: "This is our last chance and there won't be another one. We have to get this right or we will have lost the migrants forever."[58] Migrants used their organizational might to change the sending state's corporatist approach to cross-border public goods partnerships.

The Ministry of Social Development, the Ministry of Foreign Relations, and Fox's cabinet official for the President's Office for Migrants worked with frustrated migrant groups to amend the program and they made several concessions. First, preference for project selection was granted to migrants and not ordinary citizens in migrant hometowns. In practice, this meant that local residents were prohibited from proposing projects for cofinancing without the support and participation of a migrant club from the municipality. Second, political officials reversed initial course and allowed migrants to continue funding churches, plazas, rodeo rings, and other recreational projects in addition to public infrastructure and social welfare projects like schools and health clinics. And finally, the program was renamed the *3x1 Program for Migrants*. After 2002, the number of migrant clubs across the U.S. skyrocketed. Survey respondents reported overwhelmingly that they started their clubs after the 3x1 Program launched (75 percent of clubs formed between 2002 and 2008).

The exit of individuals from state control posed an interesting challenge and fundamental constraint on sending states.[59] Emigrants, no longer territorial residents of the polity, limited the sending state's capacity to use coercion, extract resources, and comply with state demands. Through the process of emigration to new political jurisdictions migrants inverted the power relationship between "state" and "society" because migrants' evolving resource base generated new political leverage— sending states wanted to harness remittances, but lacked power to control how migrants spent their savings.[60] Sending states tried to mobilize migrant resources toward particularistic goals in line with state preferences, but they were met with an organized migrant leadership that demanded autonomy over how their complementary resources were spent on projects in their hometowns. The formalization of transnational partnerships between organized migrant groups in the U.S. and the Mexican state through the 3x1 Program institutionalized ties between state and nonstate migrant actors for local development and granted HTAs considerable negotiating leverage in transnational partnerships.

SUMMARY

The network nature of international migration generated new forms of community based on shared social ties to place of origin commonly expressed in the formation of migrant hometown associations. As this chapter shows, specific historical waves of international migration are more likely to build up concentrations of migrant filial or sister communities in the destination country. In Mexico, the social network features of international migration followed a period of economic crises and U.S. immigration policy change, which led to family reunification through formal channels and through unauthorized entry to the U.S. Throughout the 1990s and 2000s as migrants settled in destination places based on social ties, proximity to other migrants built *paisanaje* community and fortified shared bonds and mutual interest to help the homeland.

This process produced HTAs in the late 1990s. While many HTAs started out with a cultural, religious, and recreation focus, many clubs amended their goals to also include public goods provision in their hometowns informally and most often autonomously. As migrants' observations and expectations for public goods access changed with time spent in the U.S., social mobility led to the acquisition of resources that made it possible to improve hometowns. Through this process migrants also recognized that greater social status could be garnered through the provision of development projects back home. Many clubs shifted focus to philanthropic investments in their places of origin through the hometown club in this period of sending state outreach and the expansion of the matching grants program at the federal level.

While many HTAs formed through grassroots mobilization, evidence presented in this chapter also showed that the sending state became an important force in the formation of new clubs and public policy formation. Sending state outreach was preceded by political and economic factors internal to Mexico, which changed local conditions that facilitated migrant intervention in public goods provision. These domestic changes incentivized the Mexican sending state to develop new ways of relating to their citizens living abroad.

Decentralization reforms spearheaded in the late 1980s and 1990s and subnational democratization over the same period impelled the creation of Mexican local, state, and federal sending outreach initiatives aimed at cultivating ties to organized migrant groups abroad. Outreach programs like the PCME, International Solidarity, and the state- and federal-level remittance matching programs encouraged hometown clubs to form throughout the U.S. and send money home for public goods projects in municipalities of origin. The growing role of migrant hometown associations in their communities of origin, along with the timing of decentralization and democratization in Mexico's political history, created an opportunity structure in which political officials looked abroad to Mexican immigrants to develop the homeland with resources acquired in the destination. With savings and social networks, organized migrants helped liberate resources for municipal officials and their public works budgets.

The institutionalization of transnational partnerships that accompanied the federal 3x1 program in 2002 did not develop either from migrant-led transnationalism or state-led outreach policies. Formal cross-border partnerships occurred at a critical juncture through a process of institutional reconfiguration. Tracing critical historical events that precipitated the federal launch of the subsequent 3x1 Program for Migrants, the chapter demonstrates how the process of decentralization and democratization in Mexico and the economic crisis that rattled the regional economies of migrant sending states were preconditions that explain Mexican government actors' interests in looking outward to the organized diaspora in the U.S. The formation of partnerships occurred in a window of time in which already-organized migrants were actively involved in hometown development projects. But the attention of public agencies in the sending state gave organized migrant groups new political leverage to negotiate policy changes that benefited the migrants. Sending state activities including the tracking of paisanos abroad, the formation of migrant affairs offices across Mexican states, and increased consular presence in the U.S. The 3x1 Program also worked to organize hometown associations where they did not exist before, which led to the widespread formation of over 1,500 active hometown clubs coproducing public goods and services with the sending state in half of all municipalities by 2013.

The historic-institutional analysis presented in this chapter provides a macrostructural picture of the conditions that led to the formation of transnational partnerships between migrant groups and the sending state. While the 3x1 Program administered the matching funds from local, state, and federal partners for local public goods, the program left project coordination entirely at the discretion of migrant groups and local government actors with no oversight from higher tiers of government. All facets of project coordination including the selection, budgeting, implementation, and oversight of projects were determined at the local level between migrant HTAs and municipal authorities. The lack of regulations regarding who made decisions on public goods projects and oversight from higher tiers of government meant that transnational partnerships varied considerably across municipalities and with many local leaders motivated to work with migrants according to electoral considerations. Local government officials and migrant clubs had to negotiate levels of engagement in project coordination across national borders, which opened up the transnational coordination of public goods process to political manipulation.

In the next three chapters, I examine why and how transnational partnership varied from place to place and over time, paying particular attention to the ways in which political institutional factors and social network relations affected the organization of coproduction partnerships. I use a processual analysis to unpack the micropolitical and social factors that combine to organize transnational partnerships. In doing so, I trace how community inclusion and government engagement interact to produce four distinct types of coproduction—substitutive, synergetic, corporatist, and substitutive partnerships—which each had important political consequences for local democratic governance across Mexican locales.

Micro-Politics of Substitutive and Synergetic Partnerships

In 2007, a group of residents in Telepi, Zacatecas, mobilized swift opposition to the new mayor when he began paving over the cobblestone streets near the central plaza. "The pavement projects were ruining the provincial feel of our town, so we made him [the mayor] stop," said Umberto, a local resident. Citizens circulated a petition throughout Telepi and collected the signatures of all those against the pavement project. A resident wrote a position piece in the local newspaper that called on the mayor to cease the project. And active members of the church group, Rotary club, and parent-teacher association organized a town hall meeting to voice opposition to the mayor's administration. The political opposition was successful and the mayor ended the pavement project. Telepitense residents used the social connections and skills they had developed during coproduction activities with previous municipal administrations to hold the mayor to account for his unpopular actions while in office. Residents mobilized collective action as a mechanism of social control and, for all those who opposed the pavement project, it made them feel politically empowered.

Citizens had serious objections to the pavement project because they enjoyed the quaintness of the main courtyard and cobblestone streets where, on weekends, sellers hawked their wares from market stalls and families strolled with their children, popsicles (*paletas*) in hand, while musicians played and friends chatted. Residents did not want their plaza any more "modernized" than it already was. Intense out-migration to the United States had brought back customs and American culture that many nonmigrant residents disliked. Since citizens had previously engaged in selecting, funding, and coordinating public goods projects with previous municipal administrations through a transnational partnership with a popular migrant club, the new mayor's dismissal of the active involvement of civil society in decision-making of public works was disconcerting to residents. Because residents had become accustomed to discussing and influencing public projects, the mayor's top-down directives were an insult to the participatory spirit in which more than 30 projects were implemented in Telepi over a six-year period. Citizens involved in coproducing public works with migrants and municipal officials came to value political deliberation, and when they felt like their participation was being threatened by a dismissive mayor, they did something about it.

What role did the transnational partnership play in residents' political engagement? How did Telepitenses develop the capacity and political will to mobilize for a cause they cared about? The political opposition organized by Telepitenses in response to the actions of an unpopular mayor and his preferred public works project offers a lens through which to analyze how synergetic transnational partnerships have unanticipated effects on citizens' political engagement in public affairs in and beyond the coproduction process. Citizens of Telepi were empowered to voice their concerns directly to the mayor and his administration because interactions with municipal officials had become routine and they learned that they could influence public decisions by speaking out.

I have two central objectives in this chapter. First, I describe the conditions under which two organizational forms of transnational partnership—synergetic and substitutive—emerge in hometown settings. I trace the transnational process of producing public goods over time to show how community inclusion and government engagement combine to produce synergetic and substitutive types. If one's research goal is the search for causal mechanisms, it is vital to study not a static network but one that changed, and then to identify dates of change. Because inclusion and engagement change over time with the expansion (and decay) of bonding and bridging social ties and the electoral incentives of political officials, so too does who is involved in the process of coproducing public goods wax and wane.

The second goal of the chapter is to identify how synergetic and substitutive partnerships affect citizens' participation in civil society and the local political process. In each case, I describe how the two types of transnational partnership, substitutive and synergetic, affect participatory engagement and government responsiveness. The two cases in this chapter represent distinct transnational partnerships in different municipal contexts but share similar organizational forms. By comparing similar partnership cases, I show how migrant social embeddedness and political institutions shape migrant-state collective action and the spillover effects of cross-border public goods provision across hometowns over time.

In the first case of El Cerrito, Guanajuato, I explain how the absence of migrant bridging ties and government engagement in the early stages of coproduction led to a more substitutive partnership. In the first two years of coproduction, the migrant group substituted for government provision of public services with the support of state and federal matching funds. But over time, migrants learned to construct social relationships with key community stakeholders through social events and recruitment activities. The construction of bridging ties and renegotiation of community membership through quotidian participation in social life of the hometown expanded who was involved in the coproduction of public works. In return, the increase in community inclusion triggered more government engagement, which changed the partnership to a more synergetic organizational form. As a result, an increase in local participation in civic and governmental affairs resulted and municipal responsiveness in El Cerrito improved.

By contrast, in the second case of Telepi, Zacatecas, members of the migrant club were more socially embedded in the hometown community from the start and the municipal administration was actively engaged in project deliberations and coordination. However, the synergetic partnership was disrupted when electoral transition introduced a mayoral administration that was uninterested in the participation of civil society in public affairs. Residents and migrants drew on the trust, reciprocity, and social network ties forged during the synergetic period to continue public works projects without municipal financing and technical support, which led to a period of substitution. Additionally, citizens censured the mayor's performance and forced him to change his behavior while he was still in office, introducing a measure of social accountability in local politics. Residents had learned how to use democratic mechanisms to voice their opposition to an unpopular mayor during the synergetic period that paid dividends at a later date.

While migration intensity, poverty levels, and club capacity are relatively constant across the cases in this chapter, sociodemographic and political characteristics of the hometowns vary. Where relevant, I identify how local historical conditions such as land tenure arrangements, political scandals, and social cleavages affect the formation and evolution of transnational partnerships through their effects on community inclusion and government engagement. I present a more detailed description of the case selection method for all the partnership cases in Data Appendix A.

SYNERGETIC AND SUBSTITUTIVE TRANSNATIONAL COPRODUCTION IN EL CERRITO, GUANAJUATO

Located 30 miles outside the Selvillo municipal county seat is El Cerrito, one of the more populated localities in the county and home to about 4,000 residents. Reymundo and Francisco, two migrants who left El Cerrito in their teens for the northern border, formed a migrant club in 2005. The acquisition of green cards and stable, well-paying jobs allowed the migrants to cross the border and visit their hometown more regularly. These visits, more frequent as the friends grew older, made them miss the traditional ways of life of the Guanajuato countryside, but also brought into sharper contrast the lack of public goods provision in their native El Cerrito. They knew El Cerrito lacked jobs, as the two migrants had emigrated with over a third of the adult male population amidst severe economic crisis in the early 1990s, but the experience of growing up in a major U.S. city with paved roads, sanitation, garbage collection, and good public schools revealed just how forgotten El Cerrito was to the municipal government. The tipping point came, though, when a schoolmate of Reymundo's was involved in a car accident and died on the side of the road due to a lack of emergency medical care. The migrants were motivated to act. When they heard about the 3x1 Program during a visit to the Mexican consulate, they decided to form a club after doing some research on the internet.

Club El Cerrito's goals were modest at the outset. The migrants hoped to complete a few projects through the 3x1 Program. But the club exceeded their expectations and coproduced more than 30 public goods projects such as paved roads, sidewalks, drainage, and a recreation area for a local school, among other projects. Additionally, the club grew from a few core members to a membership base that was about 1,000 paisanos strong, with migrant members spread out across the U.S. where Cerritenses resided.[1] In seven years, the club committed more than $2 million (USD) in collective remittances, one of the highest totals in the state of Guanajuato.[2]

Perhaps more striking to the migrants and Cerritense residents was how much more involved local residents became in public goods provision in their community as more projects were completed. Decades-old political scandals and corruption had depressed political participation in El Cerrito and community residents were divided along party lines, which negatively affected coproduction activities in the beginning. But as Reymundo, Francisco, and other migrants reintegrated into the social life of the hometown while living abroad, residents began to trust them more and felt comfortable taking part in coproduction activities with them and, later, the local government. The scaling up of community participation in public goods provision had positive spillover effects on local government engagement. As more residents became involved in project activities, municipal officials increased their involvement and recruited a resident from El Cerrito to join the administration to coordinate 3x1 projects across all of Selvillo's localities and the county seat. By 2011, residents directly engaged with municipal government officials without much involvement from the migrant club and created three new civic associations to solve local problems.

SCARCITY OF BRIDGING TIES AND THE "MAÑANA MENTALIDAD" OF MUNICIPAL GOVERNMENT

After migrating at the age of 14 with his mother Rosalia, Reymundo was miserable in the U.S.—he did not speak the English language well, and he missed his home, friends, and the slower pace of life. Everything felt foreign and awkward to him. But after he learned English, finished high school, then college, and became a teacher in San Diego, he felt more attached to the U.S. and remained connected "there," to El Cerrito. "Because I left as a teenager," Reymundo said, "the umbilical cord was still attached. I am an American citizen now. But I've never stopped being from El Cerrito." During years of public schooling in the U.S., and through friendships with immigrants and native-born Americans alike in college classrooms and in the Latino fraternity that he founded, Reymundo slowly developed an American identity while he maintained deep attachments and a few friendships in his hometown. While five of his six siblings decided to stay permanently in California, Manuel, one of his brothers, was deported and returned to El Cerrito with his wife and five-year-old son. Tragedy struck in 2008 when Reymundo's father passed away. When her husband died Rosalia returned to help Manuel with the family pig farm (*ganaderia*) and opened a small store (*abarrote*) with remittances the family had saved up in the U.S. Even though Reymundo felt strongly connected to El Cerrito—he owned a home, visited regularly, had a few close friends from elementary school and family—his absence eroded more extensive social ties in the community beyond his close circle of friends and relatives.

When the club began working with the municipal government on the first two coproduction projects, public lighting and the extension of the electricity grid, popular residents of the hometown were suspicious of the club's intentions. The residents of El Cerrito did not hold high opinions of political officials in the municipal government or the local delegate who represented their interests in the municipal administration.

Until the late 1990s, the PRI dominated municipal elections, with many in the political opposition accusing the PRI of vote buying and outright corruption. The PAN's growing base of support across Selvillo, especially in El Cerrito, was increasingly vocal about the PRI's wrongdoings. Political differences were further entrenched by local political scandal. Between 1988 and 1994, the PRI delegate of El Cerrito allegedly stole money from the patron saint festival funds and used the town's resources for political activities. The delegate and his supporters vehemently denied these allegations, but residents took sides along party lines. Although 10 years had passed and the PAN had successfully won an election during that period, Cerritenses still had misgivings about anyone in the delegate position and about political officials more generally. As a result, few residents wished to hold the office for fear that residents would blame them for any issues that might arise in the course of their tenure. A history of distrust in the local government[3] and the municipal delegate position had accumulated over the previous 15 years and created social cleavages along party lines in El Cerrito. When locals heard that some migrants from El Cerrito were working with the local government and the delegate on public lighting and electricity projects, they were skeptical about the migrants' intentions given residents' misgivings about public officials.

In addition to general distrust of political officials, El Cerrito neighbors did not have high levels of what Putnam and others refer to as social capital, trust, and norms of reciprocity in the social base of the town. Contributing to social divisions in El Cerrito was the system of land use for agricultural production, one of the pillars of economic activity in Selvillo and the surrounding area. In El Cerrito, unlike many other localities in Guanajuato, land use was not based on *ejido*, one of the hallmark achievements of President Lázaro Cárdenas's agrarian reforms in which over 18 million hectares of land were redistributed to the peasantry for communal use.[4] Rather, in 1992 with the introduction of neoliberal economic reforms, large parcels of land were sold to private companies and agricultural production was increasingly industrialized in this part of Guanajuato, which upset traditional modes of economic production and displaced Cerritenses from domestic cultivation and subsistence. The privatization of land became very expensive in El Cerrito and only a few families, including Reymundo's, owned private parcels. The change in land tenure in the early 1990s was a significant factor in the mass emigration from El Cerrito that accompanied macroeconomic crisis. Those who owned local land were viewed as elites, and El Cerrito was separated into the haves and have-nots.

Mass emigration further exacerbated social inequality in the locality because exit allowed many families to subsist on remittances from the U.S. Migrant families acquired new sources of revenue and were not dependent on employment in local agriculture. Throughout the 1990s and early 2000s, migrant households fixed up their homes, sent more children to school, and purchased creature comforts that many in El Cerrito without migrants abroad could not afford. For those residents like Jessy, a construction worker who had previously emigrated to Texas and then returned to El Cerrito because of hardships in the U.S., migrants who had "made it" in the U.S. were often "showoffs" who made life for nonmigrant families even harder than it already was. The social and political context in El Cerrito made coproduction challenging for the migrant club. Allegations of political scandal, alleged political corruption and rent-seeking that accompanied high levels of unemployment, pockets of intense poverty, and perpetual migration, which introduced jealousy and competition between migrant and nonmigrant neighbors, had reconfigured citizen-state relations in El Cerrito. The combination of these local factors created severe challenges for the cross-border provision of public goods for migrant clubs like Reymundo and Francisco's.

In 2005, most local residents who were aware of the new HTA were suspicious of the migrants' motives. Members of Club El Cerrito had migrated many years ago and although they still had a few family members in town and friendships from elementary school, the migrants lacked bridging ties to key stakeholders in the community. Jessy was someone in El Cerrito who "knew everybody" according to many residents, but not Reymundo and Francisco. He had not heard about the 3x1 Program or about what the migrant club planned to do in the town. So when he saw the migrants talking to construction crew members in El Cerrito who were there to dig holes for new electricity lines, Jessy was suspicious and asked other residents about the paisanos and the projects. No one Jessy talked to knew about the club or the project, further raising his suspicions. "Before I knew Reymundo like I know him now, I thought there must be something going on because where did the paisanos get the money for the project? And how was it happening so fast? Nothing happens fast in El Cerrito and if it involves the municipality you have to wonder because they do nothing here," he said. The lack of recognition between community stakeholders such as Jessy and migrant HTA leaders actively working to improve public goods provision in the town reflected low levels of bridging social ties.

Furthermore, pervasive mistrust of local officials responsible for public goods provision made residents suspicious of the cooperation between the migrant club and local government, even though the municipal government was not actively involved in the 3x1 project at all. Local residents did not have accurate information about who was involved in the project. From their vantage point, the migrants' cooperation with local government made them guilty by association given the history of political opportunism and scandal in El Cerrito. And gossip about the club and the migrants while they were back in the U.S. created a circle of negativity around the club early on.

Additionally, Reymundo and Francisco's long absence from the hometown, despite annual visits, had eroded their social ties beyond their close circle of friends and family. While the migrants felt connected to El Cerrito and claimed to have good intentions, residents had no reason to trust them. As Juanita, a local shop owner, told me, "People in El Cerrito keep to who they know. It's changing more now, I guess. But when Jessy and Miguel (a local schoolteacher) told us about the migrants doing projects with the municipio, I first thought they were crazy. Maybe they just don't know about politicians here anymore because they live in California." The deficiency of migrants' social ties made popular residents like Jessy publicly question whether Reymundo and Francisco had the authority to be involved in public goods provision in El Cerrito. It led others, like Juanita, to question their decision-making authority given the general skepticism locals had of political authorities in Sclvillo.

Reymundo and Francisco lamented not talking to Jessy and other residents about what the 3x1 Program was and what they wanted to do in El Cerrito before they started the projects. Reymundo said:

> People are so used to the government not delivering that we thought we had to do a quick and easy project. We extended the electrical grid to a street that had never had electricity. We did the whole project in 20 days without the municipio. And still people didn't trust us. They were so suspicious. They would say, "How come it happened so fast? They must be corrupt; they are lunatics." . . . I even had to show Jessy

the receipts and the check we wrote for 3x1 just to get them to believe that we weren't trying to steal the money that we had fundraised for the town in the U.S.[5]

The migrants learned from the first two projects that they had to communicate more effectively with locals and give residents a stake in the public projects if they wanted to succeed. "We don't want to be associated with being nontransparent. We learned that we had to inform the town what 3x1 is and who we are if we wanted to keep going with projects; otherwise it's just more gossip (*chisme*) and negativity (*negatividad*)," said Reymundo. Migrant club leaders recognized that in future projects they needed to give residents "a piece of projects that means something to them" and that the coordination of projects should be "more interactive." While Francisco and the other migrant leaders genuinely believed more active involvement of the community would help reduce suspicion and criticism of their club, they also thought that if more citizens became involved, it could stimulate more engagement from the local government. Although the migrants learned from conversations with residents about how much they disliked government officials, the migrants also did not think they could do the projects on their own without municipal matching funds.

In the first few projects, local government shirked their responsibilities and held up completion of the public lighting project, which the migrants worried would further cast doubt on their involvement in El Cerrito with residents. Reymundo said that the municipal officials "had a *mañana mentalidad*, everything was, 'We'll get it to you soon, tomorrow, tomorrow,' but nothing ever came. And since we weren't in El Cerrito we had to just keep calling and bugging them and nothing ever happened." The migrants' absence from the hometown made monitoring government activity nearly impossible. And without local residents to follow up with contractors and officials about project activities, the migrants feared they would not finish any projects, or worse, the remittances they collected from paisanos in the U.S. would disappear from the local treasury, which would surely end the club's development activities in the hometown.

While the 3x1 Program is designed to have all contributors match collective remittances one-to-one, the first municipal government (PAN) that Club El Cerrito worked with failed to deliver its 25 percent share of project costs and materials they promised the migrants as part of the 3x1 project approval process. The mayor and his administration stalled technical plans, neither delivering materials nor committing their share of matching funds. Additionally, migrant club members believed the officials tried to inflate project costs. "When we approached the mayor about the public lighting project and matching some funds for 3x1, he (the mayor) kept saying, 'Well, how much money does your club have? Tell us how much you have and then we can put together a budget.' But we were not stupid, we were not going to do that," said Reymundo. This was frustrating to the migrants because they talked to other migrant club leaders in nearby municipalities (Yuriria and Acambaro) who told them about how many projects they completed with the municipal administration through the 3x1 Program. This perplexed them since they knew Selvillo was a richer municipality and had resources to contribute to public works projects.[6]

The 2005–7 PAN administration was focused, however, on projects primarily in the county seat. Although the former mayor said he wanted to support El Cerrito and 3x1, he added, "What am I going to do, give projects to the little old ladies who live there? It is not a big population and I can do more with public resources in the *cabecera*." With skepticism growing from prominent townspeople about the migrants' involvement in public works, a reticent local government "partner," and the need to be accountable to paisanos across the U.S. who had fundraised and donated resources for the projects, Club El Cerrito worked without a municipal partner and substituted for the local government for the public lighting project, electricity project, and a street pavement project. "The longer the projects took (electricity and pavement) and we waited for the municipality to do nothing, the more the residents and paisanos in the U.S. thought we had something to hide. It was getting to be too hard. We talked about it and we said our time and reputation is more important than the municipality's 25 percent share, so we did it without them, just with state and federal matching funds," said Reymundo.

Due to internal political considerations at the local level, the initial phase of the transnational partnership was one of substitutive coproduction. For the electricity, public lighting, and pavement projects, Club El Cerrito contributed 33 percent to project costs even though the Selvillo administration had pledged support as part of the 3x1 Program approval procedure. With complementary funding from the state and federal governments, the club hired their own architect, and got help with technical planning from state-level officials they came to know at the COVAM project validation meetings. Beyond their agreement to participate in the 3x1 Program, the Selvillo municipal government was uninvolved in the early years of the club's activities. But this did not stop municipal officials from trying to take credit for projects. Residents of El Cerrito said that while the migrants were in the U.S., the municipal government had a car with a loudspeaker circulate through the town, listing the public projects they had completed in El Cerrito. When I asked the former director of social development about the credit claiming for projects, he gave me a candid response. He said, "Look, we did participate in 3x1, we let them use the municipio's truck for the projects. And we approved the projects for 3x1. It is not good if the migrants are doing projects and showing us up." With municipal elections around the corner and fiercer competition between the PRI and PAN, the local government did not want residents to perceive a municipal lack of engagement in El Cerrito.

The year 2009 marked a significant shift in the way in which coproduction projects were organized in El Cerrito and Selvillo more generally. Over the course of a year, Club El Cerrito changed how projects were selected, funded, and implemented in the hometown, which scaled up community inclusion and government engagement. Club El Cerrito recruited residents including Jessy and Miguel into club activities, an effort to get the prominent locals on "their side." The development of bridging ties to these key social actors in the hometown led to broader civic engagement and inclusion of an expanding segment of Cerritense residents in coproduction activities with the migrant club. The increase in citizen inclusion, in turn, prompted more engagement from local government in the coproduction of public goods.

CONSTRUCTING SOCIAL TIES THROUGH SOCIAL EVENTS AND CITIZEN RECRUITMENT

Manuel, Reymundo's brother and friend of migrant club leader Francisco, recommended club leadership meet with Jessy, Miguel, Dionisio, and other local residents who were critical of the club's involvement in town affairs to discuss the 3x1 Program. Since Manuel had moved back to El Cerrito, he knew who had bad-mouthed the migrant club around town. When Reymundo and Francisco approached the men during a visit to the town they decided to cohost a town hall–style meeting where the club members would come and speak directly to local residents about public goods projects. At the meeting, the migrants explained to the 70 residents in attendance what the 3x1 Program was, how it worked, and what the club hoped to accomplish moving forward.

During the meeting, Reymundo solicited volunteers to participate in the selection and implementation of projects. This effort built the club's credibility and expanded the density and heterogeneity of social ties throughout the town. About 20 residents volunteered to form a mirror association they called the Public Works Committee (PWC) to work alongside the club. Additionally, Jessy and two of his close friends, informally referred as the "Hawks" (*halcones*), appointed themselves the watchdogs of both the migrant club and political officials. This additional committee effort was meant to ensure local residents that political officials involved in any 3x1 projects would not attempt to pocket the town's resources, which was still a concern of many residents at the meeting.

The construction of new social ties to Jessy and Miguel, the veteran schoolteacher, facilitated a number of additional bridging ties to the principal of the elementary school, teachers at El Cerrito's schools, and members of the church group, all of whom the club was interested in working with on different projects. Since many in the parent-teacher association and church group knew "the Hawks," when they put in a good word for the migrants, other residents were willing to chat with club leaders about coproduction activities. The branching out of the migrant social base to community stakeholders increased the HTA's visibility, credibility, and overall reputation. As a result, residents became more involved in the everyday tasks required of coproducing public works including fundraising, selecting projects, and monitoring the implementation of projects.

In addition to constructing social ties between migrant club leaders and prominent members of El Cerrito, Reymundo and Francisco sponsored social events in the hometown that helped raise funds for development projects. They threw rodeos (*jaripeos*), hired popular local bands to play, and sold tickets at a low price so that most residents could afford to attend. In an effort to be as inclusive as possible, residents recommended that the club use chicken wire around the bleacher seating so that poor residents without tickets could still watch the events through the wire. These kinds of small details went a long way toward improving migrant-resident social relations in El Cerrito, especially with poorer citizens like Gloria. I asked her if she had attended the 3x1 meetings and spoken up about what kinds of projects she wanted for the town. She replied that she and others did not think it was appropriate to say anything about what they wanted because they did not have money to contribute to projects and did not have remittances to use for their share. But she reflected, during our chat, that when the PWC members walked around town, knocked on doors, and asked people what kinds of projects they would like, she felt more comfortable. The PWC member told her that she would not have to worry about paying if her family did not have the money and they could contribute labor or help at the fundraiser instead. Gloria felt more comfortable at this point, she said, and told the PWC member she thought drainage was a big issue in her part of town. Since the PWC members had a better understanding of the cleavages around poverty and migration in El Cerrito than the migrants did, they were able to strategize new ways to get people who were more reticent to vocalize their concerns about town issues.

The migrant club members credit a particular rodeo with really changing the townspeople's awareness of the HTA and their reputation in the town. Reymundo described the change this way:

> After working together on a few projects, we (hawks, migrant club, and PWC) all realized we had to make the projects even more inclusive. We threw a huge *jaripeo* where we got the most popular *banda* in all of Guanajuato to perform. We sold tickets in the U.S. and Mexico for $100 each (MXN pesos) and after we covered the costs of everything we made enough money to finance a recreation area for the schoolchildren. This was something the principal really wanted, and being in education, this was a project really close to my heart. And it was my elementary school too, which was special to me . . . The whole town came, like 3,000 people! It really showed people that we could do things together. Things really changed after that.

Over time, more local residents became interested in contributing to fundraising efforts for town projects, especially if it was a project they proposed. But not all projects were equally popular. Reymundo and a principal of the elementary school discussed building a computer lab at the school. When the parents heard about the idea some of them balked at the need for computers. "What do kids need with computers?" a parent remarked. But after the computer lab was installed, more parents asked the migrant club if they could have a computer lab at the schools where their children attended (middle school and elementary). To purchase more computers, the parents made food and sold dinner plates for a small fee to contribute resources to the 3x1 costs. In one of the fundraising events, the townspeople raised a hefty sum when they raffled off a mule. Social events helped raise money for public works projects, and as more townspeople became aware of and involved in projects, they felt more comfortable taking the initiative on their own.

The process of working out project selection with migrants, the PWC, and other parents had an additional social effect. Fundraisers and meetings about the projects became sites of social exchange and camaraderie for the residents of El Cerrito, which helped smooth over some of the previous political divisions across town. People who had never spoken before now had a reason to chat. The social events held for public goods projects also aided migrant club leaders' reintegration into the social life of the hometown. As one of the elementary school teachers noted, "Now, it's like they had been here. And when Reymundo comes, everyone likes to go to his parties." Over time, the paisanos' involvement in public affairs in the hometown was normalized, and increased social interactions and activities in the town helped to reintegrate their cultural membership in the community despite their residence in the U.S.

In addition to fundraising events in El Cerrito, the migrant branches continued to fundraise across the U.S. Over time, Cerritense paisanos had developed sophisticated networks that they mobilized for their social events in each branch and their fundraisers became more successful. Most raffles generated between $3,000 and $4,000 (USD). The migrants also learned after talking with other clubs in the Guanajuato federation that they could purchase trucks with lines of credit opened in the U.S. and raffle them off before they needed to make the first payment. For example, in one fundraiser, Reymundo purchased a truck in Mexico on credit, drove it back to California, and sold raffle tickets to Cerritenses in the U.S. The raffle fundraised the entire cost of the truck plus additional funds for future public projects. By 2011, Club El Cerrito had a working annual budget of about $100,000. Between 2008 and 2013, in addition to expanding social network ties throughout El Cerrito, paisanos learned how to improve participation at their fundraising events when they joined the Guanajuato state federation of migrant clubs. On both sides of the border, Club Cerrito expanded the depth and breadth of their social ties to include more participants in coproduction activities. They also held social events that helped fundraising efforts, which gave migrants and nonmigrants spaces to socialize and expand their solidaristic ties to other Cerritenses in Selvillo and the U.S.

The expansion of migrants' bridging ties to different social circles in El Cerrito through active recruitment and social events embedded migrants back into the social life of the hometown. As a result, the degree of community inclusion in coproduction activities escalated after the town hall meeting in 2009. In addition to owning homes while living abroad and supporting development projects, migrant club members were regular attendees and sponsors of parties, dinners, and meetings during their annual visits to El Cerrito. Even though the migrants were absent for much of the year, when they were in town they acted as if they still lived there and engaged in everyday activities. When they were back in the U.S., they still communicated with residents through social media, texts, phone calls, and video chats. And their social participation in the quotidian facets of Cerritense life—roasting pigs in the backyard, driving around town with friends and visiting neighbors, sitting in the plaza and catching up with old acquaintances, having beers at *jaripeos*, attending mass, visiting godparents, and gossiping—not only reduced any concerns among residents about the migrant club members' intentions in the town; this participation went a long way toward building solidarity between citizens with different economic and political backgrounds. The migrant club's sponsorship of social and cultural events brought social segments of the hometown together to socialize and chat and solve problems together in new ways.

When migrant club leaders were in El Cerrito, they altered their dress, speech, and mannerisms to reflect local customs. In my observations, these subtle changes did not seem contrived. Rather, migrant club members learned how to move in and out of rural, small-town life and engage in a form of code-switching, which helped them forge social relationships that escalated community inclusion in public goods provision. Even though migrants' experiences living abroad had changed them—they spoke English, had American citizen children, became more educated, and attained social mobility—because they maintained and constructed solidaristic social ties with different segments of local society (bridging ties), migrant club members were seen as leaders in the community, social actors with legitimate voice to negotiate and coordinate with public officials to provide public goods for their fellow Cerritenses through the transnational partnership.

COMMUNITY INCLUSION AND THE ESCALATION OF MUNICIPAL GOVERNMENT ENGAGEMENT

As migrants became more socially embedded in the hometown, expanding their bridging social ties and recruiting more active stakeholders into the coproduction process, municipal government engagement in the transnational provision of public goods also increased. Prior to more extensive citizen inclusion, local officials were virtually absent from the coproduction process, although they attempted to claim credit for the provision of public projects funded through the 3x1 Program. Witnessing how effectively the HTA worked with the town to produce projects, the new administration elected into office after the substitutive period became more engaged in coproduction activities. Local elections became more competitive in El Cerrito and the difference in vote shares between the PRI and the PAN narrowed in the 2007 municipal race. When I asked the new *Panista* mayor about the change in attitude between the previous and current administration, he said:

> We aren't a rich municipio, but we aren't a poor one either. We have a public works budget that allows us to do maybe one project in each pueblo, but most of the projects are completed in the county seat because that's where most of the people live. But when you have a really active HTA like Reymundo's, it looks bad if the municipio is not involved. The 3x1 Program gives us the extra funds we need to do projects in towns like El Cerrito, where not a lot of residents live.

As local residents participated in the coproduction process, local government became more interested in providing public works through the 3x1 Program. The mayor said, somewhat in jest, his new PAN administration did not want to compete and be "showed up" by El Cerrito's migrant club and instead wanted to work with them to improve public works using the additional matching funds from the state and federal governments.

Club Cerrito's active effort to construct social ties and recruit participation had substantial effects on not only the quality and quantity of coproduction projects, but also the extent of local government engagement and citizen-government interactions. As local government became more involved in coproduction, public officials had more occasion to discuss problems in El Cerrito and learn what Cerritenses needed in their town. Both high community inclusion and government engagement changed the substitutive transnational partnership into a more synergetic partnership. Residents' willingness to work with public officials did not happen overnight. And their skepticism of political officials never fully disappeared. Rather, in the first year of the new PAN administration, Reymundo and Francisco worked primarily with municipal officials on projects and acted as representatives of El Cerrito in their discussions and deliberations that concerned project governance.

After a few street pavement projects were successfully completed with the municipality's active involvement, some residents were more willing to interact with public officials. When migrant club members were back in the U.S., the PWC and the Hawks increasingly went to city hall and worked on technical plans with municipal engineers, collected local donations, and fundraised across town for projects the citizens wanted. In this manner, civil society leaders of El Cerrito (Miguel, Pepe, and Jessy, for example) completed another public lighting project, recreation areas for other schools, and several pavement and sidewalk projects. When workers hired by the municipality failed to report to work on time or materials did not arrive, Cerritense citizens complained directly to their contacts in the government. El Cerrito's local leaders provided much needed oversight to coproduction implementation with migrants in the U.S.

Additionally, improved community inclusiveness led to more pronounced spillovers in local political participation as well as citizen relations with the local government. Coproduction drew attention from local residents who felt increasingly comfortable contacting the HTA and PWC leaders directly to report social problems in the town. To meet citizens' requests, the PWC and the HTA asked residents to form "citizen block committees." Each organized group of neighbors fundraised and helped pay for road pavement of their respective street. Many households used family remittances from the U.S. for their contribution, while others volunteered labor or had other families cover their contribution. The PWC worked directly with political officials and block committees to fund road pavements projects throughout town. In three years, almost every road in El Cerrito was paved.

The popularity of the 3x1 Program in the community led to another political development: the El Cerrito mayor created a new municipal 3x1 Program position and hired Jessy onto his staff.[7] Jessy built connections within the local government and effective working relationships with the director of public works, the director of social development, the mayor, the director of the Office for Migrant Affairs, and the state and federal officials who approved 3x1 project proposals. Since the creation of the 3x1 municipal liaison position, Jessy has become embedded in the local municipal government, charged solely with working with citizens to coordinate coproduction projects—a kind of organizational entwining *par excellence*. As a result, a local resident who was seen as a de facto leader of the town represented El Cerrito's interests directly to the elected municipal administration. This municipal embeddedness further escalated residential involvement in public decisions about projects that affected the quality of their lives.

Moreover, as members of the PWC felt more confident in their role as community leaders, they decided to tackle some local problems on their own, independent of the 3x1 Program. After the town hall in 2009, the Hawks and the PWC worked on a series of coproduction projects with the HTA. But as more streets were paved and 3x1 signs were posted around El Cerrito, more residents wanted to voice their concerns about issues in the town. Jessy and Octavio, speaking to me over lunch one day in El Cerrito, recalled how residents texted them and posted messages on Facebook asking the new associations to help with different problems in the town, especially an uptick in crime and petty theft in a particular neighborhood. Residents contacted migrants in the U.S., the Hawks, and the PWC to complain about the crime problem and ask if they could hire more police patrols or private security for the town. Since Reymundo and Jessy had learned from a 3x1 representative at one of the COVAM meetings that this kind of project could not be funded by 3x1, residents took it upon themselves to form an additional committee to address the rise in local break-ins.

Some members from the Hawks, Club El Cerrito, the PWC, and 35 other residents formed the Public Security Committee, a kind of neighborhood watch group. They conducted foot patrols, broadcasted their presence in the neighborhood, approached the suspected thieves and threatened them with further punishment if they continued their activities. Soon after, the break-ins ended. With newfound confidence that they could solve problems on their own, members of the security committee continued to meet regularly and discussed other issues. This was an especially important development because members of the security committee included political party operatives for both the PRI and PAN who were not well acquainted.

In one of the meetings, residents discussed concerns that the doctor of the local health clinic was no longer keeping regular hours and was charging for services that were supposed to be free. Residents alleged he had also inflated the cost of medicine. Problems with the local health clinic caused serious consternation in El Cerrito because if the clinic was not open, residents had to travel 30 miles to the county seat to see a doctor and ambulances could not be counted on to travel to El Cerrito. On a few occasions, residents who were hurt when the clinic was closed had to pay for expensive taxis to get to the municipal hospital or had to travel on horseback while injured since many Cerritenses do not have their own cars. Other residents were unable to get their medicine and pregnant women often went without prenatal care when the doctor tried to charge them for routine services that were previously free. The PWC leaders organized a meeting between the clinic doctor and members of the municipal administration to coordinate a regular, consistent schedule of hours for the local clinic and the cost of services. The PWCs efforts were successful, and residents began to feel more confident going to the PWC to help with problems that surfaced in town.

The security group also began to work with members of the 2011 PRI municipal administration to bring social programs and services to El Cerrito. In 2011, the members of the Public Security Committee and the PWC worked together with the municipal government to coordinate information sessions on proper hygiene, domestic violence prevention, and nutrition for Cerritenses. By 2013, the civic associations of El Cerrito had registered with the municipal government and they worked on projects through other state-level programs beyond the 3x1 Program with and without the migrant club.

POLITICAL CONSEQUENCES OF SYNERGETIC COPRODUCTION IN EL CERRITO

In the first few years of the transnational partnership between Club El Cerrito and the Selvillo municipality, neither local residents nor municipal government officials were active contributors to the coproduction of public goods and services. The migrants were only able to complete the public lighting, electricity expansion, and some road pavement projects because they had the resources to contribute the municipalities' share of total 3x1 project costs, had complementary resources from the state and federal governments, and decided to hire their own labor, contractor, and materials when the municipality stalled project support they had previously promised but never delivered. High levels of HTA capacity allowed Club El Cerrito to substitute for municipal government engagement in coproduction activities.

Knowing that they would be unlikely to sustain the high level of engagement to compensate for an absent municipal government and involved local citizenry, the migrant club met with longtime residents outside of their bonding network of old friends and family to actively recruit key community stakeholders like Jessy, Miguel, and Pepe (leader of the Public Security Committee) into the transnational partnership. Through the formation of bridging social ties, the HTA expanded the number of local inhabitants involved in coproduction and improved the visibility and reputation of the migrant leaders of the club. Through the sponsorship of social events, such as rodeos, dances, raffles, and dinners, migrants and citizens began to work together on public goods projects, re-embedding migrants back into the social fabric of El Cerrito after having been gone for more than 15 years. As migrant leadership reinvigorated their social ties in the hometown, they were increasingly seen as cultural members of the community, which allowed them to recruit and work as collaborative partners with local residents on an array of public works projects.

As community inclusion escalated, Club El Cerrito worked extensively with local residents to fundraise, select, and coordinate all facets of public goods projects through the 3x1 Program, but without the engagement of local government. This early phase of the transnational partnership is best described as substitutive. However, as residents were increasingly involved in development projects, and political competition became fiercer between the PRI and the PAN in Selvillo, the 2007–9 municipal administration became more willing to contribute resources, offer technical planning support, hire labor, and deliberate with migrants and residents over project selection. To do so, the mayor created a new salaried position in the municipal government administration that worked directly with Club El Cerrito to coproduce public goods and services in localities throughout Selvillo.

The creation of a new participatory sphere of decision-making between migrants, residents, and municipal officials improved civic and political engagement in El Cerrito and led to the strengthening of citizen-state relations and government responsiveness. Cerritenses became more willing to work with migrants and no longer believed they had corrupt intentions. Scaling up of citizen inclusion led to the formation of three new community groups: public works, citizen block, and public security committees. Even though El Cerrito was a poor locality in a middle-income municipality with low levels of trust between residents and migrants and government officials, the coproduction process improved state-society relations and citizen political participation as a result of increased citizen inclusion that evolved over time. And, as more local residents were integrated into the coproduction process and told their representatives what they wanted and needed in their town, municipal political officials became increasingly engaged. The migrant HTA's links to the local government and residents of the town created an alternative mode of participation in which citizens had more routine inter-actions with elected officials and felt more empowered to participate in solving problems through deliberation and democratic decision-making. Citizens did not necessarily start trusting political officials, but they were willing to work with them to advance Cerritense interests through a process of social and political learning that evolved over the course of several years of coproduction activities.

Moreover, residents reported that after they became more involved in copro-duction and saw that the local government shirked their participation in the early substitutive period of coproduction, they felt compelled to vote against the PAN, even though they had been longtime PAN supporters. The PAN's vote share declined 11 percent in the El Cerrito district in the election after substitutive coproduction. The PAN still won the mayoral election, but the mayor and his new administration knew they would need to change their strategy from the previous PAN administration or face more opposition in a locality previously counted on as a Panista stronghold.

Relatedly, local government responsiveness improved in the change from sub-stitution to synergy in the transnational coproduction process. Municipal govern-ment increased the average total share of expenditures on public works by three percent as well as public works spending by $466 pesos (per capita) between the 2007–9 and 2009–11 municipal administrations. Most of the increase was attrib-uted to matching funds from the 3x1 Program's state and federal partners and dis-tributed to localities in Selvillo that had active migrant clubs including El Cerrito. The integration of a broad swath of local citizens voters into the coproduction pro-cess altered the local government's political incentives to engage in transnational activities as more citizens voiced their opinions about public goods decisions and were eager to participate in politics. Local residents participated in public life in El Cerrito at first indirectly through leadership of the HTA, but as citizen inclusion increased, more residents directly engaged in regular meetings and negotiations with elected representatives over development projects. Even though the political party of the mayor changed from PRI to PAN and back to PRI again, the synergy created between Cerritenses citizens and the local government carried over to the new PRI administrative authorities who were eager to work with the residents of El Cerrito and gain their political support.

SYNERGETIC COPRODUCTION, INTERRUPTED, IN TELEPI, ZACATECAS

Telepi is a rural municipality with about 9,000 residents located in the southwest-ern part of Zacatecas. The rural municipality is off of Route 23 and nestled between municipalities in Jalisco and Zacatecas as the geographic boundaries between the two states zig and zag in this area. Most residents live in the *cabecera municipal*, but about 500 residents are scattered across the municipality's 26 localities that locals affectionately refer to as *ranchitos*. Telepi has a long history of emigration to the U.S. Many residents are proud of the fact that relatives first went to the U.S. as *braceros* in the late 1940s and 1950s. Since then, emigration intensified during Mexico's macroeconomic crisis in the 1980s and 1990s, similar to El Cerrito, and migration has been viewed as an unfortunate necessity. Declining domestic agricultural production due to an extended draught in the 1990s and farmers' inability to compete with American corn production after the implementation of NAFTA pushed more people to leave in search of jobs or scrape by on *milpa* crops for subsistence and sale in local and regional markets. A *milpa* field typically includes a dozen complementary crops including the "three sisters" (maize, beans, and squash).

Many Telepitenses initially left for Guadalajara, but eventually went to the U.S. Since the late 1980s, Telepitenses also went straight to the U.S. to find agricultural work in California and Oklahoma and manufacturing and construction jobs in Dallas, Chicago, and Atlanta. While more than a quarter of the Telepi community emigrated to make ends meet, many residents, both migrants and nonmigrants, describe it as a necessary evil. According to one local business owner named Julia, migrants bring back American culture (for example, tattoos, bad manners, focus on income and consumerism, less religiosity), which has upset traditional culture and the local values associated with rural life.

Telepi is a poor municipality with a high migration rate according to official statistics and has one of the oldest hometown associations investing in public goods projects in the state of Zacatecas.[8] *Familias de Telepi* started as an informal group of families that all lived in the greater Los Angeles area (San Pedro, Bell Gardens, and Norwalk). Martin, an immigrant from Telepi who lived in San Pedro, formed a social group of migrants from Telepi who also lived in the area. Martin's club, called *Club Social de Telepi*, was mostly an informal group of several families who came together for social solidarity. Together the families enjoyed picnics, played soccer, and supported new migrants from Telepi when then arrived in the Los Angeles area.

About eight months after Club Social formed, Sarita and Leo, a married couple from Telepi, joined the club when they heard about it through a mutual friend at their church in San Pedro, California. Both Sarita and Leo were born and raised in Telepi and emigrated together 30 years ago. While Leo was from a farming family on the outskirts of town, Sarita was from a more prominent family who lived for generations in the center of the municipality. Her father, Ricardo, was a telegrapher who brought Morse code to the area and was considered a leader in the town who raised money for the first public light post. Sarita was a lot like her father, popular in her church group, and she was friendly with many families around town. Sarita said it was hard to leave Telepi, but the drought hurt Leo's crops and they could not see a way forward staying on the land. Reluctantly, Leo and Sarita, high school sweethearts who loved Telepi, emigrated first to Texas, where Leo's friend helped him get a job, and then to San Pedro, where he started his own small business. During their years in the U.S., Sarita and Leo started a family and had three American citizen children, two of whom served in the U.S. Army. Although she said she enjoyed her immigrant community in San Pedro where many residents from Zacatecas also lived and she knew how fortunate they were to be able to give their children opportunities they never had in Telepi (mainly, attend college), she never fully incorporated into U.S. society and always felt more "at home" in Zacatecas. In Telepi, the pace of life was slower and more traditional, which suited Sarita more than American culture in southern California. When she and Leo joined the social club, her nostalgia for rural life bloomed. As the years progressed and their children grew up and moved out of the house, the couple realized they wanted to do more for their hometown.

Part of what made the couple's cross-border involvement in Telepi possible was their ability to regularize their immigration statuses after the passage of IRCA in 1986. Soon after acquiring their green cards, the couple started to visit the hometown every summer, sometimes staying for a few months at a time with their children. Permanent residency eased the burden of crossing the border and enabled the family to maintain social relationships throughout the town. As a result of their frequent and extensive summer visits in Telepi, Sarita had both bonding and bridging social ties throughout Telepi. For example, her sister was a nun who worked in the region and still lived in Telepi. She also stayed a member of her beloved church group even from afar. Members of the church group were from all corners of Telepi and Sarita got to know many families in pueblos across town through her work in the group. Her active involvement in the local church groups was a key driving force in the development of the new hometown association that she would later form.

During one of their Christmas holiday visits, Sarita got the idea with her church friends to raise small amounts of money and donate it to the church for a new roof. The friends decided to do small fundraisers on both side of the border. Sarita and a few of her immigrant friends in Los Angeles made buttons and tamales to sell at festivals, picnics, and other social events held by Zacatecan immigrant organizations. Residence in the U.S. did not prevent Sarita from staying active in an association she had come to value and where she had made deep connections to other parishioners she left behind when they moved to the U.S.

After the church roof project, Sarita and Leo wanted to continue supporting their town. Since they had stayed in touch with friends and family across Telepi, they kept abreast of the problems in town. Friends of Sarita's who worked in the municipal government frequently complained that they had no vehicle to pick up trash and to use for public works projects in town. Eager to support the provision of a dump truck for the Telepi government, Sarita discussed the idea with the other families of Club Social in San Pedro. But while Sarita, Leo, and a few other members wanted to take on bigger public works projects, Martin and the original members of Club Social preferred the club remain more of a social group. With the blessing of the original founders of the club, Sarita, Leo, Fernando, and a few other members left the group and formed a new migrant hometown club, Familias de Telepi. Familias planned to focus exclusively on fundraising collective resources for public goods projects throughout Telepi that would help improve the residents' quality of life.

Since the late 1990s, Familias de Telepi worked to mobilize resources for public goods projects. In the early years of the club, Sarita and the members raised the money, purchased goods, and sent them back to Telepi without support or coordination with the municipal PRI government. But a trip to Telepi during the Christmas holiday in 2001 changed the scale of the club's focus and eagerness to improve social welfare in the hometown even more.

Over the Christmas holiday, Sarita and her church group went caroling in a pueblo outside the county seat. They made food and brought plates to all the poor households. House after house, Sarita and members of the church group found people living in squalor. Elderly grandparents of migrants living in the U.S. had stopped receiving remittances and had very little to eat. In one ranchito, they were invited into the home of an elderly woman whose eyesight had deteriorated so much she could not see the bugs and cockroaches embedded in the tortillas she was making for the carolers. In another home, they met an elderly man who joked he had to "fight the rats for his food." Sarita and her friends were devastated after the visit. When she returned to San Pedro in the new year, she recounted what she saw to the members of the Familias group and they all agreed they must do more for the people of Telepi whose migrant families in the U.S. had "forgotten" their relatives after living abroad for so long. Familias and the church group decided to work on an ambitious project together in the months after the caroling visit to the ranchitos of Telepi. They set out to build a nursing home (*asilo de ancianos*) for the poor, elderly residents of Telepi.

Even though Sarita was a migrant herself, she shared many of the criticisms nonmigrant residents had about the ways in which migration changed local social life. Residents bemoaned the consumerism that remittances supported and looked down on migrants' displays of wealth (designer handbags), habits (cursing), and dress (tattoos and piercings) that some residents thought migrants flaunted when they returned in December for prolonged visits. There was a great deal of pride in the rural Telepi lifestyle, and some residents were concerned Telepi boys and girls would be lured to the U.S. by materialism instead of finishing high school in town. When I asked about how migration had changed life in Telepi to a group of women in a knitting circle one afternoon, they said American culture eroded Catholic values, neighborliness, and made migrants look down on more traditional customs and practices such as *charreada* (equestrian competitions similar to an American rodeo) and patron saint festivities. Many local residents understood migration to the U.S. as necessary for families' economic well-being, but also associated the migratory process with the introduction of "modern" values and disrespect for rural, traditional modes of cultural life.

Women in the knitting circle acknowledged the tension between migration and cultural values head-on. Martina, a nonmigrant resident, said, "Listen, I understand why people leave. It is a necessarily evil. And paisanos work really hard. My friend's husband has been there [U.S.] for 10 years and he never sees his kids. It is really hard for her. But now it is like they go just for the money and the trucks, and they come back to say how much better it is there. It is not for me." Many of the women nodded their heads when Martina spoke, including Sarita. The selection of the nursing home project was reflective of this concern about migration changing social values in Telepi. Church group members thought the elderly residents who had been cared for by remittances had been "forgotten" by their families. The women identified this issue as one in which they could make a real difference. Sarita shared this view and the nursing home project became the core mission of the group. Sarita and Leo's maintenance of both bonding and bridging ties to residents throughout Telepi and their shared concerns about the disruptive nature migration had on traditional values in the hometown created a common connection and solidarity between the active residents of Telepi and Sarita, the visible ambassador of the migrant club in the hometown.

EXPANSION OF SOCIAL NETWORK TIES DURING THE NURSING HOME PROJECT

Sarita was embedded in the social base of Telepi and her concern for the people of Telepi was equally matched by her commitment to the migrant club. Sarita said, "This is not like a hobby or something to me. I take this very seriously. We take this very seriously. I will work for this club and for the people of Telepi until I am dead."[9] The breadth and depth of both bonding and bridging ties meant that local residents were highly involved in coproduction activities from the very start. Her embeddedness in Telepi after migration meant that the projects the club pursued in Telepi were framed as contributions by and for Telepitenses.

Sarita's social embeddedness was apparent after spending a few weeks in Telepi. It seemed like everyone knew her even though she lived most of the year in the U.S. When she was in town and we walked around town to different project sites, people constantly stopped to say hello or waved to her from across the street. During a bus trip to an outdoor Catholic mass for residents of several nearby municipalities, people rushed to sit next to her and ask after her family. On several occasions, I visited her house to chat and have lunch. During these visits, she either had company already or a neighbor, friend, teacher, or relative knocked on the door for a visit. Because Sarita was still perceived as a member of the community, the coproduction of public goods projects her club spearheaded was perceived by most residents as a cross-border extension of social solidarity and community. The strong base of support in the hometown also allowed migrant club members and local partners to more easily recruit residents to take on more active, leadership roles in the coproduction process with the municipal government as the number and scale of projects escalated over time.

Sarita and Leo used both their bridging ties to members of the church group and bonding ties to relatives who remained behind in Telepi as active partners in club activities. Members of the church group included her sister, Elena, the museum director, staff in the *ayuntamiento*, an owner of a popular fresh juice stall, neighbors on her block, and parents and teachers of the local technical high school. Additionally, Leo recruited his friends from high school who worked in the municipal administration and with whom he shared a migratory experience. They then became involved in the nursing home project. As Sarita, Leo, and the other club members fundraised and planned for the nursing home on the U.S. side of the border, the church group in Telepi fundraised in Mexico. The *asilo de ancianos* was a huge endeavor even with the support of the local Catholic church. Familias needed financing and technical support from the government to see the project through, since a project of this magnitude was beyond the technical capacity and economies of scale of the migrant group. Sarita decided to meet with a friend and former migrant who had returned to Telepi to work as an engineer for the PRI municipal administration. She hoped he would provide advice and perhaps technical support for the nursing home project.

Ignacio ("Nacho") was an engineer and director of social development for the municipal administration at the time he met with his old friends Sarita and Leo to discuss the nursing home in 2003. A former migrant himself with social ties to Sarita and other HTA members in the federation (his brother-in-law later became the Zacatecan Federation president), Nacho was intrigued by the 3x1 matching grants program he had heard about from his brother in the U.S. When Sarita discussed the nursing home with Nacho and recommended proposing the project through the new federal version of the 3x1 Program, he jumped at the opportunity to be involved. Nacho organized a meeting with the mayor, Sarita, Leo, and members of the church group to formally propose the nursing home project for the municipal partnership. The PRI mayor supported the idea and instructed Nacho to regularly meet with Sarita and travel to Los Angeles when necessary to plan and implement the multi-stage project. A project of this scale would need to be completed over several phases, and Nacho and the director of social development would have to use resources from several different funding streams to make the municipality's 25 percent share. Telepi was a poorer municipality without much capacity to provide more than a few public works projects a year. The 3x1 Program, with cofinancing from the state and federal governments, was viewed by the PRI administration as a new resource that could extend their public works budget beyond its limited scope.

While the planning of the nursing home project was underway, Nacho convinced the mayor to work on several additional projects with the migrant club through the 3x1 Program. Since Sarita and Leo could not be in town to help with all the planning of the nursing home, they decided, along with members of the church group, to help form a mirror club (*club espejo*) in Telepi that would work as the Telepi counterpoint to the Familias efforts in Los Angeles. One of the members of the church association, Umberto, was also the director of social communications for the Telepi government and a friend of Leo's from high school. Together with his friends and neighbors, which included a few teachers, store owners, and members of a defunct Rotary club, Umberto recruited everyone to the mirror club that planned to work together with the municipal government and Familias to implement phase one of the nursing home projects. Out of the church association, a new civic association was created to work directly with the migrant club to fundraise materials for the nursing home resident's bedrooms. As more people became involved in the project, they spun out new, smaller committees to work on particular aspects of the project that were meaningful to them.

Sarita's bonding and bridging social ties in Telepi helped to expand the number of residents involved in the coproduction process, and Umberto's connection to Sarita through the church group extended the social network of the migrants in Telepi when he recruited other active residents into the coproduction partnership through his bonding social network of close friends and family. Migrant social embeddedness in Telepi led to high levels of community inclusion in coproduction activities. As a result of their active involvement in coproduction, more residents developed skills and interest in forming their own groups to work on the nursing home project and some projects of their own. For example, the Rotary club, after they raised money for nursing home materials, decided to organize a baseball league for residents to play against other nearby towns. They used the fundraising skills they learned in the migrant club to collect resources for the baseball club's uniforms. High levels of citizen inclusion were characteristic of the transnational coproduction partnership early on and produced positive spillover effects on other forms of civic engagement in Telepi as the partnership took on more 3x1 projects with the municipal government.

A FRIEND AND FORMER MIGRANT BECOMES MAYOR

In the first phase of the nursing home project, the PRI controlled the state governorship in Zacatecas. Every year, the PRI state transferred revenues to municipalities across the state. Municipalities relied on federal and state revenue transfers to supply public works in their jurisdictions. But as Nacho came to discover, a change in the governing party of the state sometimes upset the reliability of municipal funding sources. Nacho recalled, "The [municipal] government did not have much trouble getting funds back then to do a couple projects with the migrant club, but things changed when the PRD took the state from the PRI. It got a lot harder to get money at the local level after that . . . With the state and federal 3x1 Program we saw a way to get more money for projects than relying on Ramo 20 alone [revenue-sharing funds called fund 3 and fund 4]."[10] The 3x1 Program allowed poorer municipalities including Telepi to overcome fiscal constraints to supply public goods through the amplification of public resources from the state and federal governments.

Relying on his experience as social development director, Nacho ran as the PRI candidate for mayor in the municipal election and won. He campaigned on the success of the infrastructure projects he completed with the migrant hometown club and promised to continue public goods provision throughout Telepi when elected. Even though the distribution of revenue transfers became more precarious during his mayorship, Nacho used coproduction and the 3x1 Program to liberate additional resources for municipal development during his tenure as mayor of Telepi from 2006 to 2009.

Nacho's relationship with the migrant leadership of the HTA was an important component of coproduction success during his six-year service in municipal government, first as director of social development and later as mayor. While he sought to prioritize water and electricity projects and job creation in accordance with his development plan, the HTA and local citizens had their own ideas for public projects. The migrant club, local citizen committees, and local government negotiated the selection of projects and worked in tandem at every stage from project design to hiring contractors to monitoring quality standards during implementation. While there were frequent disagreements about which projects to fund as citizens and public officials had different spending priorities, the municipal government, residents, and migrants learned to deliberate. Residents like Lula explained, "Listen, we don't always get the government to agree to all the projects we want, but they seem to try and work with us; like if they say no for a certain project this year, then maybe next year we can do it." The process of coproducing public goods created a new participatory space in which public officials and citizens negotiated project selection and planning, even when it sometimes meant citizens did not get their preferred projects funded the first time.

Nacho designed his entire budget around the 3x1 Program, leading to 30 projects over the course of the two administrations he served.[11] Public works expenditures (per capita) between 2000 and 2003 averaged $416 pesos compared to $1,082 in the following electoral cycle. By the end of Nacho's term as mayor, total public works expenditures (per capita) increased to $1,500 on average. Coproduction in Telepi increased public expenditures for public goods and services for local residents, improving government responsiveness to social spending in a poor municipality, but in which the mayor and his staff had an "entrepreneurial spirit," as one resident described them.

While Familias had special projects they promoted and pursued (the nursing home) through the 3x1 Program in Telepi, they learned in informal conversations with citizens of Telepi that people had project ideas of their own. Familias began to invite citizens—friends, family, and strangers alike—to initiate project proposals to be funded through the 3x1 Program while they worked on different phases of the nursing home. When a few residents were excited about a project, they were encouraged to form coordinating "citizen committees." Each project committee oversaw planning and project implementation in concert with municipal staff. Residents wanted ownership over their proposed projects, which was supported by the migrant club and the mayor. Over Nacho's three-year term as mayor, 10 citizen committees proposed, fundraised, and supported projects by monitoring hired contractors and making sure materials arrived on time. The invitation and recruitment of interested citizens into the coproduction process led to the creation of new civil society groups in Telepi. In response to the inclusion of the local citizenry, transnational coproduction helped activate new interest in local politics and more engagement.

Local residents appreciated the increase in civic engagement emanating from the coproduction process in addition to the projects themselves. Eduardo, the director of the technical high school, told me:

> The paisano club is kind of like an institution here . . . We had some of this kind of infrastructure before, but it didn't reach all of the communities and it was very old and needed to be redone . . . the club helps makes things happen here. We make a list of priorities and meet with the club and the mayor and we focus together on the most important ones. That is how we got the two new buses for the schoolchildren . . . we all donate some money and the parents help to collect donations from their neighbors too. It makes us feel like a real community.

The increase in civic engagement in Telepi had additional spillover effects in the municipality. Citizen committees inspired residents to form neighborhood sports clubs and a Lions Club. In addition to the Lions Club primary activities, they also fundraised and donated washers and dryers for the second stage of the nursing home project. Coproduction based on both citizen inclusion and government engagement had ripple effects. Synergetic coproduction created and scaled up citizen participation in local politics, but it also had important state-society effects. Locals who participated in citizen committees met regularly with officials in the local government and said they felt more comfortable interacting with local officials than they did before, even when they disagreed. These citizen committees would prove to have additional import in the community when the PRD, an opposition party, narrowly defeated the PRI in the contentious 2007 election.

DECLINE OF GOVERNMENT ENGAGEMENT DURING
POLITICAL PARTY TRANSITION

The PRD won the 2009 election in a close race and many residents alleged corruption. While Sarita thought of herself as a Priista, she and other club members refused to allow partisan politics to influence club business and their transnational partnership with the municipal government. As soon as Mario, the new PRD mayor, took office, Sarita and the leaders of the three new migrant clubs from Telepi (including Club Social) invited the mayor to a breakfast. At the event, the migrant club leaders hoped to discuss new coproduction projects for collaboration through the 3x1 Program. Sarita recalled that the new mayor was not receptive to their ideas. At the close of the meeting Efrain, another club leader, said they were "skeptical of this new administration" and said Mario was "dismissive" of their past accomplishments. Moreover, Sarita did not think Mario had the requisite professionalization to be an effective leader and coproduction partner. She explained, "He just wanted us to pay for the projects that he wanted. He doesn't even know what the people of Telepi want or need. I don't even think he graduated high school." Familias was not interested in funding projects dictated by the new municipal administration.

The migrants felt slighted that they were not being taken seriously after coproducing more than 30 projects in six years, more than any municipal administration had done in their tenure in Telepi. When migrants and residents began to meet after the meeting with the mayor to discuss future projects, residents were worried that citizens of Telepi would not stay active in town affairs.

The PRD government's dismissal of the projects that the migrant club suggested and the lack of recognition of the club and citizen committees' contributions to public goods provision in Telepi was not well received either by paisanos in the U.S. or residents in Telepi. Ricardo, the museum director, who had voted for the PRD mayor because he did not like the PRI candidate, said he "did not believe [anything] this mayor said." When the mayor began to pave over the cobblestone streets in the main part of town, residents used their network of social ties created during the synergetic period and mobilized against the administration's actions. Umberto explained: "All the projects the mayor wanted to do were pavement projects because they get concrete for free from the state through Coprovi (*Consejo Promotor de la Vivienda Popular*). All they have to do is pay for some labor and additional supplies. We thought the pavement projects were ruining the provincial feel of our town, so we made him stop."

Local residents circulated a petition in each of their citizen committees and took it door to door to households in their neighborhoods. A member of a citizen committee also wrote an open letter in the paper demanding that the mayor stop the pavement projects. The swift mobilization of local residents in opposition to the mayor's policy through the citizen committees was effective. The municipality suspended the concrete pavement projects in response to the political activism of local residents and civil society groups in Telepi. The trust and social network ties to a broad swath of citizens throughout Telepi generated through the synergetic transnational partnership forced the municipal government to change policy course in real time. Residents achieved a measure of social accountability by mobilizing collectively to censure the mayor's actions while in office.

While the residents put a stop to the mayor's unfavorable pavement project, the electoral transition to a new mayor and political party upset the synergetic coproduction partnerships between Familias and the other two main migrant clubs that worked with Nacho's administration. The PRD mayor declined to participate in the 3x1 Program and did not work with any migrant clubs during his tenure as mayor. However, like the Panista mayor in El Cerrito, he tried to claim credit for many of the migrant clubs' projects during the electoral campaign. In my discussion with the mayor, he told me about ten 3x1 projects he completed during his tenure, although I understood from my conversations with many residents of Telepi and 3x1 records that these projects were initiated and funded by Nacho's administration and were simply completed after Nacho left office by the PRD regime. During the substitutive period of the PRD administration, the HTAs continued to join forces with citizen groups. They worked together to purchase new drainage pipes that connected a locality to the public system and bought materials to refurbish parts of the local dam. With support from citizen committees created during the synergetic period, the migrants and local citizens completed two projects without municipal government. The only complementary input the municipality provided was right-of-way access to public land to complete the infrastructure projects. This period of low government engagement brought about by the municipal electoral transition halted participatory engagement between citizens and the state but did not affect Telepi residents' interest and desire to continue being civically engaged in local projects with migrant club partners.

POSITIVE SPILLOVER EFFECTS OF SYNERGY AND SUBSTITUTION IN TELEPI

The case of Telepi demonstrates how synergetic coproduction characterized by strong government and local citizen engagement creates new opportunities for state and nonstate actors to solve local problems through participatory action. Since Sarita had maintained membership in the social life of Telepi, she drew on the resources of her social network to recruit community residents as cooperative coproduction partners. Community participation permitted the exchange of ideas directly between citizens and local government officials and helped citizens gain ownership over the coproduction process. The contributions of the migrant club and citizen committees and the healthy engagement of local representatives led to the completion of 30 projects in six years, a marked increase in municipal public works expenditures, and the creation of new civic associations.

When an unengaged municipal administration assumed the mayorship, the organizational partnership form changed. The decline in government engagement, alongside high community inclusion, led to substitution in which migrant clubs in concert with local citizen groups provided public goods independent of the local government. During this period, the local government worked exclusively on pavement projects, but attempted to take credit for coproduction projects without contributing resources, providing public resources, or technical support.

Although the local government was uninvolved in public works provision with migrant and local civil society partners, the increase in civic engagement facilitated by the synergetic partnership had politically efficacious spillover effects in Telepi. When the mayor pursued an unpopular public project, citizen groups mobilized opposition through the social network ties that they had crafted with people around Telepi who worked on public projects with migrants and the PRI local regime. The skills that residents had developed by working together on projects was repurposed to pressure the municipal administration to end the pavement plans throughout town. Even through a period of substitution, citizens identified nonelectoral strategies to levy social control on an unpopular mayor who was dismissive of participatory governance. Locals also used the formal political process to hold the unpopular mayor and his party to account. After learning about the decision-making style of the mayor and lack of support for community civic engagement in public goods affairs, residents reelected the PRI back into the mayorship in the subsequent election. Voters casted ballots in record numbers in 2010, with over 98 percent of the voting-age population turning out to the polls. The PRI resumed the municipal presidency and the PRD experienced an 18 percent decline in vote share in Telepi.

With the ousting of the PRD administration, the synergetic partnership between Familias, citizen groups, and the municipal government resumed. The new PRI administration invited migrants and local leaders to a series of meetings even before they officially took office and sought project proposals from interested actors. Familias continued to engage with residents and the municipal government in coproduction projects through the 3x1 Program. In 2010, the third phase of the nursing home project was completed and became home to 30 elderly Telepi residents.

SUMMARY

When migrants are embedded in the social base of the hometown community or when they forge social ties to community stakeholders beyond their immediate social circles, citizen inclusion is higher and ordinary citizens are more included in the coproduction process. When government engagement is also high, migrant

HTAs' complementary remittances link them and residents directly to government representatives responsible for supplying public goods.

Attaining the "best" match of citizen inclusion and government engagement can be difficult to achieve. The case of Telepi shows how government engagement can wane, which upsets synergy and leads to more substitutive partnerships. Municipal electoral transitions between political parties may disrupt coproduction partnerships. The decline or absence of government engagement requires migrant groups and local civil society, if they are involved, to compensate for the lack of official participation. Paisanos and their partners in civil society either work together with state and federal cofinancing partners, or complete public works projects independent of the Mexican state altogether by selecting, coordinating labor and materials, and overseeing the implementation of public works.

But substitutive coproduction may still have some benefits for local democracy. We see in Telepi how citizen inclusion can become politically efficacious for democratic quality outside of the coproduction project arena. Citizen groups drew on social connections to mobilize in response to unpopular municipal decisions and exert more pressure and social control over elected officials they perceived to be behaving badly. Citizens were able to draw on social resources generated in coproduction—social ties, connections, trust, information—to hold public officials accountable for their decisions while in office. Synergy created through coproduction allowed social groups to induce a measure of popular control over local government outside the formal electoral process of electing political parties into power.

In the case of Telepi and El Cerrito, low government engagement led to periods in which the migrant club completed public works projects with very little support from the municipal administration. But as new municipal administrations transitioned in and out of office and different political parties identified electoral incentives to participate more fully, the level of government engagement changed. In El Cerrito, municipal officials ramped up engagement in coproduction as citizens became more involved in the process. As citizens worked directly with paisanos, they were more aware of political officials' performance while in office and had more complete information about public goods funding and provision. Not wanting to be outdone by the migrant HTA in El Cerrito, political officials increased their participation in the coproduction process, allowing them to interface more directly with citizens and claim credit for public goods provision through coproduction in the highly competitive municipality.

When both organizing factors of coproduction are high, more synergy often leads to improved citizen-state relations, more responsive local government, and greater civic and political engagement in migrant hometowns. When migrant social bases provide the HTA heterogeneous links in local society, residents and local government become embedded in a cooperative decision-making apparatus for public goods provision, capturing more of a plurality of societal interests.

The social ties that bind the state and society provide institutionalized channels for the negotiation and renegotiation of goals and policies.[12] This nonelectoral mode of political participation expands the institutional terrain in which citizens, migrants, and public officials communicate, negotiate, plan, budget, and implement public works projects that solve local problems through deliberative democratic mechanisms. And in some cases, as El Cerrito and Telepi demonstrate, it also increases voters' interest and willingness to participate in the formal electoral process to reward representatives for performing well while in office and punish others who are less responsive.

Effects of Violence and Economic Crisis on Hybrid Transnational Partnerships

Violence related to the drug trade had moved into the southeastern part of Jalisco when I arrived in August 2009, although I did not know that at the time. When I selected the case of Santa Catarina, I had intended to learn about a case of failure. The migrant club from Santa Catarina that completed the transnational survey reported they were inactive. When I looked more closely at survey responses, the answers to questions about resident involvement in coproduction activities was low and the club reported problems receiving funds on time from the municipal government. When I followed up with club leaders, they told me the remittances the club had deposited in the municipal treasury for their very first coproduction project—a street pavement project—had gone "missing" when the new municipal administration took office six months after they agreed to participate in the 3x1 Program. The club disbanded shortly thereafter.

I was eager to understand whether low levels of community inclusion and government engagement indicative of a fragmented partnership led to failure and the extent to which this failure had observable spillover effects on local political engagement. Conversations with paisanos from Santa Catarina confirmed initial support for the hypothesis that fragmentation left migrant clubs vulnerable to unscrupulous political actors, especially when local residents were uninvolved in coproduction activities and did not provide on-the-ground oversight. What I also learned was that residents were uninvolved in the 3x1 project because the program required municipal government engagement and residents suspected the administration was either directly or indirectly implicated in drug violence. In the case of fragmented coproduction in Santa Catarina, community inclusion was impacted by both migrant social embeddedness and drug-related violence.

Increased violence related to the drug trade was a factor that affected the organization of a transnational partnership in Santa Catarina through its negative effects on community inclusion.

In this chapter, I present two intermediary cases of transnational coproduction: synergy in Ahuacatl, Guanajuato, and fragmentation and failure in Santa Catarina, Jalisco. In each case community inclusion was impacted by migrant social embeddedness, but also by additional factors in Mexico and the United States. I contrast hybrid forms of synergetic and fragmented coproduction to show how crises in the place of origin (drug violence) and destination (the U.S. economic recession) can affect the ways in which residents and local government respond to migrant cross-border investment in hometown communities, which shapes their level of participatory engagement in project governance and public life more generally. Drug violence in Santa Catarina deterred community involvement through its effect on both community inclusion and government engagement, while the recession in the U.S. handicapped Club Ahuacatl's capacity to raise collective remittances for their hometown, which necessitated further escalation of community involvement to continue coproduction projects.

The two transnational partnerships produced different political consequences in Ahuacatl and Santa Catarina. In Ahuacatl, more residents became civically engaged in hometown public affairs and developed a new civic association to solve public goods problems with the local government *without* the financial support of the migrant club when HTA capacity waned as a result of the U.S. economic downturn. During the synergetic period, migrants created vertical links between community leaders in Ahuacatl and the municipal government in the county seat that allowed them to continue coproduction projects directly with the citizens of Ahuacatl with matching funds from the state and federal governments. In Santa Catarina, residents did not become more involved in local public affairs and the failed transnational partnership confirmed their suspicions of municipal corruption. The partnership reinforced the status quo—high levels of distrust in the local political process and low levels of participatory engagement. But in the case of Santa Catarina, the drug trade played an independent role both in the way it discouraged community involvement in club activities in 2006 and, after 2012, when it depressed civic and political engagement even more.

Drug violence and economic crisis in the U.S. are likely to play significant roles in migrant cross-border investment and coproduction of public goods through their intervening effect on community inclusion, government engagement, and club capacity as the cases in this chapter illustrate. This is especially true after 2009 when the U.S. recession severely impacted the labor market in employment sectors that heavily relied on low-wage immigrant labor including services, construction, and agriculture. Migrant clubs that had previously invested collective remittances in hometown projects had difficulty retaining club members and raising funds. Energy, time, and resources of migrant club members and leaders were severely taxed during the economic crisis, which strained their capacity to organize, coordinate, and fund public goods projects across national borders.

Additionally, after 2006 Mexican president Felipe Calderón declared war on drug trafficking and the cartels. In migrant hometown settings in Michoacán, Jalisco, Guerrero, Durango, Guanajuato, Estado de Mexico, and other central western states, criminal organizations splintered and new organizations formed, which created competition for territory and revenue in places in which the drug trade was previously less of a concern. In response to the growth of criminal activity in some high migration areas where coproduction was an everyday affair, some HTAs temporarily halted their efforts and adopted a "wait and see" approach. I learned in follow-up interviews with migrant contacts that after 2012, paisanos and municipal officials that participated in the 3x1 Program became targets for extortion by gangs. This was routine practice in parts of Guanajuato by 2012. To coproduce public goods projects, gangs required kickbacks or bribes, which were paid by the municipality and migrant groups. In other locales, some HTAs shifted their support from public infrastructure projects to public security initiatives including armed vigilante militia groups called *autodefensas* to protect their hometown communities alongside local residents. Still in other cases, I learned from key informants that some HTA members were implicated in criminal activity and had direct links to criminal organizations, with some ties forged voluntarily and others by force. Across Mexican sending communities, drug trafficking and criminal organizations affected 3x1 projects directly and indirectly through their effect on citizen and government participation in coproduction and when organized crime inserted itself into project governance.

A note about the case of Santa Catarina. Unlike in other hometown settings where I conducted fieldwork, residents of Santa Catarina were more closed off. Some residents accepted invitations for informal interviews, while others declined to chat about migration and political life in the town. I did not know before I arrived that residents were fearful that violence that stemmed from cartels had come close to Santa Catarina and they were intent to keep a low profile. Before I arrived, word had begun to spread that migrant families were being threatened, targeted for kidnappings and ransom. Given the public security concerns, I left Santa Catarina before I would have liked.[1] As a result, the case relied more on interviews with paisanos in the U.S. and fewer key informants in Santa Catarina than in other cases. Some questions I was not able to fully resolve; I note them in the presentation of the case. This case, more than others, is thus skewed toward migrants' perspectives as I was unable to learn from as many locals about how they experienced the coproduction project compared to other cases. Even though the case has limitations, I include it because it helps account for more organizational variation in transnational partnerships and reflects empirical realities in Mexico that migrants and Mexicans have been forced to confront.

FRAGMENTED COPRODUCTION IN SANTA CATARINA, JALISCO

Santa Catarina is a rural municipality in the southern region of Jalisco[2] and one of the poorest municipalities in the state. In 2000, almost 20 percent of the population over the age of 15 was illiterate and only about a quarter of the population finished primary school. In the five main localities, between 8 and 15 percent of residents lacked access to basic services such as potable water, sewerage, and electricity. The majority of residents raised cattle and other animals including pigs, sheep, and goats and grew sugar cane, sorghum, and beans. While the land was once fertile, severe drought in the late 1980s hurt agricultural production. The macroeconomic crisis in the 1990s further compounded economic hardships from low crop yields as farmers had not yet recovered from droughts that hampered their crops over the previous five years. To cope with massive economic downturn, many residents of Santa Catarina left for the U.S. By 2005, about a quarter of the working-age population was unemployed and most households had a family member who lived abroad.[3]

High rates of emigration altered society, economy, and politics in the municipality. With few prospects for economic security, the social base of Santa Catarina was dramatically altered as entire families left the municipality for permanent settlement abroad. Over the span of a decade, siblings, spouses, children, and grandparents reunited with family members in Houston, Chicago, Riverside, Los Angeles, and San Jose after several years of separation. Those who stayed behind were primarily spouses and parents of migrants who cared for children and relied on remittances sent home. Most of the other families that remained were too poor to emigrate and felt tied to land passed down to them over generations. They worked as subsistence farmers and sold any surplus crops at the local market. The households that were more economically secure in Santa Catarina were the families affiliated with the *cacique* (informal system of boss politics) that supported the PRI.

Poverty and unemployment were cause and consequence of migration in the rural municipality of about 5,000 residents. While emigration provided economic security for many families in Santa Catarina, it also meant that the economically productive workforce lived in the U.S. and parts of Santa Catarina were virtual ghost towns. Some residents I spoke to also thought migration made young men in Santa Catarina vulnerable to the drug trade. When teenagers saw how migrant families were able to improve their homes with remittances dollars and could purchase more material goods (clothes, shoes, appliances, and electronics, for example) they wanted to leave for the northern border too. But when they could not afford a *coyote* (the name given to human smugglers) to help them cross the border and did not see education as a mechanism of social mobility, many were believed to have joined local gangs with ties to larger, more organized cartel networks in Jalisco and across the eastern border in Michoacán. A priest of the local Catholic church speculated that when they no longer saw a future in Santa Catarina they became vulnerable to gang recruitment, some soon swept up into the illicit activities of the drug trade and some suffering addiction as well. He recalled a significant turning point came in Santa Catarina in 2010 when the *Cártel de Jalisco Nueva Generación* took over the region.

Increasing drug violence and criminal activity related to the trade may have played a role in levels of community inclusion in coproduction activities in 2006 and 2007 when the migrant club first sent collective remittances to Santa Catarina. But even before, Santa Catarina did not have high levels of trust and reciprocity in the community, partly attributed to the disruption to the social base of the hometown caused by substantial emigration to the U.S. over the preceding decade. Social life in in the municipality focused almost exclusively on the *fiesta patronal* activities in May and religious celebrations in December. The only other active civic association residents knew of in the town was the local church group. Some residents said there used to be a baseball team that played a few seasons against nearby municipalities, but other than that, the town was quiet and residents mostly kept to themselves.

Unlike in other municipalities where I was invited to stay in the homes of local residents and migrant families, sometimes at their insistence, some residents in Santa Catarina were more distant. When residents agreed to speak with me, I was invited into the privacy of their homes, in their stores, or I met with them in the church. On its own, this was not unusual—I frequently spent time in the households of residents in other hometown communities. But in those other communities I also sat in people's yards and accompanied them to work and weekly mass, on errands, and family visits. I also frequently joined residents for lunch in the plaza, attended family and community celebrations with them all over town, and walked with them through agricultural fields and on horseback. This occurred less frequently in Santa Catarina. Most residents and the priest spoke to me indoors. Those residents who were open to chatting with me also tried to connect me with their friends and families who were from migrant households. But when these residents reported back to me about possible meetings with other residents, many said they were "unavailable." Instead, they gave me the contact information of their family members in the U.S. and said I should contact relatives abroad who would tell me about life in Santa Catarina. I sought out their relatives in the U.S. and talked with them over the phone and after I returned to Chicago. I began to more fully understand when I spoke to migrant relatives in the U.S. that locals were simply trying to keep a low profile at the time. For many, socializing with the light-skinned American woman in town drew too much attention.

In other migrant hometowns where I conducted fieldwork, locals told me about social and political experiences in the municipality in addition to the migrants involved in hometown clubs and political officials. But for the case of Santa

Catarina I had to rely more on the secondhand accounts of migrant family members, a few shop owners who did not have any relatives abroad in the town, the local priest, and members of the church group. I never asked anyone about the drug trade while I was in the town. However, some residents volunteered to me that they thought Santa Catarina had become unsafe. They worried about public security and told me stories of locals being kidnapped for ransom. As Yessica, a friend of the priest and wife of a migrant in Riverside, told me, "Nobody trusts anybody around here and you need to look over your shoulder more these days." I learned from local residents how they made the sign of the "Z" on their hands to reference the cartel. The "Z" specifically referred to the cartel *Los Zetas*, which was rumored to be present in the region as early as 2006 as they expanded their territorial scope.

At the time I conducted my fieldwork, it was not clear to me that migrants knew about locals' concerns about illicit activities and the presence of gangs in and around Santa Catarina. Migrants never mentioned criminal violence or gang activity when I first spoke with club leaders in 2008, the year after the club became inactive. When I returned to Chicago and told club members about local fears of the drug trade dating back to late 2006 when the club was active, they said they were unaware and did not know of any families that were targeted. It could be that club leaders intentionally kept this information from me or dismissed the information as rumors, although I suspect they really did not know. The priest said he never discussed criminal activity with the migrants at any time because it was not something you talk about openly in Santa Catarina.

Migration also tangentially impacted local politics. The PRI maintained firm control of the municipal government and won most elections by double digits against a weak PAN opposition with the protracted support of a *cacique*. Before the elections in the summer of 2010, no opposition political party had won the municipal presidency. A few residents who were part of the church group believed that migration contributed to the PRI's support. As more residents left for the U.S., they said, the more people became disinterested in politics. Residents believed that people who left for the U.S. were those who cared about politics and people who remained behind were either those who were ardent Priistas and connected to the *cacique* or poor and unlikely to participate in public life beyond attendance at the annual fiestas. According to official government elections statistics, on average, about half of the voting-age population in Santa Catarina turned out to vote in the previous three elections.

CLUB SANTA CATARINA AND THE FRAGMENTATION OF HOMETOWN SOCIAL TIES

In 2005, five friends living in Chicago (Aurora and Bolingbrook, Illinois) traveled home and attended the *fiestas guadalupas* held in Santa Catarina in early

December. During their two-week visit the priest of the Catholic church approached the migrants and asked them if they would help finance a new church roof. The historic church was in disrepair and the priest was unable to raise the money needed for the roof on his own. The migrants knew many paisanos from Santa Catarina in the Chicago area and agreed to collect funds, mostly knocking on doors and taking a collection at church events in Aurora and Bolingbrook where many paisanos lived. The paisanos collected over $1,000 over the span of a few weekends from about 100 families that lived in the Chicago metro area. Miguel and Raul, two of the paisanos who visited their hometown during the festival and helped collect donations, never thought of themselves as a hometown club at the time. In fact, they organized to help raise money for the church project and thought that would be it.

Raul and Miguel were some of the few migrants who had returned for visits to Santa Catarina since departure. It was not as common in Santa Catarina as it had been in other communities I visited for migrants to return for visits and for longer stretches during the Christmas holiday season. But Raul and Miguel, unlike many of the paisanos from Santa Catarina, had secured green cards, which allowed them to traverse the U.S.-Mexican border with greater ease than undocumented paisanos. Raul married a Mexican woman from Jalisco in the 1990s who had naturalized, which granted Raul the opportunity to apply for a green card after they wed. Miguel's mother brought 12-year-old Miguel and his younger siblings to the U.S. in 1980 and rejoined their father who had found stable work in Aurora. Once he turned 18 and obtained his green card through provisions passed in IRCA, Miguel visited Santa Catarina a few times to see uncles who remained behind and worked the family's agricultural land.

Other than a few distant relatives and a few family friends who never migrated that the men kept in touch with on social media, Raul and Miguel did not have many social contacts left in the hometown. They still had houses in the town, but the houses sat empty. Most of their close friends and family had joined them in the U.S. over the last 10 years. They did not know members of the church association personally and wired the donation money directly to the pastor, who coordinated the collection of materials and hired the labor for the job. The migrants only saw the completed church roof when they returned for the annual patron saint festival in May 2007.

The paisano-financed project efforts scaled up when the priest learned about the 3x1 Program from a pastor of another church nearby. A friend told him about the hometown club in his town that partnered with the municipal government on several public works projects. The priest hoped that the paisanos who had helped him with the church could be persuaded to propose projects through the 3x1 Program and scale up their efforts. Over the phone, the priest encouraged Miguel and Raul to read about the 3x1 Program online and to ask about it at the Mexican consulate in Chicago and to their paisano friends from other municipalities in

Jalisco. Miguel and Raul asked a few paisano friends about the program and found out many Jalisciences in the U.S. were also members of a migrant club that completed projects through the 3x1 Program. Once they heard about other successful migrant clubs and the completion of projects through the program, Miguel and Raul said they would be interested in doing more projects, but they had serious reservations about working with the municipal government.

The paisanos wanted to do more projects for the town, but they were wary of proposing projects to the municipal government and did not like going to the Mexican consulate. Miguel said, "We can't raise the kind of money that would have a bigger impact in the town by knocking on doors in Illinois. We needed the help of the government to do more ambitious projects."[4] But neither local residents nor the paisanos from Santa Catarina had many favorable things to say about political officials in the municipality and on several occasions the migrants had been treated poorly by Mexican government officials at the consulate. They were reticent to formally propose a project through the 3x1 Program if it required "dealing with the government," Raul said. Moreover, they heard about the 3x1 Program secondhand and only had a cursory understanding of how the program worked and the process by which coproduction projects were implemented in municipalities.

The final decision to participate in the program was made with the support of the large network of Santa Catarina paisanos with whom Miguel and Raul had become acquainted during the collections for the church roof. Since the men were still wary about the 3x1 Program, they decided to have a meeting with other paisanos and get a sense of how interested other people were in doing projects with the Mexican government. The reluctant club leaders did not want to do it alone. At the meeting, the paisanos in attendance (about 20) decided to officially form a migrant club. Over dinner and drinks, they decided to pave the four main streets in town, which they saw were crumbling and badly in need of repair during their previous visit home.

Despite collective reservations about working with municipal officials, they said they felt reassured participating in the 3x1 Program because the state and federal governments were also involved in matching funds. The paisanos thought the involvement of higher tiers of government in the program was intended to inject more oversight into the coproduction process. The migrants did not understand that the 3x1 Program required matching contributions from the state and local governments, with the rest of project coordination falling to the migrants and the municipal government. Miguel recalled, "We didn't want to interact with any kind of government official. You have to understand that they have treated paisanos badly in the past and we often get harassed at the border." Despite their reservations, they forged ahead and agreed to ask the mayor to work with them on the project at the *fiesta patronal* in May 2007. The priest helped them organize a meeting with the mayor's administration upon their return. In the meantime, pai-sanos from the newly formed Club Santa Catarina fundraised through potlucks, picnics, and by soliciting donations door-to-door as they had done for the church roof project, and they registered their club with the Institute for Migrants Abroad.

BEGINNING AND ENDING OF THE TRANSNATIONAL PARTNERSHIP WITH THE MUNICIPAL GOVERNMENT

At the outset, it appeared that local government officials were interested in copro-duction projects with the migrant club, and migrants were cautiously optimis-tic that they would complete the pavement project. In the meeting, the migrants explained what they knew about the 3x1 Program to the mayor as he said he had not heard of the matching grants schema. The PRI mayor agreed to work with the migrants on the pavement project the club had selected. From that point, the mayor said he and his staff would finalize the budget estimates for the project and send it via email to Miguel and Raul in Chicago for final approval.

The paisanos returned to the U.S. hopeful about the project and told the other paisanos about the mayor's support of their pavement idea. The social develop-ment director of Santa Catarina sent the $3,000 project proposal. They had already raised their $3,000 contribution and wired the money to the municipal treasury while they waited for final approval from the 3x1 Program. Once approved, the migrants, back in Chicago, waited to hear about how the project progressed. That is when the worry set in. Raul and Miguel began to second-guess themselves. Raul explained:

> We had a lot of momentum going into the pavement project. I asked some residents what they thought of the street pavement idea at the *fiesta patronal* . . . they seemed in support of it. Officials put together the budget proposal and we put the money into the municipal treasury so we thought everything was going good, but we were in Chicago, we really didn't know what was happening. And then we waited and waited and waited. Nothing happened. We called the mayor's office and they never returned our calls. Our paisanos called some families to check on progress on the project, but nothing was happening and no one wanted to go . . . ask what was going on. We called the state 3x1 official, but nobody had any answers for us and told us to call a bunch of other people.[5]

For months, the migrants waited and called the director of social development in the municipality to no avail. Work commitments did not allow Miguel or Raul to visit Santa Catarina to have face-to-face conversations with the municipal admin-istration. After several failed attempts to follow up with local officials, a new mayor was elected (PRI) and prepared to take office. The club's $3,000 contribution to the proposed pavement project vanished. "No one would tell us anything," Miguel said. "We lost all the money and had to tell our paisanos that we lost the money."

Any hope Club Santa Catarina had to complete more projects with the municipal government vanished along with the money.

LACK OF MIGRANT SOCIAL EMBEDDEDNESS AND
COMMUNITY INCLUSION

Thirty years in the U.S. had depleted Miguel and Raul's social ties to people who remained in Santa Catarina, and as a result community inclusion was low during the pavement project. It was low because neither migrant had a strong bonding network back in the hometown nor did they have bridging ties to anyone other than the local priest who helped them form the club. At the *fiesta patronal*, Miguel and Raul reconnected with school friends and cousins from before they migrated. The club leaders said they had a wonderful week and caught up with people whom they had not seen in many years. Even though both men had green cards, between the two of them they had only been back to visit Santa Catarina four or five times since their migration. Furthermore, much of their social connection to the town was only to distant family that remained behind—most of their close family and friends had migrated at some point between the 1990s and early 2000s. The breadth and depth of migrant club leaders' social ties had shifted over time from the hometown to the *paisanaje* network in greater Chicago that comprised more and more of their bonding social network.

Some residents who knew about the paisanos' plans to participate in public goods provision in the hometown were ambivalent, while others did not know anything about the migrant club or the proposed project. When I asked residents in Santa Catarina if they wanted to be involved in the pavement project, some said they thought the migrants were "crazy to work with the government" and "why do they still care about the roads [here]?" Other residents confirmed that they had met the paisanos and shared casual chit-chat about people they knew in common in Chicago, but that migrants did not formally try to recruit anyone into the project process. A member of the church group, Lila, expressed what many people told me during my visit. She said it was "fine if people want to donate whatever they can, but we were only focused on church activities like cooking for the poor." Residents did not see a role for themselves in public goods provision and were agnostic about the migrant club's involvement. It was not that residents did not care about the provision of public works. When I asked them what kinds of public works projects they needed in their town, everyone had opinions about what kinds of project would improve their quality of life, namely public security and better roads. But residents reported they were not recruited to participate in the project by the migrants nor did those who knew about the project proposal approach the migrants about becoming more involved.

Miguel reported that he wanted people to believe in the club and help them with the project, but he got the impression during his visit that people "did not really seem to care." In the case of Santa Catarina, even if the migrants had been more socially embedded into the hometown community it would likely have taken more than one project to get more people involved in cross-border public goods provision. Not only did migrants not know many people who still lived in town, their only visit was usually during the week of the patron saint festival. It would have been difficult to build bridging ties in a place with deep-seated mistrust of the local government. The social and political obstacles to successful coproduction were overwhelming in the case of initial transnational coproduction in Santa Catarina.

Club Santa Catarina disbanded after the failed attempt to coproduce a pavement project with the local government through the 3x1 Program. Local residents I spoke to said they had little trust in elected officials before the failed pavement project and their suspicions were confirmed after rumors spread throughout town about the "missing" or "stolen" resources. Conversations with church members, business owners, family members of migrants, and a schoolteacher suggested efforts to coproduce public works with the municipal government confirmed what residents already suspected: the local government was corrupt. But the exposure of wrongdoing by the PRI exacerbated distrust in the local democratic process. "Look, you see why I told them they were crazy to give authorities their money," a shop owner said when I asked him about his reaction to the news the paisano funds went unaccounted for. Residents had always suspected political officials were involved in outright corruption and cronyism, but some said that the failed 3x1 project gave them "proof."

Club Santa Catarina did not muster the support of community residents in the coproduction process and local government engagement was low. The local PRI government shirked their 3x1 matching responsibilities before the state and federal governments even deposited their contributions to the pavement project in the local treasury. With the interruption of the municipal election in the midst of the project, officials in the new mayor's administration said an "accounting error" occurred during the transition in power. I neither pressed my contacts in the municipal government for more information nor spoke with members of the *cacique*. Local residents discouraged me from questioning the elite families in town who were associated with the *cacique* out of concerns for my security.

In municipal history, no opposition party had successfully defeated the PRI for the mayorship in Santa Catarina. Even though Miguel and Raul were liked by some residents, they could not get residents interested in the 3x1 project, although there is little evidence that they tried very hard to recruit them into the process and residents seemed satisfied to have the migrant club complete projects without their involvement. Even the priest who introduced the paisanos to the program, set up the meeting with the PRI administration, and completed the church roof project with paisano donations did not want to take on any kind of leadership role in the pavement project when the municipal government was formally involved through the 3x1 Program.

Miguel and Raul expressed interest in doing projects in the future but did not believe they could raise money from the paisanos after the original contributions disappeared. Some paisanos refused to work with the PRI after what happened. Upon further reflection, paisanos said they were "naive" (*ingenuo*) and "should have trusted their instincts." I asked the priest about the prospect of future projects and he also expressed reluctance given rising public security concerns:

> Paisanos work really hard in the U.S. It's a sacrifice for them and for their families. And our residents here work hard too. I don't blame our residents for not wanting to get involved in projects when officials are supposed to do it. We are a poor community. We have to do a lot for ourselves without help from anyone . . . and since the situation has worsened (referring to the drug trade), no one wants to bring any attention. Everyone tries to keep a low profile these days.[6]

The club became inactive in 2007. While Miguel and Raul still felt a strong connection to Santa Catarina, they no longer expressed those affective ties through cross-border investments in the hometown any more. Rather, in their expansive paisano network in Chicago, they continued to participate in social events with other paisanos and replicated cultural repertoires rooted in hometown social life, but in the U.S.

POLITICAL CHALLENGE FROM AN UNLIKELY
ALLIANCE AND A NEW TRANSNATIONAL
PARTNERSHIP

The PRI remained in office until a contentious election in 2010 that ended in the surprise victory of an unlikely candidate. The PAN and PRD, major opposition parties, formed an alliance and ran a mayoral candidate on a public security platform, promising to tackle the rise in drug-related violence in the area. This was a bold move as other mayors or mayoral candidates who openly challenged and confronted gangs became targets themselves, especially across the border in Michoacán in which there were both informal and formal accounts of threats to political authorities.[7] In many cases, municipal authorities had to pay "fees" (*cuotas*) to criminal organizations to conduct the everyday business of local government. In extreme cases, authorities who did not comply or challenged criminal gangs were murdered.

While details of what ultimately led to the ousting of the PRI were still unclear after the close election, for the first time in municipal history, the PRI had lost. The alliance victory was momentous. I was not in Santa Catarina in 2010 and paisanos I spoke with only had theories about how the PRD-PAN alliance candidate had managed to defeat the *cacique* and the local PRI. One theory was that the PAN-PRD candidate was funded by the *Cártel de Jalisco Nueva Generación*, which had formed earlier in the year and was quickly gaining ground in the region. Another theory was the PAN-PRD candidate had been extorted by local gangs and he paid them what they asked. Paisanos said they "heard from locals" that the gangs would leave Santa Catarina alone as long as he paid what they demanded. The most popular explanation, though, was that the political boss became a target of the drug cartel himself and he was no longer in as much a position of power and authority in Santa Catarina. Most of the theories about the PRI defeat were related, in some way, to the presence of the drug trafficking and organized criminal activity in the region and its effect on local politics.

After the PRI was defeated in 2010, a different group of paisanos from Santa Catarina formed a hometown association in 2011, despite continued concerns related to drug violence. When I spoke with the club leaders in 2011 in Chicago, Club Unido had already completed two coproduction projects through the 3x1 Program. With matching funds from the state and federal governments they successfully coproduced public lighting (street lamps) along a bridge and purchased an electrocardiogram machine for a local health clinic. Martín and Alejandra, a married couple who emigrated from Santa Catarina in the early 2000s and formed the new HTA, were not affiliated with Club Santa Catarina in any formal way, but they did donate to the church project. This gave them the idea to form a club of their own when the time was right. When the PRI lost the election, they thought this was a good time and they approached the newly elected mayor about 3x1 Program participation. They heard from some of their friends and family in Santa Catarina that locals thought highly of the new mayor, but they were still careful in how they did business with the municipal administration. They learned from the experiences of Club Santa Catarina:

> We don't put any money in the treasury. We do everything in a separate bank account. The new mayor is much better. He's an engineer and has good ideas for the town, but he has a lot of work to do trying to get security under control. It will take a long time for us to gain the trust of local residents who have seen a lot of things happen in this town. We ask them what kinds of projects they want and they tell us, but they won't donate funds or help very much . . . We have to work very hard to stay on good terms with the administration and communicate often through video chats and phone calls.[8]

Raul wished the new club the best of luck in their development projects with the new mayor, but former members of Club Santa Catarina were skeptical of the 3x1 process and the lack of accountability. By 2010, drug violence was a well-known secret in Santa Catarina and some paisanos did not want to send collective remittances back to the town because they feared that such public displays of migrant resources put themselves and locals in harm's way. As Ricardo, a paisano from Santa Catarina in Aurora, told me over the phone, "You just don't know who is who and whether doing projects and showing you have money puts a target on your back." Ricardo was surprised Club Unido had completed any projects at all and hoped the "Lord protected them."

In the case of Club Santa Catarina and their fragmented partnership with local residents and the local government, the municipal administration took advantage of migrants' physical distance and the migrants' contributions to the pavement project budget disappeared. Without more participation from local residents, the migrant HTA in Chicago was unable to exert any pressure on the officials to meet their obligations[9] and their location in the U.S. prevented them from holding local officials to account for their 3x1 contributions. Moreover, 3x1 officials lamented that they had no recourse to monitor local officials in these kinds of situations. Jaime Almaraz, a 3x1 state-level official in Jalisco and former mayor of Tuxcacuesco, Jalisco, explained to me that in situations like these in which outright corruption occurs, which he said in his experience was more rare, higher tiers of government will sometimes reimburse the club. This has happened only a few times in his recollection. Paisanos in Club Santa Catarina did not approach representatives of Sedesol for a reimbursement because they said they were done "dealing with the Mexican government. All of it."[10] The experience depleted this group of paisanos' energy and interest in cross-border investment.

The fragmented partnership in Santa Catarina was characterized by low community inclusion and government engagement. Fragmented, weak organization between paisanos, residents, and municipal government produced a context ripe for organizational corruption in Santa Catarina. This is not always what transpires from fragmentation, but it is a likely outcome. Citizens were reluctant to engage in the coproduction process and their suspicions were confirmed when the 3x1 Program resources disappeared. Without support from residents in the coproduction process, Club Santa Catarina was vulnerable. Local government officials were in a favorable position to take advantage of HTAs and their resources for their own benefit or at the behest of unscrupulous local actors involved in criminal organizations.

Corrupt, rent-seeking behaviors take many forms in the coproduction context. Public and private agents may shirk financial responsibilities and inflate project costs to extract additional resources from migrant, state, and federal partners. Political officials, local residents, and migrants collude with preferred contractors and construction companies for kickbacks and change technical plans and costs during implementation for mutual gain. Municipal government may also fail to monitor projects during implementation, which leads to poor quality or lack of project completion altogether. Although I did not witness this in any of the cases I studied for this book, I have heard from informants that in some cases migrants have colluded with governments, not simply to impose their view of what is good for the public, but to use public resources to further their own private ends. Informants' anecdotal accounts often describe some HTAs as "mano negra."[11] In the case of Santa Catarina, municipal government officials appropriated the monetary resources contributed by migrant groups. Local government officials were in a favorable position to capitalize on information asymmetries because members of the migrant club lived abroad. Without support from local resident citizens, the migrant club had limited mechanisms to monitor political officials' behavior when they were in the U.S. Fragmented partnerships characterized by limited government and resident engagement often fizzle out and fail.

The fragmented partnership revealed to the citizenry the PRI mayor's misdeeds in office. Citizens of Santa Catarina were already disillusioned with the local political process prior to coproduction; this experience compounded their disillusionment. But while political engagement was depressed in the wake of the failed 3x1 project, more citizens turned out to vote in the 2010 election than in the three previous elections. While other factors were certainly at play in citizens' decision to put their support behind the opposition candidate in 2010, paisanos thought, perhaps giving themselves too much credit, that their failed partnership had exposed government wrongdoing and citizens had punished the PRI in the next election. In the 2010 election, there was an 8 percent increase in turnout among the voting-age population compared to the previous election. Additionally, the PRI's vote share declined 5 percent as citizens shifted their support to the opposition candidate of the alliance party. It is not clear if the failure of the transnational partnership played any part in local participation. In 2009 when I visited the town, public activities, especially those that displayed income, were kept to a minimum and citizens I spoke with said they had no interest in any sphere of participatory engagement with the local government.

SYNERGETIC COPRODUCTION THROUGH THE ECONOMIC CRISIS IN AHUACATL, GUANAJUATO

Uninterested in school, Juan left his hometown of Ahuacatl, Guanajuato, in his early twenties with six years of primary education. He left for the U.S. in pursuit of his version of the American dream—find work, raise a family, and return to Ahuacatl with enough savings to build a house of his own and care for his aging parents. Finding work in the locality of Ahuacatl or the municipal county seat of Corporeo where Ahuacatl was located was difficult. With no education and no prospects for decent work, Juan had gotten into some trouble with alcohol and decided to leave for the U.S. with the hope of a fresh start. Not many residents of Ahuacatl had emigrated when Juan made the decision to go, although many citizens of Corporeo had left for the northern border and many Ahuacatlenses left later on in the late 1990s. In his town, he was a pioneer of sorts. He saw migrants from nearby municipalities leave and then return with new trucks and remittance dollars, which they used to fix up houses and start businesses. Juan wanted a chance at the same fortune. His parents were subsistence farmers, barely able to provide for their 11 children on the parcel of *ejido* land the family inherited from Juan's grandparents. Juan was the first of his siblings to leave for the U.S. and made the perilous journey with a *coyote* alone. Six of Juan's siblings eventually left for the

U.S. while four sisters and a brother remained in and around Ahuacatl to work the land with their parents.

Most residents, like Juan's family, farmed former *ejido* land, worked in the bottling plant of a popular Mexican beer company in a nearby municipality, or owned small shops and food stalls in Corporeo. Other residents of Ahuacatl traveled longer distances and worked in more economically active cities such as Irapuato, Celaya, or Leon. High levels of poverty and little attention from the municipal government meant that people had to rely on each other to solve local problems and find employment to support their families.

Despite its larger population than other localities in Corporeo, Ahuacatl was a rather tight-knit community and had a vibrant civil society before the arrival of the migrant hometown club. After a flood rattled the locality in a particularly rainy season, residents came together and collected donations across Corporeo for those who had lost possessions. In the town there was both a popular church organization that regularly met and an active and dedicated Patronato festival group. Additionally, residents had a favorable opinion of the local delegate who represented Ahuacatl to municipal authorities. Some residents affectionately called the delegate *El Guaje*.[12]

FORMATION OF CLUB AHUACATL AND THE
CHALLENGE OF WEAK CAPACITY IN THE U.S.

Juan's journey to the U.S. was not an easy one. His first trip across the border was unsuccessful and it took a few more attempts before he crossed into Texas on foot. His arrival in the U.S. was jarring. He knew not a soul and work was harder to find that he thought it would be. When times were really tough he knocked on doors and asked strangers for odd jobs. He lived in five U.S. states before he settled in San Diego, California, with his wife, Yesenia. Juan thought himself the luckiest man in the world to have found Yesenia, a Mexican woman of Nahua decent from San Luis Potosí, for he was lonely during those first 10 years in the U.S. On several occasions he was tempted to return to Ahuacatl with nothing to show for his migration. His luck changed when Juan was hired as a security guard and custodian at a private Jewish day school. Juan told me that some students and teachers joked that he was "half Catholic and half Jewish" because of his dedication to the school. By the time I came to know Juan, he had worked at the school for ten years. It was clear that the students cared about him as they practiced their Spanish with him and asked to hear about Ahuacatl and what life is life in Mexico when they saw him in the school hallways.

Once he became more settled in San Diego, Juan visited his hometown more regularly. He visited for long weekends, for a month over the summer break, and for three weeks in December. Juan was a regular figure in Ahuacatl and remained very close to his family and childhood friends. Juan became more accustomed to life in the U.S., but he never felt truly at home. He was more comfortable in Ahuacatl, near his horses, on the land, and surrounded by people who shared the same small-town values.

Unlike the migrant clubs in El Cerrito and Telepi that came together on their own, Club Ahuacatl formed at the request of local residents in 2005 and was the first hometown association in the municipality of Corporeo. After Ahuacatlenses heard about a migrant club from the nearby municipality of Acambaro that had finished several public works projects by working with the municipal administration, residents hoped paisanos including Juan who had left in the 1990s would use their social mobility to support projects for the people in Ahuacatl. Leaders in Ahuacatl asked the paisanos who returned for the annual patron saint festival to partner with them and the local government to improve living conditions in Ahuacatl through cross-border collective action.

The patron saint festival was a celebratory time in Ahuacatl when migrants trekked back to Guanajuato from all over the U.S. During the July festival, residents asked Juan, Martin, and Ramon, migrants in town for the event, to form a club and request funds from the municipal government for public works projects. El Guaje knew the paisanos families well and had a friendly relationship with Juan especially, who was a frequent visitor. While paisanos and townspeople gathered together to enjoy *música de banda*, fireworks, street food, horse races, and the religious festival of candles at the historic Catholic church, El Guaje and the leader of the local church group pulled the paisanos aside and told them about their wish to have a migrant club that helped the town, like the club they heard about in Acambaro.

The paisanos liked the idea, but they had not the first clue about how to run a club or get other paisanos in the U.S. involved. The paisanos were a bit reluctant. El Guaje, a charismatic and charming leader, reassured the migrants that they could start small; "No pressure," El Guaje told them, "it will be fun." By the end of the festival week as the migrants prepared to return to the U.S., El Guaje and the church group met with the paisanos to decide next steps for the new migrant club. The migrants agreed to fundraise in the U.S. for their first official project, which was a common area in front of the church for festivals and other social events. They also decided together that it would be a good idea to install bathrooms for patrons to use in the plaza area.

El Guaje had a plan to raise the project with the municipal administration during their next meeting with the *delegados* and gauge their level of support. Local elites, namely the doctor and the dentist who lived in Ahuacatl, had strategized with El Guaje that municipal officials might be more inclined to support residents' preferred projects if they brought the paisanos into the picture. Other residents, though, were wary of bringing the municipal government into the partnership with the migrants given the history of the soured public-private partnerships that occurred during President Salinas's National Solidarity Program (Pronasol) in Corporeo.

The eagerness of residents to work directly with the local government waned after a failed attempt at a public-private partnership for public works provision through the National Pronasol in the 1990s. Citizens in Ahuacatl told me how the resources they contributed to collaborative projects "went missing," "projects were never finished," and the people of Corporeo "no longer had confidence or really trust the municipal government." But El Guaje and other locals thought that if the paisanos proposed projects through the 3x1 Program, the additional oversight from the state and federal governments would ease the concerns of anxious Ahuacatl residents. Ahuacatl elites, who knew the mayor's family well since his wife was from Ahuacatl, thought he was different than previous administrations and would be less opportunistic with the locals and the migrant club. The mayor's social connection to Ahuacatl gave them some reassurances that he would not risk his local reputation.

ROLE OF THE STATE AND MUNICIPAL GOVERNMENTS IN THE TRANSNATIONAL PARTNERSHIP

Corporeo municipality is located in the southeastern region of Guanajuato near Selvillo. It is a middle-income municipality of about 60,000 residents. Up until 1986, the PRI maintained firm control of the municipality. But since the PAN opposition party wrested the mayorship from the PRI, the two parties have alternated power in the last eight electoral cycles. Municipal elections were hotly contested in Corporeo and Ahuacatl was considered a swing community because voters vacillated in their support for the PAN and PRI. As Oliver, a restaurant owner, said, "In Ahuacatl, we don't vote for the party, we vote for the person." The previous, current, and incoming mayors of both political parties repeated the sentiment. It was well known that during elections, the political parties worked hard for the votes of Ahuacatl and campaigned heavily in one of the most populated localities of Corporeo.

The year 2005 was the PAN mayor of Corporeo, Beto's, second year in office. When El Guaje raised the church project proposal with Beto's administration, he was not initially enthusiastic about the project, which was more social in nature and would do little to improve development goals in Ahuacatl. However, this initial meeting did reveal that he was eager to partner with the migrants on other public works projects that focused more on public infrastructure. Beto had recently heard about the 3x1 Program from another PAN mayor and knew previous PAN administrations had tried, without success, to get paisanos to form clubs and coordinate public goods provision with them using collective remittances. Beto asked to meet with Juan and El Guaje during his return visit to Ahuacatl. In the meeting, they all agreed to first work on the church project through the 3x1 Program, but then they would also collaborate on a drainage project, an essential service that was underprovided in many neighborhoods in Ahuacatl, and a problem that often wreaked havoc on the town during the rainy season when floods were more common. El Guaje urged the mayor in the meeting to reassure the residents of Ahuacatl that he would keep his word to support the church program and then move on to other coproduction projects. Beto was a young and enthusiastic mayor with aspirations to move up the party ladder and so he agreed to meet directly with the residents of Ahuacatl.

A few Ahuacatl residents were invited to the Corporeo *ayuntamiento* along with El Guaje. In the meeting, Beto reassured the citizens that they and the paisanos would stay in control of the projects and the municipality would serve in a supportive role. Beto said that he told them, "The people here in Ahuacatl trust the paisanos more. They have a kinship and connection with them and believe them more than us. We respect that." Residents also trusted Juan, leader of the migrant club, and believed he and El Guaje would serve as a conduit to the administration that represented the town's interests.

When I asked residents why they had so much confidence in Juan, many residents said they felt reassured because he had so much family in Ahuacatl and visited frequently. Since he came back often during the year and stayed for much of the summer, worked on his house and on his family's land with his kids, to some residents like Cindy, it hardly seemed like he had left at all. El Guaje and the town elites' plan—to coordinate public goods provision between the migrants and the municipal government while maintaining a clear voice in the process—worked. Mayor Beto, the director of social development, and the director of public works recognized and publicly addressed the residual mistrust between citizens and the local government. When public officials acknowledged past misdeeds of Panista mayors, the new guard of the PAN was able to extend an olive branch to the citizen voters of Ahuacatl. This effort was strategic by the savvy politicians because Ahuacatl was a swing district that had been known to make or break an election for the PAN. Political competition in Corporeo created incentives for the PAN administration to seek an edge over the PRI opposition through the provision of public goods.

At the meeting, in the presence of the residents, Beto instructed his staff to draw up technical plans, hire contractors, and source the necessary materials for the church patio. Once they received approval from the 3x1 validation committee, the project was completed in a few short weeks. Paisanos, El Guaje, and residents of Ahuacatl were proud of the project and the plaza quickly became a popular place for residents to congregate. El Guaje recalled:

> Before the paisano club and 3x1 we tried to organize and do projects for Ahuacatl, but the municipality was difficult to work with. The mayors say they will help but never do anything or it takes a really long time. But with the migrant club the government doesn't take as long to reply, we get a lot more attention from the municipal center. I think it's because they know they can get funds from the state and federal government.

FIGURE 3. Pavement project groundbreaking ceremony with mayor of Ahuacatl. Photo by author.

Residents were still wary, but hopeful the migrants would spur more financial support for public works in Ahuacatl.

On the U.S. side, the club encountered many hurdles. State public officials from Guanajuato affiliated with the Casas Guanajuato program[13] and the Mexican consulate proved an important resource for the struggling, nascent club. Juan, Ramon, and Martin had a few friends from Ahuacatl in the U.S., but paisanos were scattered all across California and Texas. The three migrants had strong bonding ties in Ahuacatl, but they did not know each other well, and their social connections to other Ahuacatl paisanos in the U.S. were even more limited. The club leaders had family who had migrated, but their social circles were not based on immigrants from their hometown in their places of settlement in the U.S. In Texas, Martin reached out to other paisanos from Ahuacatl with contact information he received from their families. Juan and Ramon reached out to paisanos in the same way in San Diego and Los Angeles. The three men conducted most of their club business over the phone and each collected donations for the project by knocking on the doors of other paisanos, most of them cold calls to strangers who shared a connection to Ahuacatl, but not to the migrant club leaders themselves.

The paisanos' weak social ties to one another and lack of ties to other paisanos from Ahuacatl and Corporeo were challenges for the migrant club. They wanted to help the residents of Ahuacatl with projects, but they were inexperienced in leading a club and fundraising. Juan, in particular, thought fundraising was awkward and he did not enjoy it. At this point, he thought the club might be able to raise the money for the church project, but then the club would disband. "It was going to be too hard to keep knocking on doors. And I'm kind of shy. I didn't feel comfortable asking people for money back then. I thought, okay, we'll do the one project that the residents want us to do and that will be it. It was taking a lot of time too," he said. Martin and Ramon had difficulty drumming up support from Ahuacatlenses in the U.S. Ramon said, "It was hard to get anyone on the phone and when we did, they didn't want to get involved in the club or donate resources." Seeing Martin frustrated, his Guanajuatense friends in Texas recommended he visit the Casa Guanajuato in Dallas and see if they could help his club get off the ground.

State officials in Texas and California became a key source of information about the 3x1 Program and the supply of contact information to paisanos from the hometown in the U.S. Personnel at the Casa Guanajuato in Dallas encouraged Martin to get his club registered at a Mexican consulate so that they could formally propose the 3x1 project to the validation committee at the next meeting in Guanajuato. They also encouraged him to contact the state Migrant Affairs Offices in Guanajuato, which would be able to help them locate other paisanos from Corporeo. With guidance from the Casa Guanajuato and Guanajuato state officials, Club Ahuacatl expanded their network of paisanos from Corporeo in the U.S. and got their club officially registered with the Institute for Mexicans Abroad at the Mexican consulate.

The state government of Guanajuato was a major gateway for the survival and expansion of Club Ahuacatl. Members of the Casa Guanajuato in Texas invited Beto to Texas and set up meetings with other paisanos from the three major localities of Corporeo. The initial visit was successful. Three additional groups of migrants agreed to form clubs and work with Beto's administration on development projects in their respective hometowns. While previous mayors of Corporeo had encouraged paisanos to support development projects in their hometown with collective remittances, migrants declined, citing the corruption in previous partnerships between citizens of Corporeo and the municipal government. Beto was pleased the relationship to some paisanos had changed during his administration and was hopeful the next administration would continue the efforts he started.

Citizens of Corporeo reelected the PAN in the July 2006 elections. Ahuacatl residents overwhelmingly supported Bricio, the PAN candidate. Bricio was the director of social development in Beto's administration and several Ahuacatl residents became acquainted with him working on the church pavement project. Bricio campaigned on a public works platform. Building on the relationship formed with the paisanos during Beto's last year in office, Bricio made the 3x1 Program a key component of his development plan. He explained:

> The best mayors, the most successful mayors who do projects for the people of their towns, are not necessarily the ones with the most revenue. There are many mayors who have resources but they can be lazy or corrupt. But municipalities that want to improve the lives of citizens without resources have to go and find the resources and manage them well (*gestion*) to do things that help make the people happy. Part of the job is finding program after program that your municipality qualifies for and get more resources. The 3x1 Program is a program like that.

Working with Ahuacatl residents and paisanos on projects through the 3x1 Program required concessions on the part of the municipal government. The church renovation project was not a priority for Beto and his team since they prioritized the provision of basic services. But they identified the need to work with the migrants and residents and support some of their wishes so they could gain their trust and continue working together on drainage and potable water projects, which the public officials cited as the most pressing needs of Ahuacatl. As a result of this collaborative approach Beto and later Bricio completed several projects with Club Ahuacatl including the church pavement and bathroom project, street pavement and sidewalk projects, and new street lamps in the town.

MIGRANT SOCIAL EMBEDDEDNESS AND COMMUNITY INCLUSION

Juan was a well-known resident of Ahuacatl even though he had lived in the U.S. for many years. He had a strong bonding social network in Ahuacatl and continued to practice cultural repertoires of community membership when he was in town. Both parents, several siblings, and friends from elementary school with whom he had remained close after his departure all lived in Ahuacatl. Once Juan landed his job at the day school, his good pay and job security allowed him to build a house for his family, Yesenia and her two sons, just as he had dreamed. He built the house across the street from his childhood home where his parents still lived and where several siblings lived nearby with their own growing families. He bought a new truck that stayed in the garage to use during his visits. He purchased land for a brother outside of town. He fixed up his parent's house. And when he came, he brought small tokens of affection to friends from elementary school and family members—Chargers baseball hats (the San Diego NFL team at the time), materials to fix up their houses, and trinkets such as little bracelets and necklaces for his nieces. He liked to take long walks or ride on his horse when he was in town to say hello to people. When I accompanied him as he went through town, store owners came outside to greet him. Despite his absence and the new luxuries social mobility offered Juan and his family, residents did not seem to begrudge his success because he shared it with them. Juan was seen as a man of Ahuacatl, even though he no longer lived there year-round. He was still a part of his hometown community and the town's favorable opinion of Juan was extended to the paisano club. This was why El Guaje and local leaders wanted Juan to run the club. They believed he would represent the people of Ahuacatl because he was still one of them.

Juan's popularity was also aided by the admiration citizens had for his older brother, Caesar. When I accompanied him into Corporeo, acquaintances who he did not know well, but who knew his brother, would yell "Brother Zamora! Órale!" Caesar lived in Celaya and he was a rodeo and party promoter throughout the region. Everyone around town knew about Caesar's parties and traveled several kilometers to attend them, especially when he booked popular banda groups. In 2007, after the migrant club had completed a few projects successfully and Juan had become more confident in his fundraising abilities, he started to throw rodeos in Ahuacatl with Caesar to fundraise for the town. When the brothers brought the popular regional social events to Ahuacatl, many residents credited the Zamora family for bringing positive attention to the small town. The rodeo gave residents something to be excited about and everyone wanted to chip in to make the event a success. The rodeo also further expanded Juan's social ties throughout Ahuacatl and to other localities in Corporeo.

Juan had both bonding and bridging ties in Ahuacatl. His bonding social ties included kin (siblings, nieces and nephews, and their friends) and fictive kin relationships (godchildren and godparents), and he had bridging ties to stakeholders in the town, such as church leaders, El Guaje and Guaje's elite friends (the dentist, doctor, and "el profesor," a retired schoolteacher who catalogued the colonial history of Corporeo), and schoolmates who were small shop owners. Furthermore, residents who were active in the church group and worked with the club also drew on their social networks to support the club's public works efforts. The paisanos' social ties and embeddedness in the town were paramount to their success scaling up community involvement in public goods provision with municipal authorities, but it became even more important when the economic crisis in the U.S. decreased the club's capacity to coproduce public works projects through the 3x1 Program.

ECONOMIC RECESSION AND THE CHALLENGE TO HTA CLUB CAPACITY

The success of 3x1 projects in Ahuacatl invigorated local residents, who had many 3x1 project ideas they wanted to see implemented in the town. In 2008, teachers from the local kindergarten asked for a meeting with El Guaje and Juan during his visit home during the Thanksgiving holiday. With the encouragement of the teachers and parents of the *jardin de niños* (kindergarten), the school group asked the migrants to help them with a problem in their school: excessive overcrowding. At the time, one teacher supervised 50 students. El Guaje suggested they build a new classroom addition to the school and hire one of the teachers who was laid off from a nearby school that recently closed. Juan and El Guaje thought it was a wonderful idea. El Guaje organized a meeting with political officials to propose the 3x1 project and Juan agreed to bring the idea back to the paisanos in the club. Shortly after, the mayor agreed and worked with his administration to submit technical plans and approval through the 3x1 Program.

The *mesa directiva* (parent-teacher association) of the school met with Corporeo's director of social development and El Guaje while Juan, Ramon, and other members of Club Ahuacatl fundraised back in the U.S. During the meeting, parents expressed concern that construction during the school year would be dangerous for the children, but they did not want to wait until July when school ended because of the elections. Everyone in the meeting worried that the elections would stall the project. Residents' concern was that if an opposition party took power there were no assurances that the new administration would complete the 3x1 school project. The residents had good reason to be concerned about party turnover because the PAN candidate running for the mayorship was very unpopular with locals. Residents thought the PRI candidate, Carlos, was going to win even though they had developed strong partisan attachments for Beto and Bricio, Panista mayors of Corporeo, whom voters in Ahuacatl credited for the improvement in public goods provision in their town.

Carlos served as mayor of Corporeo in the early 1990s and he opened the first Corona beer company bottling plant in the region, which brought many jobs to the people of Corporeo and the region. Paisanos and residents alike wanted to work with whichever party was elected, but they had concerns that Carlos's administration might not honor projects started during the PAN incumbent's last year in office. Bricio reassured everyone involved that they would start and finish the classroom project before the new administration took office. This was also a strategic decision by Bricio since he wanted to prevent the PRI administration from taking credit for his projects in order to sway unsuspecting voters during the election campaign season.

Martin, Ramon, Juan, and other paisanos tried to fundraise for the school expansion project as they had done for previous 3x1 projects. But in late 2008 and 2009 the U.S. housing crisis was in full swing. The economic crisis severely dampened the club's capacity to raise funds for their hometown. Martin, who worked in the construction industry, was worried he would lose his job and have to return to Mexico. This was the same predicament for many paisanos from Corporeo who also worked in housing construction. Club Ahuacatl was able to raise some contributions, but not the full 25 percent stipulated by the 3x1 Program. Embarrassed, Juan recalled how awful he felt when he returned to Ahuacatl and told the *mesa directiva* of the school that the paisanos were unable to raise project funds for the schoolhouse.

Members of the school group were disappointed. But they also understood too well the migrants' difficulties since many of the children in the school had parents in the U.S. who feared the loss of their jobs and ability to send home remittances. Parents offered to fundraise to help cover the remaining cost in order to continue the project. They held potluck dinners and took donations from willing families, whatever they could spare. Juan was adamant that the club never pressure the residents for money because he knew many of the families had a member in the U.S. and that times were tough. Juan was very vocal about this at the meeting I attended. Together with Juan's brother, the *mesa directiva*, El Guaje, and the church association, citizen groups offered to pitch in.

When Juan told Caesar about the decline in the club's capacity to fundraise for the school project, Caesar offered to throw the next *jaripeo* in Ahuacatl. Ahuacatl had never hosted a rodeo in their own town and everyone buzzed with excitement. Residents volunteered and sold tickets to the event all over Corporeo and nearby municipalities. Other residents posted fliers for the event in other municipalities to attract people from all over the region. The church group held a raffle for a fat calf they called "Miguel," and made food to sell at the event. The rodeo was a huge success and raised more than enough to cover the 25 percent migrant contribution to the school project. As a result of the collective mobilization of residents all across town during a decline in the club's capacity to raise 3x1 funds, construction broke ground in June and the entire project wrapped up in August. The ribbon-cutting ceremony for the schoolhouse was an emotional event for the residents of Ahuacatl who were proud of their accomplishments, and for Juan, who was unsure if his club would be able to do any more projects with paisanos' investment as they increasingly struggled to make ends meet in the U.S.

While the school classroom was being built in July, Carlos won the mayorship. Much to residents' surprise, despite PRI party turnover in municipal government, Carlos immediately set up formal meetings with Club Ahuacatl and community residents to plan 3x1 projects during his administration. At the meeting, Juan informed the mayor that Club Ahuacatl was unable to collect the remittances of paisanos in the U.S. as they had done before the economic crisis and would likely have to disband the club. By late 2009 and well into 2010, the economic crisis depressed the paisanos' ability to raise funds for coproduction projects in Ahuacatl.

Hearing of the migrant club's difficulty raising funds in the U.S., Chumo, the dentist who had been involved in earlier 3x1 projects, offered to organize a public works committee for the town. The *comite de obras* was a group of five Ahuacatl residents who wanted to keep up the momentum for public works projects even though the paisanos could no longer be actively involved in the partnership. Chumo explained that members of the *comite* "all share the same vision for the town . . . we can help the paisanos with the 25 percent and we can still do projects through the 3x1 Program." With Juan, Martin, and Ramon's blessing, the public works committee completely took over project selection, planning, and implementation efforts with the municipal government. The only involvement that Club Ahuacatl had in the coproduction process was to propose the projects to the COVAM for 3x1 Program approval so that the municipality could still quality for state and federal matching funds.

Members of the public works committee did not believe that the municipal government would still want to engage in coproduction projects if they could no longer participate in the 3x1 Program. Enrique, a member of the public works committee, reflected on how town life has changed since Club Ahuacatl began supporting projects:

> The two biggest problems in Ahuacatl are drinking water and drainage. We could not do these kinds of projects by ourselves . . . Listen, before people wanted to be involved, but having the migrant club has definitely increased residents' participation in the town . . . It is easier to get people in the town involved when there are incentives like different state or municipal programs like 3x1. When the people know they don't have to do the whole [project] by themselves and that they have the support from government officials, they are more likely to do something. Since 3x1, there are more requests for little projects. I think this is because people were not sure if the projects would actually happen, but now that they see the patio project done, and the school, and the roads, they have more confidence and will talk to our committee.

Before Club Ahuacatl, residents were active in the social life of the town, but the migrant club helped scale up participation in public works projects. This participatory engagement in coordination with public officials created new terrain for democratic decision-making outside the electoral process.

While El Guaje and prominent members of Ahuacatl were the driving forces behind the formation of the hometown association, after several projects were completed in the locality, more residents became actively involved in the 3x1 coproduction process. Juan's social embeddedness in Ahuacatl meant that his leadership in the migrant club garnered support for coproduction projects that directly involved the municipal government. Members of the town knew Juan, who was perceived as a member of the Ahuacatl community, even though he had lived abroad for more than 20 years. Since paisanos had maintained solidaristic ties with residents of the hometown beyond their immediate social circles, a more heterogeneous group of citizens were involved in the coproduction process. And as community inclusion increased with the successful completion of 3x1 projects and more residents took ownership over public projects, they had more routinized interactions with elected public officials including Beto, Bricio, Carlos, and other political officials who were part of the PAN and PRI municipal administrations.

The fierce electoral competition in Corporeo created political incentives for the municipal administration to become engaged in the coproduction process with migrants, as in the case of El Cerrito. Beto and Bricio both pursued campaign platforms based on the provision of public works. The mayors, including the PRI administration from 2009–12, viewed the 3x1 Program as an opportunity to expand social spending throughout Corporeo. The active involvement of community residents presented municipal officials with an opportunity to work with their constituents and develop relationships with stakeholders in the community. The process of coproducing public works helped to repair some of the mistrust in local government. As Gema, a local Ahuacuatl resident, told me, "It's better now, but it is always a good idea to keep a healthy distance when it comes to the Mexican government."

The combination of high community inclusion and government engagement organized synergetic coproduction in Ahuacatl. During the U.S. economic downturn, residents of Ahuacatl scaled up their participation to help the migrants overcome financial constraints to continue working on projects through the 3x1 Program. This escalation in civic participation had additional positive spillovers for democratic participation. Residents reported that their interactions with municipal officials of both parties showed them that the government responded to their needs when they made their voices heard, even if they never fully trusted politicians. Over the course of the three mayoral administrations in which Club Ahuacatl and community residents engaged in coproduction (2004–12), government spending on public works was 3 percent higher, on average, compared to the previous period (2002–04). All of the localities with an active migrant club, including Ahuacatl, received a higher distribution of public spending than they did before. Although the PAN administration did not win the 2009 election, residents continued to work effectively with Carlos's PRI administration, completing an additional four coproduction projects in Ahuacatl without collective remittances from the migrant club. As a result of the synergetic partnership forged between citizens, migrants, and political officials, 10 coproduction projects were successfully completed in Ahuacatl in Carlo's three years as mayor during the U.S. economic crisis. Coproduction created a new institutional venue through which citizens could participate more in social and political affairs of their community.

As of 2013, Club Ahuacatl continued to support the provision of public goods in Ahuacatl, but no longer with collective remittances. Juan used his status as a paisano and proposed projects through the 3x1 Program for cofinancing from the state, federal, and municipal governments, but was no more involved than that. Instead of migrants' remittance contributions, the public works committee of Ahuacatl contributed the 25 percent share for projects. Club Ahuacatl never recovered their capacity to fundraise and keep paisanos interested in coproduction activities through the economic crisis. In 2010, Martin and Ramon stopped participating in the club altogether and said it took up too much time and attention. The club became inactive in 2011 after seven years of successful coproduction in Ahuacatl, but 3x1 coproduction projects continued without them. Juan still visited several times a year and threw parties with his brother. He continued to enjoy everyday life in his hometown with friends, new and old, and his family and the people of Ahuacatl.

SUMMARY

The two cases in this chapter represent examples of intermediary organizational forms of transnational coproduction that differed in their levels of community inclusion and government engagement. But in both cases additional factors beyond electoral incentives, local-state capacity, and migrant social embeddedness impacted levels of community inclusion and government engagement.

In the PRI stronghold of Santa Catarina, local residents were uninterested in direct involvement in coproduction so long as it involved public officials who many suspected of being corrupt or in cahoots with criminal organizations. Moreover, local political officials were all but secured electoral victory by the *cacique* in town and public goods provision was not part of the electoral calculus to turn out voters in municipal elections. In Ahuacatl, migrants, especially the HTA leader who was the most visible ambassador of the migrant club in the hometown, were socially embedded, possessing both bonding and bridging ties throughout the community despite having lived in the U.S. for decades. Moreover, local government was eager to work with paisanos on projects, in Ahuacatl especially, as they thought they could benefit from the amplification of resources for public spending through the 3x1 Program in an electorally competitive locality that was known to support both PRI and PAN mayoral candidates. But when club capacity was severely contracted by the U.S. economic recession, because paisanos had helped forge network ties between community leaders in Ahuacatl and the local government through the coproduction process, 3x1 projects were able to continue with the increase in residents' ownership and leadership in local public goods provision.

In the synergetic partnership in Ahuacatl in which both inclusion and engagement were high, residents became active participants in the coproduction process with a fully engaged local government. Political officials in Corporeo supplied matching funds, proposed projects, provided technical planning and support, hired labor, and coordinated materials to the coproduction process. Because they were keen on receiving matching funds from the state and federal governments to provide public goods in a more politically competitive part of town, public officials were open to negotiation with the migrant club and resident actors. When the U.S. recession challenged Club Ahuacatl's capacity to collect resources for coproduction projects and keep club members involved in club activities on the U.S. side of the border, residents increased their involvement in public goods provision to supplement the club's investment. To do so, community members volunteered to form a public works committee, a new civic association in town, and work with the delegate and municipal officials to continue coproduction projects without the involvement of the migrant club, but still through the 3x1 Program. In sum, synergy, despite a decline in HTA club capacity, was associated with an increase in local civic and political participatory engagement.

By contrast, in Santa Catarina migrants were not as socially embedded in the town as paisano club leaders from Ahuacatl. The paisanos from Santa Catarina, who reluctantly formed a club at the request of the local priest and excited members of the paisano network in Chicago, had weak bonding and bridging social networks. High rates of out-migration coupled with over 20 years away from the hometown and few visits during those years eroded social ties to local residents. Most of the paisanos' family, close friends, schoolmates, and neighborhood acquaintances had also emigrated and either joined the paisanos in the Chicago metro area or emigrated to other parts of the U.S., namely Texas and California. In other words, paisanos bonding networks relocated with them to the U.S. and paisanos only had a few social connections to people who remained behind.

Bridging ties were also in short supply because there were few community leaders in the hometown aside from the local priest. The popular local pastor introduced migrant club leaders to parishioners when they were in town for two different religious festivals, but locals did not want to be involved and club members did not actively recruit them into project planning. Additionally, residents' mistrust of local political officials also discouraged their involvement when they learned that participation in the 3x1 Program required municipal government participation. And concerns about public security connected to the rise of criminal organizations and drug trafficking in the region further hampered local residents' interest in becoming involved in public affairs, which could potentially draw attention to the presence of remittance resources flowing into town. Relatedly, residents' concerns about the mayor's connections to nefarious activities further turned off community involvement in the transnational partnership.

In both cases in this chapter, factors beyond migrant social embeddedness and political bureaucratic capacity and competitiveness affected levels of community inclusion and government engagement. Drug violence and the U.S. economic recession had an independent effect on the organization of transnational partnerships and also through their effect on community inclusion and government engagement. Additional factors specific to the hometown setting needed to be accounted for to more fully explain variation in the organization of transnational partnerships.

In the next chapter, I present the final two cases of transnational partnership between migrant clubs and public agencies in the Mexican sending state. The cases of El Mirador and Atitlan are different than other cases in that both partnerships represent different localities that are in the *same* municipality, whereas the previous four cases were each in different municipalities. The benefit of a within-municipal case comparison is that it allows me to hold constant local bureaucratic capacity of the state and trace how migrant social embeddedness and electoral considerations in different localities shaped community inclusion and government engagement to different organizational forms of partnership (corporatist and synergetic) and to diverse political outcomes and effects on state-society relations.

Synergy and Corporatism in El Mirador and Atitlan, Comarga

"We don't need 3x1 or the paisanos, we live here. We have our own ideas about what this town needs," insisted Lydia, member of the Patron Saint Festival Association and resident of Atitlan, Comarga. After a contentious year, residents of Atitlan had enough of paisanos' directives to pay for a public goods project they had no part in choosing and of challenges to the autonomy of the Patronato as the representative voice of the community. The migrant leadership of Club Atitlan had formed an alliance with the municipal government and shut out local residents from meaningful participation in the transnational partnership that organized public goods projects through the 3x1 Program, although the migrant-state partners demanded that the Patronato contribute resources. The corporatist coproduction partnership crowded out key community stakeholders from deliberation in the selection and coordination of a 3x1 pavement project that was neither a priority for the homeowners nor something they wanted to help finance. As a result, state-society and paisano-resident relations became contentious, and residents mobilized political support for the opposition party to punish the incumbent for privileging the paisanos' remittances and voices over those who lived in the town and were represented by the Patronato.

Why were social relations between migrants and nonmigrants in Atitlan contentious? Why were residents treated as clients of the migrants and the state and not included in the coproduction process as meaningful contributors? In Atitlan, members of the hometown association lacked social bridging ties to key community stakeholders and they did not attempt to create them as they prioritized social status and political power over social solidarity with local residents. By contrast, in another locality in Comarga called El Mirador, a migrant hometown association successfully coproduced several public goods projects with the same municipal government in the same period of time. What was different in the two partnerships was that paisanos of El Mirador were still socially embedded in the hometown community after living abroad in the United States for more than 15 years. Practices of cultural membership in the hometown community and extensive bonding and bridging ties to local residents, especially migrant returnees to El Mirador, led to high levels of community inclusion. Residents were equal partners in the transnational partnership and formed a new civic association to work directly with Comarga municipal officials on a *cancha* (recreational court), *lienzo charro* (rodeo ring), street and sidewalk construction, and pavement and drainage projects. El Mirador residents routinely had face-to-face contact with municipal officials and negotiated project selection and project planning with the directors of social development and public works in the *ayuntamiento*. Even though both clubs were formed at the same time and with the encouragement of the same mayor, and had similar levels of poverty, population size, and partisan attachments, the transnational partnerships were organized differently because migrants' membership in the social community of their respective hometowns diverged.

In this chapter, I explain how low levels of community inclusion, but high levels of government engagement, organized a corporatist transnational partnership that had important consequences for political activism and state-society relations in Atitlan. I also present the partnership case of El Mirador, a locality in the same municipality as Atitlan, but one in which migrant social embeddedness in the hometown community led to higher levels of community inclusion in the provision of public goods. The comparison of two cases of transnational coproduction, which holds local-state capacity and electoral incentives constant, allows me to isolate and trace the key role that hometown-paisano social relations have in determining the structure of partnerships, which produced different political outcomes in the two hometown settings.

ATITLAN AND EL MIRADOR, COMARGA, JALISCO

The municipality of Comarga is located four hours north of Guadalajara in the northern region of Jalisco in the Sierra Madre Occidental Mountains. The municipality borders Zacatecas to the northwest and southeast. In 2005, the population was approximately 18,000; however, like many municipalities in Mexico, Comarga lost a significant portion of the economically active population to the U.S. labor market. Between 2000 and 2010, the intensity of international migration increased and changed Comarga's classification from "medium" to "high."[1] About 70 percent of the total population of Comarga lived in the country seat and the remaining citizens inhabited one of the four main localities. Differences in the provision of public goods between the county seat and Comarga's rural localities were striking.

For example, before 2005, the last time that rural communities like Atitlan and El Mirado received a public works project was when the PRI extended the electrical grid and potable water service in 1976.

According to official population statistics, Comarga is a middle-income municipality with a "medium" level of poverty, but the localities in Comarga are poorer.[2] In 2005, residents who lived on the outskirts of town lacked access to essential public goods such as drainage and sanitation. In both Atitlan and El Mirador about 8 percent of the population was illiterate. Many nonmigrant households had dirt floors and no plumbing in the home. Municipal administrations collected land taxes, license and water usage fees, and relied on revenue transfers from the state and federal governments to finance public works. But how mayors distributed those resources earmarked for public spending was entirely at the discretion of municipal officials. In Comarga, most mayors focused public resources in the county seat where the majority of the population resided. This decision left many households who lived in localities outside the town center to finance public goods on their own, often with remittance resources, which was the case in many municipalities across Mexico.[3]

El Mirador and Atitlan were two very similar localities in Comarga. In the wake of the economic crisis and drought of the 1980s and 1990s, many people left the two localities for the U.S. in search of job opportunities. They settled mostly in Texas, Oregon, California, Indiana, and Illinois. In 2000, about 15 percent of households had a member of the household living in the U.S. and between 5 and 10 percent regularly received remittances, although these households were more concentrated in the localities than the county seat. Some migrant households used a portion of remittance income to finance indoor plumbing and to build water wells because they did not have access to the public potable water system. Both locales had similar levels of emigration, household remittances, and public goods provision. El Mirador and Atitlan also had similar levels of poverty according to the Mexican Census's marginalization index and population size. In terms of sociodemographic characteristics, the two localities were very similar, although El Mirador was more remote and higher up in the mountains than Atitlan.

Both locales were also supporters of the PAN political party and voters had cast their ballots overwhelmingly for the PAN incumbent since the party's first municipal victory against the PRI in 1992. In every subsequent election, the PAN won by double-digit margins. But in the 2005, 2008, and 2011 elections, PRI candidates made serious inroads and wrested votes away from the PAN, mostly in the county seat. Since the early 2000s, localities like El Mirador and Atitlan had become even more important political districts as the PAN incumbent relied on their core supporters turning out to vote in increasingly competitive elections. In 2005, Pepe Coronado won the mayorship by a razor-thin margin against a popular PRI candidate, which put the PAN on the defensive for the first time since the early 1990s. Pepe made public works provision a central component of his campaign platform, especially in localities like Atitlan where he was born. After he won the election he put these plans into action and identified paisanos in the U.S. with remittance resources as central to the achievement of this goal. Social spending through the 3x1 Program was a political strategy to supply loyal supporters with public goods and encouraged their continued support for the PAN.

LEARNING ABOUT THE 3X1 PROGRAM FROM MUNICIPAL NEIGHBORS AND JALISCO STATE OUTREACH

The dissemination of information from Comarga's mayor and nearby political officials was integral to Pepe's exposure to the 3x1 Program and eventual participation. When Pepe observed several new public works projects in a nearby municipality, he was curious how the mayor—whom he believed worked with a similar budget and population size as Comarga—had the requisite public resources to provide so many new projects in such a short amount of time. When he asked the mayor in the Zacatecan municipality about the increase in public service delivery, officials told Pepe about their participation in the 3x1 Program and explained to him how a group of paisanos from their municipality collaborated on public projects. Members of the mayor's administration took Pepe on a tour of the public works projects they had completed throughout the town. Since Comarga had a significant population of paisanos in the U.S., Pepe was motivated to partner with them on projects and set out to expand the spending capacity of his administration through participation in the 3x1 Program.

The entrepreneurial Panista mayor contacted state-level officials in Guadalajara, the Jalisco state capital, to learn more about the 3x1 Program and how the state helped mayors locate and contact their paisanos in the U.S. It was in his correspondence with officials of the PAN governor's office where Pepe learned about the Office of Migrant Affairs, an administrative unit of the state that kept organized records of emigrants from the state of Jalisco who were in the U.S. With the support of the Migrant Affairs Office, Pepe's administration identified paisanos from Comarga across the U.S. Since the Migrant Affairs Office registered migrants in the U.S. when they visited the Mexican consulate, they supplied the Comarga municipal administration with paisanos' contact information. Pepe's new administration identified a few U.S. cities where the majority of Comarga paisanos lived, reached out to them, and organized face-to-face meetings with them in 2005.

Pepe and members of his administration visited paisanos from Comarga across the U.S. in one of his first activities after taking office. Although he was not successful in every meeting, he convinced migrants from different localities in Comarga to form a club. Two of the HTAs created during that visit were Club Atitlan and Club El Mirador. Information about the 3x1 Program and contact information of paisanos abroad allowed the mayor to recruit paisanos into a transnational partnership for public goods provision as political competition was heating up in Comarga.

FORMATION OF CLUB ATITLAN

Emilio was born in Atitlan and crossed into the U.S. with his mother when he was a newborn. She traveled alone to Texas after she separated from Emilio's father. Coming to the U.S. with a new baby and not much else, she returned to Atitlan after a few short months and reconciled with her husband when it became too hard to support herself and the baby in the U.S. Emilio spent the first 13 years of his life in Atitlan. When he was in elementary school in the 1970s, children his age attended school for half-days because the school building only had a few rooms for instruction. Younger kids went to school in the morning and older graders in the afternoons. Emilio never finished his primary education. "I was never that good in school. I got bored even though we were only there half the day! I much preferred being out in the open in the fields with my father," he said.

After Emilio's father died unexpectedly, his mother and siblings left Atitlan and immigrated again to the U.S. She did not believe she could take care of her family subsisting on the land on her own and so with most of her family had gone to the U.S. This time she went to California where her uncle lived. He found her a job in the agricultural fields of Fresno County where he worked. At the age of 13, Emilio worked with his mother in the fields and helped support the family. When his siblings were older and the family more settled in California, Emilio left and moved to Texas where many other paisanos from Comarga lived. He had grown tired of agricultural work and wanted to try something different. An old neighbor from Atitlan lived in San Antonio and he convinced Emilio to move there. Shortly after he moved to San Antonio he opened a small *abarrote* (convenience store), met his wife, and together they started a family in Texas.

It was in his store where Emilio was reunited with Esme. After more than 20 years, the two Atitlan natives recognized each other, and during their initial small talk discovered they had attended the same primary school. After a brief courtship, Esme and Emilio married. They had three children together, all born in the U.S., which they said contributed to their permanent settlement in Texas. Both Esme and Emilio became proficient English speakers and practiced with their children in the evenings. By the time I met the Atitlan natives in 2009 in Comarga, they described themselves as "Mexican American." While they had deep roots to Atitlan, they also had made the U.S. their home and had become accustomed to life in San Antonio. In many ways, Emilio and Esme had Americanized and they were proud to have done so. They cheered for their son at high school football games and celebrated American holidays with their non-Mexican neighbors as well as their hometown friends.

When Emilio, Esme, and three other migrant families from Atitlan met with Pepe and the directors of social development and communications who accompanied the mayor on his U.S. voyage, Pepe's desires to modernize Atitlan resonated immediately with the paisanos. Emilio and Esme spoke at length about the poor quality of Atitlan's roads, the lack of a recreation area, and other provisions, which they thought the residents of Atitlan needed. Emilio said he told the mayor that Atitlan was "not beautiful" and when he recalled his hometown he "felt sorry" for the people who lived there who did not have access to the same kinds of services that they had in San Antonio. It was not difficult to convince the paisanos in the meeting to form a club and partner with the mayor on projects through the 3x1 Program.

Paisanos from Atitlan who lived in San Antonio described Emilio as the "natural leader" of the group and they unanimously agreed he should be the club leader after the municipal officials returned to Comarga. Four families from Atitlan that lived in San Antonio joined the club and they recruited some of their family members to join who had recently moved to northern California and Wisconsin for more lucrative jobs. At the meeting with the Comarga administration, the mayor requested that the first project they work on together was a concrete vehicle bridge that would connect the east and west sides of Atitlan. Members of the club were ecstatic about the project proposal. Half of the families had been born on the west side of the community and knew what a hassle it had been to cross the wooden footbridge during the rainy season. The project was personal to the members of Club Atitlan. Before they had even started the project, they were excited that they would be responsible for building a bridge for the hometown.

THE CONCRETE VEHICLE BRIDGE PROJECT

The river that ran through the town of Atitlan prevented about a third of residents from access to the road that provided the main route into the county seat. Since Atitlan only had one *abarrote,* residents needed to cross the river to get to the main markets in Comarga. Residents reported that they had expressed the need for a reliable vehicle bridge for 20 years given how treacherous it was to cross the river during the rainy season. When I asked residents in Atitlan what they thought was the most important issue that faced the Atitlan community, residents said it was, before 2006, the bridge. Residents recounted how donkeys drowned, boats capsized, and neighbors needed to be rescued when their cars got stuck in the muds of the riverbed.

Pepe's parents were both born in the west side of Atitlan. So when he campaigned in Atitlan during the election, and residents broached the topic of the vehicle bridge, he promised them that if they raised matching funds to contribute to the project, he would "find the money through a program" and build the vehicle

FIGURE 4. Vehicle bridge project completed through 3x1 Program in Atitlan, Jalisco. Photo by author.

bridge for Atitlan. After he heard about the 3x1 Program from the nearby mayor in Zacatecas, Pepe saw how he could make good on his promise to the local residents. He got the idea to ask paisanos from Atitlan to form a club, raise money, and help the municipality build the bridge with matching funds from state and federal government. The group of migrants from Atitlan initially formed to help build this vehicle bridge in their hometown.

Citizens, migrant paisanos, and the municipal government all contributed funds and together they built a vehicle bridge that connected east and west Atitlan. Residents of Atitlan had worked hard collecting donations, hosting raffles, and sponsoring dinners to fundraise their portion of the budget. They had formed a bridge committee that worked alongside the town Patronato, the patron saint festival committee, to raise their contribution.[4] The involvement of the community residents was unknown to the migrant club, however. Since Emilio and Esme had not visited Atitlan in recent years and did not know many current residents, they did not know the extent of the town's effort and financial contribution to the bridge project. Beyond four migrant families in the community that the San Antonio migrants kept in touch with, neither Emilio nor other club members knew many of the people in the hometown since most of their families had rejoined them in the U.S.. While many migrants from Atitlan kept a house in the community, the houses stayed vacant but for a few days of the year when they visited.

Initially, the bridge project felt like a victory for the Patronato, residents of the west side of Atitlan, and members of the bridge committee who worked together to fundraise and make a contribution to the project. During the ribbon-cutting ceremony for the bridge in 2006, the mayor publicly thanked the paisanos for building the bridge in front of the whole town but said nothing about contributions from the Patronato or the bridge committee. He said that the bridge project was made possible by the "sacrifice" of the paisanos who left their hometown of Atitlan, but still cared for "nuestro pueblo" to build the residents a bridge. Excluding residents from public praise in favor of the migrant club was a serious misstep that generated confusion among the townspeople. The mayor's public praise for the HTA and the exclusion of their contributions upset locals involved in the bridge project who had spent time, energy, and resources fundraising with the Patronato. Atitlan resident Don Nel explained his reaction to the bridge ribbon-cutting ceremony:

> I have personally asked each and every mayor for the bridge for 20 years. When I asked this mayor, he said he knew of a new program where we can get the money we need to build the bridge. We got together in the town and formed a bridge committee and raised money with the Patronato to help pay. Why the migrants are getting the credit for the bridge I do not understand. But this is typical. No one cares about us out here.[5]

Many residents who attended the bridge ceremony were initially confused about the mayor's public focus on the paisanos for the bridge project. But confusion eventually gave way to scorn as coproduction projects continued and Emilio presumed a position of leadership and authority in Atitlan, a town he had not lived in for decades.

When I asked about the calculus for public praise of the HTA and omission of the town's contributions at the ribbon-cutting ceremony, the mayor explained his political rationale. He wanted his and future Comarga administrations to implement many coproduction projects, and he identified the 3x1 Program as the way to make the municipal budget go further. Since the municipality only had to match 25 percent of the total cost of projects, he knew they could complete several more, albeit small public works projects in Atitlan, if they kept working with the paisanos. He wanted the people of Atitlan to realize the migrants enabled access to state and federal resources that made the bridge project possible through the 3x1 Program. Public acknowledgment of the migrants' contribution, he thought, would go a long way to encourage the club to continue participating in 3x1 projects and ingratiate Emilio to the residents of Atitlan. He had not intended to make the people of the town feel excluded.

Pepe assumed a level of familiarity and trust between himself and the residents of Atitlan because he, too, was raised in the town. He was friendly with many of the community leaders, especially Daniel, who was the leader of the Patronato and his second cousin. He was well liked in Atitlan, even popular among the residents, and after many casual conversations with community members it was clear that they respected him and Pepe had earned their vote. However, Pepe rationalized that because locals "knew him" and "his character" and his parents were from Atitlan, public praise of the paisanos at the ceremony was nothing more than an overture and his platitudes toward the migrants would help the citizens of Atitlan become beneficiaries of more projects in the end.

DEPLETION OF BONDING AND BRIDGING TIES IN THE ATITLAN SOCIAL BASE

While Pepe had extensive social ties throughout the Atitlan community, the mayor did not appreciate that migrant members of the HTA were not as socially embedded in Atitlan as in other localities where he helped form HTAs such as El Mirador. The mayor and the club leader both thought residents would applaud them for the completion of the bridge. After all, the bridge was an overwhelmingly popular project that residents wanted for years and it improved the quality of life for residents who lived on the west side of town. But instead of valuing the residents and the Patronato as equal partners and contributors, political officials and the paisanos had treated the residents of Atitlan as beneficiaries. Pepe took for granted that residents supported him enough that they would not interpret his lack of recognition of their contributions as a slight. Emilio and the migrant club members also assumed residents would credit the club for the provision of the bridge and that they would thank them when they visited the town. In reality, Emilio's physical separation from Atitlan eroded his social ties to residents, but it also meant he had limited information about social relations and what public goods the majority of local citizens wanted in the hometown. Emigration and many years living and working in the U.S. left Emilio out of touch with social life in Atitlan.

Aside from the four migrant families whose relatives lived in San Antonio, Emilio and Esme lacked bonding ties with anyone else in the town. While other paisano club members reported they still kept in touch with some siblings back home and had a few acquaintances from elementary school whom they chatted with occasionally on social media, most of the club members' families had moved to the U.S. and shifted their social life and contacts to people in their destination cities. By 2006, paisanos affiliated with Club Atitlan had few connections to nonmigrant residents outside of their immediate social circle of migrant families involved with the club in Texas and California. Bridging ties were also nonexistent. Neither Emilio nor Esme had bridging ties to members of the Patronato, the de facto governing body of Atitlan, nor did either of them try to construct meaningful social relationships with Daniel or any others who were considered leaders of the Patronato.

The Patronato by all accounts was the most important social institution in the locality. Rather than recruit the Patronato into discussions about 3x1 projects or even ask the members of the social group about their perceptions of residents' desires for public projects in Atitlan, Emilio, Esme, and paisanos in the club thought they knew what the hometown needed and they did not solicit input from locals. In fact, they believed their experiences in the U.S. gave them a privileged perspective that the local townspeople could benefit from. They wanted to improve the image of the hometown and thought 3x1 projects should make it "more beautiful" and "more modern." Furthermore, Emilio had aspirations to become a leader of Atitlan and use his experiences in the U.S. to bring "prosperity" and "modernization" to his hometown.

Quickly, Emilio developed a reputation in the town as arrogant, a sentiment shared by most of the town's nonmigrant households. Residents did not have many opportunities to give him the benefit of the doubt since they only saw him in town for the bridge ribbon-cutting ceremony and at the *fiesta patronal*. Some residents thought the bridge project had inflated his ego. When Daniel and his wife, Lydia, chatted with Emilio after the bridge project, they said they approached him as an equal and told him they believed together they could accomplish many projects for Atitlan. Unfortunately, they left with an unfavorable impression. They said he seemed "full of himself" (*ser muy creído; lleno de sí mismo*) and thought he was better than them because he lived in San Antonio and they lived in rural Atitlan. Lydia imitated how he walked with a puffed-out chest around Atitlan like he was the town's "benefactor," even though it was known to everyone in Atitlan that festival funds subsidized the bridge project and the bridge committee raised funds for the project too. Members of the bridge committee, including Don Nel, recalled that when Emilio introduced himself he said he was the "president" of the migrant club that "built the bridge in the town." This rubbed Don Nel the wrong way because he was the head of the bridge committee. Emilio did not even know who he was or how he had been a vocal proponent of the bridge for decades. In short, Emilio and Esme were no longer socially embedded in the community and lacked both bonding and bridging ties in the social base of the hometown. When Emilio presented himself and the paisanos as the benefactors of the bridge project, some residents felt annoyed and it made others feel defensive about the contributions they made to the bridge project.

Emilio's interpretation of Atitlenses as clients of the paisano club was rejected by the Patronato. Members of the Patronato were elected by residents of the town and saw themselves as the leaders of the town who represented residents' interests. Even though their central activity was to organize the *fiesta patronal* and care for the town's festival resources, the Patronato members knew all the members of the community and frequently discussed problems in the town at their meetings. Residents, they said, were not interested in recreation areas and basketball courts (championed by Emilio) because they had more pressing needs.

First, residents wanted street lamps for corners of the town where "drunks" (*los borrachos*) camped out late in the evenings. Atitlan had no street lamps and it became pitch black at night, which made it difficult and sometimes dangerous for people to navigate back to their homes. Residents wanted street lamps because they thought better lighting would discourage people from congregating in dark corners and harassing residents. Second, parents of school-age children wanted to build sidewalks along the main road into Atitlan. Schoolchildren in Atitlan attended elementary and high school in the county seat and the bus dropped them off on Route 23. Children and parents had to walk down the main road into town without sidewalks and where cars sped by, which made it unsafe. Finally, half the residents of Atitlan did not have access to the public drainage system and had to expel sanitation down a stone latrine that emptied into the river a few miles downstream from the town, which often backed up. Improvements in drainage access to households in Atitlan was a public goods priority in Atitlan that most residents supported. None of these projects was proposed to Atitlenses and the paisanos were more interested in making the hometown they remember "beautiful" than either listening to or solving the problems that residents who lived in the town confronted daily.

COMMUNITY EXCLUSION AND CONFLICT IN THE ATITLAN SOCIAL BASE

During the patron saint festival, Emilio met with the newly elected PAN mayor, Antonio, who succeeded Pepe and they discussed future coproduction projects for his term. Emilio and Antonio decided together they wanted to pave streets in the town to make Atitlan "more modern." Eager to continue the partnership with the HTA forged by his predecessor, the mayor agreed to the street pavement project and worked with his administration to draw up technical plans and secure approval through the 3x1 Program. In the visit, Emilio proposed to the mayor that since migrants "visit only three or four days a year" residents of Atitlan should be required to "pay their fair share." The mayor agreed to this and told me he rationalized the requirement because it decreased the total cost of the project to the migrants and municipality. For Antonio, this was an efficiency gain and meant they could do more projects in Comarga if Atitlenses contributed resources. The two men decided to hold a meeting in Atitlan with the Patronato where they explained they would fund a road pavement project for the residents of Atitlan.

The director of social development, Jorge, invited Atitlan residents to a town hall–style meeting. At the meeting he sat at a table with Emilio and the town delegate, Ramon, at the front of the room while members of the Patronato and residents sat on benches or stood along the walls. Ramon informed them that after the success of the bridge project through the 3x1 Program, the migrant club and the municipality would begin to pave the three main crossroads of Atitlan. He told citizens that to complete the project each household would have to contribute a small share. Club Atitlan and the representative of the municipal government presented themselves as partners working together for the betterment of the Atitlan community. Emilio told those in attendance that his club would work with the mayor and with Ramon to make Atitlan a beautiful town that they could all be proud of. He invoked the language of community and encouraged the residents to "work together" to help make the town a better place. This overture did not resonate with community residents and members of the Patronato in attendance. Many residents were upset that the paisanos and municipal officials unilaterally decided they should have to pay for a project they had no say in choosing.

At the meeting, many residents in attendance were still confused about *what* the 3x1 Program was, *who* made up the HTA, and *why* the HTA and municipal officials told them they had to contribute funds to the 3x1 pavement project. The municipal administration and Emilio had never explained the 3x1 Program to residents. There was a great deal of information asymmetry between residents and the Patronato, on the one hand, and municipal officials and Emilio, on the other. Some residents were hearing about the 3x1 Program for the first time. Don Juan, a longtime resident, asked the delegate, Ramon: "If this is a federal program, why are you telling us we should be paying? I'm not paying for this." Others had heard about the program but did not know who Emilio was and did not understand what involvement the paisano club had in the federal program. Other residents began to focus on the pavement project: who decided it and how much would they need to pay? Residents wanted to know exactly what their money would pay for. As residents tried to figure out what was going on and whispered their questions to each other, Ramon, Jorge, and Emilio attempted to speak over the residents.

Daniel, president of the Patronato, stood up and moved to the front of the room. He stated he would not commit Patronato resources to the pavement project before he met with members of the association to discuss it. They would not give the paisanos and the director any decision on the spot at the meeting. Other residents were also vocal about their opposition to the project because they had never been consulted about project selection and did not believe that they should have to contribute resources to a project of a federal program. Tension between residents and paisanos escalated and the meeting adjourned without a clear resolution. After the meeting, Emilio asked me to go around town to people's houses and do damage control. He wanted me to speak to my contacts and friends in the town and persuade them to support the club. I did chat with people around town after the meeting, but I listened to their concerns. I did not attempt to influence residents' opinions of Emilio, Club Atitlan, or the 3x1 Program despite Emilio's encouragement that I do so.

In the follow-up meeting of the Patronato to discuss the 3x1 pavement project that occurred after Emilio drove back to San Antonio, members were openly frustrated that the paisanos and the political officials had formed an "alliance." "Did you see how they sat up their like they were the kings?" Carla said. "They think we will just do whatever they say we should do," said Don Juan, exasperated. At the close of the meeting to discuss the pavement project, the Patronato members arrived at a consensus. Patronato members decided they did not want "outsiders" (*fuereños, gente de afuera*) to determine what kinds of projects *residents* needed in Atitlan. At several points in the discussion, members of Patronato invoked territoriality and an "us/them" dichotomy in reference to locals who "lived here" and paisanos who "lived there." Members were resolute. Money raised by the Patronato for the annual festival should be decided by the people who live *in* the town and resources would not be earmarked for public projects sponsored by the 3x1 Program.

While initially frustrated with the tone and presentation of the 3x1 Program, the pavement project, and Club Atitlan's role in town affairs, some members said they appreciated what the paisanos were trying to do, but there was agreement that they had gone about it the wrong way. Moreover, longtime members of the Patronato were skittish about using festival funds for public projects because they tried it once before and it ended badly. The previous Patronato president used festival funds to help the local baseball team purchase new uniforms. However, after they donated the money, the team never purchased new uniforms. Some residents were upset with the Patronato and thought they should have known better than to get "scammed" (*estafado*). The Patronato worried that Atitlenses might lose trust in them if there was a repeat situation with the pavement project. At the close of the Patronato meeting, the members entrusted Daniel to reach out to the paisanos and Mayor Antonio's administration. He told them that they would only contribute Patronato resources if the majority of the townspeople agreed to it. They concluded that the best way forward was to survey the townspeople and make sure everyone was onboard with the pavement project in the spirit of community inclusion.

PAISANOS' ABSENCE AND THE DIFFICULTY OF CROSS-BORDER COMMUNICATION

The conflict continued for several months, and relations between paisanos and residents and residents and political officials continued to sour. Up to this point, political officials had pledged support to the migrant club in private, and in public they applauded their efforts and came to their defense. Community inclusion was low, but the paisano club had the full commitment and support of the municipal government that was eager to complete several 3x1 projects with the migrant club. Political officials wanted the completion of public goods projects to reflect positively on their administration. But the transnational partnership was perceived by most local residents as an alliance between the local government and the paisanos because residents' involvement in the coproduction process was minimal. Additionally, as the paisanos' local reputation became viewed as increasingly exclusionary and even bullying by some, Atitleneses' opinions of Antonio's PAN administration was also negatively affected. When municipal officials privileged Emilio's wishes, and by extension the members of Club Atitlan, over local residents' call to be part of the decision-making process, residents felt further alienated by their local government representatives. Since migrant and local officials had pressured the Patronato and residents to contribute financial resources to the pavement project, residents had become increasingly disenchanted and consternation grew in Atitlan.

Since Emilio was back in the U.S., communication between the migrant club, residents of Atitlan, and the mayor's office occurred via email. As many who use electronic mail know, this form of communication can lead to misinformation and misinterpretation of tone. This was certainly the case in the emails exchanged between Emilio, the mayor and officials in his administration, and Daniel. Part of the problem with this form of communication was that only Daniel received the emails because of his leadership position in the Patronato. Daniel forwarded the emails to other residents of the town, but because few residents had a computer with internet access in their home, most residents did not see the communications until he printed out the emails and brought them to Patronato meetings. To check email in Atitlan, residents had to use Doña Sofia's computer at the corner store, which used a dial-up connection, or they had to travel to an internet cafe in Comarga, eight kilometers away, and pay a fee.

Another problem with email for communication and conflict resolution was that Daniel did not check email as frequently as the paisanos in the U.S. He and Lydia both worked as schoolteachers in different municipalities nearby and they had two teenage sons of their own whom they were raising. By contrast, Emilio was semi-retired. He owned his *abarrote*, but he had employees to oversee the shop. He focused more time on the club and sent frequent updates about pavement project negotiations to the club listserv, Daniel, and municipal authorities. However, Daniel's slower than expected response times to Emilio's messages were misconstrued. Paisanos interpreted his silence as an attempt to stall the pavement project. Club members thought Daniel did not adequately appreciate the club's philanthropy. Emilio's nephew, for example, thought Daniel's silence suggested Atitlenses resented the paisanos' success in the U.S.

The paisanos wanted the townspeople to go along with their preferred projects and pay their small contribution "to make it fair" so that they could move on to the next 3x1 project, but within this ongoing conversation something deeper was taking place—a social rift between paisanos and nonmigrant residents of Atitlan. Paisanos spoke to each other over email and speculated that Atitlenses resented their patronage, were jealous of their success in the U.S., and blamed Daniel for not acquiescing to their demands. I was in Atitlan when Daniel received these emails, and because I regularly visited the internet café and was on the club's listserv, I read all the emails sent internally among the paisanos. In fact, I had read most of the emails before any of the local residents of Atitlan had read them and witnessed residents' first reaction to the emails when Daniel shared Emilio's messages with the townspeople in attendance at the Patronato meetings. The residents were, in short, appalled, and were quick to defend Daniel as the "true leader" and "voice of the people" of the town.

What club members in Texas failed to grasp was that the pavement project was not a priority in Atitlan and email was not a mode of everyday correspondence. The last straw came when Emilio and the brother of a local Atitlense man who lived in El Paso rhetorically questioned in a series of emails whether the Patronato really represented the "best interest" of the people of Atitlan. Paisanos in the U.S. began to call into question the need for the Patronato, which was the single most important social institution in Atitlan.

Club Atitlan and the municipal government of Comarga received approval for the street and sidewalk pavement projects from the 3x1 Program and all the funds from the coproduction partners (municipal, state, and federal governments and migrant club) had been deposited in the municipal treasury. Members of the migrant club did not understand why the townspeople refused to contribute a share to the 3x1 project via the Patronato. Emilio wrote a contentious letter to Daniel and asked, "What was the function of the Patronato . . . was it to punish the paisanos, our donations, and our sacrifices? . . . What was the role of the Patronato after all?"[6] One of Emilio's nieces, located in Texas, openly questioned the role of the Patronato: "Why was the Patronato punishing [them]? All [they] wanted was to do good things for our town." Residents of Atitlan and leaders of the Patronato became increasingly worried that the HTA and their "allies" in the municipal government wanted to steal the Patronato's money. Patronato leadership was also distressed that paisanos invoked membership in Atitlan and justified their demands for town contributions to the 3x1 pavement project. Paisanos had inserted themselves in the public affairs of Atitlan, questioned the purpose and role of the central social institution in town, attacked the integrity of their popular leader over email, and used the language of "nuestro pueblito" in an attempt to legitimate their role in decision-making in a town in which territorial residents regarded them increasingly as outsiders in response to their exclusionary practices with regard to coproduction activities.

RESIDENTS SANCTION CLUB ATITLAN FROM PARTICIPATION IN TOWN AFFAIRS

The Patronato decided to hold an emergency town hall meeting after the last slate of emails from Club Atitlan directed at Daniel. They invited everyone in the town to attend and gave everyone who wanted to an opportunity to speak their concerns. I was responsible for keeping the minutes of the meeting, which would then be relayed back to the paisanos. The meeting was standing room only. More than

50 people attended and several others stood outside the double doors and listened to the discussion. No members of the HTA were present, but two former migrants whose brothers were members of the HTA came as representatives of the club. The Patronato treasurer, Angelica, began the meeting and she expressed what many locals had expressed to me in private and in their Patronato meetings:

> I don't understand his motives [Emilio]. I saw him at City Hall talking with the officials, with Pepe, with Antonio, with Jorge. But he never came and talked to us directly. I am completely against releasing any funds to these people. We have never even seen his face before. Have you seen his face? [Asking the crowd] I am worried. What if something bad happens? Will the neighbors still have faith in the Patronato if something happens to their money? . . . Who is he [Emilio]? Is he even Mexican anymore? He does not even live here and he wants to tell us what to do with the Patronato money? No.

Lydia, Daniel's wife agreed. She was also skeptical about why the paisanos wanted residents to pay for a federal program in the first place:

> How much money does this club actually have? How do we know they . . . are not holding out and making us pay? I saw those emails that Emilio sends Daniel and he says this is how much the citizens and the Patronato have to pay. They say this is a federal program. I know it is because I see signs in Jerez, in Tlatelnango, in Tepechitlan, 3x1 signs, and do they make those citizens pay? Who does he [Emilio] think he is? . . . We live in this town. We know everyone and everyone knows us. Why don't we just go to all the neighbors and see what kinds of projects they would be interested in the Patronato supporting . . . we don't need 3x1 or the paisanos . . . we live here.

As the mood in the room shifted to resolution and residents said they were ready to take an informal vote about whether to engage in any further correspondence with the club, the brother of the migrant club members attempted to cast the club's contributions and intentions in a more favorable light. The residents proposed a motion to contribute some of the funds to the pavement project in solidarity with the paisanos but decided that they would tell the club that they needed to work together if they wanted to do any future projects. This was considered by many residents in attendance as a favorable neutral ground because they did not want to feud with the paisanos abroad.

At the close of the meeting, the Patronato decided to release half of the funds for the pavement project that was stipulated by the HTA and municipal government. By a show of hands, they agreed to donate complementary resources to the project to preserve peace. Residents characterized their contribution to the paisano project as a good faith effort that tried to restore paisano-hometown relations, but that did not fully give in to Club Atitlan's demands. Moving forward, though, residents overwhelmingly agreed that public works decisions would not be defined by the migrant club, but by the people of Atitlan who were represented by the Patronato and cared for the (town) festival funds. Daniel relayed the decision to the club in an email addressed to the paisanos of Club Atitlan, the current and former mayors of Comarga, the Atitlan delegate to the municipal government, and the directors of public works and social development.

In follow-up conversations with members of the HTA they expressed confusion with Daniel's response. They reported feeling "attacked" for their generosity by the hometowners, especially by Daniel who had become the de facto voice of Atitlense residents in cross-border communications. Some members of the HTA suggested they "withhold" funds for future coproduction projects unless the town contributed an equal share. Other members recommended Daniel be replaced as president of the Patronato. They wanted a local leader more aligned with club interests.

The events that unfolded after the completion of the bridge project between December 2008 and August 2012 exacerbated social divisions in Atitlan, especially between nonmigrant and migrant households that sided with the club. Because the HTA failed to solicit the input of the Patronato, a trusted association in the Atitlan community, and attempted to make decisions about public works projects on behalf of the people of Atitlan without consultation or inclusion in project deliberations, conflict ensued. Residents no longer recognized Emilio and Esme, and by extension members of the HTA, as members of Atitlan with the legitimate voice to make decisions on behalf of the town. Exclusion of the Patronato would not be tolerated by local residents and they decided to push back.

Club leaders neither engaged in meaningful repertoires of community membership after departure nor maintained bonding and bridging ties in the social base of the hometown that imbued them with the authority to speak on behalf of community residents with the mayor with regard to issues that concerned public life in Atitlan. Emilio and Esme did not participate in the social life of the community, except for a visit now and then. Other members of the HTA had not visited Atitlan in years. Their social base of support in the community was limited to a few migrant families in the town. Moreover, the migrant club did not attempt to forge a relationship with key stakeholders in the community (the Patronato) who were respected leaders of the community and who represented the community to the delegate and to the municipality. Whether it was intentional or not, paisanos' emails to each other and to Daniel demeaned his role as the leader of the Patronato, which was perceived by the residents of Atitlan as an affront.

The paisanos' emails were a frequent topic of conversation and gossip in town. When residents finally read printouts of the emails, some residents openly said that Emilio could no longer be trusted. Residents were open to being contributors to the coproduction process, but they wanted to be included as equal partners in deliberations about projects in their town. Residents including Don Nel, Don

Juan, Angelica, Lydia, Sofia, and others could not understand why Emilio acted like he was the "presidente municipal" of Atitlan, when, in fact, he was their paisano. Being born in Atitlan and having gone to elementary school there neither endowed Emilio with more voice in public decision-making nor made him better than the people of Atitlan.

Emilio and migrant club members enjoyed the exclusive attention of local politicians. For Emilio, community inclusion meant financial contributions, not decision-making authority. Moreover, club members valued their direct access to the elected officials of Comarga and influence in decisions about town affairs. Many paisanos described how living in the U.S. helped them see the extent to which Atitlan lacked public goods. Immigrating to the U.S. revealed how deficient public goods provision was in Atitlan and they wanted to help make it a better place than they left it. But paisanos' affective ties and altruistic goals were not apparent to the residents of Atitlan, especially members of the Patronato. Residents who said they met Emilio and talked with him when he visited town described him as "boastful" (*presumido*) and "arrogant" (*arrogante*) and attributed these character traits to attitudinal changes brought about his emigrating to the U.S.

The transnational partnership, especially the completion of the bridge project, elevated Emilio's social status among the other paisanos in the club.[7] Club members heaped praise on Emilio for his "leadership in Atitlan" and his "sacrifice." Emilio recognized the benefits that his cross-border participation had for his identity. He said, "Here (Atitlan) I am someone important. I have meetings with the mayor. I am trying to do something good. I represent the paisanos. But over there? In Texas? I just own a little store." Migrants from Atitlan hoped to use their social mobility to do something good for a town they loved from afar. But their attempts to reinsert themselves as a representative voice of the community as if they had never left was met with resistance. Members of the club were no longer perceived to be part of the social base of the Atitlan community and they did not universally represent residents' interests. Migrants did not have the authority to charge local residents for 3x1 coproduction projects. Atitlan residents were involved in their community so when they were effectively excluded from decision-making about projects that both affected their lives and required a financial contribution from them, they in turn mobilized to resist outside influence from migrants who were perceived as allied with the local government. Nonmigrant citizens who were active in the social and political life of the hometown struggled for the same access, attention, and influence that migrants had in their transnational partnership with the municipal government. When they perceived themselves to be a disadvantaged group in their own town, they decided to compete for equality through collective action. They were galvanized to take concerted action when Club Atitlan "schemed" to dislodge Daniel as leader of the Patronato and replace him with the brother of a migrant club member.

CLIENTELISTIC BREAKDOWN? THE COLLECTIVE RESPONSE OF MOBILIZED RESIDENTS OF ATITLAN

After several weeks of transnational discord between residents and paisanos in San Antonio, communications between the migrant club and the Patronato ceased. Residents of Atitlan continued to go about daily life and were under the impression that after contributing some funds to the pavement project, they had reached an understanding with the paisanos that future 3x1 projects would go through a process of collective decision-making in which residents would be equal, active participants in the selection and implementation of public goods projects. However, this is not how Emilio and other paisanos wanted to proceed. In club communications and meetings in San Antonio, Emilio and the paisanos decided that they would continue 3x1 projects in the hometown but needed new leadership in the Patronato in order to move forward with public projects and use part of the festival funds to do so. Emilio spearheaded an effort to get Ángel, a paisano's brother who farmed the family land, to run for president of the Patronato. The paisanos believed that once Daniel was no longer the leader of the Patronato, and by extension the town, and replaced with a migrant club ally, they would be able to complete many projects for Atitlan through the 3x1 Program and residents would see how important the paisanos were for the betterment of the hometown.

When Angelica, treasurer of the Patronato, heard that Ángel planned to challenge Daniel for the leadership role, she organized an informal meeting with all the heads of household in town with Ramon, the delegate, in attendance. Since Ángel had never been involved in public life before, some residents thought it was odd that he wanted to take on a leadership role out of the blue. And everyone liked the job that Daniel had done for the festival and thought he was very careful with the town's money. He had become even more respected when he was attacked by the paisanos and stood up to them for the people of the town. The Patronato's concern was not directed at Ángel, whom residents characterized as a "puppet" (*títere de la club*), but rather at the paisanos, Emilio in particular, whom they suspected to be behind the scheme.

Although Angelica and other concerned residents of Atitlan did not know for sure, their suspicions were correct. Emilio, at the urging of club members, called Ángel and encouraged him to challenge Daniel for the position so that they could do more 3x1 projects for Atitlan with Patronato resources. He had attempted to circumvent Daniel, whom Emilio believed to be the main obstacle to the use of Patronato festival money for 3x1 projects. What Emilio and members of the club never fully understood throughout the entire debacle was that residents had urged Daniel to take the leadership position. He was a humble, popular resident of the town and was highly regarded. To attack Daniel felt like an attack on everyone.

Residents of Atitlan rallied behind the Patronato. Daniel told the migrant club that their efforts to bully the Patronato in Atitlan would no longer be tolerated. The residents thanked the paisanos for their support in the bridge and road pavement and sidewalk project. And while the paisanos were always welcomed to attend the *fiesta patronal*, additional efforts to be involved in public affairs were no longer welcomed. After a year of contentious discussion over email and in person, residents believed that the municipal government and the paisanos (especially Emilio) had schemed together to misappropriate the residents' Patronato funds for official use. Club Atitlan was informally sanctioned from participating in town affairs. Ángel and his family no longer came to Patronato meetings.

CASE SUMMARY

The local government privileged the support of the HTA over local residents because they wanted to continue participating in the 3x1 Program. They believed supplying public works through the matching grants program was a clever way to extend municipal resources in the outlying community. This strategy backfired and may have cost the PAN in the next election. Citizens in Atitlan banded together and backed the opposition PRI candidate, a move designed to punish the PAN incumbent for not listening to their concerns and prioritizing the interests of the HTA. It is difficult to know how much Atitlan's political mobilization contributed to the PAN's loss (PRI vote share increased 12 percent from the 2010 to 2013 elections), but this was the goal of Atitlan voters. They wanted to punish the PAN party for privileging the HTA's contributions over the townspeople's wants and needs. The PAN's vote share declined 19 percent across the municipality and the PRI won handedly in 2013; the margin of victory was 31 percent.

The HTA's inability to forge meaningful bridging ties with the Patronato, a group of community stakeholders well regarded in Atitlan, produced a more corporatist coproduction partnership. Even though residents of Atitlan made explicit requests to be part of project deliberations, they were excluded from meaningful participation but for the request for financial support. Club Atitlan's privileged access and alliance with the local government received the full engagement of the municipality. Both PAN mayors were eager to cofinance coproduction projects through the 3x1 Program and worked hard to cultivate ties with the paisanos from Comarga in the U.S.[8] Emilio and paisanos in the U.S. enjoyed the exclusive attention of elected officials that they thought elevated their social status in Atitlan. But the perceived alliance with municipal officials and exclusion of residents from meaningful involvement in the coproduction process worsened state-society relations between paisanos and residents and between residents and municipal officials.

After the election many local residents said they were "done dealing with politicians" and "none of them can be trusted." While the HTA felt connected to their hometown and wanted to express that attachment by supporting public goods, they did not expect that physical exit complicated the ability to use voice *as if* they had never left. Migrant membership status in the social collective was far more complex. Without a concerted effort to build meaningful bridges to social elites like Daniel, Don Nel, Don Juan, and other members of the Patronato inner circle, paisanos' cross-border public goods efforts made in the name of the community ultimately reinforced political inequalities between migrants and nonmigrants and introduced more distrust in the political process. As a result, the corporatist partnership between the HTA and the local government was short-lived and Club Atitlan became inactive when the PRI administration came into office. Citizens of Atitlan reported they were more disenchanted with municipal representatives and participated less in politics than before, even if their exclusion motivated short-term political mobilization against the PAN party incumbent.

In Atitlan's more corporatist partnership, migrants' organized interests and links to a cooperative local government took precedence over competing societal interests of local residents. This arrangement produced two kinds of political effects. First, citizen exclusion compromised plural interest representation. In this context, citizens felt slighted and reacted by challenging coproduction decisions publicly, sanctioning the HTA, and making independent political demands on the state to be heard. Migrant-state corporatism in places with an active civil society increased the political participation of locals resulting from their *exclusion* in the coproduction process. Although I am reluctant to generalize from the Atitlan case alone as to the local conditions whereby citizen exclusion motivated political participation, one possibility is that places with latent or active social capital (e.g., an active social institution or citizen group like the Patronato) possess the social network ties of trust and reciprocity that can mobilize collective action more readily than places without.

Second, corporatist coproduction also caused citizens to retreat from public life and depressed political interest and engagement. Patterns of motivated inaction are often impelled by objective circumstances—people who know they cannot win often do not try.[9] Corporatist transnational partnerships are, therefore, also likely to "crowd out" citizens' interest in and ability to use democratic channels to voice their preferences for public goods. Some residents, when they are excluded from meaningful participation in coproduction activities and perceive an alliance between the HTA and local government officials, stop trying to make their voices heard, which creates political disenchantment in some migrant hometown communities. Corporatist coproduction partnerships produce different and sometimes opposing effects on local civic and political participation. They also strain state-society relations depending on preexisting social and political institutions in the hometown.

FORMATION OF CLUB EL MIRADOR

Club El Mirador was a smaller, more tightly knit group than Club Atitlan. While they only had about six core families active in club affairs, they were a dedicated and energetic group of paisanos. Core members of the club engaged in circular migration in the 1980s and 1990s and traveled across the border together. The paisanos from El Mirador worked for the same employer year after year in Illinois and Indiana, saved money, and returned home for stretches before they returned to the U.S. Before the spouses of the group joined them in the U.S., the men lived together and saved their earnings in order to send more remittances home to their families. They were "like family." Not only had many of the men grown up together and emigrated at the same time, they supported each other in the U.S. so that they could better support their families who remained behind in El Mirador, Comarga.

Temporary, circular migration between El Mirador and the U.S. became more difficult in the early 2000s when the U.S. government tightened border security in the wake of the terrorist attacks of 9/11. Paisanos from El Mirador without documents decided they would stay more permanently in the U.S. or risk capture at the border and detention by U.S. authorities. In response, Efrain, a core member of the club, decided it was the time to legalize. As soon as he met the residency requirements he naturalized and became a U.S. citizen. He then started the paperwork to petition for his spouse and children to join him in the U.S. While some of the men in the close-knit group of paisanos had acquired their green cards, others who migrated in the 1990s had no path to citizenship and remained undocumented in the U.S. For some individuals who endured longer separations from their families, this was too much of a psychological burden to bear. When crossing the U.S. border became too difficult and dangerous, some paisanos returned home with their savings and stayed in El Mirador while others settled permanently in the Midwest after being rejoined by family members.

In the summer of 2005, Marco, Efrain, and Placido met with the PAN mayor of Comarga in Chicago. The paisanos traveled from Bolingbrook, Aurora, and Gary to have dinner with the political officials at their invitation. Pepe and members of his administration came to Chicago to tell the men about the 3x1 Program, but the migrants needed no introduction. Efrain and Placido knew of the program already. The small Zacatecas municipality of Tonitlan that borders El Mirador to the east had a migrant club that worked with the municipal government on several projects. The two communities were geographically and socially close. They shared resources (a water well) and hosted festivals together since both localities were the farthest away from their respective county seats. Friends in Tonitlan had told the paisanos about their collaborative partnership with the municipality long before the municipal officials met with the paisanos in the U.S.

The club from Tonitlan had recently made plans with the municipal government to build a rodeo ring (*lienzo charro*) with cofinancing from state and federal governments. When Pepe invited the paisanos from El Mirador to form their own club, they tentatively agreed on the condition that the first collaborative project would be a rodeo ring for El Mirador so that they could enjoy competitions with neighbors in Tonitlan. *Charreada*, a collection of events involving horseback riders (*charros*) and cattle inside a ring similar to a rodeo, was popular in the region. Several families in El Mirador practiced *coleadero,* a *charrerada* event that involved steer tailing, but they often had to travel long distances to compete because El Mirador was such a remote locality. The paisanos were excited about the rodeo project. If Tonitlan was also building a rodeo ring, they could have competitions and invite other *coleadero* teams to compete in El Mirador and Tonitlan. Comarga's mayor was not initially keen on using public resources for recreation projects in El Mirador since his administration's development plan focused more on security and the provision of public services. But he eventually acquiesced with the tacit agreement that future coproduction projects would be more focused on basic service provision such as water, electricity, drainage, and road pavement.

Marco, Efrain, and Placido discussed the paisano club for several weeks after Pepe and others from his administration returned to Comarga. The men decided Placido should be the president of the club and Efrain and Marco serve as the secretary and treasurer, respectively. The paisanos decided that no decisions would be made about the club or projects without taking it to the people of El Mirador first. Pepe was eager to propose the coproduction project to the state validation committee in his first year of office, but Placido did not want to start any project without discussing plans with the residents of El Mirador, especially return migrants with whom they remained in close contact. They planned to discuss the mayor's 3x1 proposal with residents in El Mirador over the Christmas holiday when many of the paisanos planned to return for a longer visit to their hometown.

THE ROLE OF COMMUNITY MEMBERSHIP AND SOCIAL CAPITAL IN EL MIRADOR

The people of El Mirador were a close-knit, poor community. In the rural town, everybody knew everybody. High up in the mountains about a 30-minute drive from the county seat, families in El Mirador relied on each other to solve local problems. Many families relied exclusively on remittances for income and those without migrant members abroad made ends meet growing tomatoes, beans, corn, and other staple crops. Many children who worked in the fields with their parents stopped attending school altogether after they finished their primary education.

In 2005, most streets in El Mirador were dirt roads, only half the houses had access to electricity, and many lacked access to indoor plumbing and sanitation. But the residents of El Mirador had found ways to make life a little easier by working together. The town made a collective decision that the north and south sides of town alternated use of the public water system every other day to make sure all had periodic access. Parents also took turns driving the children 30 minutes down the high mountain switchbacks so that they could take the bus the rest of the way to the *secundaria*. And migrant families that were dependent on remittances supported one another with extra food when money from the U.S. failed to arrive.

This is what Placido said he missed the most when living in the U.S.: the people of El Mirador took care of each other even though no one had very much to give. Before making the difficult decision to settle permanently in the U.S. with his family, Placido always believed he would return to El Mirador. His decision to emigrate was not by choice, he explained, it was by necessity. "I thought I would be able to make enough in a few visits to come back and have enough money to fix the house and invest in the land. But it is not so easy in the U.S.," he explained, "I had to go back for years just to earn enough to buy land and care for my parents." Placido did not like living abroad. He had serious reservations about raising his sons in the big city and missed small-town, rural life in his community. His family had lived in El Mirador for many generations and were a respected family. His uncles helped pressure the PRI administration in the late 1970s to build a one-room schoolhouse for the children of El Mirador, which was applauded by local residents. It was Placido's hope he would eventually return and be able to retire in El Mirador. Working with the municipal government was one way to help the people of El Mirador have a better life, which he reasoned would make the town a nice enough place that his sons might eventually return with him one day so long as economic conditions improved in Mexico.

During the Christmas holiday Efrain visited El Mirador. Efrain was the only migrant in Club El Mirador who had acquired a green card and could cross the U.S. border to visit the hometown without a serious hardship. From the U.S., the paisanos reached out to their families and friends and coordinated a day and time for the people of the town to meet and discuss the migrant club with Efrain. It was important, Placido recalls, for Francisco, a former migrant and local farmer, to be present at the meeting. Placido and Francisco migrated together and worked alongside each other for years. They stayed close friends even after Francisco returned to El Mirador. Unhappy in the U.S., Francisco returned to live with his family despite the continued difficulty making money selling crops in the region. Francisco said, "I never liked living in the U.S. It is just too different for me. I am a rural farm boy and so was my father. I had to come back."

Francisco was admired in El Mirador. He used his migration experience to help young men find a respected smuggler to cross the border and used his connections to help people find work even though he tried to dissuade many from leaving. He and his wife also checked in on migrant families to make sure they were doing all right. Francisco had become a leader in El Mirador even though he never thought of himself that way. Placido knew this and thought very highly of Francisco. If the town was going to have a migrant club that worked with the local government to provide public goods projects, everyone agreed that Francisco should be involved every step of the way.

Francisco was initially suspicious of the government's motives and questioned why migrants should be paying for public projects. But other paisanos in town for the holiday meeting with Efrain were more willing to give the partnership a chance. Augustin, a local farmer, recalled telling his neighbors that they should hear what the mayor could do for El Mirador using the 3x1 Program and only make a decision after they heard what he had to say. Augustin was also familiar with the public projects completed in nearby Tonitlan with paisanos through the 3x1 Program and was curious what good could be brought to El Mirador through the same channels.

In the meeting, the residents agreed to support the migrant club and coproduction projects with municipal officials. They also decided to create a public works committee that was a local extension of Club El Mirador. The townspeople in attendance overwhelming supported Francisco to lead the committee with a few other volunteers. At the meeting and after further discussions throughout the holiday season, Club El Mirador and the newly formed *Comite pro Obras* alerted the mayor's office that they would propose the rodeo ring project to the 3x1 Program, register the migrant club, and begin fundraising their share of project costs in the U.S.

While Club El Mirador had only a few dedicated, core members, the network of migrants from Comarga and El Mirador was extensive. Paisanos from nearby Tonitlan also supported the club by attending their fundraising events in Chicago. Club Tonitlan was an older association and a member of the Zacatecan federation of migrant clubs in Chicago. They shared information with Efrain, Marco, and Placido about how other clubs successfully raised money, and Club El Mirador used the events of those clubs as a model. Club El Mirador's fundraising events in the U.S. started small, but eventually became grand affairs with paisanos from Comarga and beyond in attendance. The club hosted picnics with live music, held raffles, and took donations from attendees. And together with Club Tonitlan and other clubs in the Zacatecan federation they hosted fundraising *charreada* events in the U.S. using ticket and foods sales for coproduction projects. The dense networks of migrants from the region in the Chicagoland area and Club El Mirador's relationship with older, experienced clubs helped the club raise significant resources for El Mirador.

Placido and Club El Mirador quickly raised the 25 percent contribution for the first project and much more in the first few fundraising events. With Francisco leading the public works committee in El Mirador they held local meetings and visited the households in the town. They asked residents what kind of projects they would like to see the committee and the migrants propose to the municipal administration. By the following summer, they had drafted a list of several coproduction projects to work on in coordination with municipal government officials and the 3x1 Program.

Francisco increasingly served as the point of contact for the migrant club and the public works committee to the municipal government. While he initially had reservations about the partnership, he soon developed a relationship with Pepe and other members of his administration, especially the communications director and the director of public works. When he was in the county seat, he would stop in to the municipal government building (*ayuntamiento*) and check in on time-lines, budgets, hiring labor, and materials for different 3x1 projects. Francisco then convened with other members of the public works committee and they made decisions together. When it was possible, they called Placido and other members of the migrant club on cell phones and everyone discussed coproduction projects together in the U.S. and Mexico on speakerphone.

In the coproduction partnership between Club El Mirador, Comarga's munici-pal administration, and the local public works committee, the partners completed several projects during Pepe's administration. Through the 3x1 Program and effec-tive coordination between residents, paisanos, and government officials they built a rodeo ring, and recreation court, paved roads, and erected streetlights through the central part of town. When Mayor Antonio took office in 2007 the partnership continued through the municipal transition. Antonio said:

> The club in El Mirador is so easy to work with. I told the paisanos in Atitlan to call Placido and ask what they are doing up there [in the mountains] because, honestly, they tell me what projects they want and then they work with the directors [of social development and public works] and do everything down here. The trouble I have with them is telling them "no" . . . We can't do so many projects because the other localities need attention too.

From the perspective of the municipal government, working on coproduction projects in El Mirador was efficient and effective.

While the mayor could not identify what about the partnership was "easier" than the partnership with paisanos in Atitlan, the answer was community inclu-sion in the coproduction process. Paisanos from El Mirador were still socially embedded in El Mirador and drew on their extensive bonding and bridging ties to include residents in all coproduction decisions to the extent that residents wanted to be involved. For many residents I spoke with, the transnational partnership was welcomed, but they did not have the time to participate. They were happy to have Francisco, the public works committee, and the paisanos make decisions on behalf of them because they were seen as members of the El Mirador community. In short, they were trusted to speak on behalf of the community residents.

The municipal government of Comarga identified the 3x1 Program as a way to expand their budget and provide public goods and services to localities in Comarga with high emigration. Pepe's PAN administration sought out the partnership with paisanos in the U.S. and helped create the clubs in 2005. Both PAN administra-tions brought the same level of engagement to the coproduction partnerships in Atitlan and El Mirador. In El Mirador, political officials provided technical plan-ning, financial contributions, materials, labor, and contractors to support imple-mentation of the vehicle bridge, rodeo ring, public lighting, and road pavement coproduction projects. The provision of public goods through coproduction and complementary financing from state and federal 3x1 Program partners became an effective strategy, the administration surmised, for public spending on local infrastructure. They wanted the transnational partnership with all the migrant groups to work. And in the increasingly competitive municipal elections in which the PRI gained electoral ground, capturing the support of citizens in traditional PAN strongholds by improving public infrastructure in their communities was a political strategy for victory.

CASE COMPARISON: KEY ROLE OF MIGRANT SOCIAL EMBEDDEDNESS

As the two cases show, transnational partnerships were organized differently in two communities in the same municipality. In Atitlan, the social base of the migrant network was limited to a few migrant families connected to the club. Club Atitlan lacked social ties to key stakeholders in the community and excluded the Patronato from the selection, planning, and implementation of 3x1 projects. They valued the Patronato only for the resources they maintained on behalf of the town. By contrast, in El Mirador, paisanos had a more extensive social base of support and included residents in the coproduction process. The involvement of Francisco, a key bridging tie to several households throughout the town, scaled up the participation of other residents and signaled to them that the transnational partnership reflected their interests and needs. Unlike Emilio, who represented the migrant club to the residents of Atitlan but did not participate in the social life of the hometown, paisanos from El Mirador practiced cultural repertoires and were more visible in the social life of their hometown even after they had emigrated abroad.

During the summers, Placido's children lived with their grandparents in El Mirador and traveled with Efrain when he visited for *charreada* events. The members of Marco's family who remained behind were neighbors of Augustin's, and Augustin volunteered for the public works committee after Marco encouraged him to do so. The active recruitment of Francisco, a leader in El Mirador and former migrant, and the maintenance of social solidarity through bonding and bridging ties in the hometown community explained why residents were more included in the coproduction process.

Club Atitlan's insistence that residents contribute financial resources for the street pavement project was rejected by the townspeople. They were willing and eager to contribute to the bridge project because they had a strong preference for it and had proposed the project to municipal officials across several different administrations. When the mayor supported Club Atitlan's decision to demand collection of complementary resources from the townspeople, residents perceived his support of the club in a negative light and thought the administration was out of touch with the needs of Atitlenses. The municipal administration went along with the club leader's demand because he did not want to jeopardize the transnational partnership, but he was either unaware of the social cost of the alliance with the paisano club or did not anticipate it would lead to a worsening of state-society relations and political opposition to the administration. Moreover, the club's decision to speak on behalf of the community in coproduction decisions without mutual recognition from hometown residents of their continued membership resulted in consternation and contestation in Atitlan.

The more synergetic partnership in El Mirador characterized by community inclusion and government engagement produced different social and political consequences than in Atitlan. The active involvement of residents in coproduction routinized interactions with political officials. Citizens of El Mirador started to believe that they could accomplish something by working together with the local government and the paisanos. Personal political efficacy was improved through the participation in the transnational partnership. Residents began to value democratic engagement because they witnessed firsthand how citizens' quality of life was improved through participatory action. Municipal officials visited El Mirador to prepare technical plans for projects and workers hired by the government showed up on time. Projects that the public works committee and Club El Mirador proposed to the government were completed in the town. Citizens were more empowered and checked the budget, observed the arrival of physical materials according to a predetermined timeline, and monitored workers to ensure quality and completion. When materials did not arrive on schedule, residents in El Mirador visited the *ayuntamiento* and let the officials know. On occasion, some residents volunteered their own labor to help the municipal contractors.

In short, the involvement of local residents produced more participatory action including the deliberation in project selection, information exchange, and more regular interactions between elected officials and ordinary citizens. And while occasionally citizens and officials did not agree and miscommunications occurred, both residents and citizens valued the partnership and recognized the benefits of negotiation. Municipal officials, for example, acknowledged the administration had to make concessions. Pepe explained:

> We let them tell us what they need and we do it. Enrique [director of public works] and I can't use the whole budget in El Mirador because we have other localities, but we know Francisco and other people in the town well enough now that we can say, okay, this time we do this, but next time about how this project. Like with the water. We really need to extend the town's access to water, but that is a big project. The citizens wanted smaller projects first and then we decided to tackle the big water project in several phases.

The nature of the migrant social base in each town in the same municipality shaped the organization of the partnership and the corresponding changes in democratic participation and state-society relations.

SUMMARY

Not all coproduction partnerships are organized such that many local citizens are included in the process or the local government is fully engaged. When one of these two organizing factors is variable, transnational partnerships are more likely to approximate fragmented or corporatist coproduction. In these two organizational forms, low citizen involvement based on weak social ties to migrant members of hometown clubs depresses the representativeness of local interests in public goods provision.

Coproduction partnerships in El Mirador and Atitlan in Comarga, Jalisco, were organized differently even though both clubs were created with the encouragement and support of the municipal PAN government. The difference in the nature of the partnership in the two communities can be traced to differences in the degree to which migrants remained embedded in the social base of the hometown. In El Mirador, migrants maintained more extensive bonding and bridging ties in the hometown and were inclusive of local residence participation in most aspects of coproduction project planning and implementation. As such, citizens worked closely with political officials and interactions between state and society in El Mirador became more routinized and productive. Citizens became more involved in everyday affairs of El Mirador and worked collaboratively with the local government to identify and execute public goods projects that improved local residents' quality of life. In turn, the responsiveness of elected officials to their constituents in a remote locality where residents seldom encountered, much less worked alongside, public officials in decision-making concerning public works also improved as a result of the synergy created by transnational coproduction.

By contrast, migrants from Atitlan were not well integrated into the social base of their hometown community after departure. They did not take steps to forge bridging ties with key stakeholders in the community even after community leaders requested to be more meaningfully involved in the coproduction process. Worried that they would alienate the paisanos from future 3x1 projects, the municipal government allied themselves with Club Atitlan, which further alienated citizens from coproduction. Despite short-term political mobilization in reaction to exclusion from coproduction to punish the incumbent political party, citizens' political interest and engagement in Atitlan declined. More corporatist coproduction in which migrant clubs' preferences for public goods were aligned with local government interests crowded out citizen engagement.

In cases like Atitlan, citizen exclusion from coproduction reinforced social and political inequalities in the hometown based on social mobility acquired through international migration. When paisanos positioned themselves as more knowledgeable and capable of making decisions on behalf of a town in which they no longer physically resided, this further created social division between residents and emigrants. Residents did not believe that the migratory experience had elevated the social status of the paisanos and they resented the implication that because they stayed in Atitlan they were more backward and incapable of selecting and advocating for projects that improved their quality of life.

Analyzing the dynamics and organizational variation of transnational coproduction partnerships through case studies illuminates how migrant HTAs' mobilization of collective remittances for hometown development has important spillover effects for democratic governance and participation. My chief purpose is to draw attention to the ways in which coproduction is configured and how different organizational forms of coproduction correspond to political outcomes in places with emigration. In doing so, I trace how community inclusion and government engagement interact at different levels to determine synergetic, corporatist, fragmented, and substitutive coproduction types. Through the cases I show how the organization of types changes as the social and political context in hometowns shape and are shaped by migrant-state interactions.

In the next chapter, I turn to a more systematic assessment of how transnational partnerships affect democratic governance and examine how generalizable the findings are across all municipalities and within only those cases that have partnerships. Using original survey data, longitudinal survey data from the Mexican Family Life Survey, and panel data on all Mexican municipalities from 1990 to 2013, I show how cumulative participation in transnational partnerships through the 3x1 Program leads to substantial effects on citizen engagement in formal and informal politics and government responsiveness.

Systematic Effects of Transnational Partnerships on Local Governance

In many decentralized democracies like Mexico, migrant social actors step in to supply public goods when the state lacks sufficient resources or the political will to do so on its own. Migrants' cross-border investment often improves citizens' access to essential goods such as drinking water, paved roads, and bridges, but the process of coordinating service provision also produces significant political consequences in the near and long term. I argue in chapter 1 that when transnational partnerships include residents and local government is engaged, it creates a synergetic partnership. Synergetic partnerships produce new participatory spaces in which residents, migrants, and elected representatives interact, deliberate, and negotiate policy decisions about public goods provision. In this new participatory sphere, state and society become entwined, improving government responsiveness and citizens' interest and engagement in civic and political activities. When the two main factors combine differently, corporatist, substitutive, and fragmented partnerships are more likely to emerge and have different consequences.

In the previous three chapters, I trace the political and social processes that organize partnership differently and link types to political effects. The political consequences include worsening of state-society relations, political disenchantment, corruption, and offloading of responsibility for public goods onto migrant clubs. I also show how partnership types change when social interactions between migrants, residents, and political officials change over time, especially during periods of political party transition in local office. But how well does the theory hold up at meso and macro levels of empirical scrutiny? Are transnational partnerships organized into the types hypothesized in a representative set of cases? Are different types of partnerships associated with changes in political and civic participation and government responsiveness? More generally, how systematic are the political effects of different transnational partnerships across places that have them and compared to all Mexican municipalities?

In this chapter, I examine these questions at two levels of aggregation using multiple data sources and statistical analyses. First, using original survey data of a representative sample of migrant-state partnerships, I examine how partnerships are organized. I use principal component and cluster analysis to observe whether partnership types are associated with different political effects in origin communities. In this part of the analysis, I focus on short-term effects given the cross-sectional nature of the survey data. This data represents only a snapshot in time for each partnership. The before-and-after effects focus on the most recent projects and immediate political outcomes. I find that in synergetic and corporatist partnerships, government spending on public works increases, but the duration of the spending increases depends on the level of community inclusion. In substitutive partnerships, the share of government spending on public goods decreases and local citizens become disenchanted with local politics as they become less likely to participate in local elections the longer that such partnerships continue. Fragmented partnerships are more likely to be associated with partnership failure and a worsening of public opinions of government performance.

Next, using panel and longitudinal data from the Mexican Family Life Survey (MxFLS), I examine whether transnational partnerships, regardless of organizational type, change the incidence and frequency of civic and political engagement at the local level. I operationalize civic engagement as local citizen participation in civic associations of varying sorts (social, political, religious) and political engagement as participation in municipal elections. The panel data does not permit the evaluation of how organizational types affect civic and political engagement in the universe of municipal cases of 3x1 participation due to a lack of information on community inclusion and government engagement. To address this data limitation, I move beyond a cross-section of partnerships surveyed at one point in time and investigate how cumulative participation in the program and the frequency of public goods projects affects local governance using panel data. With the addition of a longer observation window from 1990 to 2013 and data on civic engagement from 2000–13 provided by the MxFLS, I can more clearly address how preexisting histories of political and civic participation affect transnational partnerships and, in turn, how those partnerships affect political and civic participation and government responsiveness at the municipal level.

The addition of the MxFLS longitudinal data provides a fruitful opportunity to examine changes in the incidence, type, and frequency of community civic engagement while holding all other factors constant. I find that in places in which partnerships approximate synergy and substitution, the habitual engagement of municipalities in transnational partnerships are associated with more citizens participating in municipal elections and civic associations. Overall, in synergetic and substitutive partnerships civic and political participation increases. Additionally, findings reveal that municipalities that participate in the 3x1 Program are more likely to consistently devote more budgetary resources to programmatic spending. The increase in government social spending in response to transnational partnerships signals improvements in government responsiveness in the realm of public goods provision. Taken together, results suggest that more frequent and consistent coproduction activities that bring residents, migrants, and political officials into more routine contact increase civic and political engagement and government responsiveness in local democratic governance. This finding lends further support to the social learning hypothesis I advance in chapter 1.

SURVEYING MEXICAN TRANSNATIONAL PARTNERSHIPS

Most research on Mexican migrant hometown associations in the United States is based on qualitative interviews with select clubs and ethnography in communities of origin.[1] In the Mexican context, case-based research has primarily examined HTAs from the traditional sending states of Michoacán, Zacatecas, Jalisco, and Puebla and to a lesser extent the southern indigenous states of Oaxaca and Chiapas.[2] There are two surveys that examine a larger cross-section of migrant HTAs.[3] While these surveys enrich our understanding of migrant clubs even more, they lack representativeness because they are isolated to geographic areas of the U.S. and are limited because they do not ask about the structure of transnational partnerships with sending-state governments. Given the lack of systematic data, I developed a national original survey instrument and disseminated it to all registered leaders of Mexican HTAs in the U.S. in the fall of 2008.

The survey questionnaire includes a combination of multiple-choice, open answer, and rank order questions written in Spanish and asks about club formation, goals, and structure, leadership and membership characteristics, transnational partnerships, and 3x1 Program participation, among other themes. The questionnaire was informed by 30 interviews with migrant club leadership in Los Angeles, San Diego, Chicago, Indiana, and North Carolina. Of the 800 associations that self-identified as hometown clubs and registered their clubs with the Mexican government in 2008, 500 listed up-to-date contact information and were sent a paper survey through the U.S. Postal Service. With support from the University of Chicago Survey Lab, surveys were collected and coded through July 2009 with a 50 percent response rate (n = 250).[4] I describe additional details about the transnational survey instrument and sampling strategy in Data Appendix B.

Since migrant clubs are located in the U.S. but provide public goods in their hometowns in Mexico, I also collected data that characterizes migrant sending and destination places. Taken together, this data creates a transnational statistical profile for each club respondent in the survey sample. To my knowledge, this is the first survey to incorporate destination and origin place characteristics in a transnational research design. For each migrant HTA respondent, I compiled sociodemographic and political data for each side of the transnational dyad between destination city and state and origin municipality and state. Data was collected from the American Communities Survey (ACS), Mexican Census (CONAPO), National Institute of Statistic and Geography (INEGI), and Center of Research for Development (CIDAC). This step allows me to assess whether features of the origin and destination also affect partnership dynamics.

I use a three-pronged approach to examine how well survey respondents' transnational partnerships with the Mexican sending state reflect different organization types—synergetic, corporatist, substitutive, and fragmented partnerships. In the first stage, I use transnational survey data to construct a composite index of community inclusion and government engagement, the two multidimensional factors—I hypothesize—that organize coproduction partnerships and whose combination determines political outcomes. This data provides a window into factors that may affect coproduction partnerships at home and abroad as well as characteristics of the HTA. I use principal component analysis (PCA) to reduce highly correlated variables reflective of the multiple dimensions of community inclusion and government engagement. I also develop an indicator for migrant club capacity and examine whether club structure, membership size, and leadership characteristics, for example, are associated with levels of community inclusion and government engagement.

In the second stage, I use the indicators for inclusion, engagement, and club capacity, among other sociodemographic and political characteristics, in a cluster analysis and observe how configurations of all these multiple attributes group together to form groups or clusters of migrant partnerships. In the final stage of the survey analysis, I conduct multivariate statistical analyses to understand how partnership types affect civic and political participation and government responsiveness in the short term. Data Appendix C presents more detailed information on PCA and cluster analysis and Data Appendix D provides more information on the panel analysis.

COMMUNITY INCLUSION AND GOVERNMENT ENGAGEMENT

The survey asks questions about how migrant clubs integrate local citizens into the coproduction process with the Mexican government. The questions asked migrant clubs how often local citizens in the hometown: (1) volunteered labor; (2) helped select projects; (3) donated resources (monetary or in-kind); (4) monitored projects during and after implementation; (5) discussed project-related activities with municipal officials (i.e., hiring laborers and contractors, timelines, technical plans); (6) participated in local committees or mirror clubs (*clubes espejo*); (7) were involved in the creation of the HTA; and the extent to which (8) the HTA perceived problems working with local citizens and citizen groups; and (9) whether other social, religious, business, and civic associations were involved in the provision of public goods with the HTA. Together, these questions comprise the index for community inclusion created using PCA.

With a combination of survey questions and 3x1 Program data I also construct an index for government engagement. Since sometimes more than one HTA participates in coproduction in a given year, each survey respondent's club name was matched against the 3x1 Program dataset and only the corresponding club information was extracted. Survey questions used to approximate government engagement included questions about municipal government involvement in and frequency of (1) selecting projects; (2) creating the migrant club; (3) providing matching funds and project materials in a timely manner; (4) problems working with the municipal government; (5) matching 25 percent or more of total project costs; and (6) failure to successfully complete coproduction projects.[5] The survey also asked whether the HTA respondent was able to (7) access officials; (8) participate in decision-making; and (9) influence negotiations with municipal officials.

A few factors are consistently associated with more community involvement in transnational partnerships. First, the mayor's political party affiliation is an important factor. Both the PRI and PAN are more likely to be the municipal party in power in places characterized by high levels of community involvement in transnational public goods projects. Second, community inclusion increases as more projects are designated for localities outside the county seat. This suggests that inclusion is more likely in places with less population density and therefore a smaller social base to mobilize collective action.[6] Third, places in which religious organizations have been actively involved in providing social welfare are more likely to have higher levels of community involvement. The role of churches both in providing social welfare to the community and in the formation of HTAs has been documented in other studies of migrant HTAs and is further supported by the survey findings.[7] An active church association and affiliate groups are important preexisting social factors associated with community inclusion. Finally, a higher level of migrant club capacity is positively associated with community inclusion. Clubs with a larger membership base, resources, regular meetings and formal organizational structure, membership in a state-level federation of clubs, and leadership skills are likely to be more inclusive of local residents in transnational partnerships. I discuss migrant club capacity in more depth in the next section.

There are a few important attributes of municipalities that have higher levels of government engagement in coproduction partnerships. Consistent with hypotheses presented in chapter 1, municipalities that have fewer fiscal constraints and therefore more budgetary capacity to invest public resources in coproduction are more likely to have higher levels on the government engagement index. I also posit that political officials facing more competition from opposition parties in local elections are likely to engage in transnational partnerships; however, neither the closeness of elections nor party fragmentation is associated with government engagement. Rather, years since the PRI was in power is highly correlated with government engagement. Municipal officeholders in places that have only recently transitioned to democracy—meaning an opposition party (PAN, PRD, Green, Worker, or alliance party, for example) has only recently won a municipal election—are likely to be more engaged in partnerships. This suggests that municipalities in which an opposition party has a shorter institutional memory and experience governing in local office are more likely to engage in partnerships. One interpretation of this finding is that transnational partnerships with migrants help to expand the incumbent party's electoral base of support in places in which the PRI has a long-standing foothold in the municipality. Municipalities with higher levels of government engagement are also those with higher levels of international migration, lower levels of poverty, larger populations, more citizen turnout in local elections, and migrant clubs that have high levels of club capacity. Places in which the local government is more highly engaged are no more likely to be associated with a particular political party nor are they associated with any particular characteristics of the U.S. destination.

MIGRANT HOMETOWN ASSOCIATION CAPACITY TO COPRODUCE PUBLIC GOODS

During interviews with migrant club leaders that informed the survey questionnaire, several leaders remarked that being in a U.S. city where there are many immigrants, other hometown clubs, and state-level federations of migrant clubs created a network of people to converse with, exchange information, and compare experiences about cross-border partnerships and club activities. In follow-up discussions with migrant club leaders who participated in the survey, and interviews with 3x1 officials in the U.S. and Mexico, several people explained to me that migrants learned tips on how to organize their clubs from training programs administered by the Mexican consulate and in discussions with other migrant club leaders in nearby municipalities to their hometowns in Mexico. For example, club leaders learned how to structure their club, employ methods for making decisions, develop a mission statement and bylaws, collect dues, and fundraise. Information shared between migrants and Mexican state officials in the U.S. and Mexico proved to be an important factor in how clubs set up and ran their associations and coordinated projects in their respective hometowns.

Given the number of clubs that described the importance of club capacity to their partnerships and evidence in the previous analysis that indicators of club capacity highly correlate with both community inclusion and government engagement, I also construct on indicator of club capacity using PCA. Several survey questions ask HTAs about club leadership characteristics, organizational structure and decision-making, membership characteristics, and club activities.

I have found a few factors that are associated with club capacity. First, not surprisingly, U.S. cities with a larger Mexican foreign-born population are more likely to have clubs with higher levels of club capacity. Second, clubs that have previous experience providing public goods projects in the hometown, independent of the Mexican sending state and the 3x1 Program, are associated with higher levels of club capacity. Third, clubs that have participated in the 3x1 Program for several years (prior to the year they took the survey) have higher club capacity scores. Finally, survey respondents that report mimicking some aspects of other HTAs' organizational structure and decision-making also have higher capacity scores. Taken together, this evidence suggest more support for the social learning hypothesis, or organizational isomorphism, at the migrant club level. Organizational isomorphism means that migrant clubs may become similarly structured to other clubs resulting from imitation or development under similar conditions or constraints. Clubs that have the opportunity to learn from each other and adopt best practices are able to improve their capacity to provide public goods and collaborate with state and local partners more effectively. Migrant club capacity is an important determinate of higher levels of community inclusion and government engagement and must be accounted for in the multivariate analysis accordingly. Place-based characteristics such as the density of the Mexican immigrant population in the destination city and concentration of other hometown clubs are important indicators of clubs with higher capacity.

Many club leaders also described how they struggled to retain members' interest in club activities, which required extensive energy and time. The case of Ahuacatl illustrates this sentiment. Migrant leaders described having to frequently plead (some used the word "harass") paisanos to donate resources and take part in the planning and execution of transnational projects. In fact, in several follow-up phone calls, migrant club leaders asked me if I could share information about how other clubs who took the survey ran their associations so that they could learn how to retain membership involvement and better navigate the difficult process of coordinating public goods projects across national borders.[8] Many club leaders told me they were frustrated trying to rally the support of paisanos in the U.S. or were becoming aggravated working with political officials in Mexico. Many leaders also shared that they felt isolated in more rural U.S. destinations. Leaders lamented how they wished they were in closer proximity to metropolitan cities like Los Angeles, Chicago, Atlanta, Dallas, Houston, and San Jose so that they could be closer to other migrant clubs and participate in state-level HTA federations. That being said, for some clubs, a high level of club capacity was achievable in new destination areas and with a smaller core group of families or club leadership in lieu of a large paisano membership organization. A dedicated membership base was more feasible, some leaders reported, when they also had strong support from local residents and political officials back in the hometown. Developing and maintaining a strong network of paisano support in the U.S., which was key to determining high levels of club capacity, was partially dependent on preexisting community inclusion and government engagement suggesting a feedback effect or an endogenous relationship.

The results of the cluster analysis and interview data confirmed feedback effects inherent in transnational partnerships like those described above. Migrant clubs with high club capacity were not necessarily those that were more socially embedded in the community and therefore more likely to include residents in the coproduction process. Nor were they necessarily the clubs that motivated political actors to engage in partnerships and complete their obligations. This is consistent with evidence in the case of Santa Catarina. But clubs that drew on the social resources in the social base of the hometown were able to overcome club capacity issues and learned new ways to encourage members to become more interested in club activities. Moreover, clubs learned about the benefits of community inclusion when they exchanged information with other clubs. Clubs that did not recruit local residents into the coproduction process implemented new outreach activities in the hometown when other club leaders described to them the value of local resident participation. Information sharing across migrant clubs both influenced the level of HTA capacity and had feedback effects on community inclusion and engagement.

Finally, analysis of the structure of migrant clubs revealed that despite many migrants' best intentions and recruitment efforts, sometimes local residents did not want to engage in coproduction with migrant and state actors. While the multivariate analysis did not reveal that poverty or political histories were systematically associated with community inclusion, it is quite likely that long histories of distrust in political officials, especially in authoritarian enclaves, and places in which residents have fewer resources, skills, and time to participate in projects contribute to low levels of community inclusion despite a migrant club that has a higher capacity for public goods provision.

The case of Club Jilotepec from the state of Mexico and located in San Jose, California, supports this interpretation of the data. The club formed in 2008 with only a few members and grew to 30 active members and over 100 extended members over the span of a calendar year. They fundraised through picnics and raffles and had the support of a large migrant network in San Jose. The club held regular meetings and most of the leadership had lawful permanent residency status (green card holders), which allowed them to visit the hometown at least once a year, sometimes more. Despite strong bonding ties to many migrant families in their hometown of 895 residents and consistent efforts to recruit residents into the partnership, club leaders explained that locals remained uninterested in their club activities. Migrants suggested that local residents were too politically apathetic to participate in any activities that involve the local PRI government, which was perceived to be too untrustworthy to partner with on coproduction projects. For Club Jilotepec, this was frustrating because they recognized that a lack of community involvement—that is, a lack of more "eyes and ears" on the ground—made them vulnerable to unscrupulous political officials. Since we spoke in 2009, community residents were content to be the beneficiaries of completed projects but remained uninvolved in the transnational partnership despite migrant club members' active efforts to recruit them into coproduction activities.

Community inclusion, government engagement, and club capacity are important factors involved in the organization of transnational partnerships in migrant hometown communities. But do the key factors analyzed in the case studies and survey combine to create stable transnational partnership types consistent with the framework presented in chapter 1?

IDENTIFYING TYPES OF TRANSNATIONAL PARTNERSHIP USING SURVEY DATA

I use cluster analysis to identify different clusters or "types" of transnational partnership using the original survey data. With this method, I differentiate and compare partnership types and examine the set of characteristics that are more associated with each type or cluster. Overall, the cluster analysis confirms that partnerships vary according to combinations of different levels of community inclusion and government engagement while holding migrant club capacity constant. Including sociodemographic and political characteristics of origin and destination, I consistently observe the formation of four stable partnership clusters: synergy (high community inclusion / high government engagement), corporatist (low community inclusion / high government engagement), substitutive (high community inclusion / low government engagement), and fragmented (low community inclusion / low government engagement).[9]

Additionally, since we learn in the previous analysis that migrant club capacity is an important attribute of both government engagement and community inclusion, I also relax the assumption that club capacity is constant and include the club capacity index as an additional variable in the cluster analysis. The objective here is to observe whether club capacity has an independent effect on how coproduction partnerships group together. When I include the index for club capacity (resources, leadership characteristics, organizational structure, membership size), an additional partnership type emerges along with synergetic, corporatist, substitutive, and fragmented partnerships. In this additional cluster, clubs with more capacity but low levels of community inclusion and government engagement form an additional, stable partnership type. I refer to this type of partnership as *apex partnerships* since migrant clubs complete the lion's share of project coordination with minimal support from residents and political officials in their hometowns.

Cluster analysis, while underutilized in sociological studies of international migration, gives me an opportunity to externally validate my claim that migrant-state partnerships organizationally vary beyond the small number of cases I examine in the field. This additional methodological step provides more compelling evidence that transnational coproduction partnership types are more likely to be associated with different political consequences. Moreover, informed by the interview data with migrant club leaders, I also had reason to suspect that levels of club capacity would affect partnership dynamics. The combination of inductive and deductive reasoning pushed me to analyze the role of capacity in the organization of partnerships. As a result, an additional hybrid partnership form emerged from the empirical data whose political consequences could also be analyzed along with the four main coproduction types that I originally theorized.

POLITICAL PARTICIPATION AND
GOVERNMENT SPENDING BEFORE AND AFTER
TRANSNATIONAL PARTNERSHIPS

The cluster analysis consistently reveals four partnership types: 55 cases of synergetic partnership, 69 cases of fragmented partnership, 51 cases of substitutive partnership, and 38 cases of corporatist partnership. Of the 250 club respondents, 37 were in places with *usos y costumbres* for which no political outcomes were available for analysis. For the 213 partnerships cases for which complete data is available, I use multivariate regression and assess the change in how many local citizens of voting age took part in municipal elections and the change in government spending on public works before and after the transnational partnerships, holding all other factors constant. Voter turnout and government social spending represent two key indicators of local democratic participation and government responsiveness.[10] I also assess how partnerships affect civic and political participation using survey questions and data from the MxFLS. Data Appendix D contains more detailed information about model specifications, explanatory variables, and controls.

SYNERGETIC PARTNERSHIPS

In one group of partnerships, clubs had higher levels of community inclusion and government engagement consistent with the synergetic type of coproduction. In these partnerships, residents in the hometown were more frequently involved in volunteering labor, selecting projects, donating resources or labor, monitoring project implementation and upkeep, and discussing project activities with municipal officials. Residents were also regularly involved in issues such as hiring laborers and contractors for projects, timelines for completion, technical plans, and local committees or mirror clubs. The local government was also more likely to engage in selecting projects, providing the requisite matching funds in full and in a timely manner, and completing projects according to the timeline when migrant clubs had more frequent access to and negotiating leverage with political officials. Results also reveal that synergetic partnerships were those in which the municipal government had more local-state capacity and were also more likely to be characterized by medium levels of international migration and poverty. Synergetic partnerships were no more likely to be associated with a particular political party of the incumbent.

In the 55 cases that approximate synergetic partnerships, there was no systematic change in the number of citizens participating in local elections in the period immediately following the most recent coproduction project. Places with synergy were no more likely to experience more citizens turning out to vote in local elections than in municipalities with other kinds of partnerships in the electoral period immediately following the most recent coproduction project. I offer four interpretations of the nonfinding for voter turnout.

First, the citizens and citizen groups that were active partners in transnational public goods provision already may have been those individuals who turned out to vote in local elections, which explained why there was no systematic changes in voter turnout in the election immediately after the most recent coproduction project. Second, it could be that the number of citizens involved in partnership who voted were simply too small a number to be observed in the aggregate. Third, and by contrast, citizens included in partnerships may have been those who did not regularly participate in politics and required more time and information to develop political interest and personal efficacy before going to the polls. Finally, citizens are often motivated to participate in elections when they are unhappy and have recourse to punish the incumbent for poor performance in office. Citizens who became active, equal partners in the provision of public goods and helped set the spending agenda, selected projects, and interacted with government partners may have chosen to focus their political activity on nonelectoral forms of political engagement because they perceived local officeholders to have performed well in office.

While there is no observable relationship between the 55 cases of synergy and short-term voter turnout, there is an indication that local citizens became more involved in nonelectoral forms of participation and there were also indications of short-term, positive effects on government responsiveness. Survey results also showed that local citizens became more involved in community affairs beyond public goods projects and more active in local politics after synergetic coproduction. In terms of the effect that synergetic partnerships have on local government performance, clubs report that after the most recent transnational project, they "agree" and "strongly agree" that municipal officials were more trustworthy, more responsive to the needs of the local citizenry, and delivered on their promises to the community more consistently.

Synergetic partnerships are also more associated with increases in the share of total public spending on public goods and services in those municipalities in which clubs participate more frequently. On average, with each additional project completed through a synergetic partnership, the share of public spending increases by 1.2 percent in the electoral period immediately following the coproduction project. As synergetic partnerships continue in municipalities, local government is more responsive to programmatic spending on public works. While there is no association between incidence of synergetic partnerships and the party affiliation of the incumbent mayor, after repeated cases of synergy, it is more likely that the PRI is the party in power and less likely that the PAN is the municipal incumbent.

Club Nochistlan, a large club with 250 members located in Los Angeles, California, formed in 1997 and spent 11 years coordinating public goods provision in their hometown in the state of Zacatecas independently and through the federal 3x1 Program. After Club Nochistlan completed their very first project with the municipal government through the 3x1 Program, they reported that while reaction from local residents and civic associations in the hometown was very positive, local officials were more difficult to work with and the club had an unfavorable opinion of them. However, over time and after the completion of several more projects, the club noted that access to the mayor and his staff and the club's ability to influence decision-making improved considerably. In 2009 and later in 2010, club leaders described the partnership with the local government and citizens in a positive light. One club leader said she considered the transnational partnership to now be an important "local institution" for the provision of public goods regardless of the political party of the mayor in power. When I reviewed the changes in public spending on public works in Nochistlan for the years in which the club completed 3x1 projects, every additional year of project activity was associated with a $126 peso increase (per capita) in municipal spending on public works. The survey data on synergetic partnerships supports the findings from the case study analysis: civic engagement in community activities in and beyond coproduction activities, nonelectoral forms of political participation, and government responsiveness improve with synergetic partnerships.

CORPORATIST PARTNERSHIPS

The 38 cases of corporatist partnerships were those characterized by low levels of community inclusion, but higher levels of local government engagement. In the short term, places with more corporatist partnerships are associated with more citizens participating in local elections. On average, 5 percent more citizens turn out to vote in municipalities with corporatist partnerships than in other partnership types. But while more people turn out to vote, there is no *change* in voter turnout in the electoral period immediately following the partnership, all other things being equal. As the analysis of government engagement reveals, citizens are more likely to turn out to vote in municipal elections compared to other partnership communities. Moreover, HTA leaders are no more likely to agree or disagree that citizens become more civically or politically involved in the hometown in the period after transnational partnerships.

HTA leaders' impressions of club involvement in local governance and political officials' performance is more positive. HTA leaders are more likely to "agree" and "strongly agree" that transnational partnerships give them more access to political officials and grant them decision-making authority and influence during negotiations with local officials. Leaders are also more likely to perceive local government to be more responsive, trustworthy, and perform their duties consistency well. HTA leaders' perceptions are supported by municipal budget data. In places with corporatist partnerships, the local government is more likely to spend more (4 percent) on public works in the electoral cycle after the partnership and even more than in synergetic partnerships following the most recent coproduction project. The positive spending effects disappear, however, after repeated municipal engagement in partnerships. The data suggests that increases in government spending on public goods is more likely confined to the electoral period right after the active partnership, which may suggest political opportunism. One interesting association uncovered in this analysis is that places with more corporatist partnerships are more likely located in PRD municipalities.

While corporatist partnerships are more associated with active, engaged local government that works cooperatively with migrant clubs, the public spending returns to local citizens that occur in the periods directly after partnerships are short-lived. This provides some initial evidence that corporatist partnerships may benefit local government in politically expedient ways but do little to improve government responsiveness over the longer term. The lack of social inclusion in partnerships also suggests that while migrant-state relations are cooperative, residents have little say in how public goods decisions are made and how resources are allocated. Community exclusion may lead to some short-term political activism, as the case of Atitlan reveals, but over a larger number of corporatist cases, the finding in the aggregate is that these types of partnership are more likely to reinforce the status quo level of political participation or lead to a worsening of resident involvement in community and political affairs in the hometown.

SUBSTITUTIVE PARTNERSHIPS

The 51 cases of substitutive partnership characterized by high levels of community involvement, but low levels of government support, produced mixed results for civic and political engagement and government responsiveness. Local citizens in these locales turned out to vote less in substitutive partnerships compared to other places before partnerships and there was no change in voter turnout afterward. However, as substitutive partnerships continued over time, there was a significant decline in citizen voting behaviors. In places with repeated substitution, voter turnout declined by 11 percent. This is a significant decrease in the citizen population participating in elections. Survey results revealed no systematic association between civic engagement after substitutive partnerships.

Additionally, local government officials in substitutive partnerships spent 3 percent less on public goods and had significantly fewer 3x1 projects compared to other types of partnerships in the short run. Municipal governments involved in these partnerships are also more likely to fall short of their full 25 percent matching contribution to migrant clubs. In substitutive partnerships, municipal government matched less than one-to-one with other cofinancing partners (state, federal, and migrant partners). Survey data suggests that HTA leaders' perceptions of government responsiveness were also more negative after coproduction activities. Leaders are more likely to "disagree" and "strongly disagree" that municipal officials did their jobs consistently well, were responsive to citizens' needs, and were more trustworthy after experiences in coordinating public goods. Leaders' perceptions of changes in citizens' involvement in civic and community affairs, however, were considerably more favorable. After the most recent projects, migrant leaders were more likely to "strongly agree" that residents become more politically active and engaged in civic affairs.

While substitutive partnerships may be inclusive of the local citizenry through processes of social learning or because migrants are embedded in the social base of the hometown, a lack of government engagement has depressive effects on public spending and negative consequences for electoral participation in the short run. Survey findings suggested that while migrant clubs were able to use their collective resources to improve public goods provision with the help of local residents, partnerships do little to improve *local government* performance, depress voter turnout, and have no effects on citizen engagement beyond coproduction projects. Substitutive partnerships may scale up citizen participation in voting eventually, which may, in turn, encourage local government to be more responsiveness as the case of El Cerrito illustrates in chapter 3. Longitudinal data is necessary to uncover the durability of political effects within cases and across cases over time.

FRAGMENTED PARTNERSHIPS

The 69 cases of fragmented partnership produced more negative political consequences in the period after migrant partnerships with the local government than in other coproduction types. In municipalities with fragmented coproduction, which are more likely to be characterized by low community inclusion and government engagement, partnerships had a much shorter lifespan than other types of partnerships. They were not only more likely to be clubs that reported being temporarily or permanently inactive, they were also more likely to have completed only one project through the 3x1 Program. HTA leaders in fragmented partnerships were also more likely to perceive negative consequences after their involvement in public goods provision. Leaders were more likely to "strongly disagree" that government officials are more responsive, reliable, and trustworthy and leaders report a higher frequency of not finishing public goods projects "often" or "very often."

Leaders' perceptions of citizen involvement in community and political activities were also more unfavorable. Survey data suggests that HTAs are more likely to "strongly disagree" that in the period right after the most recent 3x1 project, citizens were more engaged in local politics and community activities. Unlike in other partnership cases in which the length of time a club leader resides in the U.S. has no systematic effect in organizing partnerships or political consequences, HTA leaders in fragmented partnerships were more likely to reside in the U.S. for longer periods of time. In fragmented partnerships, leaders are more likely to live in the U.S. for more than 20 years than in other types of partnerships.

Taken together, results of fragmented partnerships suggest few opportunities to improve local democratic governance in the short run. Cases of fragmented coproduction were more likely to fail without local social resources and more state capacity involved in coproduction activities. The data also reveals that citizens are more likely to become politically disenchanted and are less likely to participate in civic and political affairs in the period following fragmented coproduction activities.

APEX PARTNERSHIPS

In the framework I present in chapter 1, the level of HTA capacity is held constant. When I relaxed the assumption that HTA club capacity was similar across cases, the data revealed a hybrid form of coproduction. This partnership grouping was characterized by low levels of community inclusion and government engagement but high levels of HTA capacity through which to provide local public goods without much support from other social and political actors. In these cases of coproduction, cofinancing from state and federal partners helped coproduce public works projects, but the HTA was the "apex" provider of public goods, which allowed local government to be less responsive for service provision and shirk a core responsibility of local office.

In the survey sample, 31 partnerships were apex partnerships. In apex partnerships, HTA leaders reported near unanimous disagreement that municipal government officials became more responsive, reliable, and trustworthy after coproduction projects were implemented. These clubs were also more likely to report the local government was less cooperative, and clubs had consistently more problems completing projects and receiving matching contributions in a timely manner compared to other kinds of partnerships. Club leaders in apex partnerships were also more likely to "disagree" or "strongly disagree" that participation in public goods provision gives migrants more influence and decision-making authority in local governance. Data shows that while migrant clubs were able to complete public goods projects in their hometowns with less engagement from the local citizenry and municipal government, apex clubs faced considerable obstacles to successfully completing coproduction projects.

There are some limitations in the survey analysis that suggest more caution when drawing conclusions. First, the number of cases of each partnership type is small, which limits confidence in the generalizability of findings. Second, the survey data is a representative sample of migrant partnerships, but only from a snapshot in time. Many of the projects that club leaders were referencing when completing the before-and-after questions on the survey occurred between 2007 and 2009, although some referenced project experiences from earlier time periods. As such, migrant clubs' reflections on how political engagement and government performance changed after coproduction projects only reflect the kind of project in that snapshot of time. As we learned in the comparative case studies, the type of partnership is likely to change over time through social learning. It is quite likely the case that some of the partnerships surveyed, especially those in the very early years of coproducing public goods with the Mexican state, changed organizational forms in later periods. To address these limitations in the survey analysis, I also assessed with multivariate statistics how repeated partnerships affect political outcomes over a longer time horizon for each type of partnership. As the results show, habitual engagement between migrants, citizens, and the local government does produce important changes over time, but a longer observation window is necessary to draw more confidence in the conclusions.[11]

A final limitation of the cluster analysis is that the unit of observation is the club year for the most recent before-and-after period, but the political outcomes are aggregated at the municipal level of observation. Data is unavailable at the locality level where many clubs focus their coproduction activities. To isolate the effects of the survey respondent and political effects in the municipality, I controlled for whether there were any other hometown associations in the municipal year. I also restricted the 3x1 coproduction data and municipal spending data to the specific survey respondent by matching the name of migrant club listed in the 3x1 Program data. Nonetheless, I was unable to completely isolate how the survey respondent's coproduction partnership produced changes in local civic and political engagement and government responsiveness, especially when there were other hometown clubs active in the municipality in the same time period. In the HTA survey sample, 27 percent of the sample were in municipalities with other active 3x1 partnerships in the same time period as the club observations. More micro-level data at the locality level would be necessary to completely rule out the possibility that different partnerships had counteracting effects on political and civic engagement and government responsiveness. Cross-checking the survey data with data from the universe of partnership cases in the 3x1 data was an important step as it showed that partnerships types can vary in the same municipality and caution must be exercised when interpreting club-level results using municipal political outcome variables.

The survey provides a window into how partnerships are organized and how this organizational variation is associated with different political effects in a cross-section of partnership cases. Without the survey data and PCA and cluster analysis, it would have been difficult to validate whether partnerships are structured differently. Small-n case studies cannot control for the multitude of factors that likely affect partnerships. Moreover, 3x1 Program data does not have the detailed information about the nature of partnerships to assess organizational variation. The survey analysis is the first opportunity to examine organizational variation in partnership types in the specific social, economic, and political contexts of U.S. destinations and Mexican origins.

In the final stage of the empirical analysis in this chapter, I turn to panel data and statistical analysis to determine the long-term political consequences of transnational partnerships. I assess if places with transnational partnerships have a systematic effect on voter turnout and government responsiveness compared to municipalities that never participated in the 3x1 Program between 1990 and 2013. I also compare a subset of 3x1 participating municipalities. In that analysis, I analyze how municipalities that frequently engage in coproduction compare to those that participate less frequently between 2002 and 2013, the active period of the 3x1 Program. In this part of the statistical analysis, I move up a level of aggregation from club level to municipal level exclusively and examine the political effects across all transnational partnership types. Using longitudinal data from the Mexican Family Life Survey and 3x1 Program project data at the municipal level, I assess how 3x1 Program participation and the number of coproduction projects affect civic and political participation and government responsiveness across migrant hometowns.

PANEL ANALYSIS USING 3X1 PROGRAM AND MUNICIPAL DATA

To test the hypothesis that transnational partnerships affect political and civic participation and government responsiveness, I must operationalize partnerships and political outcomes. I rely on municipal participation in the 3x1 Program to account for places that formally engage in the coproduction of public goods and services between the Mexican sending state and organized migrant hometown associations.[12] As I describe in chapter 2, the 3x1 Program is a federally administered social spending program that matches the collective remittances of migrant HTAs, three-to-one, at the local, state, and federal levels of government. While financing from all three levels of the Mexican government and migrant collective remittances fund project costs, all other aspects of project coordination occur at the municipal level. Project selection, planning, technical support, labor, materials, implementation, and monitoring are coordinated between municipal government officials and migrant hometown groups. I construct several indicators for

3x1 Program participation. Additional data on the main explanatory variables and controls is presented in Data Appendix D.

Data for the analysis includes annual municipal participation and project data in the 3x1 Program from 2002, the first year of the program, to 2013, the most recent year for which complete data is available. The *Secretaría de Desarrollo Social,* the Ministry of Social Development (Sedesol), maintains a database of all approved 3x1 projects. The database contains annual data on project location, type, funding sources and amounts, and total number of projects for each participating municipality. The unit of analysis is the municipal-year observation. Sedesol does not report information about projects that were proposed, but not approved, by state-level project validation committees.[13]

The project proposal process generally proceeds as follows. First, HTAs and local government officials agree to submit a proposal for approval to a Validation Committee (COVAM), which exists in every Mexican state. The COVAM is made up of two individuals for each kind of coproduction partner including municipal, state, federal, and migrant partners. The representative body typically meets one to three times a year to approve project proposals depending on the number of proposals in each Mexican state. After the COVAM approves or rejects proposals, each cofinancing partner deposits 25 percent of the total project costs into an independent banking account or the municipal treasury. The migrant HTA and local government authorities plan, hire labor, implement, and monitor projects at variable levels of engagement.

Between 2002 and 2013, 1,234 municipalities participated at least once in the 3x1 Program, which is half (50.2 percent) of all Mexican municipalities. In 2008, for example, while 539 different municipalities participated, only 87 municipalities were participating in the program for the first time. The number of new municipalities starting the program for the first time decreases over the duration of the program. This indicates that a large number of municipalities repeatedly participate rather than indicating more diffuse policy adoption across municipalities between 2002 and 2013.[14]

MEASURING LOCAL CIVIC AND POLITICAL PARTICIPATION AND GOVERNMENT RESPONSIVENESS

Researchers have different approaches for conceptualizing and measuring democratic governance. Scholarship on political democracy ranges from regime change and democratic consolidation,[15] democratic quality in terms of how well democracy performs given some normative standards (for example, procedural minimums including participation and competition),[16] the effects of democracy on other indicators such as economic growth and wars, and government institutional performance.[17] Since I am interested in how transnational partnerships affect local democracy across standard benchmarks, I measure political effects that provide insight into procedural and results facets of democracy. The dependent variables of interest are political participation in elections, civic engagement in community activities and associations, and government responsiveness in terms of spending on social welfare and public works programs.

POLITICAL PARTICIPATION

Political participation refers to the extent to which citizens exercise formal voting rights as well as organize, assemble, protest, lobby, join political parties and civil society organizations, and otherwise influence the decision-making process. Democratic quality is high when citizens participate in the political process, deliberate policy issues, communicate with and demand accountability from elected representatives, and monitor the conduct of political officials. Greater formal participation makes democratic systems, in theory, more responsive to a larger share of the population. In this analysis, I restrict the focus to formal political participation and measure how many citizens of voting age cast a vote in local elections. The focus on nonmigrant citizen voting reflects the importance of electoral participation in studies of democratic participation and governance. Additionally, reliable panel indicators for more informal forms of political participation (for example, rallies, protests, and petitions) are scarce.

CIVIC ENGAGEMENT

The MxFLS data allows me to assess how 3x1 Program participation affects non-electoral forms of political and civic engagement in addition to voting. I observe whether transnational partnerships explain changes in the frequency of community-level activities and the incidence and kind of civic associations such as social, religious, and political associations. I hypothesize that community inclusion is an important factor in organizing partnerships and that more citizen involvement increases information sharing, political interest, and awareness of government actions and behaviors while in office. Places in which the incidence of community activities increase during periods of municipal participation in the 3x1 Program provide a window into how partnerships may have positive spillovers on different forms of civic and political engagement.

Changes in levels of community activities that are positively associated with the incidence and frequency of 3x1 Program participation and the number of 3x1 projects suggest higher levels of community inclusion. I anticipate that more community inclusion may be indicative of both the role of preexisting civic associations in transnational projects and the creation of new kinds of citizen activities. Over time and with repeated social interactions between citizens, migrants, and political officials, citizens' routinized interactions will lead to more regular participation in the local civic and public affairs. In addition to analyzing the independent effects of coproduction on civic and political activities, I also evaluate whether civic engagement has a conditional effect on political participation. For example, if 3x1 participation is associated with increases in community civic activities, I expect that this may further increase citizens' interest and engagement in the formal electoral process. To capture the likelihood of a conditional effect, I estimate interactions between community civic engagement and 3x1 participation on voter turnout.

The MxFLS is a longitudinal, multi-thematic survey taken over three panel waves (2002, 2005–2006, 2009–2012). The survey is helpful for my purposes because in addition to an individual and household survey, there is also a community sample. The community survey includes questions about community activities across a random sample of Mexican municipalities. Using the MxFLS sample, I match municipal survey respondents with all the municipalities in the panel dataset used earlier in the chapter. Over the three panels of the MxFLS, the total number of respondent municipalities for which comprehensive data is available is 272 municipalities with some missing data. About 30 percent of MxFLS municipalities participated in the 3x1 Program during the period of study. The survey questionnaire includes a battery of questions related to community activities including whether the community organizes activities, meetings, and assemblies, and the type of community activities organized including religious, political, social, or other. The survey also collects data on whether activities are more recent and how many occur over the preceding 12-month period.[18]

GOVERNMENT RESPONSIVENESS

Government responsiveness to the needs, interests, expectations, and demands of citizens[19] provides additional insight into the results dimension of transnational partnerships. Across Mexican municipalities, public goods provision is the central responsibility of local government and citizens base their evaluations of government performance on access to public works. Mexican municipalities are responsible for the provision of public goods and services and citizens know whom to reward and blame for this core responsibility.[20] As per Article 115 of the Mexican Constitution, municipalities have exclusive authority over (1) provision of drinking water, drainage, and sewage systems; (2) public lighting; (3) cleaning, collection, removal, treatment and disposal of waste materials; (4) markets and supply centers; (5) cemeteries and monuments; (6) slaughterhouses; (7) streets, parks, and gardens; and (8) public security and safety. Survey data shows that citizens know the issue areas that are the exclusive domain of municipal government, can differentiate between state and local government policy responsibilities, and report that public utility provision (especially water and sewerage) are the "most important" municipal problems.[21]

By the same token, municipal presidents know that receiving credit for public goods provision is a key factor in determining citizens' evaluation of their performance while in office. Municipalities rely on a combination of federal and state transfers and local sources of revenues to finance public goods and services. Some revenue transfers sent to municipalities are based on objective criteria including population size, poverty, and relative need, but other disbursements may be politically motivated.[22] Municipal presidents maintain discretion concerning how resources are spent once they arrive from state and federal transfers. Because participation in the 3x1 Program provides amplifying funds for municipal government to finance public works, transnational partnerships are likely to affect government responsiveness.

I evaluate the extent to which 3x1 participation achieves benefits for citizens in participating municipalities by analyzing changes in government spending as an indicator of their responsiveness to coproduction. Specifically, I analyze how 3x1 participation affects municipal spending on public works (per capita) and the share of the total budget devoted to social spending. These measures are instructive because they reveal the share of funds being distributed for public works and any possible spending leakages that may occur from cofinancing from coproduction partners. For example, because I know the total budget for each 3x1 project, I can examine the difference in total municipal contributions that should be spent on 3x1 projects and actual expenditures by looking at different spending categories in the municipal budget for each three-year electoral period of a single political party in power.

If political officials were more responsive to citizen demands for public works, we would expect 3x1 Program participation to increase the spending on public works as opposed to increases on personal salaries or debt services. Moreover, when municipalities match program contributions one-to-one with state, federal, and migrant partners, we should expect municipal expenditures and shares of public works to increase. No change in public expenditures would provide evidence that 3x1 participation is subsidizing public works spending that municipalities would have spent in the absence of program participation. A decrease would suggest that political officials are offloading responsibility to migrant (and state and federal government) partners and spending less than they would have spent without coproduction financing. A negative change in spending implies 3x1 Program participation is allowing municipalities to shirk their coproduction financing obligations and spend what they would have spent on public works in other budget areas. Finally, if total expenditures increase, but not a concomitant increase in public works spending, we may deduce a spending leakage in response to 3x1 participation.[23] In other words, we may infer that municipalities are shifting expenditures to other categories in response to program participation and away from social welfare spending, which is one of the primary objectives of the federal 3x1 Program.

Civic and political participation and government responsiveness are three dimensions of governance likely affected by transnational coproduction facilitated by participation in the 3x1 Program. Assessing the extent to which municipal participation in the 3x1 Program affects multiple dimensions of democratic governance provides some insight into what some scholars refer to as vertical accountability.[24] Vertical accountability refers to citizens' awareness and access to information about representatives' political actions and decisions while in office, their evaluation of the justifications officials provide for their actions, and their interest and capacity to impose consequences on representatives through participation in the democratic process.

SYSTEMATIC EFFECTS ON LOCAL DEMOCRATIC ENGAGEMENT AND GOVERNMENT RESPONSIVENESS

Using a difference-in-difference approach, I analyze first whether municipal participation in the 3x1 Program has systematic effects on voter turnout and government responsiveness compared to municipalities that never participated in the program from 1990 to 2013. Results show that 3x1 municipalities are more likely to experience significant changes in voter turnout and government spending than nonparticipating municipalities. I illustrate these findings in Figure 5. Specifically, more frequent participation in the 3x1 Program significantly increases political participation compared to municipalities that never participate. In the subset of municipal cases that participate at some point between 2002 and 2013, those that participate in the 3x1 Program less frequently have less citizens turning out to vote, holding all other factors constant. For every year of participation in the 3x1 Program, the number of citizens turning out to vote increases by about 2 percent. Among the municipalities that participate in the 3x1 Program, the average frequency of annual participation is four years. For these municipalities, every four years of participation leads to an 8 percent increase in the voting-age citizenry turning out to vote in municipal elections. If a municipality participates in the 3x1 Program 10 times, for example (about 10 percent of the participating sample), the increase in voter turnout increases by about 20 percent. Since the voting-age population that turns out to vote is a relatively stable percentage in municipalities over time, the fact that participating in the 3x1 Program produces significant turnout effects is somewhat surprising and provides compelling evidence that transnational partnerships have important consequences on local electoral politics.

The results also show that municipalities that participate in the 3x1 Program and that coproduce a higher number of public goods projects increase the odds of having recent community activities (the reference group is not having any recent activity). For every additional year of municipal participation in the 3x1 Program and for each additional coproduction project that is implemented, the odds that local residents take part in community activities increase by 68 percent and 60 percent, respectively. The more that the migrant hometown participates in the 3x1 Program and has more projects, the higher the odds of having local civic engagement.

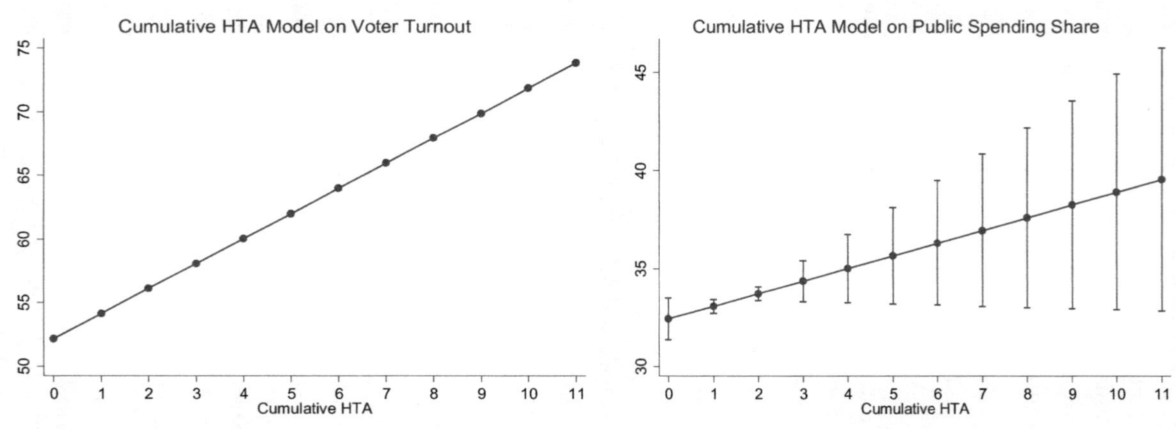

FIGURE 5. Marginal effect of cumulative 3x1 participation on voter turnout and government responsiveness. Source: Calculations using data sourced from INEGI Simbad, INE, Conapo, and Sedesol.

While we cannot infer that recent community activities are a direct indication of community inclusion in coproduction projects, these findings offer initial support that transnational partnerships play some positive spillover role in more citizens becoming involved in the civic affairs of their community compared to places that do not participate in the 3x1 Program. Additionally, results suggest additional support for the social learning hypothesis. As municipalities participate more in the 3x1 Program and complete more coproduction projects, the odds that community activities increase to 10 or more increase by 16.5 percent. However, in places in which the citizenry is *already* highly engaged in civic associations and activities that predate 3x1 participation, there is no evidence that additional coproduction projects further increase civic engagement. In other words, additional 3x1 projects lead to higher propensities for community engagement in places with lower initial levels of civic engagement but have no effect in places in which the citizenry was already highly active in civic associations.

The final analyses using the MxFLS examines if 3x1 participation enhances political participation (voting) *conditional on civic engagement.* In other words, I observe how civic engagement and 3x1 participation together affect voter turnout. While the panel data shows that more people turn out to vote in municipalities that participate in 3x1 projects, the MxFLS data more directly tests whether increases in citizen participation in local elections are conditional on transnational partnerships that also spur more civic engagement in local community affairs. Results reported in Data Appendix D confirm the important condition role of civic engagement on coproduction projects and their political effects.

The number of citizens that turn out to vote in elections increases by an additional 4 percent when nonmigrant citizens engage in more than 10 community activities in the preceding year. The positive effect of civic engagement *and* 3x1 participation holds across other indicators of 3x1 Program participation. For every additional project completed through the 3x1 Program, voter turnout increases by an additional 3 to 5 percent, depending on the level of civic engagement in the hometown. For example, in places with at least 50 community activities (a quarter of the sample), voter turnout increases by 3.4 percent for each additional 3x1 project completed. In municipalities with high levels of civic engagement and that complete at least three public works projects through the 3x1 Program, we would expect voter turnout to increase about 10 percent. When community activities reach 100 (7 percent of the sample), voter turnout increases by 5.4 percent for every coproduction project completed. Figure 6 plots the marginal effects of program participation conditional on different levels of local civic engagement.

Results also show that the frequency of participation in the 3x1 Program and the number of coproduction projects have important effects on voter turnout given the type of civic engagement in migrant hometowns. When there are more social and religious kinds of community activities, each additional coproduction project increases the percent of citizens voting by about 2 percent (1.7 and

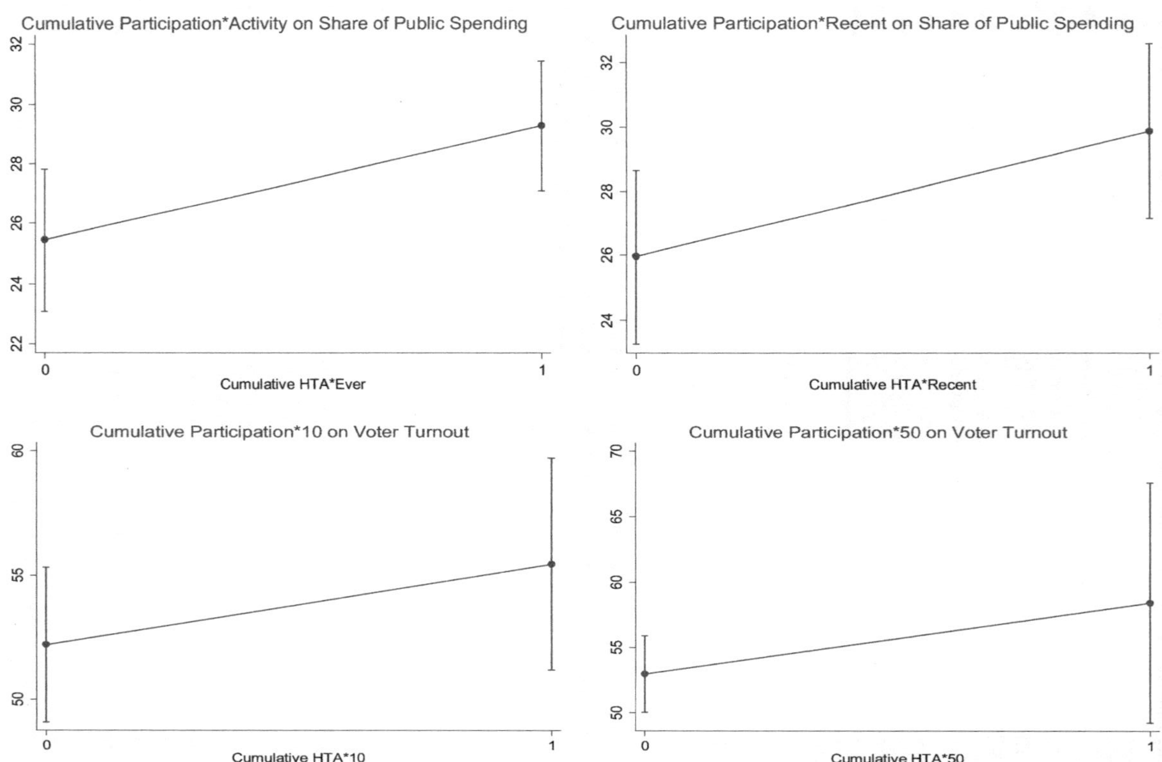

FIGURE 6. Marginal effect of cumulative 3x1 participation and civic engagement on voter turnout and government responsiveness.
SOURCE: Calculations using data sourced from Mexican Family Life Survey and panel data from INEGI Simbad, INE, Conapo, and Sedesol.

1.8 percent respectively). Taken together, the interaction models confirm that the positive spillover effects on political participation in municipal elections are conditional on citizens' active participation in community civic affairs and magnify the positive effects that transnational partnerships have on nonmigrant citizens' engagement in local governance.

The central findings for government responsiveness are generally less sanguine. When a municipality participates in the 3x1 Program, there is a decrease in total spending in the municipal budget and spending on public goods and services. Places that participate in the 3x1 Program are likely to spend $37 pesos (per capita) *less* on public works and $50 pesos (per capita) *less* on total spending across all categories compared to municipalities that never participate in the 3x1 Program. The only gains to citizens in terms of government spending on public goods from transnational coproduction occur when municipalities are consistently engaging in the 3x1 Program over time, which is consistent with the survey findings presented earlier in the chapter. From one electoral cycle to the next (about three years), municipalities that habitually participate in the 3x1 Program spend about $21 pesos (per capita) more on public works and increase the total share of the municipal budget by about 2 percent. When municipalities participate once or have more limited engagement in coproduction, officials are more likely to allow 3x1 spending to subsidize for municipal spending on public works.

Municipal public spending as a share of total spending also suffers when municipalities participate in the 3x1 Program less consistently. The share of public works spending declines by almost 5 percent for municipalities that participate infrequently. By comparison, in those municipalities that participate more habitually, municipal spending increases, but very minimally. For example, in the election year after 3x1 participation, municipalities are likely to allocate only about 0.5 percent more of their total budget expenditures to public works and are only likely to spend an additional 0.37 percent with each subsequent year of participation. To put this in perspective, consider a municipality with the mean level of expenditures. The average municipality spends about 30 percent of their total municipal budget on public goods and services. If average total expenditures per capita are $1,912 pesos and mean public works expenditures are about $626, participating in the 3x1 Program once corresponds to an additional $11 pesos of spending on public works per citizen. This amounts to about $1 USD more on public works spending per capita, which is negligible. But if a municipality participates six times, for example, public works expenditures increase by almost 2 percent. When municipalities participate once or only a handful of times, financial contributions from state, federal, and migrant partners subsidize local public works budgets at best and decrease programmatic spending at worst. Improvements in municipal social spending only occur with more frequent, consistent participation in the 3x1 Program over time and even then, on average, social spending increases only amount to a few additional dollars per citizen.

The findings on municipal spending in response to transnational coproduction reveal that in the absence of continuous participation in the 3x1 Program, municipal government partners have an incentive to offload public works spending on organized migrant groups. Even in cases in which municipalities are habitual participants, on average, political authorities increase social welfare spending very little beyond what they commit to cofinancing public works through the 3x1 Program. In other words, beyond meeting their obligations to match coproduction project budgets in very active 3x1 municipalities, political officials are not reorganizing their municipal budgets to increase social welfare spending significantly. In those municipalities that participate in the 3x1 Program more erratically, municipal government is less responsive to the citizenry in social welfare spending than if they never participated in the program at all.

What characteristics do 3x1 participating municipalities that have the highest changes in social spending allocations share? Additional analysis shows that the places that have the highest increase in the share of public spending on public works are the poorest municipalities in the sample. Taking the results from the public spending models above into consideration, on average, when a municipality that is designated as "poor" or "very poor" by the Mexican census's marginalization index participates in the 3x1 Program 10 times, for example, the share of the total municipal budget spent on public works increases by 3 percent. For a relatively poor municipality this is a considerable increase, but this is not a majority of municipal cases.

There are two other noteworthy results. First, when poor and very poor municipalities are participating in the 3x1 Program, the data shows they are spending more of their total budgets on public goods and services than when they are not participating in the program. Results show that relatively poorer municipalities spend more on public goods (per capita) relative to richer municipalities during active periods of program participation. Second, municipalities that are the most likely to participate the most frequently in 3x1 projects (6, 8, and 10 times) are not the poorest municipalities in Mexico. Rather, they are more likely to have a medium level of poverty according to the national marginalization index.

One policy implication from these results is that the 3x1 Program helps the worst-off Mexicans gain more access to essential public goods and services, but poorer municipalities are not participating with the same frequency as relatively wealthier locales. This may suggest that the 3x1 Program is regressive and leads to a widening of inequality in access to public goods and services in response to high levels of out-migration. However, there is an important exception to this. Since 85 percent of projects are distributed to poorer localities outside the county seat, 3x1 participation is helping poor, rural citizens gain more access to public goods in middle-income municipalities. In turn, in middle-income municipalities where poorer residents often live in outlying localities with worse public goods provision, 3x1 participation is likely encouraging a more egalitarian distribution of public resources. Finally, if more marginalized citizens are more civically and politically engaged in local politics as a result of 3x1 participation, perhaps concerns about widening inequality or the regressive nature of the program may be somewhat tempered. When marginalized citizens and citizen groups become more involved in local governance, they are using democratic channels to represent their interests and demand better government performance, which may have more long-lasting political consequences such as empowering poorer, more marginalized citizens to use their voice and demand better government performance from local officials.

While spending on public works increases in municipalities that habitually participate in the 3x1 Program, I do not observe a one-to-one increase in public spending *and* total expenditures. The accounting anomaly suggests municipal spending leakages in the presence of state and federal 3x1 matching funds. On average, municipalities that participate in coproduction with state, federal, and migrant club partners are not allocating all of the matching funds to public spending. Rather, matching funds allow municipal officials to change how they allocate spending across budget categories. When I consider each expenditure category of the municipal budget, results show that 3x1 not only *decreases* total expenditures, but that program participation leads to increases in debt and "other" municipal spending. This suggests that municipal officials are allocating some of the 3x1 monies to finance other parts of their budget such as debt obligations in lieu of spending all the money on public works and social welfare programs.[25]

However, the cumulative effects from continuous participation in the 3x1 Program produce opposite effects. More participation in the 3x1 program leads municipal officials to pay down less debt over time. This may occur because there is less debt to pay down or because officials are become more responsive to the citizenry and financing more public works projects the longer they engage in transnational partnerships with migrant clubs. So while social spending on public works only increases a small amount, about $2 USD per citizen on average, municipalities that participate in the 3x1 Program frequently change how they choose to allocate public resources across different categories of the municipal budget.

The effects of 3x1 participation and civic engagement on government responsiveness using data from the MxFLS are consistent with findings from the panel analysis, but the magnitude of the effect is stronger. More recent community engagement is associated with a 4 percent increase in the share of social spending on public works in the municipal budget. The strongest conditional effects of 3x1 participation and civic engagement are in changes to municipal spending on public works as a share of the total budget. Municipal governments spend more of their total budgets on public works as a function of participation in the 3x1 Program when community activities reach 50 cumulative projects. But at low levels of community involvement (10 activities), municipal governments allow 3x1 participation to subsidize social spending. These findings suggest that in places in which local civic engagement is high, 3x1 participation increases municipal spending even more on public goods and services including electricity, potable water, streets and roads, and other public infrastructures. At lower levels of civic engagement, however, 3x1 Program participation lets local public officials off the hook for public spending and decreases their responsiveness to the public.

Consistent results from two different data sources provide compelling evidence of the returns to social spending and civic and political participation in places that have transnational partnerships with an engaged, active citizenry. As more citizens become actively engaged in coproduction activities and in community and political affairs more generally, local government becomes more responsive to citizens' demands for public goods and social welfare spending. As civic engagement increases, the positive effects of 3x1 participation are amplified. Participation in the 3x1 Program spurs more civic engagement and, in turn, more civic engagement increases voter turnout in local political participation, all other things being equal. This account indicates evidence of a "virtuous circle" stemming from cumulative, repeated engagement in coproduction activities where state and nonstate actors learn new ways to deliberate and cooperate in the fuzzy space between the public and private spheres of local governance.[26]

The more that migrant, resident, and government actors work together to provide public goods and are more generally active in local civic and political affairs, the more likely coproduction activities strengthen municipal government responsiveness. Even though elected officials are often only increasing public goods spending by 2 and 3 percent, they are doing so in response to citizens demanding programmatic spending increases, especially in localities that exist outside the municipal center. Survey results show that local citizens consistently identify public goods provision as the most pressing municipal concern when asked about government performance. When citizens are actively involved in deliberations about the distribution of public funds, more spending on public goods occurs in lieu of increases in other budget categories including debt spending, payroll salaries, or targeted transfers to citizens in return for political support. Additionally, citizen deliberation in public decisions about how much municipal budgets spend on what kinds of public goods and services increases regular interactions between citizens and the representatives they elect to serve. As more citizens become regularly involved in spending and allocation decisions concerning public goods, more equitable decisions are made that benefit a broader swath of the local citizenry in and beyond heavily populated town centers.

TESTING ALTERNATIVE HYPOTHESES

I argue that how much money migrants send collectively is not as important for understanding the effects of transnational coproduction on local governance as variation in the organization forms of partnerships. But this is an empirical question. Maybe it is the case that when migrant clubs propose projects with higher budgets that commit them to invest more money, local officials change their behavior. Perhaps when migrant clubs propose more coproduction projects, government responsiveness and local citizens' civic and political engagement improve. I examine these alternative hypotheses and ask: Are places that have more 3x1 projects or higher 3x1 expenditures more likely to observe changes in democratic functioning regardless of how transnational partnerships are organized?

Using the panel dataset, I examine how the total number of annual projects and 3x1 spending across municipalities affect civic and political participation and government responsiveness. Results show total 3x1 spending has a statistical effect on voter turnout, but the effects are overall negative and not substantively significant (see Data Appendix D). On average, total 3x1 Program expenditures lead to a decline in the number of voters turning out to cast a ballot in municipal elections by 0.3 percent. Those municipalities where 3x1 expenditures surpass $50,000 will see a decline in voter turnout by as much as 2.5 percent, but there are few municipalities with annual expenditures that high. There are no significant effects for the number of total projects on political and civic participation or government spending.

These findings suggest that how much money migrant groups and their coproduction partners spend on public works is not the key for understanding how transnational collective action affects local democratic governance. Rather, the frequency of program participation and the nature of the involvement of local civil society and municipal government shed more light on the political consequences at the local level. Interestingly, in places with higher than average spending through the 3x1 Program we see less formal engagement in municipal politics. I argue that how citizens are included and local government is engaged in partnerships and the frequency of interaction between migrant, political officials, and residents explains a great deal more of the variation in local democratic governance over time and place than how much money migrants send home in collective remittances for public goods provision.

SUMMARY

Migrant transnational partnerships are politically consequential for migrant places of origin. As more people leave their communities of origin, form migrant clubs, and partner with the sending state, more citizens take part in the formal electoral process, especially with more frequent, engaged coproduction activities across borders and in places with more robust civil society. As the survey analysis reveals, when citizens take part in partnerships with an engaged local government repeatedly, more citizens take part in formal and informal modes of political participation. Moreover, when transnational coproduction creates civic engagement and builds on social assets available in the hometown, local democratic engagement improves even more.

The effects of partnerships on government responsiveness are more mixed. Survey results show that substitutive partnerships subsidize public works spending for local governments but increase the share of government social spending in corporatist and synergetic partnerships over time. The more positive effects on democratic governance emanating from transnational partnerships are realized with repeated participation in the 3x1 Program, lending more support to the hypothesis that social and political learning occurs through the repeated process of transnational engagement in local public goods provision.

Findings from this chapter suggest that municipal 3x1 participation, in part, makes citizens more aware of and better informed about government officials' decisions in office. When territorial and extraterritorial citizens alike engage in coproduction activities, the relational context serves as a "school of democracy." And as the active civic and political engagement of the local citizenry improves, it has positive spillovers on government performance. The results suggest that transnational partnerships that are more inclusive of the local citizenry and spur civic engagement are also likely to induce a measure of vertical accountability—mechanisms that enable citizens as electors to evaluate government performance through formal channels like voting. Migrant collective action in hometown development has an additive effect on both civic engagement and political turnout. But the results also suggest that synergy is not the only kind of partnership important for affecting democratic engagement. Repeated, cumulative participation in coproduction spurs civic and political engagement and government responsiveness. Transnational partnerships structurally vary across cases and over time, producing short-term consequences for local democracy. But the most profound changes from partnerships occur over a longer time horizon in which organizational variation of partnerships is likely to change through repeated, cumulative participation in the coproduction of public goods across national borders.

Conclusion

The Paradox of Cross-Border Politics

In places where roads are not paved, few sidewalks exist, and drainage and sanitation are in short supply, citizens gain better access to these and other public goods when nonstate actors step in to complement and substitute for state action. In developing countries and transition regimes, citizens often have to rely on nonstate actors such as faith-based associations, private companies, nongovernmental organizations, neighborhood associations, sectarian groups, and migrant hometown associations to fill the gap in public goods provision. As this book shows, migrants and their organized social groups abroad pool their resources to invest in public goods provision in places in which they maintain shared connections and attachments. In doing so, this practice enabled by international migration creates a mechanism by which citizens can enjoy better access to public goods but it also produces unintended, yet profound political consequences for local democracy.

When migrants organize partnerships with public agencies in the sending state to improve local development, cross-border collective action also changes who participates, and how they participate, in local democracy. Under certain conditions, the process scales up civic and political engagement and strengthens government responsiveness. Under other conditions, though, transnational partnerships reinforce elite power relations, social and political cleavages, and political disenchantment. Mobilizing collective remittance resources for development projects back home creates political opportunities for migrants to participate and make decisions in local public affairs. But exercising the privilege of speaking with and for a community in which some members no longer physically reside raises fundamental social and political questions about who belongs and which voices should shape decisions that impact everyone in a political jurisdiction. Examining the transnational practice of providing public goods generates new insights into the ways in which international migration changes how citizens participate in local democracy, meanings of citizenship, and belonging in a world with millions of people on the move.

While there are several different kinds of nonstate actors involved in public goods provision, this book places the politics of migrant actors and the intermediary institutions of transnational public-private partnerships front and center. Public goods provision is a core function of subnational government in decentralized political systems like Mexico; therefore, when migrant social actors become involved in decisions that concern public welfare and resources, it blurs the boundaries between public and private spheres. The blurring of boundaries between who provides public goods and how they are provided is not a neutral, technocratic policy issue.[1] Rather, it is substantially consequential for political life in ways that have been poorly understood.

I attend to the political consequences of transnational partnerships in the strategic case of Mexico. Specifically, I study the process of coordinating public goods provision across the public-private divide, that is, between migrant hometown associations and public officials in the sending state, and highlight the ramifications of the process for three important political outcomes that bear directly on the quality of local democracy: civic and political participation, government responsiveness, and state-society relations. There are many dimensions of local democracy that transnational migration is likely to affect, but in the previous chapters, I examine democratic engagement at the local level and government officials' responses to transnational forms of collective action.

The book tackles the emergence, variation, and effect of migrant transnational partnerships at multiple levels of analysis, using original data collection and a mixed methodological approach. I find that while migrant resources create vertical links to sending states keen on courting resources earned abroad for public projects back home, the structure of migrant social ties and migrants' ability to negotiate meanings of belonging and membership in the hometown is also a critical determinant of democratic effects. By focusing much-needed attention on the intersection of social and political actors and institutions, I show how migrants' horizontal and vertical ties in the origin community create new modes of political participation. Social and political relations in the migrant transnational network shape the organization of cross-border collective action and the political consequences that result.

Specifically, migrant social embeddedness and political institutions at origin organize transnational partnerships differently. When partnerships are inclusive of the local citizenry and local government is engaged, the process of public goods provision creates more participatory governance. But when migrant groups are no longer embedded in the social fabric of the hometown or fail to forge ties to key stakeholders in the community and recruit them into the decision-making process, social exclusion stokes inequalities and sometimes depresses local political engagement. How migrants navigate the boundaries of social and cultural membership in their hometowns (when membership is no longer based on territorial residence) has different implications for democratic governance or what Dahl refers to as polyarchy.[2]

When countries experience substantial emigration, paying close attention to how existing local democracies function requires looking beyond domestic political borders and the messy space between the artificial walls of the "public" and "private."[3] Transnational actors, especially migrants and their organized social groups, transform how citizens engage the local government by inserting themselves back in local democracy, especially when newfound resources acquired abroad grant them decision-making opportunities in local politics not afforded to those without them. Aiming analytic attention at migrants' cross-border practices shows how decentralized democracies with substantial emigration actually work. We see with new lenses how migrant intervention in the hometown after departure upsets, reinforces, and transforms the ways in which citizens engage in local democracies and interface with elected representatives. We also see the ways in which acquiring a bargaining voice in democratic politics is enabled by remittances and not by territorial residence alone, which complicates traditional ideas of citizenship that are circumscribed by the political boundaries of the nation-state.

When migrants leave their countries seeking political freedom, economic opportunities, and family reunification, the people and places they leave behind rarely fall completely out of view. Certainly not all migrants are "transmigrants" taking action, making decisions, and developing subjectivities and identities in two or more nation-states.[4] All people everywhere do not lead transnational lives, and among those who do there is considerable variation in the sources and types of practices they engage in across borders. As important research shows, individuals and foreign-born groups embrace different "ways of being" and "ways of belonging" in transnational social fields.[5] But despite exit from the places of their birth, migrants continue to participate in quotidian and revolutionary practices in their places of origin that affect social, political, and economic life at home.[6]

CORE FINDINGS

The empirical heart of the book examines when, why, and how transnational partnerships emerge and transform local democratic governance. I find in the Mexican case that since the 1980s, neoliberal market reforms advocated by development banks including the World Bank and International Monetary Fund prescribed a reduced role for the state in social safety nets and decentralization reforms that offloaded the responsibility of public goods to subnational levels of government.[7] Concurrently, state retrenchment and decentering administrative authority opened up opportunities for domestic, international, and transnational nonstate actors and organizations to step in and assume a greater role in social welfare and public infrastructure provision. Political openings in former authoritarian states like Mexico meant more freedom for civic associations, including those in transnational civil society, to solve local problems through collective action without fear of state reprisal. Additionally, fiercer political competition meant more opportunities for opposition political parties to wrangle power and authority away from dominant parties such as the PRI and represent new constituencies, including migrant constituencies abroad.[8]

Moreover, since the late 1990s and early 2000s supranational organizations including the United Nations have sponsored migration and development initiatives in which government stakeholders, business elites, migrant organizations, and policy experts exchange best practices and the practical challenges of economic development. Directing increasing attention at the migration-development nexus, supranational organizations identified family and collective remittances as possible sources to fight poverty and fuel income-generating enterprises.[9] State retrenchment and decentralization efforts coupled with the rise in a "migration-development" discursive agenda encouraged policymakers to look to their diasporas for much-needed financial and human capital.

While the analysis in chapter 2 shows that macrostructural factors created the conditions of possibility for migrant cross-border involvement in local development, it also revealed that transnational partnerships are not necessarily automatic outgrowths of international migration. Rather, organized Mexican migrant groups' grassroots mobilization preceded the coordination of public policies to channel collective remittance resources for community development. Country-specific historic factors were critical antecedents to the creation of transnational public-private partnerships. But migrant hometown associations' bottom-up organizing and the sending state's top-down outreach to migrants during a period of democratization and decentralization produced feedback effects that facilitated the widespread adoption of coproduction partnerships as a strategy for public goods provision at the local level.

While a majority of municipalities participate in the 3x1 Program, a closer look at transnational partnerships using surveys, interviews, and comparative fieldwork shows that they are organized differently from place to place and over time. Partnerships vary in the degree to which local citizens are involved and local government engages in the coproduction process. Understanding this organizational variation provides a key window into why the political consequences also vary across and within migrant hometown communities.

The case studies show how migrants are embedded in varying degrees in the social bases of their origin communities after departure. The structure of pre-migration social networks determines, in part, the nature of the partnerships they build across international borders because migrant social networks vary in the extent to which they maintain bonding and bridging ties. More heterogeneous social ties reflect more social resources. They also reflect the variation of societal interests represented in negotiations, interactions, and decisions made between political officials and the local citizenry. When migrant social bases include both bonding and bridging ties in the hometown community, transnational coproduction is more likely to be inclusive and more egalitarian because it represents more of a plurality of societal interests. Since migrants are physically absent, they must draw on a wide array of social resources in the community for the coprovision of public goods to be most successful.

Although local government is administratively and politically responsible for provision, not all local government officials respond to coproduction opportunities with the same interest and engagement. The political institutional context creates different incentives for local political officials' engagement in partnerships with migrants. Moreover, in the Mexican context, municipal presidents (equivalent to mayors) are barred from individual reelection after serving a three-year term. Political incentives to participate in transnational partnerships reflect political parties' strategies for winning and maintaining office, and disruptions in party representation at the local level during periods of electoral transition interrupt how partnerships continue. The case of Telepi shows how this process unfolds through the change in political party in municipal office.

It is the dynamic interaction between community inclusion and government engagement that organizes coproduction partnerships differently, making them more synergetic, fragmented, corporatist, and substitutive. These four ideal typical forms of coproduction emerge from the interaction of migrant social networks and local political context. This is why migrant social groups that are otherwise similar, with the same resources, same size club, organizational capacity, and destination locale in the U.S., produce different consequences for local democracy.

The survey cluster analysis and statistical analysis using the Mexican Family Life Survey and panel data in chapter 6 provide a closer look into how partnerships vary and how emergent variation is associated with different short- and long-term effects on democratic functioning and state-society relations. When we telescope away from the organizational variation to assess the systematic effects of partnerships, the key finding is that repeated, continuous participation leads to more citizen participation in municipal elections and engagement in community activities such as neighborhood associations, religious groups, and social and civic associations like the Rotary and Lions clubs.

Finally, the panel analysis shows that transnational partnerships that occur in locales with preexisting endowments of social capital have more pronounced effects on democratic governance. In places where citizens are more engaged in community civic activities, local government devotes more public resources to social welfare spending. But preexisting bridging ties that enable more trust and cooperation between migrants and stay-at-homes are not a necessary condition for partnerships to succeed. Rather, the data shows that migrants who renegotiate their membership in the hometown and construct social ties to key community stakeholders learn how to effectively deliberate and cooperate through repeated interactions over multiple projects. The social learning process that accompanies doing development projects with migrant and state partners helps scale up citizen interest and engagement in local democracy, giving more marginalized groups new avenues to discuss and make demands on their political representatives.

In places where transnational partnerships are more erratic and have less community involvement, transnational partnerships subsidize and substitute for government social welfare spending. Continuous participation in coproduction activities that draw on the social resources and assets of origin communities experiences the highest gains in democratic engagement and responsive government. By focusing on multiple dimensions of local democratic quality and the organizational variation in transnational partnerships, empirical results from both qualitative and quantitative data provide compelling evidence that migrant partnerships not only improve citizens' access to public goods, they also enhance participatory governance when migrants' social ties are multiplex.[10]

EMIGRANT CITIZENSHIP

Migrant involvement in public goods provision decouples substantive citizenship—that is, forms of civic and political participation—from territorial residence. Political and civic participation without territorial residence challenges neat conceptions of the nation-state as a bounded political territory with fixed populations[11] because migrant collective action complicates membership and belonging in the political community. These questions about membership, belonging, and ultimately citizenship emerge because the foray by migrants into collective action for development is in the public domain of the hometown and substantive, legitimate participation in the public, political sphere is predicated on belonging.[12]

As Levitt and Glick Schiller (2004) argue, there are differences between "ways of being"—ongoing cross-border activities—and "ways of belonging"—practices signaling an identity with another people or place. The results of this book reveal the need to pay careful attention to how particular kinds of transnational practices take belonging for granted. Membership in the hometown political community is not guaranteed after exit. International migration involves connections that cross territorial units, and while immigrants may be oriented toward their hometowns and those immigrants have an affiliation and affection with it, connectivity and social collectivity are analytically and practically distinct.[13] Migrants have the power and legitimacy to use collective voice in political life in origin communities in which they no longer continuously reside when they renegotiate their cultural membership in the hometown community. When migrants are no longer perceived as members of the social and political community, but participate in public, political life as if they were territorial residents, nonmigrant citizens react to migrants' intervention either by struggling for recognition through democratic channels of participation or, in some cases, by retreating from political life and becoming more disengaged from civil society and politics. Exclusion often makes people stop trying to be relevant actors in local political affairs.

In some instances, as the case of Atitlan shows, the competition for recognition between extraterritorial migrants and territorial citizens can result in new social divisions and sources of political inequality that mobilize political activism in the short run, but ultimately displace nonmigrants' interest and engagement in local politics as coproduction activities become more corporatist and, often, clientelistic. But when migrants renegotiate their social membership by constructing social ties with local stakeholders, recruiting residents into the coproduction process, and practicing cultural repertoires of community, these inclusive practices affirm social solidarity between migrant and nonmigrant citizens and legitimate migrants' local authority. The case of El Cerrito provides compelling evidence of these processes taking shape over time.

Cross-border social solidarity between migrant and nonmigrant citizens enables substantive participation in the public sphere of decision-making around public goods provision. While these struggles for group recognition and boundary-making can occur when organized migrant groups wield resources to be used in the local public domain, the sending state's emigrant policies facilitate and foreclose migrant groups' entrance into local political processes. The Mexican sending state, for example, does not allow extraterritorial citizens to vote in local elections, and although such citizens maintain certain rights and protections from the sending state while abroad (dual nationality, expatriate voting in national elections), their rights to participate and affect *local* politics are otherwise limited relative to Mexican territorial nationals.[14] Mobilizing their collective remittances resources for development projects is one way in which migrants channel their interests and ambitions and affect the democratic process, even if the political effects are unintended.

De jure citizenship or legal status citizenship is a guarantee extended by the country of origin to its nationals abroad. Even after departure the state promises emigrants that should they want or need to return and remain, they have indefinite permission to do so in the territorial space of the homeland. But while emigrants maintain the right to return, their substantive citizenship, and their ability to participate as full rather than nominal citizens in the public and political life of the home country, remains predicated on political belonging.[15] When migrants use collective resources and voice in the political affairs of their hometowns, they practice not just *de jure* citizenship but *substantive* citizenship as well. Legal scholar Kim Barry argues: "Citizenship is embedded in, as well as constitutive of, community, and its legitimacy depends on that community's approval."[16] The findings in this book buttress Barry's theoretical contention and explore the implications of migrant *transnational* public goods provision across borders for meanings and practices of emigrant citizenship.

Migrant membership in the hometown political community is a question that is contested, negotiated, and defined when migrants contribute resources and help make decisions about public goods provision from beyond national borders. Migrants' legitimate participation in development processes in countries of origin is predicated on being socially embedded after exit because the structure of social ties and practices of solidarity effectuate membership in the political community.

THE PARADOX AND POLITICS OF CROSS-BORDER COLLECTIVE ACTION

Understanding the conditions under which citizens use voice, loyalty, and exit tells us a great deal about the quality of local democratic institutions as mechanisms of political and social accountability in places beset by significant emigration. How citizens respond to government performance reveals the likelihood that government officials will respond to citizen dissatisfaction or lose out to the competition. Albert Hirschman explored these processes through his seminal exit-voice-loyalty triptych.

In Hirschman's framework, exit and voice are mutually exclusive options and loyalty reflects citizens' efforts to preserve the status quo. Either people "exit" the political system and take their support elsewhere or they use "voice" to try and change the behavior of the target, in this case the state. In the context of international migration, exit is a physical act. Migrants leave their countries of origin for greener pastures when the state has failed them. For migrants, it is exit that creates the condition of possibility for voice. By emigrating and voting with their feet abroad, migrants are able to save and send remittances. Migrants' collective resources create opportunities to participate in local government affairs from abroad. But to understand migrant cross-border collective action in the hometown, Hirschman's "loyalty" concept must be refashioned to capture not just the preservation of the status quo of loyal citizens remaining behind, but as a necessary precondition for migrants' cross-border engagement.

As scores of studies in the transnational migration literature show, not all migrants maintain the same level of attachment to homeplace nor do they sustain the same kinds of transnational and translocal practices and passions across international borders. Those migrants who do choose to engage in cross-border conversations, information sharing, remittance sending, and public goods provision, for example, are those for whom loyalty is a given or has been cultivated by the sending state through outreach initiatives. The goal of this book is not to explain who is loyal and how much loyalty they have for the people and places they leave behind in Mexico or other countries of origin. Rather, I argue that loyalty is a precondition for cross-border collective action. The migrants I study in this book are loyal to their hometowns, even if the use of voice and exit may be mired in conflict in some places and received with more open arms in others. The starting point for this book is based on migrants' shared connections and loyalty to their places of origin. The variation I explain is focused, instead, on how migrant groups' ability to exercise voice and exit *simultaneously* is enabled and constrained by the social and political relationships that preexist in hometowns and is transformed by the process of cross-border collective action.

I posed a question at the beginning of this book. Can loyal migrants exercise voice and exit simultaneously? The answer this book provides is, well, yes and no. Although migrants form hometown clubs, pool resources, and work together to provide public goods projects in their places of origin, they are no longer territorial residents yet maintain legal personhood. Territorial citizens are ascribed full membership status regardless of whether they participate in the political and social affairs of their town because they are denizens. Citizenship grants migrants certain rights to substantively participate in home country affairs from beyond national borders even though they are not directly subject to the policies they help enact precisely because they left and migrated abroad for a chance at a better life. But emigration constrains migrants' collective participation in local public affairs when they are no longer socially embedded in the hometown nor perceived as members who still belong in the political community. Feeling socially connected to a hometown does not necessarily evoke consensus over meanings of belonging and membership and legitimate voice is contingent on renegotiating cultural membership after exit.[17] This is the paradox of cross-border collective action in local democracy and development.

Although many immigrants lack full membership in the destination country because they lack legal status citizenship, exercising voice in the home country may be one of only a handful of ways in which those who want to can engage in political life. For immigrants who wish to feel part of a polity, to be valued, to be included in a political and social community, investing in hometown development with remittances gives them an opportunity to participate in a political system as if they had never left. In many ways, migrants channel their political, social, and economic grievances in the destination country to the homeland where their substantive citizenship is not completely barred.[18] But when voice in public affairs is materially conditioned by remittances and exit, some migrants are met with opposition from local residents who no longer identify them and their groups as legitimate members of the local political community with the authority to speak with and for the citizenry.

The "right" combination of exit, voice, and loyalty is difficult to achieve and transnational partnerships between migrants, states, and local citizens often fail, exacerbate inequalities, and reinforce elite power relations. It is not enough for migrants to be socially connected; they must also be able to overcome perceived status differences that arise when migrants leave their places or origin for richer countries abroad. Examining the process of coordinating public goods across the public-private divide reinforces how nonstate actors,[19] be they nongovernmental organizations (NGOs), sectarian and religious organizations, or migrant clubs, can nurture trust and cooperation and scale up local participation when they build on social assets and work through preexisting institutions in project recipient communities. But negotiating the complex terrain of local politics and the transnational social network to make local democracy work from abroad is a high bar for migrants and their groups to clear.

MOVING BEYOND THE MEXICAN CASE

The findings of this research underscore the importance of studying the sources of variation in transnational practices across geography and time. How migrants engage in hometown development is unlikely to be the same in Mexico as it is in China or Ghana or the Philippines and beyond.[20] This variation is rooted in differences in the nature and composition of migratory streams, social networks, and other factors that are endemic to origin and sending states. Origin countries vary in the intensity of ethnolinguistic fractionalization, state capacity, sociodemographic characteristics of emigrants, and political regime dynamics, for example. Moreover, destination countries vary in the degree of civil liberties and freedom to associate into collective groups. And sending states develop vastly different emigrant incorporation strategies to their diasporas abroad. Migrant social ties are a key factor in explaining the kinds of migrant cross-border partnerships that prevail, but they are also determined, in part, by the ways in which sending and destination states make room for nonstate migrant actors to intervene.

The findings of this book illustrate the importance of unpacking the role of "the state" and migrant transnational social network ties simultaneously to better understand the roots and feedback effects and organizational dynamics of transnational public-private partnerships. When considering migrant development practices and the emigrant outreach initiatives of sending states across countries, researchers would be wise to heed sociologist David FitzGerald's call to analyze from a neopluralist perspective; that is, one in which "the state" is disaggregated into multi-level constituent units wherein political actors at different levels of government compete for their interests.[21] When researchers unpack sending states' competing interests in this way, more variation across and within emigrant outreach policies may be explained. For example, Gamlen and colleagues have begun to typologize sending states' "diaspora engagement" policies according to whether they are more aimed at discursively producing a state-centric diaspora, extending rights to the diaspora that legitimate sending-state sovereignty, and extracting obligations from loyal emigrants abroad.[22]

Disaggregating (local, state, national) state interests according to these three categories eventuates the identification of patterns across diverse sending states according to whether emigration policies are more exploitative, generous, or engaged in extracting obligations with or without also granting social and political rights to the diaspora living abroad.[23] As researchers identify the emigrant/diaspora engagement policies that differentially enable and constrain migrants' interest in developing their countries of origin through the extension of social rights, representation, national belonging and citizenship, what Bhagwati has called the "web of rights and obligations,"[24] we can more easily compare and contrast transnational partnerships across more diverse institutional terrains.

The neopluralist state perspective will also necessitate a closer evaluation of the domestic political environment across sending countries. This should include assessing the extent to which political systems are decentralized, institutions consolidated, and state capacity sufficiently coherent bureaucratically to enable public-private partnership with organized migrant groups to bloom and succeed. And as this book shows, a neopluralist state approach will also need to consider the nature of social relations in and across migrant hometowns. In doing so, researchers are likely to gain new insights into why some governments have been able to formally engage their organized diasporas abroad in various matching grants and co-development policies with grassroots migrant associations, and why other sending states are more likely to partner with more elite business and nongovernment organizations. A neopluralist, comparative approach would also shed additional light on why some country cases pursue a more laissez-faire approach to emigrant outreach and home country development.[25]

Beyond Mexico, how migrants pursue public goods initiatives with minimal or no material or symbolic support from public agencies in sending or destination countries continues to be an area ripe for further study. There is also very little accumulated knowledge concerning how migrant intervention in public goods provision across diverse countries of origin produces political and development consequences at the subnational and national levels. Research shows that migrant HTAs have worked independently and oftentimes at cross-purposes with local and state governments, and with the tacit support of sending states in the production of infrastructure and social welfare. But how well the theoretical framework I present here explains political consequences beyond the Mexican case to other country cases with (and without) cofinancing programs is as yet unknown.

I hope future scholarship will assess the external validity of the framework I offer in other country contexts. In testing the theory across more (or less) democratic sending and receiving country contexts, ethnically heterogeneous groups and migrant classes, for example, the theory may need to be amended to reflect a wider constellation of political and social incentives and network ties that govern cross-border public-private partnerships. The comparative framework may also be used to classify more hybrid forms of transnational public-private partnership for development beyond migrant hometown associations to include other kinds of migrant actors such as business elites and entrepreneurs and transnational sectarian and religious-based organizations with migrant leadership in countries with substantial emigration and engaged diasporas as diverse as India, China, Vietnam, Cambodia, Lebanon, Syria, and the Philippines.

As I describe in the introduction, the Mexican case is unique in that the state and federal governments developed a social spending program to match migrants' collective resources for community development ends that other emigration states have attempted to emulate in a variety of ways. It is as yet unclear how an end to the 3x1 Program would affect migrant groups' ability to finance public goods or the extent to which the spillover effects on social capital and civic and political engagement would be able to mobilize collection action for public goods provision, or other objectives, in the absence of the state's involvement. This question will be of importance in the Mexican context as increasing political competition at the national level leaves open the question of whether the federal 3x1 Program will continue through political party representation in the presidency. As of July 2018, the PRD will command the presidency for the first time in Mexican political history, and relative to other major political parties (PAN and PRI) it is underrepresented in coproduction partnerships at the municipal level.

Furthermore, as Hirschman's principle of conservation and mutation of social energy makes clear, collective action in one endeavor, even when it fails, can be mobilized for new purposes and political uses in future time periods.[26] If the 3x1 Program and transnational coproduction partnership ceased to exist, the positive spillovers from more inclusive partnerships such as improved political efficacy and interest in politics could be transformed and used in alternative participatory spheres at a later date and for other purposes. The long-term consequences of migrant partnerships for local democracy remain to be seen.

CIVIL SOCIETY, SOCIAL ACCOUNTABILITY, AND TRANSNATIONAL COPRODUCTION

Beyond the role that democracy—narrowly understood as elections—has on government performance, this research shows how nonelectoral modes of engagement affect democratic quality. Political participation, which includes a range of activities that have the intent or effect of influencing government action either directly by affecting the making or implementation of policy or indirectly by influencing the selection of people who make those policies, also improves government responsiveness.[27] Through pestering, protesting, petitioning, and *coproducing public works* with public agencies, resident and extraterritorial citizens work to improve their lot in life. These participatory strategies can be complementary to robust political competition,[28] and these strategies influence local government responsiveness directly when migrant-state coproduction is synergetic and ongoing.[29] When citizens and migrant groups assume more than the "watchdog" function, they break the state's monopoly on the responsibility of public goods provision and directly participate in this core function of local government.[30]

Being open to the role of migrant coproducer explains changes in political and civic participation even in places where we would expect substantial emigration to have more depressing effects.

Coproduction partnerships also serve as an additional collective mechanism in the provision of public goods and services, but when they approximate synergy they also expand the institutional terrain in which citizens and local representatives deliberate to solve local problems through nonelectoral channels. External social groups like migrant hometown associations mobilize new networks of engagement and collective action across the public-private "divide."[31] These inclusive and engaging public-private partnerships generate alternative locales for negotiations about the distribution of resources. Synergetic migrant-state coproduction improves development, but it also introduces new mechanisms of accountability through social action.

Social accountability refers to a broad range of actions beyond voting that citizens, communities, and civic society organizations can use to hold government officials and bureaucrats accountable.[32] The range of activities include citizen participation in public policy making, participatory budgeting, public expenditure tracking, monitoring public service delivery, advisory boards, lobbying, and advocacy campaigns. Citizens' direct involvement in managing public resources, selecting projects designed to meet their needs, and monitoring the implementation of projects is a novel mode of political participation that can be an effective means of exacting social accountability that is complementary to electoral institutions of formal political accountability, especially when they are weak or absent.[33]

Electoral competition is a major mechanism of organizational "recuperation," although voice is another significant alternative to this mechanism and can come into play either when political competition is unavailable or as a complement to it. Choosing projects, finalizing budgets, developing technical plans, and obtaining appropriate permits, for example, are not without the normal complications that accompany decision-making among multiple actors—coproduction partnerships are an arena for both contestation and compromise. How migrant clubs position themselves vis-a-vis the state and how the local state positions itself vis-a-vis the citizenry have important consequences for state-society relations. These kinds of messy processes are what we should expect in local democracies where citizens and political representatives are learning to interact in some places for the first time after protracted authoritarian rule. Negotiating mechanisms that incorporate the voices of more marginalized groups is the very essence of democratic decision-making.

But what of migrant sending communities and countries of origin in which a weak state is incapable or unwilling to provide even the most basic public good: public security? I focus exclusively on public infrastructure and social welfare provision and only discuss one case of a failed partnership in which a corrupt, weak local-state apparatus led to the demise of the transnational partnership in the context of rising violence related to the drug trade. There are many countries around the world in which a weak and predatory state is anathema to external social actors' involvement in state functions and the introduction of new forms of social accountability. What does the transnational public provision of goods and services look like in places where social order is not a given? The Mexican case provides another window into these questions after 2006 in which rising violence spread in the central western plateau states with high levels of migration.

RISING VIOLENCE, MUNICIPAL GOVERNANCE, AND PUBLIC GOODS PROVISION

On January 2, 2016, Gisela Mota was murdered by four armed gunmen in her home one day after being sworn in as mayor of Temixco, Morelos. Four weeks into her campaign, Aidé Nava González, a mayoral candidate for the municipality of Ahuacuotzingo, Guerrero, was decapitated and left with a *narcomanta*, a warning message, directed at other political candidates. This was after González's husband, Francisco Quiñónez Ramírez, who was the mayor of Ahuacuotzingo from 2009 to 2012, announced his plans to run again and was murdered in 2014 ahead of the election. Three weeks after Rogelio Sánchez Galán won the mayoral election in Jerecuaro, Guanajuato, he was shot dead at a bus stop. The list goes on and on. Over the last decade, hired killers called *sicarios* have killed more than 100 mayors and mayoral candidates, making Mexico the third-highest country with assassinated mayors in the world.[34]

Drug-related violence in Mexico escalated in 2006 after Panista president Calderón announced a militarized war on the drug cartels. Cartels have been competing for territory, fighting for political power, and scouring new sources of revenue throughout Mexico in response to the crackdown on the drug trade. Migratory flows, remittance transfers, and transnational partnerships have not been immune to the rise in drug-related violence throughout the country. Many individuals, families, and HTAs have responded in strategic albeit different ways. In some cases, migrants have diverted their remittance resources earned abroad away from public infrastructure and community development projects and toward financing public security and social order, a different and essential public good. In others, HTAs ceased to invest transnationally in their communities of origin when security concerns became too threatening.

Migrants in the U.S. have had to adapt their investment strategies in Mexico in response to drug-related violence. When the Los Rojos in Morelos, Knights Templar (KTO) in Michoacán, and the Jalisco New Generation cartels, among others, identified municipal government coffers as new opportunities to control resources, cofinancing public goods with migrant groups was imperiled. In addition to extortion, kidnapping for ransom, and the drug trade, criminal organizations started to compete for political control of municipal government. The gangs that worked for the larger cartel organizations threatened and murdered mayoral candidates and mayors in office were sent somber warnings of what would happen when they do not comply with the cartel's demands.

Additionally, cartels and gangs associated with larger criminal networks forced mayors to yield percentages of their annual budgets to them, which affected their fiscal capacity to provide public goods including public security, public infrastructure, and social welfare independently and in cooperation with migrant HTAs. Cartels have also demanded contracts for building public projects and the selection of municipal police chiefs. Servando "La Tuta" Gómez, former leader of the KTO cartel before his capture in 2015, was known to meet face to face with mayors to make his demands. In other egregious cases, individuals who were directly affiliated with the cartels became municipal mayors. While in office they reportedly ordered the assassinations of individuals of the political opposition and of other individuals with whom they had personal vendettas. The mayors were also alleged to have siphoned public resources to fund the KTO in the municipalities of Parácuaro, Aguililla, Apatzingán and Tacámbaro, Michoacán.[35] News articles, photos, videos, and eyewitness testimony suggest this also became common practice across municipalities in southern Jalisco and Guanajuato as early as 2012. Cartel competition for political control of local government has sown terror across municipalities in Mexico and disrupted political officials' interest and capacity to provide public works with and without migrant groups.

The rise and horror of *La Violencia* throughout Mexico has direct and indirect effects on the local governance of public goods and migrant transnational partnerships as the case of Santa Catarina shows. Migrant families have been murdered and targeted for kidnappings in which gangs demanded remittances as ransoms. Public insecurity and generalized fear have thwarted civic engagement as citizens have opted to stay safe by keeping low profiles and out of public spaces. This fear has depressed community participation generally and in transnational partnerships, specifically. Migrant leadership of hometown associations in high crime areas has also halted coproduction activities in response to the rise in criminal organizations and violence in hometown communities. Until some migrant leaders feel conditions have improved and their activities will not put residents and paisanos in harm's way, many choose to suspend coproduction partnerships with public agencies.

Furthermore, my discussions with migrant leaders of HTAs in Guanajuato and Jalisco reveal that criminal organizations have seized upon the 3x1 Program to extract revenue.[36] Extracting a percentage of the matching funds from migrant, municipal, state, and federal partners, cartels and their gang affiliates have identified the federal program as a lucrative revenue stream. Local gangs require bribes for the completion of 3x1 projects as well as kickbacks from labor and building contractors hired for coproduction projects. In other cases, criminal organizations have required municipal officials and migrants to inflate the cost of 3x1 projects at the project proposal stage and then skimmed the money directly from the municipal treasury once it has been deposited by coproduction partners. Finally, some municipal administrators have fabricated HTAs, referred to informally as "ghost clubs," to propose public goods projects and then delivered matching funds directly to criminal organizations. Since 2012 and likely before, the 3x1 Program has been co-opted by criminal organizations in some Mexican municipalities, especially in those in southern Guanajuato, Jalisco, Morelos, Michoacán, and Guerrero, which has discouraged the formation and continuation of many coproduction partnerships. And as the case of Santa Catarina shows, violence has also affected the organization of partnerships through its impact on the level of community inclusion and government engagement in the 3x1 Program.

How drug-related violence and public security concerns systematically impact partnerships is a known unknown. In many cases, HTAs temporarily stop their efforts and take a "wait and see" approach. In one of the synergetic partnerships I present in this book, a municipal official was allegedly extorted by the KTO in 2013, which demanded a percentage of matching funds destined for public works projects through the 3x1 Program. Since gang leadership changed so frequently, paisanos had trouble identifying who the culprit was and the extent to which the continuation of 3x1 projects put members of their club and the public works committee in danger. In response, they decided to "lay low" until a new municipal administration came into power. In the meantime, the club sought out alternative state and federal programs to the 3x1 Program to finance social welfare in the hometown in less conspicuous ways.

By contrast, in other cases, especially in the state of Michoacán where the KTO has savagely attacked municipal authorities and migrant families, citizens have said enough is enough. In hard-hit regions where the state has failed to ensure public security and social order, locals and migrants abroad have taken up arms in the collective struggle against violence and property seizure. HTAs have also diversified their activities to support *autodefensas* in Mexico. *Autodefensas* are self-defense public security forces akin to militias that use violence to challenge criminal organizations themselves. Leaders and members of the *autodefensas* movement have links to migration and hometown associations.[37] For example, the leader of the militia movement in Michoacán, Jose Manuel Mireles, is a former migrant from Sacramento, California, who returned to fight the militias when migrants' wives and schoolgirls as young as 12 years old were being systematically raped by KTO members. The second in command, Antonio Torres Gonzalez, who is known as "El Americano" because he was born in the U.S., joined Mireles's militia after he was kidnapped on an annual visit to his hometown and held for $150,000 ransom. Many members of *autodefensas* are migrants who have returned to their hometowns voluntarily or forcibly by the U.S. government through deportation and taken up arms for income or for revenge against the cartels who have terrorized families in their hometowns.

Many migrant returnees, individuals deported from the U.S., and leaders of hometown associations in conjunction with nonmigrant citizens have mobilized in response to the violence plaguing their communities. Since HTAs are unable to cofinance public security measures through the 3x1 Program, many associations have chosen to fund the militias using collective remittances in lieu of investment in public infrastructure and social welfare projects. Since their formation, these militias have been effective at disrupting the KTO's operations and restoring some social order, efforts the Mexican military and local and state police forces have been unable to do in many high migration areas around the country.

Working together, migrants and residents have been effective at regaining some social order through transnational collective action. In response to the rise in violence and weak state capacity to supply public security and enforcement, migrants have mobilized the skills, remittance resources, and social network connections facilitated by public-private partnerships to invest time, energy, and resources away from public infrastructure and social welfare provision and toward the provision of public security. The role of migrant civic associations, transnational partnerships, and return migration has important implications for the study of public goods provision and state capacity. Researchers must focus attention on how endowments of social capital created by transnational collective action affect state capacity and public insecurity in conflict and postconflict states in Mexico and beyond. And because there is the possibility that armed militia, including *autodefensas*, may "turn bad," researchers will need to better interrogate how international migration and remittances enable and constrain threats to public security and social order.

The Mexican case also calls attention to more general concerns about the likelihood of achieving development and public goods provision that improves citizens' quality of life in weak states. As migrant remittances surpass $600 billion worldwide with over $400 billion flowing directly to developing countries in 2016, many in the donor community are celebrating remittance-led development as the next solution to underdevelopment. Additionally, participatory development and cogovernance arrangement made possible by the range of nonstate actors and intermediary institutions involved in public goods provision have filled in where market failures and state provision left many without a modicum of social welfare. But remittance-led participatory development faces extreme obstacles if states cannot even ensure public security and social order. For migration to have positive effects on public goods provision and local democracy through cross-border collective action, the state must be willing and able to restore security. If not, the collective action and financial and social resources mobilized for development may next be used to challenge the state for authority in other public domains. It may also be used for transnational social mobilization to resist home country regimes as migrants from Syria, Yemen, and other countries did with varying levels of success during the Arab Spring.[38]

Comparative Fieldwork in Mexico

In chapters 3, 4, and 5, I traced the micro-foundations of transnational partnerships across six cases. Cases, in this context, refer to different transnational partnerships between migrant hometown associations and municipal governments in Mexico. In each of the cases, I analyzed the process through which one or more public goods projects were completed with cofinancing from the Mexican municipal, state, and federal governments and migrant club partners in the 3x1 Program. The central objective of the case studies was to trace how local social and political factors shaped community inclusion and government engagement over time and combined to produce different organizational types of coproduction. Since I was in each town for only a few months, in addition to firsthand observations, informal chats, and in-depth interviews with key actors, I also conducted retrospective interviews with relevant migrant, citizen, and political actors. This combination of data collection in real-time and actors' reflections on previous projects helped me to develop a more complete picture of how the coproduction process transpired over time.

I selected six cases for in-depth fieldwork that exhibited variation on both community inclusion and government engagement. The multi-sited, comparative fieldwork occurred in the states of Jalisco (Comarga and Santa Catarina), Guanajuato (Ahuacatl and Selvillo), and Zacatecas (Telepi). Four partnership cases were in four different municipalities, but in one of the municipalities in Jalisco, I studied two transnational partnerships in different localities in the same municipality. Originally, I planned to only study a partnership based in Atitlan, a locality located outside the county seat of the municipality of Comarga, but during my fieldwork, locals and political officials recommended I visit another locality that also had a migrant club that formed at the same time but had gone through a different experience during the coproduction process. This proved to be a fruitful, albeit spontaneous addition to the analysis. Since I studied variation in partnerships within one municipality, government engagement was held constant, but the level of community inclusion varied substantially across the partnerships. The case comparison in two different localities in the

Government Engagement	Community Inclusion: High	Community Inclusion: Low
High	*Synergetic* El Cerrito Ahuacatl El Mirador Telepi	*Corporatist* Atitlan
Low	*Substitutive* El Cerrito Telepi	*Fragmented* Santa Catarina

FIGURE 7. Schematic table showing the distribution of comparative case studies by transnational partnership type.

same municipality showed me why and how migrant social embeddedness varied, led to different kinds of community inclusion, and resulted in different partnership types and political effects.

First and foremost, the cases selected for fieldwork exhibited variation in levels of community inclusion and government engagement according to how migrant leadership responded to questions in the original transnational survey. The survey included several questions about the frequency with which local residents participated in the selection of projects, volunteered their labor, contributed resources, monitored projects during and after implementation, and interacted with municipal officials. The survey also asked about when and how the club came together, sociodemographic characteristics of migrant club leadership, and included several questions about the involvement of municipal government officials. These and other survey questions provided an indication of the extent of local government and resident involvement in the coproduction process, and information about migrant club capacity, structure, and membership size. To complement this data, I also collected sociodemographic, fiscal, political, and 3x1 Program characteristics for each municipality in which a migrant club reported coproduction activities. I evaluated how levels of migration and poverty, state capacity (municipal tax revenues), political party affiliation, and population size varied across partnership cases. Additionally, I analyzed 3x1 Program data for each partnership case including the number and types of projects, budget expenditures, and frequency of program participation. I used all of the data from multiple sources to formulate a comprehensive profile of 250 transnational partnerships that represented clubs that took the survey.

Once I had complete data for all the survey respondents and their corresponding municipalities and localities of origin, I stratified the sample based on the composite indices

I created for community inclusion and government engagement (see Data Appendix C). Next, using difference of means tests, I analyzed whether political, fiscal, and sociodemographic characteristics were correlated with levels of community inclusion and government engagement. I identified cases that had different combinations of community inclusion and government engagement and analyzed whether levels of poverty, local-bureaucratic capacity, party affiliation of the municipal incumbent, population size, migration intensity, club capacity, method of club formation, and leadership characteristics were statistically related to the inclusion and engagement indices using t-tests and ANOVA. Finally, I selected a group of partnerships that varied in their levels of community inclusion and government engagement but represented the average case in terms of the survey sample respondents that had high and low levels. I then contacted the club leaders and asked follow-up questions about their survey participation and discussed my plans to conduct fieldwork in Mexico.

On a preliminary trip, I visited several municipalities to assess the feasibility of more extended fieldwork. Based on observations and discussions with key informants, I selected five municipalities in Guanajuato, Zacatecas, and Jalisco, three traditional high-migration states, to conduct comparative case analysis. Initially, I hoped to conduct fieldwork in Michoacán and Durango, but during my discussions with migrant club leaders and local informants, I was persuaded that the uptick in violence in these states made it unsafe for me to stay in the towns. In addition to the five municipalities I discuss at length in the chapters, I also made trips to San Luis Potosí and Colima to visit two municipalities for a few days that had active and failed transnational partnerships.

The partnerships and their places of origin ultimately selected for fieldwork shared several similarities. First, they were all municipalities that had similar levels and history of migration intensity. In all but one municipality, there was a history of migration dating back to the Bracero period (1942–64), and a spike in migration during the late 1980s and early 1990s in response to macroeconomic crises and the downturn in agricultural production. In all of the municipalities of origin, migration intensity according to the INEGI index that accounts for the percent of households with a migrant abroad, return migration, household remittances, and circular migration was classified as "medium" or "high." In many cases, between 10 and 50 percent of households in the county seat or locality had received remittances from the United States in the five-year period between 2000 and 2005.

Second, in all of the partnerships, the migrant club reported similar levels of club capacity, meaning the club had a core group of dedicated club members, ability to fundraise collective resources from paisanos, and an organizational structure for decision-making. Additionally, a few of the clubs were members of a state-level federation of migrant clubs in which information was exchanged between migrant club leaders that helped improve fundraising and navigating bureaucratic paperwork involved in the 3x1 Program. Moreover, most of the migrant club leaders had benefitted from the passage of the Immigration Reform and Control Act of 1986 and either became lawful permanent residents (LPRs) themselves or another member of the club leadership circle was an LPR and able to traverse the U.S.-Mexican border with relative ease. In most cases, the clubs selected for in-depth analysis had all formed in the early 2000s, except for the case of *Familias de Telepi*, which formed in the early 1990s. Finally, most of the club leaders had been in the U.S. for 10 years or longer, but the age at which they arrived in the U.S. differed, which I discuss more in

TABLE 1. Characteristics of Case Study Transnational Partnerships.

	Santa Catarina	Atitlan	Telepi	El Cerrito	Ahuacatl	El Mirador
Sociodemographic Characteristics	Fragmented	Corporatist	Synergetic→ Substitutive	Substitutive→ Synergetic	Synergetic→ Inactive	Synergetic
Total Population in County Seat	10,000	18,000	9,000	95,000	60,000	18,000
Number of Localities	5	24	35	47	8	24
Projects in County Seat	Yes	No	Yes	No	No	No
Total Population	4,951	361	8,954	3,904	3,700	380
Poverty Index	High	Medium	High	Low	High	High
Migration Intensity Index	Medium	Medium	High	High	Medium	Medium
Local Political Context						
Local-State Capacity	Poor with budget constraints; severe public security threats from drug trade; PAN mayor has university degree, previous mayors only high school; authoritarian enclave	Middle income; depends on state and federal programs for public works budget; mayor received professional training at state level; engineers on staff	Poor with severe budget constraints; public works director engineer; PRD staff minimal training; allegations of PRD electoral corruption	Middle-income municipality; focus budget expenditures on county seat; engineers on staff to provide technical project support; extensive migrant outreach initiatives	Middle income; depends on state and federal programs for public works budget; mayor is career politician; engineers on staff; state outreach	Middle income; depends on state and federal programs for public works budget; mayor received professional training at state level; engineers on staff

Political Party in Power Party ID of Opposition Winner	PRI→PAN/PRD PAN-PRD Alliance victory after runoff 2010–2013	PAN→PRI PRI 2012–2015	PRI→PRD→PRI PRD 2007–2010	PAN→PRI→PAN PRI 2009–2012	PAN→PRI PRI	PAN→PRI PRI 2012–2015
Political Competition	Recently Competitive	PAN Stronghold	PRI Stronghold	Competitive	Competitive	PAN Stronghold
Year of First Opposition Victory	2010	1992	2007	1992	1986	1992
Migrant Hometown Association						
Year Formed	2005	2005	1990	2005	2005	2005
Origin	Club came together at the request of locals and church	Mayor asked paisanos to form club	Club came together on their own	Club came together on their own	Local residents asked club to form	Mayor asked paisanos to form club
Club Capacity	High	Low	High	High	Low	High
Length of Time in the U.S.	18 years	45 years	30 years	15 years	20 years	20 years
Club Membership Size	5 core decision-makers; 200–500 members in Chicago metro	1 leader; loose coalition of 50 members in TX & CA	5 core families; +1,000 supporters in S. CA & Central Valley	3 leaders; 15 core members; +1,000 supporters (4 cities)	3 leaders; + loose coalition of 30 members in TX & CA	3 leader; 6 core families + supporters from nearby town

SOURCE: Data compiled from fieldwork, in-person and telephone interviews, survey instrument, Sedesol, and Institute of National Elections.

the chapters. Leadership educational attainment was not correlated with either community inclusion or government engagement.

Finally, I examined hometowns with high or medium levels of poverty as measured by the Mexican census's marginalization index. I use the language of hometown in this context because in some partnership cases, projects benefitted the entire municipality (Telepi and Santa Catarina), but in others, the partnership coproduced public goods for a locality outside the county seat (Ahuacatl, Atitlan, El Mirador, El Cerrito). The marginalization index accounted for the percent of households with dirt floors, illiteracy, access to water and electricity, income that was two standard deviations below the mean household income, and other factors in the year 2000. In all of the *municipalities* of origin, marginalization was classified as "medium" or "low," but the localities were worse off and were classified as having "high" or "medium" levels of poverty. I indicate the poverty classification for the relevant geography in Table 1. I allowed other characteristics to vary across transnational partnership type including level of political competition, party affiliation of the incumbent between 2008 and 2010, club membership size, population size, government capacity to provide public goods, and U.S. city where the migrant club was based. There was no clear statistical relationship between community inclusion and government engagement and these characteristics. Nonetheless, I selected cases where there was some variation on these indicators in the event there was more to be gleaned about how these characteristics shaped partnerships while I was in the field.

The six cases selected for fieldwork approximate different combinations of community inclusiveness and government engagement and organize transnational partnerships into four types—synergetic (high/high), substitutive (high/low), corporatist (low/high), and fragmented (low/low). The cases provide an example of each kind of partnership, but because interactions and relationships forged between migrant, political, and local actors were ongoing, the degree of community inclusiveness and government engagement sometimes changed. In each case, I highlight (chapters 3 and 4) how and why the two main factors that organized the partnerships increased and decreased over time and approximated more intermediate partnership forms. I did not conduct in-depth analysis of a "pure" substitutive partnership type. Initially, I selected the case of Telepi to investigate substitutive coproduction since at the time the migrant club leader who completed the survey responded that they exhibited low levels of government engagement and higher levels of community inclusion. However, I learned during my fieldwork more about the history of transnational coproduction in the hometown and how political party turnover disrupted a six-year synergetic partnership. I was able to observe in real-time the breakdown of a synergetic partnership to a substitutive partnership as a result of local political conditions and chose the case for that reason.

Moreover, I selected the case of El Cerrito as emblematic of a synergetic partnership but learned during fieldwork that the case was best described as substitutive up to the year prior to my arrival in the town. I was able to witness firsthand how an increase in community inclusion led to increased government engagement, and the improvement in citizen-state relations and political participation that occurred as a direct result.

Transnational Matched Survey Data Instrument

The Mexican government maintains a database of immigrant organizations updated annually at the Institute for Mexicans Abroad (IME).[1] When HTAs propose 3x1 projects, either individual HTAs or the state-level federations, they are members of register with the IME. The IME collects contact information for each club and federation, which is available for public use. In September 2008, we contacted every registered HTA in the database. Of the 3,000 organizations listed, 800 self-identified as hometown clubs, and of those, 500 clubs had correct contact information. We contacted all 500 clubs by telephone to verify mailing address, explain the purpose of the survey, answer questions, and encourage club leaders to participate.[2] After the initial round of calls, 500 active and inactive clubs with correct contact information were sent a hard-copy mail survey and small gift of appreciation. The total number of failed-to-contact potential respondents was 250. Of those failed-to-contact respondents, we identified approximately 80 clubs that existed "on paper" but did not have any membership or activities. These so-called "ghost clubs" were not targeted for the survey. For those clubs that did not wish to provide a home mailing address but wanted to participate in the survey, an exact copy of the mail survey was electronically administered to migrant club leaders through the Survey Monkey application online tool.

Surveys were mailed to prospective HTA respondents over a five-week period with a short break during the general presidential election in November 2008. Throughout this period, the University of Chicago Survey Lab telephoned prospective respondents again to confirm receipt of the survey, encourage participation, and answer questions. Surveys were collected through July 2009 with a 50 percent response rate (n = 250).[3] To assess whether the population of survey respondents was systematically different from the population of attempt-to-contact nonrespondents, I conducted difference of means tests on socioeconomic indicators based on the nonrespondent contact addresses. For example, I examined whether poverty, foreign-born population, and population density based on the listed zip code of the potential respondent revealed whether those who did not respond to the survey were more likely to be in poorer locales, more rural areas, or lived in places with less for-eign-born population. Data for the statistical tests was collected from the American Com-munities Survey. Statistical tests on these indicators did not reveal sampling bias.

Additionally, some of the HTA respondents we contacted reported that their clubs were no longer active. I recontacted leaders of clubs that reported failed or stalled partnerships to better understand the nature of partnership collapse. Respondents were also given the option to call me or the survey lab to provide more detailed information about club activi-ties. I purchased a cellular phone exclusively for survey respondents to call and discuss the survey or anything else they wanted to discuss about cross-border participation. About 50 club leaders called during the dissemination period of the survey. On several occasions, these calls led to longer, more formal telephone interviews that lasted from 30 minutes to over an hour.

The survey asked questions about when, where, and why the club formed, sociodemo-graphic characteristics of club leadership, membership, and organizational structure, and experiences providing public goods and services in Mexican hometowns. Additionally, I also asked about the geographic location of the Mexican hometown where the club sup-ported development projects and the U.S. destination where the majority of club members lived. Geographic information on the sending and receiving places in the U.S. and Mexico presented an opportunity to match club-level data in transnational space, so to speak. Situ-ating the club in the transnational dyad of sending and receiving place allowed me to create a global picture of the club. Using the panel dataset described in chapter 6 and Appendix D and additional data collected from the American Communities Survey from the U.S. Cen-sus, I compiled information about each Mexican municipality of origin and U.S. city where the respondent club was situated.

The transnational matched survey sample contains respondents from 24 of Mexico's 31 states (about half from Jalisco, Zacatecas, Guanajuato, and Michoacán) as well as the federal district. Survey respondent clubs were located in half of U.S. states (25) and the majority were based in the traditional immigrant receiving states of California, Texas, and Illinois. While three quarters of the sample formed after 2002, 17 percent of the sample formed be-tween 1990 and 2001, and 6 percent before 1990.[4]

One of the limitations of the original transnational survey is the selection method for identifying migrant hometown associations engaged in remittance-funded public goods projects. I selected potential respondents from the universe of clubs that officially registered with IME at Mexican consulates and self-identified as a migrant hometown club, about 800 clubs total in 2008. However, by some estimates, this number only represents between a quarter and half of all migrant clubs in existence at the time. There are a few notable impli-cations of this selection problem in need of more discussion.

First, it is likely the case that smaller, more informal clubs that are more likely to au-tonomously invest resources in origin locales are less likely to register with the IME because development projects are not coordinated with any level of the sending state. It is also likely the case that clubs that were more fragmented or only participated in coproduction part-nerships once would be less likely to register with the consulate. As such, more substitutive and fragmented cases would be underrepresented in the IME database and censored by the selection protocol I used to identify survey participants.

Second, clubs from Oaxaca and Chiapas where the traditional system of self-governance called *usos y costumbres* is practiced may not have registered their clubs at the same rate as club from other states where this form of government is less practiced. In traditional systems of self-government, the separation between government, civil society, and ethno-religious institutions including the cargo system are not neat. There would be less formal government participation and thus less need to register the transnational partnership with IME. The underrepresentation of clubs from Oaxaca and other *usos y costumbres* origin locales may likely bias the recording of synergetic partnerships. Given these real-world limitations, the identification and selection of migrant clubs from the IME database for participation in the survey was the best option in order to contact as many clubs as possible. That being said, it is an imperfect club selection strategy and likely biases the results toward more formal clubs with greater club capacity and those from traditional municipalities governed by elected representatives from organized political parties.

Principal Component and Cluster Analysis Using Survey Data

In chapter 6, I assessed how transnational partnerships were organized and whether synergetic, corporatist, substitutive, and fragmented partnerships were more likely associated with more civic and political participation and government responsiveness. I asked whether the interaction of community inclusion and government engagement organized coproduction in the forms hypothesized and assessed if different partnerships were linked to observable political outcomes. In addition to the two central factors organizing coproduction, the chapter also paid special attention to the ways in which HTA club capacity may have affected transnational partnerships. I relaxed the assumption that HTA club capacity was constant and analyzed how differences across HTAs affected community inclusion and government engagement as well as the possibility that club capacity had an independent effect on the formation of coproduction types. Table 2 presents select descriptive statistics of the survey sample.

PRINCIPAL COMPONENT ANALYSIS

Principal component analysis (PCA) is a mathematical procedure for transforming a number of possibly correlated variables into a smaller number of uncorrelated variables called principal components.[1] PCA identifies a linear combination of variables that maximizes the variance from the selected variables. The objective of the technique is to reduce the number of highly correlated variables to a smaller number of principal components without sacrificing information. Since both community inclusion and government engagement are multidimensional conceptual constructs approximated by several variables, the PCA technique simplifies the number of variables into a composite index, making it easier to compare values in a cross-section of Mexican migrant hometown associations.

TABLE 2. Descriptive Statistics of Transnational Survey.

	Summary Statistics			
	Mean	SD	Min	Max
Index				
Community Inclusion	2.498	1.119	1	4
Government Engagement	2.502	1.127	1	4
Club Capacity	2.512	1.118	1	4
Sociodemographic				
Poverty Index	−0.555	0.702	−1.993	3.192
International Migration Index	0.879	0.936	−1.031	3.689
Politics				
Margin of Victory	24.48	17.51	0.681	99.81
Effective Number of Parties	2.473	0.556	1	4.061
Voter Turnout	53.39	10.07	12.15	75.40
Observations		250		

SOURCE: Calculations using data sourced from original survey, INEGI Simbad, INE, Conapo, and Sedesol.

CONSTRUCTING THE COMMUNITY INCLUSION PRINCIPAL COMPONENT

The survey asked questions about how migrant clubs integrated local citizens into the co-production process with the Mexican government. Questions asked migrant clubs how often local citizens in the hometown: (1) volunteered labor; (2) helped select projects; (3) donated resources (monetary or in-kind); (4) monitored projects during and after implementation; (5) discussed project-related activities with municipal officials (i.e., hiring laborers and contractors, timelines, technical plans); (6) participated in local committees or mirror clubs (*clubes espejo*); (7) were involved in the creation of the HTA; and the extent to which (8) the HTA perceived problems working with local citizens and citizen groups; and (9) whether other social, religious, business, and civic associations were involved in the provision of public goods with the HTA. Survey questions related to community inclusion were then transformed into consistent forms to conduct PCA, positively coded,[2] and tested for internal consistency.[3]

CONSTRUCTING THE GOVERNMENT ENGAGEMENT PRINCIPAL COMPONENT

I also evaluated different dimensions of government engagement using survey questions and data from the Mexican panel municipal database (see Data Appendix D). Since sometimes more than one HTA participated in coproduction in a given year, each survey respondent club name was matched against the 3x1 Program dataset and only the corresponding club information was extracted. Survey questions used to approximate government engagement included questions about municipal government involvement in and frequency of (1) selecting projects; (2) creating the migrant club; (3) providing matching funds and project materials in a timely manner; (4) problems working with the municipal government;

(5) matching 25 percent or more of total project costs; and (6) failure to successfully complete coproduction projects.[4] The survey also asked whether the HTA survey respondent was able to (7) access officials; (8) participate in decision-making; and (9) influence negotiations with municipal officials. Questions and variables related to municipal government engagement were transformed into consistent forms, positively coded, and tested for internal consistency. The specific linear combination of these variables used to create the community inclusion and government engagement indices are housed on my professional website, but not included in the appendix due to space constraints.

For both inclusion and engagement, the variance explained by the first (main) component is substantial (eigenvalues >1). This means that the first component explains more variance than any of the individual variables that helped construct the index. The eigenvalue thus reports the index of strength of each component. Using the main component for each index, which is a continuous number, I next transformed the index into a categorical variable based on different cut points or levels based on deviance from the mean value of the index. For example, if the survey respondent's government engagement level was 1.5 (out of a maximum of 4), engagement would be considered "low." If another survey respondent's engagement score was 3.5, the engagement score would be coded "high." I tested several different cut points including both tertile (low, medium, and high) and quartile cut points (very low, low, high, very high). There is very little difference in how the data clustered when using tertile or quartile cut points. In the interest of ease of interpretation, I used a quartile cut point to signal low and high levels of inclusion and engagement. Low and high scores for each index are based on whether the continuous component is above or below the mean value.

CONSTRUCTING THE HOMETOWN ASSOCIATION CLUB CAPACITY PRINCIPAL COMPONENT

Several survey questions asked respondent HTAs about club leadership characteristics, organizational structure and decision-making, and club activities that approximated club capacity.[5] Sociodemographic questions included: (1) employment status; (2) marital status; (3) educational attainment; and (4) number of years living uninterrupted in the U.S. for each migrant club leader completing the survey.[6] I included additional questions in the index that related to club organizational structure including whether the club (5) invested in public works project independently (e.g., without cofinancing from the local, state, or federal government); (6) had membership in a state-level federation of migrant clubs; and the club's (7) the total membership base size; (8) number of core, active leaders; (9) method of club decision-making and leadership selection (for example, by informal consensus, committee, or formal voting process); and (10) whether the club modeled any aspect of their associational activities by watching or learning from other migrant clubs. Finally, the club capacity index included indicators of how frequently the club (11) met to discuss club affairs and (12) fundraised. The PCA shows that the main component of the HTA club capacity index explained a substantial proportion of the variance (eigenvalues >1). Using the continuous component, I created categorical variables from a quartile cut representing levels of HTA club capacity in a similar fashion as community inclusion and government engagement.

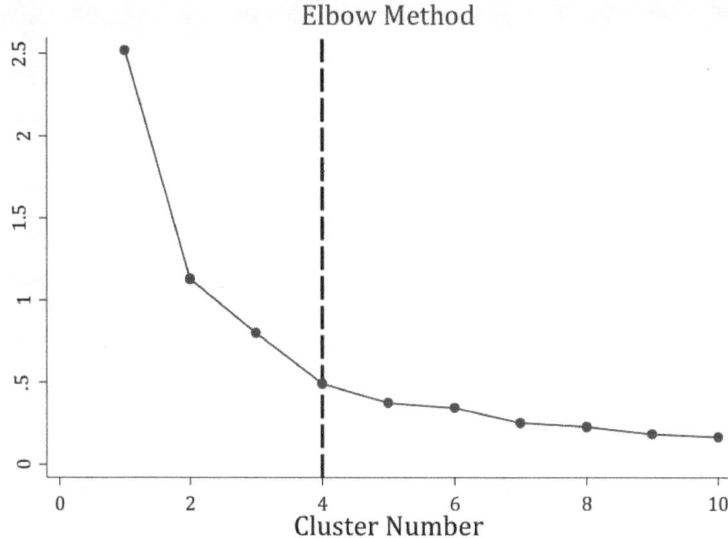

FIGURE 8. Elbow method displaying four stable clusters. Source: Kmeans calculations using data sourced from original survey and panel data from INEGI Simbad, INE, Conapo, and Sedesol.

CLUSTER ANALYSIS USING PRINCIPAL COMPONENTS

Cluster analysis is a technique to identify groupings or clusters of observational data. The technique determines groups based on information found in the data that describes data points and their relationships. The clusters that form from the data reflect how similar the data points are to one another within each distinct cluster and how different the data points are from the objects in other clusters groups. In the survey sample, levels of community inclusion and government engagement for each HTA respondent served as the individual data points. The greater the similarity within a group (the distance or tightness between points) and difference between groups, the more distinct the clustering.[7] When clusters are tighter the researcher can be more confident that the cluster represents something meaningful, in this case, transnational coproduction types.

I used a "kmeans" (nonhierarchical) cluster analysis and examined the formation of clusters of coproduction types based on the interactions of different values of community inclusion and government engagement. Specifically, this method determined if clusters of coproduction types emerged from the survey data and approximated synergy and fragmentation, which reflect "extreme" values of inclusion and engagement, as well as two intermediary partnership types, corporatist and substitutive, which reflected variable levels (high/low, low/high) of inclusion and engagement. Kmeans clustering is called a centroid approach. A centroid approach uses an algorithm (kmeans algorithm) to cluster data points by a single mean vector. In other words, each data point belongs to the cluster with the nearest mean value. Since I had theoretical expectations that community inclusion and

TABLE 3. Descriptive Statistics of Organizational Types of Coproduction.

	Substitution		Fragmentation		Corporatism		Synergy	
	Mean	SD	Mean	SD	Mean	SD	Mean	SD
Index								
Community Inclusion	3.137	0.348	1.478	0.503	1.553	0.504	3.836	0.373
Government Engagement	1.922	0.796	1.478	0.503	3.211	0.413	3.836	0.373
Club Capacity	2.765	0.971	1.870	0.954	2.289	0.956	3.236	1.053
Sociodemographic								
Poverty	−0.457	0.784	−0.514	0.597	−0.713	0.587	−0.587	0.807
International Migration	0.974	0.871	0.842	0.813	0.976	1.060	0.769	1.051
Politics								
Margin of Victory	22.98	13.32	24.24	17.55	26.34	22.10	24.93	17.79
Number of Parties	2.451	0.420	2.537	0.563	2.474	0.710	2.408	0.545
Voter Turnout	52.71	8.111	51.35	10.39	58.50	9.219	53.19	11.01
Observations	51		69		38		55	

SOURCE: Calculations using data sourced from original survey, INEGI Simbad, INE, Conapo, and Sedesol.

government engagement produced four main partnerships types, kmeans clustering was a more appropriate method than other clustering approaches.[8]

In the cluster analysis, I observed how different values of community inclusion and government engagement clustered together in combinations that approximate the four organizational types: synergetic (high/high), fragmented (low/low), corporatist (low/high), and substitutive (high/low). In this application, the (k) number of groups specified the number of clusters detected in the observations. Four clusters may be inappropriate, however, if more (or less) coproduction types existed in the data. I ran several diagnostics to determine the most appropriate number of k clusters: the rule of thumb method (square root of n/2), elbow method (minimizes the within sum of squares such that all points in each cluster are very close), and silhouette method (using the difference between the within-cluster tightness and separations from the rest). After I ran the cluster analysis several times with each method to achieve stability (about 10 times), four clusters repeatedly emerged in the data.[9] Even when I relaxed the categories from high/low to high/medium/low, four stable clusters that mimicked hypothesized transnational types clustered in the data. I present the elbow method diagram showing four main clusters in Figure 8.

MULTIVARIATE REGRESSIONS EXAMINING THE POLITICAL CONSEQUENCES OF PARTNERSHIP TYPES USING TRANSNATIONAL SURVEY DATA

Table 3 presents descriptive statistics for each transnational partnership type that emerged from the cluster analysis. Using the panel data from chapter 6, I matched the Mexican municipality with the survey respondent and analyzed how the club's most recent 3x1 project period correlated with changes in political participation measured by the percent of the voting-age population casting a ballot in the next municipal election year and government responsiveness measured by municipal spending on public works (per capita) and municipal public works spending as a share of total budget spending. Since the municipal panel data was time-series, I observed political indicators before, during, and after the period in which coproduction occurred that allowed me to create indicators for public works spending changes and voter turnout changes over the project observation period. Since both dependent variables were continuous, I used standard OLS estimations and included state-fixed effects to control for time-invariant unobservable factors at the state level. These data are not presented due to space constraints, but they are available in the online supplementary file on my professional website for download or by request.

Mexican Panel Data, Mexican Family Life Survey, and Statistical Analyses

MEASURING TRANSNATIONAL PARTNERSHIPS WITH 3X1 PROGRAM DATA

Using the Sedesol 3x1 Program database, I constructed four measures of municipal participation in the 3x1 Program. Measuring program participation was not a straightforward endeavor in the context of the 3x1 Program since there was neither uniform start time across program participants nor continual participation by each municipality. Mexican municipalities started, stopped, and reentered the program annually throughout the observation period. These measures permitted a closer examination of temporal dynamics of 3x1 participation. For example, I assessed the municipal effects of participation, electoral-cycle effects of participation (shorter term effects), and cumulative participation (effects accumulating over a longer time period). Municipal elections in Mexico are staggered across states every three years.

The first major measure ("program treatment") was the baseline indicator for the treatment effect, that is, participation in the 3x1 Program. "Program treatment" was a dichotomous variable taking the value of 1 if a municipality participated in the program *at least once* between 2002 and 2013, and zero otherwise. The second major indicator of program participation reflected short-run effects of program participation ("electoral cycle"). Three treatment variables represent whether the municipality participated at any point in the present electoral cycle (current cycle), the previous electoral cycle (last three years), and the previous electoral cycle before that (last six years). I did not report the cycle models, but the results are available to interested readers upon request. Finally, since municipalities entered and exited the program annually, the last treatment indicator was a continuous variable ("cumulative treatment") that measured the frequency of program participation over the entire program period. Cumulative treatment was a continuous variable that provided insight into the frequency of municipal participation in the 3x1 Program. The relevant reference group combined all municipalities that participated, but less frequently, and municipalities that never participated in the 3x1 Program to isolate the comparison of

TABLE 4. Descriptive Statistics of Panel Dataset.

	Full Sample		3x1 Participation	
	Mean	SD	Mean	SD
3x1 Participation				
DiD Treatment	0.12	0.33	0.25	0.43
Cumulative 3x1	0.46	1.39	1.75	2.25
Sociodemographic				
Poverty Index	0.00	1.00	−0.20	0.85
Poverty Index Squared	0.99	1.27	0.77	1.06
International Migration Index	0.02	0.98	0.33	1.04
Literacy Rate	78.63	11.15	84.38	7.13
Indigenous Population	19.99	31.42	12.97	25.39
Total Population (log)	8.84	1.53	9.21	1.40
Politics				
Margin of Victory	21.40	21.53	26.43	24.69
Effective Number of Parties	2.63	1.02	2.45	1.08
Voter Turnout	58.48	16.68	54.41	16.35
Incumbent Win	53.54	49.87	51.01	50.00
PRI	53.48	49.88	70.44	45.63
PRD	9.22	28.93	8.20	27.43
PAN	17.27	37.80	14.28	34.99
OTHER	20.04	40.03	7.08	25.65
PRI Vote Share	46.96	20.69	37.62	21.45
PRD Vote Share	15.90	16.97	14.13	15.84
PAN Vote Share	22.36	18.51	27.02	17.62
Public Finance				
Tax Revenue Per Cap	2,324	1,909	2,856	1,869
Expenditure Per Cap	1,912	2,234	3,321	2,157
Public Spending Per Cap	626	872	1,096	967
Observations	58,972		14,808	

NOTE: 3x1 participation includes all municipalities that participate in the 3x1 Program at least once between 2002 and 2013. The full sample includes all Mexican municipalities from 1990 to 2013.

SOURCE: Calculations using data sourced from INEGI Simbad, INE, Conapo, and Sedesol.

cumulative treatment compared to all other municipalities. For all other treatment indicators, the control group remained municipal nonparticipants in the 3x1 Program.

Formal political participation ("voter turnout") represented the percentage of the citizen voting-age population casting a vote in municipal elections in the given election year. This data was adjusted to reflect the migrant population living abroad. Voter turnout data was calculated using the CIDAC database of municipal elections for the period from 1990 to 2013 and state-level elections data for select years. Mexican municipal elections occurred every three years in a staggered electoral calendar across Mexican states during the observation period. I examined the effects of 3x1 participation on annual municipal observations, but I also converted the observations into three-year election cycles for ease of interpretation. Table 4 presents select summary statistics for the 3x1 panel dataset sample.

COMMUNITY CIVIC ENGAGEMENT

I also constructed indicators of civic engagement from the survey questions. "Recent activity," "religious," "political," "social," and "other" were all dichotomous variables that indicated if there were recent community activities and meetings that occurred in the previous 12-month period before the survey, and the types of community activities that were present in the community, respectively.[1] I focused the analysis on recent community activities to try and isolate the effects of treatment in the corresponding period of observation. Additionally, "activity level" was a continuous variable reflecting the total numbers of activities for which residents are most recently involved. Finally, "high activity level" was a dichotomous indicator that took the value of 1 if the community had greater than or equal to different thresholds of community activity (greater than or equal to 10; 20; 30; 50; and greater than or equal to 100 activities), and zero otherwise. These variables were labeled high activity level 1 through 5. The minimum number of activities was zero and the maximum was 800. In the sample, 46 percent had at least 10 activities, 25 percent of the sample had 20 or more, 14 percent 30 or more, 11 percent 50 or more, and 7 percent more than 100 activities. I coded the activity level as different dichotomous variables for ease of interpretation of interaction coefficients. Observations for all indicators of civic engagement reflected community activities before 2002 (wave 1), between 2002 and 2004 (wave 2), and between 2005 and 2008 (wave 3). This yielded three separate observations for the civic engagement variables.

GOVERNMENT RESPONSIVENESS

I included three measures that proxied for government responsiveness. The first measure was an indicator of annual municipal expenditures on public goods and services (per capita). The second measure was an indicator of total expenditures (per capita), which included expenditures for debt, personal salaries, general services, materials and supplies, aid, assets, and "other" expenditures. I included total expenditures since some indirect costs of coproduction were likely included in other expenditure categories (e.g., materials and supplies). This variable also helped disclose whether and if total expenditures were increasing as a result of program participation, but not to public works, which would have suggested possible spending leakages as a result of program participation. The third measure was the annual share of total expenditures spent on public works. Annual municipal public finance data came from the Mexico's *Instituto Nacional de Estadistica y Geografia* (INEGI) *Sistema Estatal y Municipal Base de Datos* (Simbad).

DIFFERENCE IN DIFFERENCE AND FIXED EFFECTS MODELS

A key objective of the quantitative analyses was to mitigate the threat of selection bias often present when using quasi-experimental data. This form of bias occurs either when program participation is voluntary or when a municipal participant is selected into the program based on preexisting characteristics that may also be related to outcomes of interest. When such nonrandom selection occurs, if Mexican municipalities participating in the program are characterized by having systematically lower (higher) levels on democracy indicators, then any difference observed on political outcomes between treatment (3x1 Program participant) and control group (nonparticipation) may reflect pre-program biases and not necessarily the effect of the 3x1 Program on local democracy. Researchers use a variety of statistical techniques to analyze "treatment effects models" using observational data, where a policy of interest such as municipal participation in the 3x1 Program is the treatment variable.[2]

Confronted with observational data in which self-selection into treatment may be confounded with the outcomes of interest, I used the difference-in-difference estimator (DiD) to mitigate this form of bias as much as possible in the absence of randomized controlled municipal participation in the 3x1 Program.[3] The DiD estimator is a simple and powerful tool for estimating treatment effects with observational data, and panel data is often best suited to maximize the method and generate causal inference.[4] DiD measured the difference on democracy indicators between municipalities that participated in the 3x1 Program (treatment group) and those that did not participate (control group) before and after the start of the federal 3x1 Program in 2002. As such, it required repeated observations of the units over time to compare the *difference in the differences between treatment and control groups before and after program participation.* As Buckley and Shang (2003) argue, this strategy helps ensure that any variables remaining constant over time (but unobserved) and correlated with both the decision to participate in the program and the outcomes of interest will not bias the estimated effect.

The panel dataset included data for all Mexican municipalities between 1990 and 2013 (24 years).[5] The time series included a 12-year pre-treatment period to analyze prior trends before possible selection into the 3x1 Program. It also included an additional 11 years of post-treatment observations in which some Mexican municipalities participated in the 3x1 Program and some did not. This allowed examination of how program participation affected the average change in different dimensions of democracy across all Mexican municipalities.

In addition to the standard assumptions of ordinary least squares (OLS) models, a key assumption of the DiD estimator was that average changes in democratic functioning were assumed to be the same for both the control group and the treatment group had they never participated in the 3x1 Program.[6] In other words, the *difference in the differences* showed that whatever would have happened to the control group over time was what would have happened to the treatment group in the absence of municipal participation in the 3x1 Program. Participation in the 3x1 Program was more likely in places with higher levels of migration. This was consistent across all of the three 3x1 participation measures. Moreover, local democracy had a nonlinear relationship with international migration. These statistics provided some initial evidence that 3x1 participation may have offset or reversed the general negative impacts on local democracy from international migration.[7] In specifications in which the dependent variable was continuous, OLS was used to estimate treatment effects. Logistic regression was used when the outcome variable was dichotomous.

CONTROLLING FOR CONFOUNDERS

In the statistical analysis, I included several socioeconomic, demographic, and political conditions likely to affect voter turnout for both 3x1 municipal participants and nonparticipants. I also included additional covariates hypothesized to influence both the baseline change common to all units of observation and the amount of change predicted by the 3x1 participation.

First, "poverty" (and its quadratic term) was a continuous index of marginalization. The index of marginalization accounts for the percent of the municipal population that lived without primary education, drainage or toilet, electricity, piped water, and that were over the age of 8 and illiterate. It also included the percent of the population that lived with over-crowding, earthen floor, income below poverty level, and in locations with less than 5,000 people. Second, "international migration" was a continuous index variable that summarized the percent of households that received migrant remittances, had circular migrants, and had a member of the household living abroad in the previous five years. The migration index allowed me to analyze how the intensity of individual emigration in municipalities (family remittances, return migration, and absence of household members) affected democracy.

Third, I included a measure of the percent of the population that spoke an indigenous language ("indigenous"), since previous research showed that ethno-linguistic fractional-ization affected public goods provision and democratic quality.[8] Fourth, percent of the total population over the age of 12 that was literate ("literacy") served as a proxy for political participation. Literacy is often correlated with both informal and formal forms of political participation in Mexico and the United States.[9] Finally, log of the total population over the age of 15 was the final sociodemographic control included in all specifications. Population size served as a good proxy for both budget constraints of the municipal government and poverty. Migration, socioeconomic, and demographic indicators were obtained from the Mexican National Census, including the *Censo General de Población y Vivienda* (Mexican National Census conducted every 10 years), *Conteo de Población y Vivienda* (updated every five years), and INEGI.

Political variables were included to control for local government's interest and ability to provide public goods. For example, electoral competition affected trends in political par-ticipation and government responsiveness.[10] I included the lagged effective number of par-ties in all specifications with the exception of when the dependent variable of interest was electoral competition (margin of victory and effective number of parties) to control for this fact. Also, since different political parties provided public goods based on different political strategies,[11] I included the party label of the municipal incumbent lagged one electoral cycle in all specifications.

Finally, to control for municipal government's capacity to provide public goods I includ-ed a lagged measure of total revenues (per capita). Total revenues measured government budget constraint and included all sources of funding for municipal government including state, federal, and locally sourced revenue. This measure was also sourced from the INEGI Simbad database of municipal public finance. Taken together, the political variables served as a proxy indicator of government engagement, one of the main factors, I argued, that pro-duced variation on organizational forms of transnational coproduction. The panel dataset for Mexican municipalities did not provide an opportunity to assess the effect of citizen inclusion in the coproduction process because it lacked reliable estimates for civic engage-ment in community activities, but I examined this later in chapter 6 using longitudinal survey data from the Mexican Family Life Survey.

Figure 9 graphs the time trends between 1990 and 2013 by treatment and control group for voter turnout. The figure shows that pre-treatment trends are similar and stable before 2002, and the trends become different after 2002. Limitations still remained using the DiD,

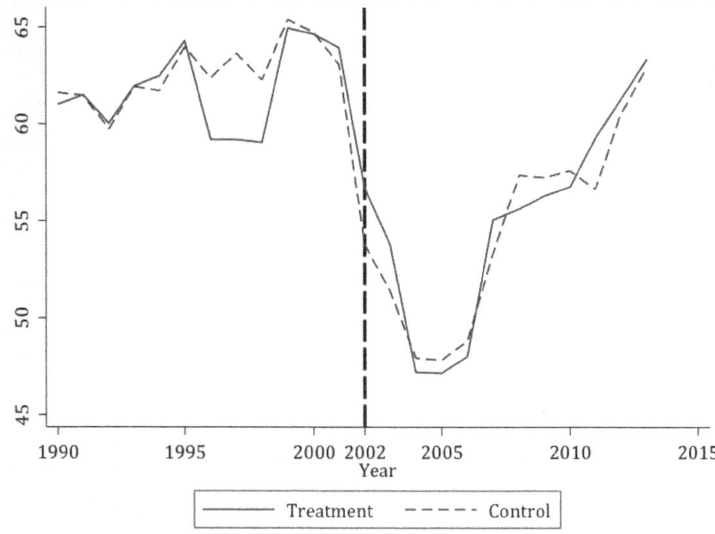

FIGURE 9. Voter turnout trend by treatment and control. Source: Calculations using data sourced from INEGI Simbad, INE, Conapo, and Sedesol.

however. Although the DiD models mitigated irregularities in the frequency and starting time of participation, the DiD models only captured the average treatment effects of 3x1 participation. The results for the DiD models are reported in Tables 5 and 6. I also tested fixed effects models with a municipal-linear time trend and a state-linear time trend, although only the municipal results are reported.[12] Using different indicators of 3x1 participation reflected fluctuations in the specific linear trend that allowed me to better isolate the causal effects from 3x1 Program participation.[13] The results are consistent in both the municipal- and state-specific linear time trend models. Finally, I examined the cumulative effects of 3x1 Program participation on government responsiveness and voter turnout. Those findings, which include year fixed effects and the municipal linear time trend, are presented in Tables 7 and 8.

MEXICAN FAMILY LIFE SURVEY MULTIVARIATE REGRESSION ANALYSIS

Civic engagement indicators were sourced from the MxFLS, while all other socioeconomic, demographic, public finance, political, and 3x1 Program indicators were sourced from the panel dataset. All of the same controls were included in the civic engagement models; however, controls were averaged for the pre-survey period for each panel wave. Similar to earlier specifications, I created a mean lag of each confounder leading up to the year in which the second and third panel waves observe municipal responses. Since I had comprehensive data on all Mexican municipalities before and after the start of the 3x1 Program period, I also examined whether survey respondents were systematically different on indicators of democracy prior to the observation period. Results yielded no concerns of selection bias.[14]

TABLE 5. Difference in Difference Models, 3x1 Program Participation on Voter Turnout.

3x1 Participation	3.040***	2.628***
	(0.225)	(0.215)
2002 Dummy	−8.990***	−9.075***
	(0.339)	(0.334)
3x1*2002 Dummy	−1.051**	−1.403***
	(0.326)	(0.325)
Poverty	0.948***	0.944***
	(0.174)	(0.172)
Poverty Squared	−0.379***	−0.411***
	(0.075)	(0.074)
Migration Index	0.095	−
	(0.094)	−
Migrant Percentage	−	1.508***
	−	(0.084)
Literacy Rate	0.255***	0.248***
	(0.017)	(0.017)
Indigenous Population	0.076***	0.095***
	(0.004)	(0.004)
Population (log)	−3.690***	−3.608***
	(0.078)	(0.078)
Number of Parties	2.118***	2.080***
	(0.088)	(0.088)
PRI	−0.109	−0.178
	(0.230)	(0.227)
PRD	2.869***	2.491***
	(0.316)	(0.313)
PAN	2.813***	2.734***
	(0.265)	(0.262)
Tax Revenue (per capita)	0.001***	0.000***
	(0.000)	(0.000)
Constant	67.561***	67.144***
	(1.621)	(1.590)
Observations	34,655	35,296

Robust standard errors in parentheses. +$p < 0.1$; *$p < 0.05$; **$p < 0.01$; ***$p < 0.001$. All models include state and time fixed effects.

SOURCE: Calculations using data sourced from INEGI Simbad, INE, Conapo, and Sedesol.

Several treatment variables indicated 3x1 Program participation. First, "treatment" was a dichotomous variable equal to 1 if the municipality participated in the 3x1 Program in any year in the period before the survey years, and zero otherwise. Note, no municipalities in the MxFLS participated in the 3x1 Program in the first panel wave, the first year of the federal program. Second, a cumulative treatment indicator ("cumulative treatment") was incorporated to reflect the total number of years the municipality participated in the 3x1 Program between panel waves 2 and 3. Finally, since the 3x1 Program database contained information regarding the number of projects annually completed, I also included a continuous count

TABLE 6. Difference in Difference Models, 3x1 Program Participation on Government Responsiveness.

	Public Spending Per Capita	Share of Public Spending over Total Expenditure	Public Spending Per Capita	Share of Public Spending over Total Expenditure
3x1 Program	36.911***	1.740***	49.899***	2.574***
	(5.133)	(0.273)	(4.865)	(0.262)
2002 Dummy	275.255***	13.558***	282.353***	13.930***
	(17.057)	(0.366)	(16.689)	(0.364)
3x1*2002 Dummy	−61.887***	−4.728***	−93.816***	−5.297***
	(13.137)	(0.351)	(13.418)	(0.350)
Poverty	238.177***	8.829***	246.457***	8.982***
	(9.479)	(0.208)	(9.338)	(0.206)
Poverty Squared	30.006***	−0.587***	25.415***	−0.666***
	(3.788)	(0.092)	(3.674)	(0.090)
Migration Index	37.116***	1.288***	–	–
	(3.763)	(0.100)	–	–
Migrant Percentage	–	–	63.606***	0.703***
	–	–	(8.096)	(0.102)
Literacy Rate	8.808***	0.250***	9.151***	0.251***
	(0.840)	(0.020)	(0.824)	(0.020)
Indigenous Population	0.051	0.003	0.032	−0.008+
	(0.199)	(0.005)	(0.197)	(0.005)
Population (log)	21.429***	1.560***	21.564***	1.438***
	(3.899)	(0.085)	(3.716)	(0.084)
Number of Parties	38.093***	1.738***	36.881***	1.730***
	(3.430)	(0.102)	(3.394)	(0.101)
Voter Turnout	−0.528*	−0.024***	−0.928***	−0.030***
	(0.209)	(0.005)	(0.210)	(0.005)
PRI	68.845***	2.556***	63.098***	2.417***
	(6.376)	(0.238)	(6.329)	(0.236)
PRD	107.838***	3.468***	102.239***	3.553***
	(10.758)	(0.378)	(10.822)	(0.376)
PAN	56.757***	1.616***	52.250***	1.531***
	(9.081)	(0.287)	(8.987)	(0.285)
Tax Revenue (per cap.)	0.315***	−0.001***	0.300***	−0.001***
	(0.009)	(0.000)	(0.009)	(0.000)
Constant	1,050.394***	−15.061***	1,070.912***	−14.046***
	(76.393)	(1.897)	(74.447)	(1.837)
Observations	31,958	31,958	32,511	32,511

Robust standard errors in parentheses. +p < 0.1; *p < 0.05; **p < 0.01; ***p < 0.001. All models include state and time fixed effects.

SOURCE: Calculations using data sourced from INEGI Simbad, INE, Conapo, and Sedesol.

TABLE 7. Fixed Effects Models, 3x1 Cumulative 3x1 Participation on Voter Turnout with Municipal Time Trend.

	Voter Turnout	
3x1 Cumulative Participation	1.971***	1.751***
	(0.455)	(0.449)
Poverty	22.892*	19.447*
	(9.007)	(9.188)
Poverty Squared	−11.786**	−10.966**
	(4.076)	(4.000)
Migration Index	4.157	−
	(4.032)	−
Migrant Percentage	−	4.963***
	−	(0.802)
Literacy Rate	−1.828**	−1.969**
	(0.668)	(0.660)
Indigenous Population	0.972+	1.001+
	(0.507)	(0.527)
Population (log)	48.325***	7.559
	(9.531)	(11.993)
Number of Parties	4.982***	4.848***
	(0.377)	(0.371)
PRI	−2.580***	−1.568*
	(0.619)	(0.632)
PRD	−0.581	0.675
	(0.830)	(0.849)
PAN	−0.341	0.703
	(0.823)	(0.857)
Tax Revenue (per capita)	0.001**	0.000*
	(0.000)	(0.000)
Constant	−260.739***	130.290
	(76.633)	(108.070)
Observations	10,042	10,087

Robust standard errors in parentheses. +p < 0.1; *p < 0.05; **p < 0.01; ***p < 0.001.

SOURCE: Calculations using data sourced from INEGI Simbad, INE, Conapo, and Sedesol.

variable for the number of total coproduction projects ("cumulative projects"). Results for the models that analyze how 3x1 Program participation and civic engagement interact to change voter turnout and government responsiveness are reported in Table 9 and Table 10.

HETEROGENEOUS TREATMENT EFFECTS

I learned from the data that program participation varied according to when a municipality started the program and the duration of program participation, which may have affected democratic participation and government responsiveness. The program flexibility in the

TABLE 8. Fixed Effects Models, 3x1 Cumulative 3x1 Participation on Government Responsiveness with Municipal Time Trend.

	Public Spending Per Capita	Share of Public Spending over Total Expenditure	Public Spending Per Capita	Share of Public Spending over Total Expenditure
3x1 Participation	15.285	0.371*	10.805	0.338+
	(10.412)	(0.171)	(10.345)	(0.173)
Poverty	327.681*	5.857*	289.717+	5.835*
	(149.571)	(2.329)	(151.674)	(2.344)
Poverty Squared	70.431	−1.230	91.368+	−0.885
	(53.658)	(0.853)	(54.134)	(0.821)
Migration Index	−13.411	−1.524+	–	–
	(53.227)	(0.790)	–	–
Migrant Percentage	–	–	46.078*	0.481+
	–	–	(19.669)	(0.279)
Literacy Rate	63.527***	0.267	58.101***	0.175
	(13.174)	(0.217)	(13.054)	(0.211)
Indigenous Population	25.255+	0.388+	26.573+	0.395+
	(14.924)	(0.228)	(14.635)	(0.220)
Population (log)	−588.712**	6.445*	−624.897**	6.046+
	(226.905)	(3.269)	(228.258)	(3.284)
Number of Parties	4.568	−0.142	4.165	−0.125
	(8.463)	(0.208)	(8.514)	(0.208)
Voter Turnout	2.380***	0.032**	2.209***	0.029*
	(0.611)	(0.012)	(0.607)	(0.012)
PRI	58.397*	1.701**	65.289*	1.752***
	(29.164)	(0.519)	(29.119)	(0.522)
PRD	31.963	1.630*	42.752	1.700*
	(40.406)	(0.752)	(40.217)	(0.758)
PAN	85.903*	1.880**	91.089*	1.846**
	(41.629)	(0.683)	(41.424)	(0.685)
Tax Rev. (per capita)	0.214***	0.001***	0.212***	0.001***
	(0.027)	(0.000)	(0.027)	(0.000)
Constant	−789.937	−58.320+	2.364	−47.345
	(2,257.191)	(32.868)	(2,296.995)	(32.863)
Observations	9,382	9,382	9,425	9,425

Robust standard errors in parentheses. +p < 0.1; *p < 0.05; **p < 0.01; ***p < 0.001.

SOURCE: Calculations using data sourced from INEGI Simbad, INE, Conapo, and Sedesol.

starting and stopping of program participation necessitated capturing this heterogeneity of treatment dynamics with the inclusion of interactions between treatment indicators and additional covariates.[15] I explored heterogeneous treatment effects by testing if, first, exposure to treatment—the possibility that the intervention itself—affected outcomes, and if, second, treatment effects varied with time and duration.

TABLE 9. Conditional Effects of 3x1 Participation, Project Levels, and Civic Engagement on Voter Turnout.

	3x1 Participation					3x1 Cumulative Projects				
3x1	0.017	0.063*	0.063*	0.028	0.039	0.011	0.008	0.009	0.000	0.007
	(0.038)	(0.030)	(0.029)	(0.046)	(0.035)	(0.008)	(0.005)	(0.005)	(0.004)	(0.005)
Number of Parties	0.021	0.03	0.028	0.033	0.033	0.022	0.026	0.025	0.029	0.03
	(0.023)	(0.023)	(0.023)	(0.021)	(0.021)	(0.023)	(0.023)	(0.023)	(0.020)	(0.021)
Poverty	0.093+	0.086	0.089	0.08	0.09	0.072	0.075	0.08	0.079	0.081
	(0.055)	(0.057)	(0.057)	(0.054)	(0.057)	(0.057)	(0.057)	(0.057)	(0.054)	(0.056)
Poverty Squared	0.028	0.018	0.018	0.011	0.01	0.019	0.015	0.014	0.009	0.007
	(0.022)	(0.024)	(0.024)	(0.022)	(0.022)	(0.023)	(0.023)	(0.023)	(0.021)	(0.021)
Migration Index	−0.017	−0.022	−0.02	−0.031+	−0.026	−0.014	−0.014	−0.011	−0.027	−0.02
	(0.020)	(0.021)	(0.020)	(0.018)	(0.018)	(0.021)	(0.021)	(0.020)	(0.017)	(0.018)
Literacy Rate	1.232*	1.327*	1.328*	1.375**	1.503**	1.163*	1.175+	1.216*	1.374*	1.399*
	(0.545)	(0.587)	(0.587)	(0.517)	(0.562)	(0.586)	(0.612)	(0.613)	(0.545)	(0.572)
Indigenous Pop.	0.284*	0.292*	0.294*	0.279*	0.300*	0.296*	0.277*	0.284*	0.276*	0.294*
	(0.121)	(0.130)	(0.130)	(0.131)	(0.127)	(0.132)	(0.133)	(0.133)	(0.128)	(0.125)
Population (log)	−0.003	−0.004	−0.002	0.003	0.006	−0.004	−0.004	−0.001	0.002	0.006
	(0.015)	(0.015)	(0.015)	(0.013)	(0.013)	(0.015)	(0.015)	(0.015)	(0.013)	(0.013)
Tax Rev. (per cap.)	0.000	0.000	0.000	0.000	0.000	0.000	0.000	0.000	0.000	0.000
	(0.000)	(0.000)	(0.000)	(0.000)	(0.000)	(0.000)	(0.000)	(0.000)	(0.000)	(0.000)
10+ Activities	−0.073*					−0.038				
	(0.035)					(0.031)				
3x1*10+ Activities	0.112*					−0.001				
	(0.052)					(0.011)				
50+ Activities		0.02				0.004				

		(0.046)						(0.045)		
3x1*50+ Activities		0.017						0.034**		
		(0.091)						(0.012)		
100+ Activities			0.02						0.011	
			(0.037)						(0.037)	
3x1*100+ Activities			0.059						0.054*	
			(0.047)						(0.022)	
Social Activities				0.025						0.022
				(0.042)						(0.035)
3x1*Social Activities				0.042						0.017*
				(0.054)						(0.008)
Religious Activities					−0.007					−0.005
					(0.032)					(0.029)
3x1*Rel. Activities					0.049					0.018+
					(0.044)					(0.010)
Constant	−0.537	−0.655	−0.677	−0.788+	−0.899+	−0.483	−0.505	−0.571	−0.76	−0.797
	(0.477)	(0.509)	(0.508)	(0.458)	(0.502)	(0.506)	(0.524)	(0.524)	(0.471)	(0.507)
Observations	143	143	145	168	169	143	143	145	168	169

Robust standard errors in parentheses. +p < 0.1; *p < 0.05; **p < 0.01; ***p < 0.001. All models include state and time fixed effects.

source: Calculations using data sourced from Mexican Family Life Survey (MxFLS) and panel data from INEGI Simbad, INE, Conapo, and Sedesol.

TABLE 10. Conditional Effects of 3x1 Participation, Project Levels, and Civic Engagement on Government Responsiveness.

	3x1 Cumulative Participation				3x1 Participation			
3x1 Treatment	−2.269	−1.965	2.726*	2.070*	−7.994*	−4.346	3.623	2.410
	(1.453)	(1.689)	(1.305)	(0.855)	(3.056)	(4.441)	(3.193)	(2.359)
Community Act.	−0.047				−0.927			
	(2.070)				(2.191)			
Cum. 3x1* Comm. Act.	3.791*				9.504***			
	(1.499)				(3.226)			
Number of Parties	0.870	0.053	0.186	−0.078	0.730	0.220	0.329	0.055
	(1.556)	(1.691)	(1.812)	(1.833)	(1.538)	(1.682)	(1.816)	(1.842)
Poverty	7.894+	10.716*	14.973**	15.150***	8.508+	10.857*	15.287***	15.277***
	(4.731)	(5.100)	(4.745)	(4.711)	(4.680)	(5.070)	(4.661)	(4.633)
Poverty Squared	−0.304	0.328	2.697	3.004+	−0.061	0.379	2.874	3.099+
	(1.747)	(2.079)	(1.806)	(1.759)	(1.728)	(2.069)	(1.757)	(1.712)
Migration Index	−0.617	−0.664	−0.428	−0.133	−0.417	−0.073	0.229	0.524
	(1.120)	(1.047)	(1.270)	(1.215)	(1.181)	(1.117)	(1.330)	(1.293)
Literacy Rate	−0.813+	−0.654	−0.341	−0.390	−0.821*	−0.688	−0.411	−0.440
	(0.418)	(0.434)	(0.466)	(0.449)	(0.412)	(0.434)	(0.465)	(0.454)
Indigenous Population	−0.163+	−0.160	−0.114	−0.118	−0.188*	−0.171	−0.135	−0.134
	(0.084)	(0.109)	(0.100)	(0.098)	(0.085)	(0.110)	(0.099)	(0.098)
Population (log)	1.572*	1.667+	0.987	1.051	1.638*	1.832+	1.216	1.227

	(1)	(2)	(3)	(4)	(5)	(6)	(7)	(8)
	(0.761)	(0.921)	(0.932)	(0.919)	(0.787)	(0.934)	(0.939)	(0.931)
Tax Rev. (per capita)	−0.003	−0.002	−0.002	−0.002	−0.003	−0.002	−0.002	−0.002
	(0.002)	(0.002)	(0.002)	(0.002)	(0.002)	(0.002)	(0.002)	(0.002)
Recent Comm. Activity		−2.977				−2.505		
		(3.630)				(3.863)		
3x1*Recent Comm. Act.		4.006*				6.926		
		(1.990)				(5.124)		
10+Activities			2.456				2.043	
			(2.384)				(2.498)	
3x1*10+Activities			−1.207				−1.359	
			(1.599)				(4.178)	
50+Activities				−0.421				−1.383
				(3.083)				(3.165)
3x1*50+Activities				3.911				6.858+
				(2.438)				(3.659)
Constant	89.347*	79.888*	55.295	60.506	91.510*	80.967*	59.618	63.509
	(36.206)	(36.655)	(40.775)	(38.921)	(35.647)	(36.647)	(40.696)	(39.375)
Observations	219	167	143	143	219	167	143	143

Robust standard errors in parentheses. +p < 0.1; *p < 0.05; **p < 0.01; ***p < 0.001. All models include state and time fixed effects.

SOURCE: Calculations using data sourced from Mexican Family Life Survey (MxFLS) and panel data from INEGI Simbad, INE, Conapo, and Sedesol.

TABLE 11. Heterogeneous Treatment Effects Models, 3x1 Program Participation.

| | | Government Responsiveness | |
	Voter Turnout	Public Spending	Share of Public Spending
Frequency Interactions			
3x1*Irregular	−1.5	14.89	−0.441
	(1.161)	(75.240)	(1.042)
3x1*Habitual	−2.011[+]	−72.99	−0.817
	(1.219)	(73.100)	(1.053)
Time Interactions			
3x1*2006–2009	3.359***	51.48*	−0.0413
	(0.633)	(24.310)	(0.521)
3x1*2010–2013	8.695***	157.4***	1.806***
	(0.698)	(34.910)	(0.661)
3x1 Participation	−3.844***	32.08	1.411
	(1.156)	(69.310)	(1.026)
Poverty	7.971***	−120.0*	1.947
	(1.566)	(48.130)	(1.259)
Poverty Squared	−0.952[+]	102.3***	1.950***
	(0.527)	(24.370)	(0.485)
Migration Index	1.279*	29.85	1.514**
	(0.649)	(27.910)	(0.559)
Literacy Rate	−0.169***	3.957**	0.693***
	(0.044)	(1.336)	(0.041)
Indigenous Population	0.0485	11.68***	0.134*
	(0.080)	(2.590)	(0.066)
Population (log)	22.94***	−328.0***	−3.130*
	(1.890)	(60.240)	(1.291)
Number of Parties	4.115***	29.35***	0.347*
	(0.187)	(4.676)	(0.136)
Voter Turnout	−	−0.174	−0.00905
	−	(0.303)	(0.009)
PRI	−3.498***	112.1***	4.573***
	(0.272)	(7.943)	(0.331)
PRD	−0.0618	134.1***	3.789***
	(0.421)	(14.510)	(0.492)
PAN	−0.587[+]	109.2***	3.467***
	(0.340)	(13.330)	(0.397)
Tax Rev. (per capita)	−0.00159***	0.255***	0.000475***
	(0.000)	(0.020)	(0.000)
Constant	−145.3***	2,067***	−9.196
	(17.510)	(548.800)	(11.950)
Observations	34,655	31,958	31,958

Robust standard errors in parentheses. +p < 0.1; *p < 0.05; **p < 0.01; ***p < 0.001. All models include state and time fixed effects.

SOURCE: Calculations using data sourced from INEGI Simbad, INE, Conapo, and Sedesol.

TABLE 12. Fixed Effects Models, 3x1 Municipal Spending and
Project Totals on Voter Turnout.

	Voter Turnout	
3x1 Municipal Spending	−0.501[+]	−
	(0.276)	−
3x1 Municipal Projects	−	−0.053
	−	(0.037)
Poverty	5.781[+]	5.779[+]
	(3.027)	(3.027)
Poverty Squared	−1.281	−1.272
	(0.927)	(0.928)
Migration Index	−0.009	0.008
	(0.979)	(0.976)
Literacy Rate	−0.620*	−0.625*
	(0.262)	(0.262)
Indigenous Population	0.422*	0.423*
	(0.213)	(0.214)
Population (log)	23.079**	23.071**
	(3.986)	(3.995)
Number of Parties	4.926**	4.924**
	(0.332)	(0.332)
PRI	−3.130***	−3.138***
	(0.612)	(0.612)
PRD	−1.415[+]	−1.428[+]
	(0.811)	(0.811)
PAN	−0.769	−0.786
	(0.825)	(0.824)
Tax Revenue (per capita)	0.000[+]	0.000[+]
	(0.000)	(0.000)
Constant	−138.511***	−138.114***
	(40.849)	(40.933)
Observations	10,042	

Robust standard errors in parentheses. $+p < 0.1$; $^*p < 0.05$; $^{**}p < 0.01$;
$^{***}p < 0.001$. All models include state and time fixed effects.

SOURCE: Calculations using data sourced from INEGI Simbad, INE, Conapo, and Sedesol.

Results indicated that the timing and duration of program participation produced treatment effects on voter turnout, party competition, and incumbent winning probability, party vote share, and municipal spending. The late participation (2006–13) in the 3x1 Program was associated with a 3–8 percent increase in voter turnout, when compared with early participation (2002–5). The effect was stronger in 2010–13 than in 2006–10. The timing and duration of program participation also produced effects on government responsiveness: the public works spending (per capita) and public works spending as a share of total spending (per capita). Municipalities that participated in 3x1 after year 2010 were more likely to spend $157 pesos (per capita) on public works than those who participated in the early period, between 2002 and 2006. These late program adopters were also likely to spend 1.8 percent more of the total budget on public works. This finding suggested that municipalities entering the program in the later period enjoyed greater returns on municipal spending on public works and enhanced political competition. Heterogeneous effects models are reported in Table 11. The fixed effects specifications that model the effect of 3x1 Program spending and number of total projects on voter turnout and government spending are presented in Table 12.

NOTES

INTRODUCTION

1. Municipalities are the lowest level of government below the state and federal governments in Mexico's three-tiered federal system. Each municipality is governed by a municipal president (*presidente municipal*), akin to a mayor, who heads a municipal council. Citizens elect the municipal mayor to a three-year term by plurality and incumbents cannot run for immediate reelection. Most municipalities designate one town as the *cabecera municipal* (similar to a county seat in a U.S. township) where the majority of the local population resides. The municipal population not residing in the county seat is spread out across outlying communities referred to as localities (*localidades*). For example, in the municipality of Tlatelnango in Zacatecas, 65 percent of the population resides in the county seat of the same name, while the remaining population is scattered across 75 localities. I use "local" and "municipal" interchangeably to refer to the territorially based lowest tier of government. I use "outlying village" and "locality" to reference villages situated outside municipal county seats, but within the political jurisdiction of the municipal government.

2. Moya 2005.

3. Iskander 2010; Portes and Fernandez-Kelly 2015; Lacroix 2016; Pries and Sezgin 2012.

4. Strode and Grant 2004.

5. On clientelism and distributive politics see Stokes et al. 2013 and Nichter 2008 for the case of turnout-buying.

6. About a quarter of the Mexican population lives in localities with less than 2,500 inhabitants. These rural towns are most often classified as "poor" or "very poor" by the Mexican census. Of the 25 million inhabitants of localities akin to outlying villages or hamlets, 14 percent are located in the vicinity of cities, 9 percent near municipal county seats with population between 2,500 and 15,000 inhabitants, 44 percent are remote from cities and county seats, and 33 percent are in isolation (Conapo 2000). See www.conapo.gob.mx/es/CONAPO/Localidades_rurales.

7. Different terms that refer to countrymen and women are used throughout the world including paisano/a, paesano/a, and son/daughter of the soil, for example.

8. I am referencing here initial endowments of social capital. See, for example, Putnam et al. 1993; Boix and Posner 1998; Coleman 1990; Lin 2001; Heller 1996; Woolcock and Narayan 2000; Knack and Keefer 1997; Portes 1998.

9. In this context legitimacy concerns the ability to defend or justify something, in this case migrant participation, rather than legitimacy in terms of conformity to rules or laws.

10. International Organization for Migration, *Global Migration Trends Factsheet,* 2015.

11. Wilkerson 2010.

12. Tiebout 1956; Hirschman 1978.

13. Bauböck 2003: 705.

14. Basch, Glick Schiller, and Szanton Blanc 1994; Portes, Guarnizo, and Landolt 1999; Durand, Parrado, and Massey 1996; Levitt 1998, 2001; Itzigsohn 2000; Pries 2001; Guarnizo, Portes, and Haller 2003; Smith 2006; Waldinger 2015.

15. Andrews 2018.

16. Levitt and Glick Schiller 2004.

17. Moya 2005; Wyman 1993; Levitt 2001.

18. Soehl and Waldinger 2010.

19. Moya 2005.

20. Massey et al. 1987; Massey and Zenteno 1999; Massey and Espinosa 1997; Garip 2016.

21. Massey et al. 1987; FitzGerald 2008; Mines 1981.

22. Massey et al. 1987: 143 (emphasis in original).

23. Duquette-Rury and Bada 2013; author's survey results also presented in chapter 6.

24. Goldring 1998.

25. *World Bank Migration and Remittances Factbook,* 2016.

26. Ibid., iv.

27. Kapur 2004; Yang 2011; Adams and Page 2005.

28. Durand, Parrado, and Massey 1996; Taylor 1999; Yang 2011.

29. Adams and Page 2005; Acosta et al. 2008; Singer 2010; Kapur and McHale 2005; Kapur 2010; Fajnzylber and Lopez 2008; Giuliano and Ruiz-Arranz 2009; Chami et al. 2008; Docquier and Lodigiani 2010; Catrinescu et al. 2009; Batista and Vicente 2011.

30. Kapur 2004.

31. Levitt 1998, 2001.

32. Levitt 1998.

33. Levitt 2001; Page 2007; Pérez-Armendáriz and Crow 2010.

34. Lacroix 2014; Carling 2014.

35. Goldring 1998; Waldinger 2015; Mahmud 2014.

36. Zelizer and Tilly 2006.

37. Smith 2006; Mazzucato and Kabki 2009; Levitt 2001; Waldinger 2015; Grillo and Ricchio 2004.

38. Abdih et al. 2012; Ahmed 2012; Escriba-Folch, Meseguer, and Wright 2015.

39. Goodman and Hiskey 2008; Bravo 2009; Cordova and Hiskey 2015; Piper 2009; Rother 2009; Ahmed 2012; O'Mahony 2013; Perez-Armendaríz and Crow 2010; Duquette-Rury and Chen 2018.

40. Pérez-Armendaríz and Crow 2010; Pérez-Armendaríz 2014; Careja and Emmenegger 2012; Duquette-Rury, Waldinger, and Lim 2018. For research on migrant involvement in campaign finance, lobbying, serving in elected office, and voting from abroad in national elections see Kapur 2010; Lafleur 2013; Nyblade and O'Mahony 2014.

41. Goldring 1998; Portes 1999; Levitt 2001; Østergaard-Nielsen 2003; Burgess 2005, 2012. 2016; Smith 2006; Fox and Bada 2008; Danielson 2018; Smith and Bakker 2008; Bada 2014.

42. Portes 1999; Østergaard-Nielsen 2003; Fox and Bada 2008; Itzigsohn and Villacres 2008.

43. Levitt 2001; Smith 2006.

44. Burgess 2005, 2016; Bada 2014.

45. Østergaard-Nielsen 2003; Waldinger, Popkin, and Magana 2008; Mazzucato and Kabki 2009.

46. Meseguer and Aparicio 2012; Aparicio and Meseguer 2012; Simpser et al. 2016.

47. Waldinger and FitzGerald 2004; FitzGerald 2008; Smith and Bakker 2008; Délano 2011, 2018; Lacroix 2016.

48. Simper et al. 2016.

49. Levi 1988.

50. Olson [1965] 2007.

51. Ostrom and Ostrom 1977; Ostrom 1990.

52. Dahl 1971.

53. Bardhan and Mookherjee 2000; Besley and Burgess 2002; Grindle 2007; Ndegwa and Levy 2004; Larsen and Ribot 2004; Giraudy 2010; Falleti 2010; Bohlken 2016; Smith and Revell 2016; Przeworski, Stokes, and Manin 1999. For evidence of political manipulation of social spending in decentralized Mexico see, for example, Diaz-Cayeros, Estevez, and Magaloni 2016

54. Bird 1993; Oates 1972; Blair 2000; Besley 2006.

55. Falletti 2010.

56. O'Donnell 1988.

57. Diaz-Cayeros, Magaloni, and Ruiz-Euler 2014; Hagopian and Mainwaring, 2005; Levitsky and Murillo 2005; Helmke and Levitsky 2006; Smith 2005.

58. Dahl 1971; Schmitter 2004; Evans 1996; Ostrom 1996.

59. Almond and Verba 1963; Verba and Nie 1972; Verba, Schlozman, and Brady 1995; Campbell 2003; Ackerman 2004; Peruzzotti and Smulovitz 2006; Fox 2007.

60. Verba et al. 1995.

61. Tocqueville [1835] 2000; Lipset 1960; Almond and Verba 1963; Verba and Nie 1972; Dahl 1989; Putnam 1993; Verba, Schlozman, and Brady 1995.

62. Putnam 1993; Fukuyama 1999.

63. Fukuyama 1999; Boix and Posner 1998.

64. Holzner 2010.

65. Grindle 2007; Cleary 2010; Diaz-Cayeros, Magaloni, and Ruiz-Euler 2014; Ackerman 2004; Tendler 1997; Ostrom 1996; Evans 1996; Cornwall and Coelho 2007; Diamond and Plattner 1999; Goetz and Jenkins 2001; Heller 2001; Avritzer 2002; Fung and Wright 2003; Auyero 1999; Fox and Aranda 1996; Wampler 2007; Peruzzotti and Smulovitz 2006; Duquette-Rury 2016.

66. Heller 2001; Evans 1996; Baiocchi 2001, 2003.

67. Ostrom 1996; Evans 1996; Tendler 1997; Gaventa 2004; Ackerman 2004; Pritchett and Woolcock 2004; Goldfrank 2011; McNulty 2011.

68. Cornwall and Coelho 2007.

69. Evans 1996; Ostrom 1996.

70. Levitt 2001; Smith 2006; Lacroix 2014; Smith and Bakker 2008.

71. Lacroix 2014: 665; Carling 2014: 1459. See also Goldring 1998; Levitt 2001; Smith 2006; Duquette-Rury 2016.

72. Hirschman 1970.

73. Levitt and Lamba-Nieves 2011.

74. Aparicio and Meseguer 2012; Meseguer and Aparicio 2012; Goldring 1998; Danielson 2018; Bada 2014; Smith and Bakker 2008.

75. For exceptions see FitzGerald 2006 and Lacroix 2014.

76. There is an extensive literature on Mexican hometown associations, specifically, and hometown associations in other parts of the world based on single country cases or associations. For a historical overview of immigrant organizations, see Moya 2005; for the historical legacy of Mexican mutual aid societies linked to contemporary hometown associations in the United States, see Pycior 2014. On HTAs in Europe see Østergaard-Nielsen 2001; Soysal 1994; Caglar 2006; Hersant and Toumarkine 2005; Lacroix 2014, 2016. On HTAs and "Sons/Daughters of the Soil" on the African continent see Barkan, McNulty, and Ayeni 1991: Honey and Okafor 1998; Trager 2001; Henry and Mohan 2003; Page 2007; Mazzucato and Kabki 2009; Mercer, Page and Evans 2009; Beauchemin and Schoumaker 2009; Hickey 2011; Chauvet et al. 2013; McKenzie and Yang 2015. On HTAs from the Latin America and the Caribbean, the Philippines, and East Asia see Maeyama 1979; Okamura 2014; Hirabayashi 1986; Levitt 1997, 2001; Nyiri 2001; Paul and Gammage 2004; Orozco 2006; Silva 2006; Waldinger et al. 2008; Itzigsohn and Villacrés 2008; Loebach 2016. For Mexican HTAs see Smith and Guarnizo 1998; Goldring 1998; Orozco 2002, 2003; Zabin and Escala 2002; Moctezuma Longoria 2002; Alarcon 2002; Bada 2003; Fox and Rivera-Salgado 2004; Rivera-Salgado and Escala Rabadán 2004; López and Ángel 2004; Lanly and Valenzuela 2004; Orozco and Lapointe 2004; Escala Rabadán, Bada, and Rivera-Salgado 2006; Stephen 2007; Orozco and Welle 2005; Frias, Ibarra, and Soto 2006; Smith 1998, 2006; Duquette-Rury and Bada 2013; Duquette-Rury 2014.

77. Thomas Lacroix's extensive research on what he calls "hometown transnationalism" and "hometown organizations" shares this view.

78. Hirschman 1978.

79. Cornwall and Coelho 2003; Mansbridge 2000.

80. Duquette-Rury 2014.

81. World Bank Group 2016.

82. Conapo 2000, 2010.

83. Lipset 1960; Przeworski et al. 2000.

84. Instituto Nacional de Estadística y Geografía (Inegi) 2013.

85. Duquette-Rury 2014.

86. Author's calculations using Sedesol's database of 3x1 Program projects, 2002–13.

87. Seawright 2016.

88. Duquette 2011.

89. Jalisco has the lion's share of coproduction projects with 5,264, Zacatecas 3,372, and Guanajuato with 1,769 completed projects as of 2013.

90. In more populated outlying localities, residents select a delegate (*delegado*) who represents their interests in municipal government. The position is not a salaried, full-time position and the delegate most often serves as a liaison in an informal capacity.

1. LOCAL DEMOCRATIC GOVERNANCE AND TRANSNATIONAL MIGRANT PARTICIPATION

1. Staniland's research on the role of politicized and unpoliticized social bases in the construction and transformation of insurgent organization and rebellion was helpful to my thinking on migrant social embeddedness. See Staniland 2014.

2. Emirbayer and Goodwin 1994.

3. Goldring 1998.

4. Levitt 2001; Goodman and Hiskey 2008; Pérez-Armendariz and Crow 2010.

5. In Mexico, HTAs support public goods in different geographic contexts. Some HTAs invest in projects in one or more localities in their municipality of origin, while others may focus their efforts exclusively in the county seat (Duquette-Rury and Bada 2013). The geography of projects is determined, in part, by negotiations between the HTA and the municipal government as well as the membership base of the HTA, which reflects the concentration of paisanos in the destination.

6. Young 2002.

7. In this way, migrant HTAs may come to represent the collective preferences of local residents much like political parties.

8. This includes *compradazgo*. *Compradazgo* is a word in Spanish that literally translates to "coparenthood" or "godparenthood," both of which are fictive kinship relationships with origins in the Roman Catholic Church. At birth, biological parents select "compadres" and "comadres" (also referred to as *padrinos* and *madrinas*) to serve as coparents to the child. *Compradazgo* often formalizes preexisting friendships and lifelong bonds between compadres (close friends). Often compadres and godparents provide political protection and economic support for their godchildren and the whole family.

9. Putnam 2000. Granovetter (1983) refers to bridging ties as "weak" social ties that link to more distant acquaintances moving in different social circles.

10. Woolcock and Narayan 2000.

11. See Woolcock and Narayan 2000.

12. See Gaventa 2004 and Cornwall and Coelho 2007 for a discussion of inclusion of marginalized groups in participatory spheres.

13. Putnam 2000: 22–23.

14. Cohen 2002.

15. Binder et al. 2008: 10. See also Lamont 1992, 2000.

16. Anderson 2006.

17. Lamont 2000.

18. Other nonstate actors keen on disrupting coproduction for personal gain may include local mafia and drug-related and non-drug-related criminal gangs, and political bosses working for the electoral victory of select political parties and candidates.

19. Staniland 2012: 36.

20. Weber 1978.

21. See Tsai 2007 for important research on the role of informal institutions of accountability in nondemocratic settings.

22. Ziblatt 2008.

23. Mann 1984.

24. Pearlman 2014: 41.

25. Meseguer and Aparicio's research suggests a political bias in coproduction partnerships depending on partisan identity of the incumbent and the degree of political competition. They find that, regardless of the objective social welfare needs of a locality, local officials are more likely to engage and support coproduction projects in partisan strongholds than in places with more contested elections. See Meseguer and Aparicio 2012; Aparicio and Meseguer 2012.

26. Bueno de Mesquita et al. 2005.

27. Recent research from Simpser et al. 2016 reveals that coproduction spending through the 3x1 Program follows a local political budget cycle. Municipalities that participate in the 3x1 Program are more likely to engage in coproduction projects in pre-election and election years, periods when public infrastructure projects are visible to the voting public and incumbents can take credit for service provision.

28. This conceptual relationship space follows the spirit of Dahl 1971 and Koopmans 2005.

29. Fragmented coproduction need not result in co-optation, although I suggest it is likely. Low inclusion and engagement may produce coproduction partnerships that fizzle or fail after the completion of a single project.

30. There are many cases in which HTAs privately supply public goods without any complementary involvement of public agencies in the sending state; however, treatment of this kind of remittance-led provision is beyond the scope of this book. In this vein, HTAs are akin to nonstate providers (NSP) of social welfare. See Cammett and MacLean 2011 for more discussion of NSP social welfare provision in the global South.

31. I describe how additional factors such as HTA capacity, drug violence, and the U.S. recession affect coproduction partnerships in chapters 4, 6, and the conclusion.

2. DECENTRALIZATION, DEMOCRATIZATION, AND THE FEEDBACK EFFECTS OF SENDING-STATE OUTREACH

1. Cornelius 2001.

2. Garip 2016.

3. Lawful permanent residents (green card holders) have the right to petition for minor children and unmarried sons and daughters over the age of 21 through normal immigration channels.

4. Gonzalez-Barrera and Lopez 2013.

5. Durand and Massey 2003.

6. Massey 2008.

7. Riosmena and Massey 2012.

8. Donato et al. 2007.

9. Smith and Guarnizo 1998; Goldring 1998; Orozco 2003; Zabin and Escala 2002; Moctezuma Longoria 2002; Alarcón 2002; Bada 2003; Fox and Rivera-Salgado 2004; Rivera-Salgado and Escala Rabadán 2004; López and Ángel 2004; Lanly and Valenzuela 2004; Orozco and Lapointe 2004; Escala Rabadán et al. 2006; Stephen 2007; Orozco and Welle 2005; Frias, Ibarra and Soto 2006; Smith 1998, 2006; Duquette-Rury and Bada 2013. See Bada 2013 for a rich history of Mexican HTAs in the United States.

10. Escala-Rabadán, Bada, and Rivera-Salgado 2006.

11. Author's data analysis from Sedesol's 3x1 dataset.

12. FitzGerald 2008a, 2008b.

13. Duquette-Rury and Bada 2013.

14. In some *usos y costumbres* hometowns, migrants who do not fulfill their social obligations to the community may be sanctioned by not being allowed to be buried in the place of their birth.

15. Author's original survey data.

16. Levitt 2001; Smith 2006.

17. Goldring 1998; Waldinger et al. 2008.

18. Woods 1994; Henry and Mohan 2003; Lentz 1994.

19. Itzigsohn and Saucedo 2002 refer to this as "reactive transnationalism."

20. Zelizer and Tilly 2006; Lacroix 2014.

21. A *sexenio* is the term limit of the president of Mexico. Presidential terms in Mexico are restricted to a single six-year term and the individual is prohibited from serving in the president post again.

22. Smith and Bakker 2008.

23. The word *pocho* literally means fruit that has become rotten or discolored.

24. See Sherman 1999; Cano and Délano 2007; Garcia y Griego 1990, 1993; Garcia y Griego and Campos 1988; Ayon 2005; and FitzGerald 2008a for a history of Mexican emigration policy.

25. FitzGerald 2008a.

26. Délano 2011.

27. Decentralization policies refer to the set of policy reforms that transfer resources, authority, or responsibilities from national to subnational levels of government, which accompany a move toward a free market economy in the context of the neoliberal market agenda. Rodriguez (1997) and Falleti (2003) describe fiscal decentralization as the set of policies that increase the revenues of subnational political units (municipal or state level) through higher levels of revenue-sharing schemes from the central government, the creation of new subnational taxes, or the delegation of taxing responsibility. Administrative decentralization includes the set of policies that transfer the administration and delivery of particular social services to subnational levels of government, which typically include the devolution of decision-making authority. Political decentralization describes the set of constitutional amendments and electoral reforms that open up new spaces for political representation and devolve electoral capacities to subnational actors. In the realm of political decentralization mayors and governors previously appointed by the presidency became popularly elected.

28. Rodriguez 1997: 47.

29. Magaloni et al. 2007.

30. Dresser 1993.

31. Ibid., 96.

32. Sherman 1999.

33. See FitzGerald 2000 for an extended discussion of the International Solidarity Program.

34. Personal communications with personnel in migrant affairs offices in Zacatecas, Guanajuato, and Jalisco.

35. Orozco and Walle 2005.

36. Rodriguez 1997: 77.

37. Hiskey 2003.

38. Diaz-Cayeros et al. 2016.

39. Personal communication with consulate representatives, Chicago, IL March 2008.

40. Personal communication with former directors of the state-level offices for migrant affairs in Guanajuato, Jalisco, Zacatecas, and San Luis Potosi.

41. Courchene and Díaz-Cayeros (2000) argues that states theoretically retained the capacity to levy income, payroll, and sales taxes and all other taxes not explicitly listed in Article 73 of the Constitution, but taxes on foreign trade, natural resources, banks, insurance, excise taxes on electricity, tobacco, natural gas, matches, alcohol, forestry, and beer remained in control of the federal government. In exchange for states refraining from using their own tax authority, the federal treasury transferred shares of the tax revenue (*participaciones*) directly to the states and these transfers increasingly came to constitute the most important source of municipal financing.

42. Grindle 2007.

43. Ibid., 88.

44. Courchene and Díaz-Cayeros 2000.

45. See Magaloni et al. 2007; Rodriguez and Ward 1998; Rodriguez 1997.

46. Lujambio 2001.

47. Quoted in Iskander 2010: 251.

48. For a rich and dynamic presentation of the process by which the 3x1 policy was created, negotiated, and amended over time in Mexico, see Iskander 2010.

49. Interviews with state-level officials in Zacatecas, August 2010.

50. Iskander 2010.

51. Telephone interviews with officials in Casas Guanajuato organization in Texas, November 2008.

52. Pa'l Norte DAGCE agency newsletter 1994.

53. Fox claimed 33 Casas Guanajuato in his presidential campaign addresses.

54. Iskander 2010.

55. Iskander 2010.

56. Quoted in Iskander 2010: 289.

57. Personal interview June 25, 2009, Zacatecas.

58. Quoted in Iskander 2010: 291.

59. Zolberg 1999.

60. Waldinger 2015.

3. MICRO-POLITICS OF SUBSTITUTIVE AND SYNERGETIC PARTNERSHIPS

1. Reymundo and Francisco credit the expansion of club membership to the ability to keep track of friends, relatives, and acquaintances moving to different parts of the United States through social media, the Mexican consulate, and the Office of Migrant Affairs in Selvillo, which kept detailed records of paisanos' whereabouts in the U.S. who were originally from the municipality. Reymundo, Francisco, and Octavio, core leaders of the club, contacted Cerritenses and asked them to set up club "branches" in cities where concentrations of paisanos settled, including California, Texas, Colorado, Georgia, and Illinois. The branches were primarily focused on fundraising activities, including door-knocking, picnics, dances, and raffles to collect money for public goods projects. Migrant club leaders along with a board of directors (*mesa directiva*) coordinated fundraising, project selection, and approvals through the 3x1 Program Validation Committees called COVAM.

2. As of 2013, the Club has coproduced the sixth highest number of projects through the 3x1 Program.

3. Like many municipalities, El Cerrito has a community delegate (*delegado*) that represents the town in municipal government.

4. See Kouri 2015 for a rich historical account of Cardenismo and the invention of the *ejido* in Mexico.

5. All face-to-face interviews with key informants occurred between April and June 2009.

6. Selvillo is classified as a middle-income municipality by INEGI.

7. The mayor requested permission from local council officials (*regidores*) to create a municipal 3x1 position. The 3x1 liaison receives a municipal salary for overseeing all 3x1 Program activities.

8. INEGI Conteo de Población y Vivienda 2005.

9. Face-to-face interviews with key informants in Telepi occurred between April and June 2009.

10. Face-to-face interview in Telepi, March 2009. Face-to-face interviews with Sarita and Leo took place between March 2009 and December 2009 in Telepi and over the phone when they returned to California.

11. There are a few HTAs that sporadically engage in coproduction in Telepi and one additional HTA that has had a long-term presence in the municipality.

12. Evans 1996.

4. EFFECTS OF VIOLENCE AND ECONOMIC CRISIS ON HYBRID TRANSNATIONAL PARTNERSHIPS

1. I did not choose the transnational partnership case in Santa Catarina because it had drug violence. In fact, I was unaware of the precarious conditions in the hometown when I selected the case and began the fieldwork in the summer of 2009. Had I known then what I learned in the field and subsequently, I would not have exposed local residents of the town to any unwanted attention that my presence may have brought.

2. "Rural" is classified as a population of less than 10,000 people.

3. All sociodemographic and economic information is taken from the INEGI municipality database called SIMBAD.

4. Interview with Miguel, September 2010.

5. All face-to-face interviews occurred in Santa Catarina in August 2009. I conducted several follow-up telephone interviews with club leaders and residents in Santa Catarina in September and October 2009 and face-to-face interviews in Chicago with Raul and Miguel in 2009 and 2010.

6. Interview with the pastor, August 2009.

7. Andrea Bocanegra, "Confirma SSP amenazas del narco a 8 presidentes municipales de Michoacán," Andrea Bocanegra, *Marmor Informa,* August 8, 2017, www.marmorinforma.mx/confirma-ssp-amenazas-del-narco-8-presidentes-municipales-michoacan/. See also "Matan a alcalde de Michoacán que denunciaba pagos de cuotas al 'narco,'" *Aristegue Noticias,* November 8, 2013, https://aristeguinoticias.com/0811/mexico/matan-a-alcalde-de-michoacan-que-denunciaba-al-narco/.

8. Interview with club leaders in Chicago, IL, July 2010.

9. Even with more citizen engagement, corruption may not have been thwarted, suggesting more citizen inclusion may not necessarily prevent corruption by rent-seeking politicians.

10. Interview with Miguel, Chicago, IL, September 2010.

11. In this context *mano negra* means suspicious of wrongdoing.

12. In colloquial Spanish, *guaje* can refer to a "fool," but in this context it is the nickname locals gave the municipal delegate to describe his physical appearance. *Guajes* are very long, thin pods from the wild tamarind tree that grows throughout the region. El Guaje was a tall, thin man with a zesty sense of humor.

13. Recall from chapter 2 that the Casas Guanajuato are nonprofit 501(c)3 organizations that serve as community centers and provide educational, cultural, and recreational support and services to the Guanajuato migrant community in the United States. Casas Guanajuato are located throughout the U.S., but older, more established sites are located in Dallas, Texas, San Diego, and Los Angeles.

5. SYNERGY AND CORPORATISM IN EL MIRADOR AND ATITLAN, COMARGA

1. INEGI, Censo General de Población y Vivienda 2000.

2. INEGI, Censo General de Población y Vivienda 2010. INEGI uses the marginalization index to categorize municipalities as very high, high, medium, low, and very low levels of marginalization. The marginalization index is a scalar index that reflects households' access to essential public goods provision, income distribution, basic amenities in dwellings including the number of households with earthen (dirt) floors and piping, and literacy.

3. Adida and Girod 2011.

4. The Patronato is the local association responsible for planning and executing the annual patron saint festival in Atitlan. The festival is the most important social event of the year.

5. Face-to-face interview in Atitlan, March 2009. All interviews in the municipality were conducted during fieldwork between March and August 2009.

6. Email correspondence dated April 5, 2009.

7. Emilio told me he had political aspirations of his own in Mexico. Many former migrants have successfully campaigned and won mayoral office after they returned to their hometowns.

8. HTAs created by the administration in the same period are still active and successfully coproducing in three other communities in Comarga. Local political participation and state-society relations have improved as a result of more synergetic coproduction in these places, where government engagement was consistent, but community inclusion was higher.

9. Piven and Cloward 1997: 276.

6. SYSTEMATIC EFFECTS OF TRANSNATIONAL PARTNERSHIPS ON LOCAL GOVERNANCE

1. See Bada 2014 and Smith 2006.

2. Goldring 2002; Zabin and Escala 2002; Lanly and Valenzuela 2004; Smith 2006; Smith and Bakker 2008; Bada 2014; Fox and Rivera-Salgado 2004; Alarcón 2000.

3. Orozco 2003; Portes, Escobar, and Arana 2008; Portes, Escobar and Radford 2007.

4. About 25 surveys had missing data.

5. These data were taken directly from Sedesol's 3x1 database for the most recent project in which each club was involved. Separate from the variables that formed the government engagement index, I also collected all the available 3x1 data for each survey club respondent for the full time period, 2002–13. HTA survey responses were cross-checked with 3x1 data to ensure an additional measure of reliability.

6. Olson [1965] 2007.

7. FitzGerald 2008a.

8. All of the club leaders who participated in the survey could indicate if they wished to receive a copy of the survey results via email at the close of the project.

9. Filiz Garip's (2016) use and presentation of cluster analysis in her research on Mexican migration streams inspired this methodological step. I appreciate her leadership in the use of cluster analysis in the sociological study of international migration.

10. In addition to running OLS, I also ran logit models for each coproduction type separately and I evaluated the degree to which coproduction types are statistically and substantively different across the types using multiple methods including T-test and ANOVA tests. The full specifications with coproduction types as categorical dependent variables including all theoretically relevant controls were also evaluated. The results were consistent. I do not report the findings here, but they are available upon request.

11. Heterogeneous regression model results are not reported here due to space limitations, but are available upon request. In these models, I compare how partnerships occurring in different program periods—for example, "early program adopters" versus "late program adopters," and more and less "habitual program participants"—vary in their political outcomes.

12. This strategy excludes municipalities that may engage in informal forms of coproduction outside of the 3x1 Program as well as cases in which migrant HTAs may provide public goods without any involvement of local government. There is no data that helps to capture these additional cases, unfortunately.

13. Sedesol does not report information about projects that were proposed, but not approved, by the validation committees that oversee project proposals (*Comite de Validation y Atención a Migrantes* or COVAM), which is a limitation of the data. Interviews with personnel at COVAM meetings in 2009, 2010, and 2011 in Guanajuato, Zacatecas, and Jalisco suggest that projects are typically rejected because (1) local government fails to sign on to overseeing projects, (2) previous projects have not been completed as proposed in earlier periods, and (3) the HTA has outstanding contributions from previous projects (Simpser et al. 2016).

14. Aaron Malone, PhD candidate in geography at Colorado, is conducting dissertation research on the spatial diffusion of policy adoption of the 3x1 Program across Mexico. His research is consistent with the findings described here. See Malone and Durden 2018.

15. Diamond 1999.

16. Schumpeter 1947; Dahl 1971; Collier and Levitsky 1997; Diamond and Plattner 1999; Przeworski et al. 2000; Mainwaring, Brinks, and Pérez-Liñán 2007; Altman and Pérez-Liñán 2002.

17. Putnam et al. 1993.

18. Additional information about the Mexican Family Life Survey is available at www.ennvih-mxfls.org/english/index.html.

19. Diamond and Morlino 2005: xxix.

20. Mizrahi 1998; Cleary and Stokes 2006; Cleary 2010.

21. Cleary 2010.

22. Cleary 2010: 115.

23. Simpser et al. 2016.

24. Diamond and Morlino 2005.

25. This is consistent with results in Simpser et al. 2016.

26. Putnam et al. 1993.

CONCLUSION: THE PARADOX OF CROSS-BORDER POLITICS

1. Cammett and MacLean 2011: 7–8.

2. Dahl 1971.

3. Ostrom 1996.

4. Basch et al. 1994.

5. Levitt and Glick Schiller 2004.

6. See Moss 2016 for the case of transnational uprising during the Arab Spring.

7. Bardhan and Mookherjee 2006; Grindle 2007; Falleti 2010.

8. Cammett and MacLean 2011.

9. Global Forum on Migration and Development, 2007–2018.

10. I thank David FitzGerald for suggesting this characterization of migrant social ties to me.

11. Barry 2006: 17.

12. Bloemraad 2006.

13. Waldinger 2015: 32. See also Levitt 2001 and Goldring 1998.

14. Fitzgerald 2006.

15. Barry 2006: 34; Bloemraad 2006: 9.

16. Barry 2006: 25.

17. Waldinger et al. 2008.

18. Andrews 2018.

19. Cammett and MacLean 2014.

20. Tusalem 2018; Mazzucato and Kabki 2009; Zhou and Lee 2013; Agarwala 2015.

21. Fitzgerald 2006.

22. Gamlen 2006; Délano and Gamlen 2014.

23. See Diossa-Jimenez's forthcoming dissertation for an explication of emigration policies in Latin America.

24. Bhagwati 2003.

25. A growing literature examines the causes and consequences of emigrant state development policies and destination country codevelopment policies across countries as diverse as Morocco, the Philippines, Turkey, Mexico, Mauritius, Algeria, Bulgaria, Colombia, Ecuador, Mali, Romania, Senegal, Ghana, India, Serbia, Spain, France, and the Netherlands to name a few (see Nyberg-Sorensen et al. 2002; Vezzoli and Lacroix 2010; Schmelz 2009; Orozco 2003; Baraulina et al. 2007; de Haas 2006; Østergaard-Nielsen 2009; Lacomba and Cloquell 2014; Iskander 2010; Lacroix 2014).

26. Hirschman 1984.

27. Verba, Schlozman, and Brady 1995; Verba and Nie 1987.

28. Hirschman 1970.

29. Putnam et al. 1993; Verba et al. 1995.

30. Tendler 1997; Fox 2007; Ackerman 2004.

31. Ostrom 1996; Evans 1996; Tendler 1997.

32. Peruzzotti and Smulovitz 2006.

33. Tsai 2007.

34. Ioan Grillo, "Why Cartels Are Killing Mexico's Mayors," *New York Times,* January 15, 2016. See also Trejo and Ley 2016, 2017 on the role of partisan politics in the escalation of violent murders of subnational political officials.

35. Justice in Mexico 2016. See https://justiceinmexico.org/three-michoacan-mayors-indicted-another-appears-in-images-with-la-tuta/.

36. Key paisano informants from Jalisco and Guanajuato, telephone interviews in July 2013, May 2014, and August 2016.

37. See Guerra and Asencio 2015; Rivera Velázquez 2014; Fuentes Díaz and Paleta Pérez 2015; Orozco-Aleman and Gonzalez-Lozano 2017; Phillips 2017; Trejo and Ley 2016, 2017 on *autodefensas* and the vigilante movement in Mexico. See also Meseguer, Ley, and Ibarra-Olivo 2017; Basu and Pearlman 2017; Pérez-Armendáriz and Duquette-Rury 2019 on migration and violence in Mexico.

38. Moss 2016.

DATA APPENDIX B

1. Many Mexican HTAs choose not to register with the IME for a host of reasons. Future research might address similarities and differences between registered and nonregistered clubs through snowball sampling methods. This is beyond the scope of this book.

2. With generous financial support from the National Science Foundation SBE grant SES-0819245, I contracted the University of Chicago Survey Lab to contact potential survey respondents. The results were coded by hand by me and a research assistant.

3. About 25 surveys had missing data.

4. Three quarters of the survey sample is between one and seven years old, while a quarter of the sample is older than seven years. The oldest club formed in 1969.

DATA APPENDIX C

1. See Jolliffe 1986.

2. For instance, categorical variables were transformed into dichotomous variables for each main category and continuous variables transformed into dichotomous variables using the first quantile as the cut point.

3. We use the conventional test of Cronbach's alpha (alpha >0.7).

4. These data were taken directly from Sedesol's 3x1 database for the most recent project in which each club was involved. Separate from the variables that formed the government engagement index, we also collected all the available 3x1 data for each survey club respondent for the full time period, 2002–2013.

5. Different facets that characterize a migrant club's overall capacity—for example, revenue generation activities, leadership characteristics, and organizational structure—together explain most of the variance on capacity.

6. I did not ask respondents explicitly about their legal status in the United States because I did not want to cause them anxiety. This is a limitation of the data that is important to acknowledge. I recognize that club leadership is likely to change. All of the indices thus reflect the current period of club activities, creating a snapshot of organizational form of coproduction and not reflective of the dynamism that is inherent to these partnerships.

7. Tan, Steinbach, and Kumar 2005. For information about the kmeans algorithm, see Kanungo et al. 2002.

8. Kmeans cluster analysis program in STATA initially creates the k clusters according to an arbitrary procedure. The program calculates the means or centroids of each of the clusters. If one of the observations is closer to the centroid of another cluster, then the observation is made a member of that cluster. This process is repeated until none of the observations are reassigned to a different cluster. Unlike hierarchical cluster analysis, kmeans clustering does not produce all possible clusters of n observations. I have also run the analysis by assigning a type of coproduction based on low, high, medium values of the continuous index using a quartile cut point. I then ran interaction models with community inclusion and government engagement and controlled for all other factors likely to affect the organization of partnerships and observed how the interactions affected measures of democracy. The results are similar to the findings in the cluster analysis section, increasing confidence. These data are not reported, but available by request.

9. I tried several numbers of clusters (2, 3, 5, 6, and 10) using all three diagnostic methods. Four clusters emerged repeatedly as the "tightest" clusters with each method. The cluster analysis was also conducted using continuous values for all indices, but I use the categorical variables for ease of interpretation and explanation. The results hold using the continuous values. I also note for the reader that additional variables were included in the cluster analysis including poverty and migration intensity, which did not produce significant changes in the clusters. As I detail in later sections, poverty and migration are associated with particular kinds of coproduction, but not in their formation.

DATA APPENDIX D

1. Each record includes the year that the survey was taken for each panel wave.

2. For example, researchers employ Heckman selection models, instrumental variable approaches, difference-in-difference estimations, and nonparametric propensity score matching methods.

3. Results on OLS specifications, which are in all likelihood extremely biased, are available by request.

4. See Ashenfelter 1978; Buckley and Shang 2003; Imbens and Wooldridge 2009. For excellent examples of the application of DiD approaches to observational data, see Card and Krueger 2000; Hastings 2004; Watson 2006.

5. I would like to thank Zeke Chen for outstanding research assistance on data collection, cleaning, coding, and analysis.

6. This is also referred to as the parallel trend assumption. Data on pre-program period should show that the difference between treated and control is stable, not necessarily that the trends are precisely parallel. Moreover, data on post-program periods should show that the difference between treated and control occurs concurrent with program participation. All fixed effects DiD models were subjected to an AR (1) disturbance in the event of serial autocorrelation and estimated with bootstrapping. No significant differences were found in these specifications.

7. We also conducted Heckman selection models to observe selection into the 3x1 Program and political outcomes of interest. The results are not reported but are available by request.

8. Alesina, Baqir, and Easterly 1997.

9. For representative examples see Cleary 2010 and Verba et al. 1995.

10. Hiskey 2003; Cleary 2010.

11. Two strands of the distributive politics literature point to different political rationale for public goods provision (Aparicio and Meseguer 2012; Meseguer and Aparicio 2012). On the one hand, in competitive multiparty political systems, the size of the coalition of voters required for victory is small, and targeted spending is likely more effective than programmatic spending on public goods (Bueno de Mesquita et al. 2005). Conversely, in less competitive locales, programmatic spending on public goods, which by definition are non-rivalrous and nonexclusionary, benefit a larger number of voters and increase the likelihood of securing a winning coalition. On the other hand, other research contends that politicians use public projects to target politically competitive localities in order to win over swing voters, optimizing electoral returns (Cox and McCubbins 1986; Calvo and Murillo 2004; Kitschelt and Wilkinson 2007; Diaz Cayeros, Estevez, and Magaloni 2016). The competitiveness of local elections is likely to affect public goods provision either because politicians seek to reward core supporters in less competitive locales or win over swing voters in more competitive locales.

12. We evaluate both state and municipal linear trends.

13. Zeke Chen, STATA wizard, figured out how to code the time interactions for treatments with state and municipal fixed effects. The calculations sometimes took days to run. I thank him for his patience.

14. Durbin-Wu-Hausman tests were run to test for the possibility of endogeneity.

15. Imbens and Wooldridge 2007.

BIBLIOGRAPHY

Abdih, Yasser, Ralph Chami, Jihad Dagher, and Peter Montiel. "Remittances and Institutions: Are Remittances a Curse?" *World Development* 40, no. 4 (2012): 657–66.

Acevedo, Jesse. "Move, Work, Save, Send: The Political Economy of Migration and Remittances." PhD diss., University of California, 2016.

Ackerman, John. "Co-Governance for Accountability: Beyond 'Exit' and 'Voice.'" *World Development* 32, no. 3 (2004): 447–63.

Acosta, Pablo, Pablo Fajnzylber, and J. Humberto Lopez. "Remittances and Household Behavior: Evidence from Latin America." In *Remittances and Development: Lessons from Latin America*, edited by Pablo Fajnzylber and J. Humberto Lopez, 133–70. Washington, DC: World Bank, 2008.

Adams Jr., Richard H., and John Page. "Do International Migration and Remittances Reduce Poverty in Developing Countries?" *World Development* 33, no. 10 (2005): 1645–69.

Adida, Claire L., and Desha M. Girod. "Do Migrants Improve Their Hometowns? Remittances and Access to Public Services in Mexico, 1995–2000." *Comparative Political Studies* 44, no. 1 (2011): 3–27.

Agarwala, Rina. "Tapping the Indian Diaspora for Indian Development." In *The State and the Grassroots: Immigrant Transnational Organizations in Four Continents*, edited by Alejandro Portes and Patricia Fernandez-Kelly, 84–110. New York: Berghahn Books, 2015.

Ahmed, Faisal Z. "The Perils of Unearned Foreign Income: Aid, Remittances, and Government Survival." *American Political Science Review* 106, no. 1 (2012): 146–65.

Alarcón, Rafael. "The Development of Hometown Associations in the United States and the Use of Social Remittances in Mexico." In *Sending Money Home: Hispanic Remittances and Community Development*, edited by Rodolfo O. de la Garza and Briant Lindsay Lowell, 101–39. Lanham, MD: Rowman and Littlefield, 2002.

Alesina, Alberto, Reza Baqir, and William Easterly. "Public Goods and Ethnic Divisions." *Quarterly Journal of Economics* 114, no. 4 (1999): 1243–84.

Almond, Gabriel, and Sidney Verba. *The Civic Culture: Political Attitudes and Democracy in Five Nations.* Thousand Oaks, CA: Sage, 1963.

Altman, David, and Aníbal Pérez-Liñán. "Assessing the Quality of Democracy: Freedom, Competitiveness and Participation in Eighteen Latin American Countries." *Democratization* 9, no. 2 (2002): 85–100.

Anderson, Benedict. *Imagined Communities: Reflections on the Origin and Spread of Nationalism.* New York: Verso Books, 2006.

Andrews, Abigail. *Undocumented Politics: Place, Gender, and the Pathways of Mexican Migrants.* Oakland: University of California Press, 2018.

Aparicio, Francisco Javier, and Covadonga Meseguer. "Collective Remittances and the State: The 3×1 Program in Mexican Municipalities." *World Development* 40, no. 1 (2012): 206–22.

Ashenfelter, Orley. "Estimating the Effect of Training Programs on Earnings." *Review of Economics and Statistics* 60, no. 1 (1978): 47.

Auyero, Javier. "'From the Client's Point of View': How Poor People Perceive and Evaluate Political Clientelism." *Theory and Society* 28, no. 2 (1999): 297–334.

Avritzer, Leonardo. "Modelos de Deliberação Democrática: Uma Análise do Orçamento Participativo No Brasil." In *Democratizar a Democracia: Os Caminhos da Democracia Participativa*, edited by Boaventura de Sousa Santos, 561–98. Rio de Janeiro: Civilização Brasileira, 2002.

———. "The Different Designs of Public Participation in Brazil: Deliberation, Power Sharing and Public Ratification." *Critical Policy Studies* 6, no. 2 (2012): 113–27.

Ayón, David R. "Mexican Policy and Émigré Communities in the U.S." Background paper presented at the conference "Mexican Migrant Social and Civic Participation in the United States," Woodrow Wilson International Center for Scholars, Washington, DC, 2005.

Bada, Xochitl. "Mexican Hometown Associations." *Citizen Action in the Americas* 5 (March 2003): 1–10.

———. "From National to Topophilic Attachments: Continuities and Changes in Chicago's Mexican Migrant Organizations." *Latino Studies* 11, no. 1 (2013): 28–54.

———. *Mexican Hometown Associations in Chicagoacán: From Local to Transnational Civic Engagement.* New Brunswick, NJ: Rutgers University Press, 2014.

Baiocchi, Gianpaolo. "Participation, Activism, and Politics: The Porto Alegre Experiment and Deliberative Democratic Theory." *Politics & Society* 29, no. 1 (2001): 43–72.

———, ed. *Radicals in Power: The Workers' Party and Experiments in Urban Democracy in Brazil.* New York: Zed Books, 2003.

Baraulina, Tatjana, Michael Bommes, Tanja El-Cherkeh, Heike Daume, and Florin Vadean. "Egyptian, Afghan, and Serbian Diaspora Communities in Germany: How Do They Contribute to Their Country of Origin?" *HWWI Research Papers Migration—Migration Research Group* 3 (2007): 5.

Bardhan, Pranab K., and Dilip Mookherjee. "Capture and Governance at Local and National Levels." *American Economic Review* 90, no. 2 (2000): 135–39.

———. "Decentralization, Corruption, and Government Accountability." *International Handbook on the Economics of Corruption* 6 (2006): 161–88.

Barkan, Joel D., Michael L. McNulty, and M.A.O. Ayeni. "Hometown Voluntary Associations, Local Development, and the Emergence of Civil Society in Western Nigeria." *Journal of Modern African Studies* 29, no. 3 (1991): 457–80.

Barry, Kim. "Home and Away: The Construction of Citizenship in an Emigration Context." *New York University Law Review* 81, no. 1 (2006): 11-59.

Basch, Linda, Nina Glick Schiller, and Cristina Szanton Blanc. *Nations Unbound: Transnational Projects, Postcolonial Predicaments, and Deterritorialized Nation-States.* Amsterdam: Gordon and Breach, Amsterdam 1994.

Basu, Sukanya, and Sarah Pearlman. "Violence and Migration: Evidence from Mexico's Drug War." *Iza Journal of Development and Migration* 7, no. 1 (2017): 18.

Batista, Catia, and Pedro C. Vicente. "Do Migrants Improve Governance at Home? Evidence from a Voting Experiment." *World Bank Economic Review* 25, no. 1 (2011): 77–104.

Bauböck, Rainer. "Towards a Political Theory of Migrant Transnationalism." *International Migration Review* 37, no. 3 (2003): 705.

Beauchemin, Cris, and Bruno Schoumaker. "Are Migrant Associations Actors in Local Development? A National Event-History Analysis in Rural Burkina Faso." *World Development* 37, no. 12 (2009): 1897–913.

Besley, Timothy. *Principled Agents?: The Political Economy of Good Government.* Oxford University Press on Demand, 2006.

——— and Robin Burgess. "The Political Economy of Government Responsiveness: Theory and Evidence From India." *Quarterly Journal of Economics* 117, no. 4 (2002): 1415–51.

Bhagwati, Jagdish. "Borders beyond Control." *Foreign Affairs* 82 (2003): 98–104.

Binder, Amy, Mary Blair-Loy, John Evans, Kwai Ng, and Michael Schudson. "Introduction: the Diversity of Culture." *Annals of the American Academy of Political and Social Science* 619, no. 1 (2008): 6–14.

Bird, Richard M. "Threading the Fiscal Labyrinth: Some Issues in Fiscal Decentralization." *Tax Policy in the Real World* 46, no. 2 (1993): 141–62.

Blair, Harry. "Participation and Accountability at the Periphery: Democratic Local Governance in Six Countries." *World Development* 28, no. 1 (2000): 21–39.

Bloemraad, Irene. *Becoming a Citizen: Incorporating Immigrants and Refugees in the United States and Canada.* Berkeley: University of California Press, 2006.

Bohlken, Anjali Thomas. *Democratization from Above: The Logic of Local Democracy in the Developing World.* Cambridge: Cambridge University Press, 2016.

Boix, Carles, and Daniel N. Posner. "Social Capital: Explaining Its Origins and Effects on Government Performance." *British Journal of Political Science* 28, no. 4 (1998): 686–93.

Bosniak, Linda. "Citizenship Denationalized." *Indiana Journal of Global Legal Studies* (2000): 447–509.

Bravo, Jorge. "Emigración y Compromiso Político en México." *Política y Gobierno* 16, no. 1b (2009).

Buckley, Jack, and Yin Shang. "Estimating Policy and Program Effects with Observational Data: the 'Differences-in-Differences' Estimator." *Practical Assessment, Research & Evaluation* 8, no. 24 (2003): 1–10.

Bueno de Mesquita, Bruce, Alastair Smith, James D. Morrow, and Randolph M. Siverson. *The Logic of Political Survival.* Cambridge, MA: MIT Press, 2005.

Burgess, Katrina. "Migrant Philanthropy and Local Governance in Mexico." In *New Patterns for Mexico: Remittances, Philanthropic Giving, and Equitable Development,* edited by Barbara Merz. Global Equity Initiative, Harvard University, 2005.

———. "Collective Remittances and Migrant-State Collaboration in Mexico and El Salvador." *Latin American Politics and Society* 54, no. 4 (2012): 119–46.

———. "Organized Migrants and Accountability from Afar." *Latin American Research Review* 51, no. 2 (2016): 150–73.

Caglar, Ayse. "Hometown Associations, the Rescaling of State Spatiality and Migrant Grassroots Transnationalism." *Global Networks* 6, no. 1 (2006): 1–22.

Calvo, Ernesto, and Maria Victoria Murillo. "Who Delivers? Partisan Clients in the Argentine Electoral Market." *American Journal of Political Science* 48, no. 4 (2004): 742–57.

Cammett, Melani Claire, and Lauren M. MacLean. "Introduction: The Political Consequences of Non-State Social Welfare in the Global South." *Studies in Comparative International Development* 46, no. 1 (2011): 1–21.

———, eds. *The Politics of Non-State Social Welfare.* Ithaca, NY: Cornell University Press, 2014.

Campbell, Tim. *The Quiet Revolution: Decentralization and the Rise of Political Participation in Latin American Cities.* Pittsburgh: University of Pittsburgh Press, 2003.

Cano, Gustavo, and Alexandra Délano. "The Mexican Government and Organised Mexican Immigrants in the United States: A Historical Analysis of Political Transnationalism 1848–2005." *Journal of Ethnic and Migration Studies* 33, no. 5 (2007): 695–725.

Card, David, and A. B. Krueger. "Minimum Wages and Employment: A Case Study of the Fast-Food Industry in New Jersey and Pennsylvania: Reply." *American Economic Review* 90, no. 5 (2000): 1397–420.

Careja, Romana, and Patrick Emmenegger. "Making Democratic Citizens: The Effects of Migration Experience on Political Attitudes in Central and Eastern Europe." *Comparative Political Studies* 45, no. 7 (2012): 875–902.

Carling, Jørgen. "Scripting Remittances: Making Sense of Money Transfers in Transnational Relationships." *International Migration Review* 48, no. 1 (2014).

Catrinescu, Natalia, Miguel Leon-Ledesma, Matloob Piracha, and Bryce Quillin. "Remittances, Institutions, and Economic Growth." *World Development* 37, no. 1 (2009): 81–92.

Chami, Ralph, Adolfo Barajas, Thomas Cosimano, Connel Fullenkamp, Michael Gapen, and Peter Montiel. *Macroeconomic Consequences of Remittances.* Washington, DC: International Monetary Fund, 2008.

Chauvet, Lisa, Flore Gubert, and Sandrine Mesplé-Somps. "Aid, Remittances, Medical Brain Drain and Child Mortality: Evidence Using Inter and Intra-Country Data." *Journal of Development Studies* 49, no. 6 (2013): 801–18.

Cleary, Matthew R. *The Sources of Democratic Responsiveness in Mexico.* Notre Dame, IN: University of Notre Dame Press, 2010.

———, and Susan Stokes. *Democracy and the Culture of Skepticism: The Politics of Trust in Argentina and Mexico.* New York: Russell Sage Foundation, 2006.

Cohen, Cathy. 2002. "Social Capital, Intervening Institutions, and Political Power." In *Social Capital and Poor Communities,* edited by S. Saegert, J.P. Thompson, and M.R. Warren, 267–89. New York: Russell Sage Foundation.

Coleman, James S. *Foundations of Social Theory*. Cambridge, MA: Belknap Press of Harvard University Press, 1990.

Collier, David, and Steven Levitsky. "Democracy with Adjectives: Conceptual Innovation in Comparative Research." *World Politics* 49, no. 3 (1997): 430–51.

Conapo, Consejo Nacional de Población, Migración México-Estados Unidos. *Temas de Salud*. México, Df, 1990–2010.

Conapo, Consejo Nacional de Población, Distribución Territorial. *Localidades Rurales*, 2000, 2010.

Córdova, Abby, and Jonathan Hiskey. "Shaping Politics at Home: Cross-Border Social Ties and Local-Level Political Engagement." *Comparative Political Studies* 48, no. 11 (2015): 1454–87.

Cornelius, Wayne A. "Death at the Border: Efficacy and Unintended Consequences of U.S. Immigration Control Policy." *Population and Development Review* 27, no. 4 (2001): 661–85.

Cornwall, Andrea, and Vera Schatten Coelho, eds. *Spaces for Change: The Politics of Citizen Participation in New Democratic Arenas*, vol. 4. New York: Zed Books, 2007.

Courchene, Thomas, Alberto Díaz-Cayeros, and Steven B. Webb. "Historical Forces: Geographical and Political." In *Achievements and Challenges of Fiscal Decentralization: Lessons from Mexico*, edited by Marcelo M. Guigale and Stephen B. Webb, 123–38. Washington, DC: World Bank, 2000.

Cox, Gary W., and Mathew D. McCubbins. "Electoral Politics as a Redistributive Game." *Journal of Politics* 48, no. 2 (1986): 370–89.

Dahl, Robert Alan. *Polyarchy: Participation and Opposition*. New Haven, CT: Yale University Press, 1971.

———. *Democracy and Its Critics*. New Haven, CT: Yale University Press, 1989.

Danielson, Michael S. *Emigrants Get Political: Mexican Migrants Engage Their Home Towns*. New York: Oxford University Press, 2018.

De Haas, Hein. "Migration, Remittances and Regional Development in Southern Morocco." *Geoforum* 37, no. 4 (2006): 565–80.

Délano, Alexandra. *Mexico and Its Diaspora in the United States: Policies of Emigration since 1848*. Cambridge: Cambridge University Press, 2011.

———. *From Here and There: Diaspora Policies, Integration, and Social Rights beyond Borders*. New York: Oxford University Press, 2018.

——— and Alan Gamlen. "Comparing and Theorizing State–Diaspora Relations." *Political Geography* 41 (2014): 43–53.

Diamond, Larry. *Developing Democracy: Toward Consolidation*. Baltimore: Johns Hopkins University Press, 1999.

Diamond, Larry Jay, and Marc F. Plattner. *Democratization in Africa*. Baltimore: Johns Hopkins University Press, 1999.

Diamond, Larry Jay, and Leonardo Morlino. "An Overview." *Journal of Democracy* 15, no. 4 (2004): 20–31.

Diamond, Larry, and Leonardo Morlino, eds. *Assessing the Quality of Democracy*. Baltimore: Johns Hopkins University Press, 2005.

Díaz-Cayeros, Alberto, Beatriz Magaloni, and Alexander Ruiz-Euler. "Traditional Governance, Citizen Engagement, and Local Public Goods: Evidence from Mexico." *World Development* 53 (2014): 80–93.

Diaz-Cayeros, Alberto, Federico Estevez, and Beatriz Magaloni. *The Political Logic of Poverty Relief: Electoral Strategies and Social Policy in Mexico*. Cambridge: Cambridge University Press, 2016.

Docquier, Frédéric, and Elisabetta Lodigiani. "Skilled Migration and Business Networks." *Open Economies Review* 21, no. 4 (2010): 565–88.

Donato, Katharine M., Michael Aguilera, and Chizuko Wakabayashi. "Immigration Policy and Employment Conditions of U.S. Immigrants from Mexico, Nicaragua, and the Dominican Republic 1." *International Migration* 43, no. 5 (2005): 5–29.

Donato, Katharine M., Charles M. Tolbert, Alfred Nucci, and Yukio Kawano. "Recent Immigrant Settlement in the Nonmetropolitan United States: Evidence from Internal Census Data." *Rural Sociology* 72, no. 4 (2007): 537–59.

Dresser, D. "Exporting Conflict: Transboundary Consequences of Mexican Politics." *The California-Mexico Connection*, edited by Abraham F. Lowenthal and Katrina Burgess. Stanford, CA: Stanford University Press, 1993.

Duquette, Lauren. *Making Democracy Work from Abroad: Remittances, Hometown Associations and Migrant-State Coproduction of Public Goods in Mexico*. Chicago: University of Chicago Press, 2011.

Duquette-Rury, Lauren. "Collective Remittances and Transnational Coproduction: The 3×1 Program for Migrants and Household Access to Public Goods in Mexico." *Studies in Comparative International Development* 49, no. 1 (2014): 112–39.

———. "Migrant Transnational Participation: How Citizen Inclusion and Government Engagement Matter for Local Democratic Development in Mexico." *American Sociological Review* 81, no. 4 (2016): 771–99.

Duquette-Rury, Lauren, and Xóchitl Bada. "Continuity and Change in Mexican Migrant Hometown Associations: Evidence from New Survey Research." *Migraciones Internacionales* 7, no. 1 (2013).

Duquette-Rury, Lauren, and Zhenxiang Chen. "Does International Migration Affect Political Participation? Evidence from Multiple Data Sources across Mexican Municipalities, 1990–2013." *International Migration Review* (2018). https://doi.org/10.1177/0197918318774499.

Durand, Jorge, Emilio A. Parrado, and Douglas S. Massey. "Migradollars and Development: A Reconsideration of the Mexican Case." *International Migration Review* 30, no. 2 (1996): 423–444.

Emirbayer, Mustafa, and Jeff Goodwin. "Network Analysis, Culture, and the Problem of Agency." *American Journal of Sociology* 99, no. 6 (1994): 1411–54.

Escala-Rabadán, Luis, Xóchitl Bada, and Gaspar Rivera-Salgado. "Mexican Migrant Civic and Political Participation in the U.S.: The Case of Hometown Associations in Los Angeles and Chicago." *Norteamérica: Revista Académica del Cisan-Unam* 1, no. 2 (2006).

Escriba-Folch, Abel, Covadonga Meseguer, and Joseph Wright. "Remittances and Democratization." *International Studies Quarterly* 59, no. 3 (2015): 571–86.

Evans, Peter. "Government Action, Social Capital and Development: Reviewing the Evidence on Synergy." *World Development* 24, no. 6 (1996): 1119–32.

Fajnzylber, Pablo, and J. Humberto Lopez, eds. *Remittances and Development: Lessons from Latin America*. Washington, DC: World Bank, 2008.

Falleti, Tulia Gabriela. "Governing Governors: Coalitions and Sequences of Decentralization in Argentina, Colombia, and Mexico." PhD diss., Northwestern University, 2003.

———. *Decentralization and Subnational Politics in Latin America.* Cambridge: Cambridge University Press, 2010.

FitzGerald, David. *Negotiating Extra-Territorial Citizenship: Mexican Migration and the Transnational Politics of Community.* Center for Comparative Immigration, University of California San Diego, 2000.

———. "Rethinking Emigrant Citizenship." *NYU Law Review* 81 (2006): 90.

———. *A Nation of Emigrants: How Mexico Manages Its Migration.* Berkeley: University of California Press, 2008.

———. "Colonies of the Little Motherland: Membership, Space, and Time in Mexican Migrant Hometown Associations." *Comparative Studies in Society and History* 50, no. 1 (2008): 145–69.

Fox, Jonathan A. *Accountability Politics: Power and Voice in Rural Mexico.* Oxford: Oxford University Press, 2007.

Fox, Jonathan A., and Josefina Aranda. "Decentralization and Rural Development in Mexico: Community Participation in Oaxaca's Municipal Funds Program." Center for U.S.-Mexican Studies, University of California San Diego, 1996.

Fox, Jonathan, and Xochitl Bada. "Migrant Organization and Hometown Impacts in Rural Mexico." *Journal of Agrarian Change* 8, nos. 2–3 (2008): 435–61.

Fox, Jonathan, and Gaspar Rivera-Salgado. "Building Civil Society Among Indigenous Migrants." In *Indigenous Mexican Migrants in the United States,* 1–65. Center for U.S.-Mexican Studies, University of California San Diego, 2004.

Frías, Nina, Mónica Ibarra, and L. Rivera Soto. "La Organización Comunitaria. Actor Ausente en la Reglamentación del Programa 3x1 para Migrantes en Hidalgo." In *El Programa 3x1 para Migrantes.¿Primera Política Transnacional en México?,* edited by R. Fernández, R. García, and Y. A. Vila, 160–210. Mexico City: Miguel Angel Porrua, 2006.

Fuentes Díaz, Antonio, and Guillermo Paleta Pérez. "Violencia y Autodefensas Comunitarias en Michoacán, México." *Iconos: Revista de Ciencias Sociales* 53 (2015): 171–86.

Fukuyama, Francis. "Social Capital and Civil Society." Prepared for the International Monetary Fund Conference on Second-Generation Reforms. Washington, DC: IMF, 1999. www.imf.org/external/pubs/ft/seminar/1999/reforms/fukuyama.htm.

———. *The Great Disruption: Human Nature and the Reconstitution of Social Order.* London: Profile, 1999.

Fung, Archon, and Erik Olin Wright. *Deepening Democracy: Institutional Innovations in Empowered Participatory Governance,* vol. 4. New York: Verso, 2003.

Gamio, Manuel. *Mexican Immigration to the United States.* New York: Arno Press, 1930.

Gamlen, Alan. "Diaspora Engagement Policies: What Are They and What Kinds of States Use Them?" Centre on Migration, Policy and Society, Working Paper no. 32. University of Oxford, 2006.

García Y Griego, Manuel. "La Migración Internacional y las Proyecciones de la Población de México: Un Ensayo Metodológico." In *Seminario de Análisis y Evaluación de Datos de Población, México,* 1–17. El Colmex, 1990.

———. "La Emigración Mexicana y el Tlc en América del Norte: Dos Argumentos." In *Liberación Económica y Libre Comercio en América del Norte*, edited by G. Vega Cánovas, 213–38. México City: El Colegio de México, 1993.

——— and Mónica Verea Campos. *México y Estados Unidos Frente a la Migración de Indocumentados*. Coordinación de Humanidades, no. 301.32872073 G3, 1988.

Garip, Filiz. "The Impact of Migration and Remittances on Wealth Accumulation and Distribution in Rural Thailand." *Demography* 51, no. 2 (2014): 673–98.

———. *On the Move: Changing Mechanisms of Mexico–U.S. Migration*. Princeton, NJ: Princeton University Press, 2016.

Gaventa, John. "Towards Participatory Governance: Assessing the Transformative Possibilities." In *Participation: From Tyranny to Transformation*, edited by Samuel Hickey and Giles Mohan, 25–41. London: Zed Books, 2004.

Giraudy, Agustina. "The Politics of Subnational Undemocratic Regime Reproduction in Argentina and Mexico." *Journal of Politics in Latin America* 2, no. 2 (2010): 53–84.

Giuliano, Paola, and Marta Ruiz-Arranz. "Remittances, Financial Development, and Growth." *Journal of Development Economics* 90, no. 1 (2009): 144–52.

Goetz, Anne Marie, and Rob Jenkins. "Hybrid Forms of Accountability: Citizen Engagement in Institutions of Public-Sector Oversight in India." *Public Management Review* 3, no. 3 (2001): 363–83.

Goldfrank, Benjamin. *Deepening Local Democracy in Latin America: Participation, Decentralization, and the Left*. University Park: Penn State University Press, 2011.

Goldring, Luin. "The Power of Status in Transnational Social Fields." *Transnationalism from Below* 6 (1998): 165–95.

———. "The Mexican State and Transmigrant Organizations: Negotiating the Boundaries of Membership and Participation." *Latin American Research Review* (2002): 55–99.

———. "Family and Collective Remittances to Mexico: A Multi-Dimensional Typology." *Development and Change* 35, no. 4 (2004): 799–840.

Gonzalez-Barrera, Ana, and Mark Hugo Lopez. "A Demographic Portrait of Mexican-Origin Hispanics in the United States." Washington, DC: Pew Hispanic Center, 2013.

Goodman, Gary L., and Jonathan T. Hiskey. "Exit without Leaving: Political Disengagement in High Migration Municipalities in Mexico." *Comparative Politics* 40, no. 2 (2008): 169–88.

Granovetter, Mark. "The Strength of Weak Ties: A Network Theory Revisited." *Sociological Theory* 1, no. 6 (1983): 201–33.

Grillo, Ralph, and Bruno Riccio. "Translocal Development: Italy–Senegal." *Population, Space and Place* 10, no. 2 (2004): 99–111.

Grillo, Ioan. "Why Cartels Are Killing Mexico's Mayors." *New York Times*, 16 January 2016.

Grindle, Merilee S. "Good Enough Governance Revisited." *Development Policy Review* 25, no. 5 (2007): 533–74.

———. *Going Local: Decentralization, Democratization, and the Promise of Good Governance*. Princeton, NJ: Princeton University Press, 2009.

Guarnizo, Luis Eduardo, Alejandro Portes, and William Haller. "Assimilation and Transnationalism: Determinants of Transnational Political Action among Contemporary Migrants." *American Journal of Sociology* 108, no. 6 (2003): 1211–48.

Hagopian, Frances, and Scott P. Mainwaring, eds. *The Third Wave of Democratization in Latin America: Advances and Setbacks*. Cambridge: Cambridge University Press, 2005.

Hastings, Justine S. "Vertical Relationships and Competition in Retail Gasoline Markets: Empirical Evidence from Contract Changes in Southern California." *American Economic Review* 94, no. 1 (2004): 317–28.

Heller, Patrick. "Social Capital as a Product of Class Mobilization and State Intervention: Industrial Workers in Kerala, India." *World Development* 24, no. 6 (1996): 1055–71.

———. "Moving the State: The Politics of Democratic Decentralization in Kerala, South Africa, and Porto Alegre." *Politics & Society* 29, no. 1 (2001): 131–63.

Helmke, Gretchen, and Steven Levitsky, eds. *Informal Institutions and Democracy: Lessons from Latin America*. Baltimore: Johns Hopkins University Press, 2006.

Henry, Leroi, and Giles Mohan. "Making Homes: The Ghanaian Diaspora, Institutions and Development." *Journal of International Development* 15, no. 5 (2003): 611–22.

Hersant, Jeanne, and Alexandre Toumarkine. "Hometown Organisations in Turkey: An Overview." *European Journal of Turkish Studies: Social Sciences on Contemporary Turkey* 2 (2005).

Hickey, Sam. "Toward a Progressive Politics of Belonging? Insights from a Pastoralist 'Hometown' Association." *Africa Today* 57, no. 4 (2011): 28–47.

Hirabayashi, Lane Ryo. "The Migrant Village Association in Latin America: A Comparative Analysis." *Latin American Research Review* 21, no. 3 (1986): 7–29.

Hirschman, Albert O. *Exit, Voice, and Loyalty: Responses to Decline in Firms, Organizations, and States*, vol. 25. Cambridge, MA: Harvard University Press, 1970.

———. "Exit, Voice, and the State." *World Politics* 31, no. 1 (1978): 90–107.

———. *Getting Ahead Collectively: Grassroots Experiences from Latin America*. Oxford: Pergamon Press, 1984.

Hiskey, Jonathan T. "Demand-Based Development and Local Electoral Environments in Mexico." *Comparative Politics* 36, no. 1 (2003): 41–59.

Hollander, Barry A. "Tuning Out or Tuning Elsewhere? Partisanship, Polarization, and Media Migration from 1998 to 2006." *Journalism & Mass Communication Quarterly* 85, no. 1 (2008): 23–40.

Holzner, Claudio A. *Poverty of Democracy: The Institutional Roots of Political Participation in Mexico*. Pittsburgh: University of Pittsburgh Press, 2010.

Honey, Rex, and Stanley I. Okafor, eds. *Hometown Associations: Indigenous Knowledge and Development in Nigeria*. London: Intermediate Technology, 1998.

Imbens, Guido W., and Jeffrey M. Wooldridge. "Recent Developments in the Econometrics of Program Evaluation." *Journal of Economic Literature* 47, no. 1 (2009): 5–86.

Instituto Nacional de Estadística y Geografía (INEGI). Sistema Estatal y Municipal de Bases de Datos, 1990–2013.

Instituto Nacional de Estadística y Geografía (INEGI). Conteo de Población y Vivienda, 1995, 2005.

Instituto Nacional de Estadística y Geografía (INEGI). Censo de Población y Vivienda, 1990, 2000, 2010.

International Organization for Migration. *Handbook on Establishing Effective Labour Migration Policies in Countries of Origin and Destination*. Geneva: International Organization for Migration, 2006.

———. *Global Migration Trends Factsheet, 2015.*

Iskander, Natasha. "Social Learning as a Productive Project: The Tres Por Uno (Three for One) Experience at Zacatecas, Mexico." In *Migration, Remittances and Development*, 249–64. Paris: OECD, 2005.

———. *Creative State: Forty Years of Migration and Development Policy in Morocco and Mexico.* Ithaca, NY: Cornell University Press, 2010.

Itzigsohn, José. "Immigration and the Boundaries of Citizenship: The Institutions of Immigrants' Political Transnationalism." *International Migration Review* 34, no. 4 (2000): 1126–54.

Itzigsohn, José, and Silvia Giorguli Saucedo. "Immigrant Incorporation and Sociocultural Transnationalism." *International Migration Review* 36, no. 3 (2002): 766–98.

Itzigsohn, José, and Daniela Villacrés. "Migrant Political Transnationalism and the Practice of Democracy: Dominican External Voting Rights and Salvadoran Hometown Associations." *Ethnic and Racial Studies* 31, no. 4 (2008): 664–86.

Kanungo, Tapas, David M. Mount, Nathan S. Netanyahu, Christine D. Piatko, Ruth Silverman, and Angela Y. Wu. "An Efficient k-means Clustering Algorithm: Analysis and Implementation." *IEEE Transactions on Pattern Analysis & Machine Intelligence* 7 (2002): 881–92.

Kapur, Devesh. *Remittances: The New Development Mantra.* United Nations Conference on Trade and Development, no. 19. G-24 Discussion Paper Series, 2004.

———. *Diaspora, Development, and Democracy: The Domestic Impact of International Migration from India.* Princeton, NJ: Princeton University Press, 2010.

——— and John McHale. *Give Us Your Best and Brightest: The Global Hunt for Talent and Its Impact on the Developing World.* Washington, DC: Center for Global Development, 2005.

Kitschelt, Herbert, and Steven I. Wilkinson, eds. *Patrons, Clients and Policies: Patterns of Democratic Accountability and Political Competition.* Cambridge: Cambridge University Press, 2007.

Knack, Stephen, and Philip Keefer. "Does Social Capital Have an Economic Payoff? A Cross-Country Investigation." *Quarterly Journal of Economics* 112, no. 4 (1997): 1251–88.

Koopmans, Ruud, ed. *Contested Citizenship: Immigration and Cultural Diversity in Europe*, vol. 25. Minneapolis: University of Minnesota Press, 2005.

Kourí, Emilio. "La Invención del Ejido." *Revista NEXOS*, January 2015.

Lacomba, Joan, and Alexis Cloquell. "Migrants, Associations and Home Country Development: Implications for Discussions on Transnationalism." *New Diversities* 16, no. 2 (2014): 21–37.

Lacroix, Thomas. "Conceptualizing Transnational Engagements: A Structure and Agency Perspective on Hometown Transnationalism." *International Migration Review* 48, no. 3 (2014): 643–79.

——— *Hometown Transnationalism.* London: Palgrave Macmillan, 2016.

Lafleur, Jean-Michel. *Transnational Politics and the State: The External Voting Rights of Diasporas.* Abingdon: Routledge, 2013.

Lamont, Michèle. *Money, Morals, and Manners: The Culture of the French and the American Upper-Middle Class.* Chicago: University of Chicago Press, 1992.

————. *The Dignity of Working Men: Morality and the Boundaries of Race, Class, and Immigration*. Cambridge, MA: Russell Sage at Harvard University Press, 2000.

Lanly, G., and M. B. Valenzuela. "Clubes de Migrantes Oriundos Mexicanos en los Estados Unidos: La Política Transnacional de la Nueva Sociedad Civil Migrante [Mexican hometown associations in the United States: The transnational politics of the new migrant civil society]." Guadalajara: Universidad de Guadalajara, Centro Universitario de Ciencias Económico Administrativas, 2004.

Larson, Anne M., and Jesse C. Ribot. "Democratic Decentralisation through a Natural Resource Lens: An Introduction." *European Journal of Development Research* 16, no. 1 (2004): 1–25.

Lentz, Carola. "Home, Death and Leadership: Discourses of an Educated Elite from North-Western Ghana." *Social Anthropology* 2, no. 2 (1994): 149–69.

Levitsky, Steven, and María Victoria Murillo. *Argentine Democracy: The Politics of Institutional Weakness*. University Park: Penn State University Press, 2005.

Levitt, Peggy. "Social Remittances: Migration Driven Local-Level Forms of Cultural Diffusion." *International Migration Review* 32, no. 4 (1998): 926–48.

————. "Transnational Migration: Taking Stock and Future Directions." *Global Networks* 1, no. 3 (2001): 195–216.

Levitt, Peggy, and Nina Glick Schiller. "Conceptualizing Simultaneity: A Transnational Social Field Perspective on Society." *International Migration Review* 38, no. 3 (2004): 1002–39.

Levitt, Peggy, and Deepak Lamba-Nieves. "Social Remittances Revisited." *Journal of Ethnic and Migration Studies* 37, no. 1 (2011): 1–22.

Levy, Brian, and Sahr John Kpundeh, eds. *Building State Capacity in Africa: New Approaches, Emerging Lessons*. Washington, DC: World Bank, 2004.

Lin, Nan. *Social Capital: A Theory of Social Structure and Action*. Cambridge: Cambridge University Press, 2001.

Lipset, Seymour Martin. *Political Man: The Social Bases of Politics*. Baltimore: Johns Hopkins University Press, 1960.

Loebach, Peter. "Space and a Damaged Place: Philippine Migrant Transnational Engagement Following the Guinsaugon Landslide Disaster." *Population, Space and Place* 22, no. 6 (2016): 526–38.

López, Victor, and Miguel Ángel. "Conducta Electoral y Estratos Económicos: El Voto de los Sectores Populares en Chile." *Política* 43 (2004).

Lujambio, Alonso. *Adiós a la Excepcionalidad: Régimen Presidencial y Gobierno Dividido en México*. CLASCO, 2001.

Maeyama, Takashi. "Ethnicity, Secret Societies, and Associations: The Japanese in Brazil." *Comparative Studies in Society and History* 21, no. 4 (1979): 589–610.

Magaloni, Beatriz, Alberto Diaz-Cayeros, and Federico Estévez. "Clientelism and Portfolio Diversification: A Model of Electoral Investment with Applications to Mexico." In *Patrons, Clients, and Policies: Patterns of Democratic Accountability and Political Competition*, edited by Herbert Kitschelt, 185–205. Cambridge: Cambridge University Press, 2007.

Mahmud, Hasan. "'It's My Money': Social Class and the Perception of Remittances among Bangladeshi Migrants in Japan." *Current Sociology* 62, no. 3 (2014): 412–30.

Mainwaring, Scott, Daniel Brinks, and Aníbal Pérez-Liñán. "Classifying Political Regimes in Latin America, 1945–2004." In *Regimes and Democracy in Latin America: Theories and Methods*, edited by Gerardo L. Munck, 123–60. New York: Oxford University Presss, 2007.

Malone, Aaron, and Durden, T. Elizabeth. "Who Drives Diaspora Development? Replication of Mexico's 3×1 Program in Yucatán." *Journal of Latin American Geography* 17, no. 1 (2018): 139–65.

Mann, Michael. "The Autonomous Power of the State: Its Origins, Mechanisms and Results." *European Journal of Sociology/Archives Européennes de Sociologie* 25, no. 2 (1984): 185–213.

Mansbridge, Jane. "What Does a Representative Do? Descriptive Representation in Communicative Settings of Distrust, Uncrystallized Interests, and Historically Denigrated Status." *Citizenship in Diverse Societies* 26 (2000): 99–124.

Massey, Douglas S., ed. *New Faces in New Places: The Changing Geography of American Immigration*. New York: Russell Sage Foundation, 2008.

Massey, Douglas S., and Kristin E. Espinosa, "What's Driving Mexico-U.S. Migration? A Theoretical, Empirical, and Policy Analysis." *American Journal of Sociology* 102, no. 4 (1997): 939–99.

Massey, Douglas S., and Rene M. Zenteno. "The Dynamics of Mass Migration." *Proceedings of the National Academy of Sciences* 96, no. 9 (1999): 5328–35.

Massey, Douglas S., Rafael Alarcón, Jorge Durand, and Humberto González. *Return to Aztlan: The Social Process of International Migration from Western Mexico*, vol. 1. Berkeley: University of California Press, 1987.

Massey, Douglas S., Joaquin Arango, Graeme Hugo, Ali Kouaouci, Adela Pellegrino, and J. Edward Taylor. "An Evaluation of International Migration Theory: The North American Case." *Population and Development Review* 20, no. 4 (1994): 699–751.

Mazzucato, Valentina, and Mirjam Kabki. "Small Is Beautiful: The Micro-Politics of Transnational Relationships between Ghanaian Hometown Associations and Communities Back Home." *Global Networks* 9, no. 2 (2009): 227–51.

McKenzie, David, and Dean Yang. "Evidence on Policies to Increase the Development Impacts of International Migration." *World Bank Research Observer* 30, no. 2 (2015): 155–92.

McNulty, Stephanie. *Voice and Vote: Decentralization and Participation in Post-Fujimori Peru*. Stanford, CA: Stanford University Press, 2011.

Mercer, Claire, Ben Page, and Martin Evans. "Unsettling Connections: Transnational Networks, Development and African Home Associations." *Global Networks* 9, no. 2 (2009): 141–61.

Meseguer, Covadonga, and Francisco Javier Aparicio. "Migration and Distributive Politics: The Political Economy of Mexico's 3×1 Program." *Latin American Politics and Society* 54, no. 4 (2012): 147–78.

Meseguer, Covadonga, Sandra Ley, and J. Eduardo Ibarra-Olivo. "Sending Money Home in Times of Crime: The Case of Mexico." *Journal of Ethnic and Migration Studies* 43, no. 13 (2017): 2169–92.

Mines, Richard. *Developing a Community Tradition of Migration: A Field Study in Rural Zacatecas, Mexico, and California Settlement Areas*. Center for U.S.–Mexican Studies, University of California San Diego, 1981.

Mizrahi, Yemile. "Dilemmas of the Opposition in Government: Chihuahua and Baja California." *Mexican Studies / Estudios Mexicanos* 14, no. 1 (1998): 151–89.

Moctezuma Longoria, Miguel. "Iniciativa de Reforma a la Constitución Política del Estado Libre y Soberano de Zacatecas Sobre el Ejercito Pleno de los Derechos Políticos de los Migrantes." Autonomous University of Zacatecas, Zacatecas, México, 2002.

Moss, Dana M. "Transnational Repression, Diaspora Mobilization, and the Case of the Arab Spring." *Social Problems* 63, no. 4 (2016): 480–98.

Moya, Jose C. "Immigrants and Associations: A Global and Historical Perspective." *Journal of Ethnic and Migration Studies* 31, no. 5 (2005): 833–64.

Ndegwa, Sahr, and Brian Levy. "The Politics of Decentralization in Africa: A Comparative Analysis." In *Building State Capacity in Africa: New Approaches, Emerging Lessons*, 283–322. Washington, DC: World Bank, 2004.

Nichter, Simeon. "Vote Buying or Turnout Buying? Machine Politics and the Secret Ballot." *American Political Science Review* 102, no. 1 (2008): 19–31.

Nyberg–Sørensen, Ninna, Nicholas Van Hear, and Poul Engberg–Pedersen. "The Migration-Development Nexus Evidence and Policy Options: State-of-the-Art Overview." *International Migration* 40, no. 5 (2002): 3–47.

Nyblade, Benjamin, and Angela O'Mahony. "Migrants' Remittances and Home Country Elections: Cross-National and Subnational Evidence." *Studies in Comparative International Development* 49, no. 1 (2014): 44–66.

Nyíri, Pál. "Expatriating Is Patriotic? The Discourse on 'New Migrants' in the People's Republic of China and Identity Construction Among Recent Migrants from the PRC." *Journal of Ethnic and Migration Studies* 27, no. 4 (2001): 635–53.

O'Donnell, Guillermo. "Challenges to Democratization in Brazil." *World Policy Journal* 5, no. 2 (1988): 281–300.

O'Mahony, Angela. "Political Investment: Remittances and Elections." *British Journal of Political Science* 43, no. 4 (2013). 799–820.

Oates, Wallace E. *Fiscal Federalism*. New York: Harcourt Brace Jovanovich, 1972.

Okamura, Jonathan Y. "Filipino Hometown Associations in Hawaii." In *Asian American Family Life and Community*, edited by Franklin Ng, 89–101. New York: Routledge, 2014.

Olson, Mancur. "The Logic of Collective Action [1965]." *Contemporary Sociological Theory* 2 (2007): 111.

Orozco, Manuel. "Globalization and Migration: The Impact of Family Remittances in Latin America." *Latin American Politics and Society* 44, no. 2 (2002): 41–66.

———. *Hometown Associations and Their Present and Future Partnerships: New Development Opportunities*. Washington, DC: Inter-American Development Bank, 2003.

———. *International Flows of Remittances: Cost, Competition and Financial Access in Latin America and the Caribbean—Toward An Industry Scorecard*. Washington, DC: Inter-American Development Bank, 2006.

Orozco, Manuel, and Michelle Lapointe. "Mexican Hometown Associations and Development Opportunities." *Journal of International Affairs* 57, no. 2 (2004): 31–51.

Orozco, Manuel, and Katherine Welle. *Hometown Associations and Development: A Look at Ownership, Sustainability, Correspondence, and Replicability*. Washington, DC: Inter-American Development Bank, 2005.

Orozco-Aleman, Sandra, and Heriberto Gonzalez-Lozano. "Drug Violence and Migration Flows: Lessons from the Mexican Drug War." *Journal of Human Resources* 52, no. 3 (2017): 71–49.

Østergaard-Nielsen, Eva. "Diasporas in World Politics." In *Non-State Actors in World Politics*, 218–34. London: Palgrave Macmillan, 2001.

———. "The Politics of Migrants' Transnational Political Practices." *International Migration Review* 37, no. 3 (2003): 760–86.

———. "Mobilising the Moroccans: Policies and Perceptions of Transnational Co-Development Engagement among Moroccan Migrants in Catalonia." *Journal of Ethnic and Migration Studies* 35, no. 10 (2009): 1623–41.

Ostrom, Elinor. *Governing the Commons*. Cambridge: Cambridge University Press, 1990.

———. "Crossing the Great Divide: Coproduction, Synergy, and Development." *World Development* 24, no. 6 (1996): 1073–87.

Ostrom, Vincent, and Elinor Ostrom. "Public Goods and Public Choices." Workshop in Political Theory and Policy Analysis, Indiana University, 1977.

Page, Ben. "Slow Going: The Mortuary, Modernity and the Hometown Association in Bali-Nyonga, Cameroon." *Africa* 77, no. 3 (2007): 419–41.

Paul, Alison, and Sarah Gammage. "Hometown Associations and Development: The Case of El Salvador." Destination, DC Working Paper no. 3, 2004.

Pearlman, Wendy. "Competing for Lebanon's Diaspora: Transnationalism and Domestic Struggles in a Weak State." *International Migration Review* 48, no. 1 (2014): 34–75.

Pérez-Armendáriz, Clarisa. "Cross-Border Discussions and Political Behavior in Migrant-Sending Countries." *Studies in Comparative International Development* 49, no. 1 (2014): 67–88.

Pérez-Armendáriz, Clarisa, and David Crow. "Do Migrants Remit Democracy? International Migration, Political Beliefs, and Behavior in Mexico." *Comparative Political Studies* 43, no. 1 (2010): 119–48.

Pérez-Armendáriz, Clarisa, and Lauren Duquette-Rury. "The 3×1 Program for Migrants and Vigilante Groups in Contemporary Mexico." *Journal of Ethnic and Migration Studies*. Published online July 3, 2019. https://doi.org/10.1080/1369183X.2019.1623345.

Peruzzotti, Enrique, and Catalina Smulovitz, eds. *Enforcing the Rule of Law: Social Accountability in the New Latin American Democracies*. Pittsburgh: University of Pittsburgh Press, 2006.

Phillips, Brian J. "Inequality and the Emergence of Vigilante Organizations: the Case of Mexican Autodefensas." *Comparative Political Studies* 50, no. 10 (2017): 1358–89.

Piper, Nicola. "The Complex Interconnections of the Migration–Development Nexus: A Social Perspective." *Population, Space and Place* 15, no. 2 (2009): 93–101.

Piven, Frances Fox, and Richard A. Cloward. *The Breaking of the American Social Compact*. New York: New Press, 1997.

Portes, Alejandro. "Social Capital: Its Origins and Applications in Modern Sociology." *Annual Review of Sociology* 24, no. 1 (1998): 1–24.

———. "Conclusion: Towards a New World the Origins and Effects of Transnational Activities." *Ethnic and Racial Studies* 22, no. 2 (1999): 463–77.

Portes, Alejandro, and Patricia Fernández-Kelly, eds. *The State and the Grassroots: Immigrant Transnational Organizations in Four Continents*. New York: Berghahn Books, 2015.

Portes, Alejandro, Luis E. Guarnizo, and Patricia Landolt. "The Study of Transnationalism: Pitfalls and Promise of an Emergent Research Field." *Ethnic and Racial Studies* 22, no. 2 (1999): 217–37.

Portes, Alejandro, Cristina Escobar, and Renelinda Arana. "Bridging the Gap: Transnational and Ethnic Organizations in the Political Incorporation of Immigrants in the United States." *Ethnic and Racial Studies* 31, no. 6 (2008): 1056–90.

Portes, Alejandro, Cristina Escobar, and Alexandria Walton Radford. "Immigrant Transnational Organizations and Development: A Comparative Study." *International Migration Review* 41, no. 1 (2007): 242–81.

Pries, Ludger. "The Disruption of Social and Geographic Space: Mexican-U.S. Migration and the Emergence of Transnational Social Spaces." *International Sociology* 16, no. 1 (2001): 55–74.

——— and Zeynep Sezgin, eds. *Cross-Border Migrant Organizations in Comparative Perspective*. Springer, 2012.

Pritchett, Lant, and Michael Woolcock. "Solutions When the Solution Is the Problem: Arraying the Disarray in Development." *World Development* 32, no. 2 (2004): 191–212.

Przeworski, Adam, Michael E. Alvarez, José Antonio Cheibub, and Fernando Limongi. *Democracy and Development: Political Institutions and Well-being in the World, 1950–1990*, vol. 3. Cambridge: Cambridge University Press, 2000.

Przeworski, Adam, Susan C. Stokes, and Bernard Manin, eds. *Democracy, Accountability, and Representation*, vol. 2. Cambridge: Cambridge University Press, 1999.

Putnam, Robert D. "Bowling Alone: America's Declining Social Capital." In *Culture and Politics: A Reader*, edited by Lane Crothers and Charles Lockhardt, 223–34. New York: Palgrave Macmillan, 2000.

———, Robert Leonardi, and Raffaella Y. Nanetti. *Making Democracy Work: Civic Traditions in Modern Italy*. Princeton, NJ: Princeton University Press, 1993.

Pycior, Julie Leininger. *Democratic Renewal and the Mutual Aid Legacy of U.S. Mexicans*. College Station: Texas A&M University Press, 2014.

Ratha, Dilip, Christian Eigen-Zucchi, and Sonia Plaza. *Migration and Remittances Factbook 2016*. Washington, DC: World Bank, 2016.

Reichert, Joshua S. "The Migrant Syndrome: Seasonal U.S. Wage Labor and Rural Development in Central Mexico." *Human Organization* 40, no. 1 (1981): 56–66.

Riosmena, Fernando, and Douglas S. Massey. "Pathways to El Norte: Origins, Destinations, and Characteristics of Mexican Migrants to the United States." *International Migration Review* 46, no. 1 (2012): 3–36.

Rivera-Salgado, Gaspar, and Luis Escala Rabadán. "Identidad Colectiva y Estrategias Organizativas Entre Migrantes Mexicanos Indígenas y Mestizos." In *Indígenas Mexicanos Migrantes en los Estados Unidos, México, H. Cámara de Diputados de la LIX Legislatura*, edited by Jonathan Fox and Gaspar Rivera-Salgado, Universidad de California, Santa Cruz, Universidad de Zacatecas. Mexico City: Miguel Ángel Pórrua, 2004.

Rivera Velázquez, Jaime. *Crimen Organizado y Autodefensas en México: El Caso de Michoacán*. FES Seguridad, Perspectivas 2014. http://library.fes.de/pdf-files/bueros/la-seguridad/10845.pdf.

Rodríguez, Victoria. *Decentralization in Mexico: From Reforma Municipal to Solidaridad to Nuevo Federalismo*. Boulder, CO: Westview, 1997.

Rosenstone, Steven J., and John Hansen. *Mobilization, Participation, and Democracy in America*. London: Macmillan, 1993.

Rother, Stefan. "Changed in Migration? Philippine Return Migrants and Undemocratic Remittances." *European Journal of East Asian Studies* 8, no. 2 (2009): 245–74.

Seawright, Jason. *Multi-Method Social Science: Combining Qualitative and Quantitative Tools*. Cambridge: Cambridge University Press, 2016.

Schiller, Nina Glick, Linda Basch, and Cristina Blanc-Szanton. "Transnationalism: A New Analytic Framework for Understanding Migration." *Annals of the New York Academy of Sciences* 645, no. 1 (1992): 1–24.

Schmelz, A. *The Ghanaian Diaspora in Germany: Its Contribution to Development in Ghana*. GTZ, Migration and Development, 2009. www.migration4development.org/sites/m4d.emakinaeu.net/files/The_Ghanaian_diaspora_in_Germany.pdf.

Schmitter, Philippe C. "The Ambiguous Virtues of Accountability." *Journal of Democracy* 15, no. 4 (2004): 47–60.

Schumpeter, Joseph A. "The Creative Response in Economic History." *Journal of Economic History* 7, no. 2 (1947): 149–59.

Seawright, Jason. *Multi-Method Social Science: Combining Qualitative and Quantitative Tools*. Cambridge: Cambridge University Press, 2016.

Sherman, Mark Andrew. "Some Thoughts on Restoration, Reintegration, and Justice in the Transnational Context." *Fordham International Law Journal* 23 (1999): 1397.

Silva, Jon. "Engaging Diaspora Communities in Development: An Investigation of Filipino Hometown Associations in Canada." PhD diss., Public Policy Program, Simon Fraser University, 2006.

Simpser, Alberto, Lauren Duquette-Rury, Jose Hernandez Company, and Juan Fernando Ibarra. "The Political Economy of Social Spending by Local Government: A Study of the 3×1 Program in Mexico." *Latin American Research Review* 51, no. 1 (2016): 62–83.

Singer, David Andrew. "Migrant Remittances and Exchange Rate Regimes in the Developing World." *American Political Science Review* 104, no. 2 (2010): 307–23.

Smith, Heidi Jane M., and Keith D. Revell. "Micro-Incentives and Municipal Behavior: Political Decentralization and Fiscal Federalism in Argentina and Mexico." *World Development* 77 (2016): 231–48.

Smith, Michael P., and Matt Bakker. *Citizenship across Borders: The Political Transnationalism of El Migrante*, vol. 77. Ithaca, NY: Cornell University Press, 2008.

Smith, Michael P., and Luis Eduardo Guarnizo, eds. *Transnationalism from Below*, vol. 6. Piscataway, NJ: Transaction, 1998.

Smith, Peter H. *Democracy in Latin America: Political Change in Comparative Perspective*. New York: Oxford University Press, 2005.

Smith, Robert C. "Transnational Localities: Community, Technology and the Politics of Membership within the Context of Mexico–U.S. Migration." In *Transnationalism from Below: Comparative Urban and Community Research*, edited by Michael Peter Smith and Luis Eduardo Guarnizo, 196–241. New York: Routledge, 1998.

———. *Mexican New York*. Berkeley: University of California Press, 2006.

Smulovitz, Catalina, and Enrique Peruzzotti. "Societal Accountability in Latin America." *Journal of Democracy* 11, no. 4 (2000): 147–58.

Soehl, Thomas, and Roger Waldinger. "Making the Connection: Latino Immigrants and Their Cross-Border Ties." *Ethnic and Racial Studies* 33, no. 9 (2010): 1489–510.

Soysal, Yasemin Nuhoglu. *Limits of Citizenship: Migrants and Postnational Membership in Europe.* Chicago: University of Chicago Press, 1994.

Staniland, Paul. "States, Insurgents, and Wartime Political Orders." *Perspectives on Politics* 10, no. 2 (2012): 243–64.

———. *Networks of Rebellion: Explaining Insurgent Cohesion and Collapse.* Ithaca, NY: Cornell University Press, 2014.

Stokes, Susan Carol, Thad Dunning, Marcelo Nazareno, and Valeria Brusco. *Brokers, Voters, and Clientelism: The Puzzle of Distributive Politics.* New York: Cambridge University Press, 2013.

Strode, Ann, and Kitty Barrett-Grant. *Understanding the Institutional Dynamics of South Africa's Response to the HIV/AIDS Pandemic.* Cape Town: Idasa, 2004.

Suárez-Orozco, Marcelo, and Carola Suárez-Orozco. "Some Conceptual Considerations in the Interdisciplinary Study of Immigrant Children." In *Immigrant Voices: In Search of Educational Equity,* edited by Enrique T. Tueba and Lilia I. Bartolomé, 17–36. Lanham, MD: Rowman and Littlefield, 2000.

Tan, Pang-Ning, Michael Steinbach, and Vipin Kumar. *Introduction to Data Mining.* Boston: Addison-Wesley Longman, 2005.

Taylor, Edward J. "The New Economics of Labour Migration and the Role of Remittances in the Migration Process." *International Migration* 37, no. 1 (1999): 63–88.

Tendler, Judith. *Good Government in the Tropics.* Baltimore: Johns Hopkins University Press, 1997.

Tiebout, Charles M. "A Pure Theory of Local Expenditures." *Journal of Political Economy* 64, no. 5 (1956): 416–24.

Tocqueville, Alexis de, and Henry Reeve. *Democracy in America.* New York: Bantam Books, 2000 [1835].

Trager, Lillian. *Yoruba Hometowns: Community, Identity, and Development in Nigeria.* Boulder, CO: Lynne Rienner, 2001.

Trejo, Guillermo, and Sandra Ley. "Federalism, Drugs, and Violence: Why Intergovernmental Partisan Conflict Stimulated Inter-Cartel Violence in Mexico." *Política y Gobierno* 23, no. 1 (2016): 9–52.

———. "Why Did Drug Cartels Go to War in Mexico? Subnational Party Alternation, the Breakdown of Criminal Protection, and the Onset of Large-Scale Violence." *Comparative Political Studies* 51, no. 7 (2017): 900–37.

Tsai, Lily L. *Accountability without Democracy: Solidary Groups and Public Goods Provision in Rural China.* Cambridge: Cambridge University Press, 2007.

Tusalem, Rollin F. "Do Migrant Remittances Improve the Quality of Government? Evidence from the Philippines." *Asian Journal of Comparative Politics.* Published online March 7, 2018. https://doi.org/10.1177/2057891118757694.

Verba, Sidney, and Norman H. Nie. *Participation in America: Social Equality and Political Democracy.* New York: Harper & Row, 1972.

Verba, Sidney, and Norman H. Nie. *Participation in America: Political Democracy and Social Equality.* Chicago: University of Chicago Press, 1987.

Verba, Sidney, Kay Lehman Schlozman, and Henry E. Brady. *Voice and Equality: Civic Voluntarism in American Politics*. Cambridge, MA: Harvard University Press, 1995.

Vezzoli, Simona, and Thomas Lacroix. "Building Bonds for Migration and Development: Diaspora Engagement Policies of Ghana, India and Serbia." PhD diss., International Migration Institute, Gesellschaft für Technische Zusammenarbeit (GTZ), 2010.

Waldinger, Roger. *The Cross-Border Connection: Immigrants, Emigrants, and Their Homelands*. Cambridge, MA: Harvard University Press, 2015.

Waldinger, Roger, and David FitzGerald. "Transnationalism in Question." *American Journal of Sociology* 109, no. 5 (2004): 1177–95.

Waldinger, Roger, Eric Popkin, and Hector Aquiles Magana. "Conflict and Contestation in the Cross-Border Community: Hometown Associations Reassessed." *Ethnic and Racial Studies* 31, no. 5 (2008): 843–70.

Wampler, Brian. *Participatory Budgeting in Brazil: Contestation, Cooperation, and Accountability*. University Park: Penn State University Press, 2007.

Watson, Tara. "Public Health Investments and the Infant Mortality Gap: Evidence from Federal Sanitation Interventions on US Indian Reservations." *Journal of Public Economics* 90, no. 8–9 (2006): 1537–60.

Weber, Max. *Economy and Society: An Outline of Interpretive Sociology*, vol. 1. Berkeley: University of California Press, 1978.

Wilkerson, Isabel. *The Warmth of Other Suns: The Epic Story of America's Great Migration*. New York: Random House, 2010.

Woods, Dwayne. "Elites, Ethnicity, and 'Home Town' Associations in the Côte d'Ivoire: An Historical Analysis of State–Society Links." *Africa* 64, no. 4 (1994): 465–83.

Woolcock, Michael, and Deepa Narayan. "Social Capital: Implications for Development Theory, Research, and Policy." *World Bank Research Observer* 15, no. 2 (2000): 225–49.

World Bank Group. 2016. *Migration and Remittances Factbook 2016, Third Edition*. Washington, DC: World Bank.

Wyman, Mark. *Round-Trip to America: The Immigrants Return to Europe, 1880–1930*. Ithaca, NY: Cornell University Press, 1993.

Yang, Dean. "Migrant Remittances." *Journal of Economic Perspectives* 25, no. 3 (2011): 129–52.

Young, Iris Marion. *Inclusion and Democracy*. Oxford: Oxford University Press, 2002.

Zabin, Carol, and Luis Escala. "From Civic Association to Political Participation: Mexican Hometown Associations and Mexican Immigrant Political Empowerment in Los Angeles." *Frontera Norte* 14, no. 27 (2002).

Zelizer, Viviana A., and Charles Tilly. "Relations and Categories." *Psychology of Learning and Motivation* 47 (2006): 1–31.

Zhou, Min, and Rennie Lee. "Transnationalism and Community Building: Chinese Immigrant Organizations in the United States." *Annals of the American Academy of Political and Social Science* 647, no. 1 (2013): 22–49.

Ziblatt, Daniel. "Why Some Cities Provide More Public Goods than Others: A Subnational Comparison of the Provision of Public Goods in German Cities in 1912." *Studies in Comparative International Development* 43, nos. 3–4 (2008): 273–89.

Zolberg, Aristide R. "The Politics of Immigration Policy: An Externalist Perspective." *American Behavioral Scientist* 42, no. 9 (1999): 1276–79.

INDEX